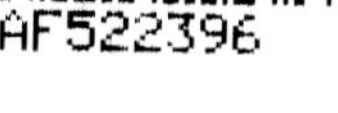

ANMOL PUBLICATIONS
AKASHDEEP PUBLISHING HOUSE
NEW DELHI - BANGLORE

INVESTMENT MANAGEMENT

INVESTMENT MANAGEMENT

INCLUDING PORTFOLIO MANAGEMENT & SECURITY ANALYSIS

Prof. V. Gangadhar
Dept. of Commerce &
Business Management
Kakatiya University,
WARANGAL.

Dr. G. Ramesh Babu
Lecturer in Commerce
S.S.R. Jyothi College,
KHAMMAM.

ANMOL PUBLICATIONS PVT. LTD.
NEW DELHI - 110 002 (INDIA)

ANMOL PUBLICATIONS PVT. LTD.
4374/4B, Ansari Road, Daryaganj
New Delhi - 110 002
Ph.: 23261597, 23278000
Visit us at: www.anmolpublications.com

Investment Management

First Published, 2003

Reprint, 2006

PRINTED IN INDIA

Published by J.L. Kumar for Anmol Publications Pvt. Ltd., New Delhi - 110 002 and Printed at Mehra Offset Press, Delhi.

CONTENTS

PREFACE

Investment Management is a subject of growing importance and interest. Investment is the sacrifice for the future *reward*. Investment decision is a trade off between *risk and return*. The entire globe is based on Risk and Return. Investing is an activity that is of interest to many individuals regardless of occupation or income level.

In this book an attempt is made to give a comprehensive coverage of the Investment Management, Security Analysis and Portfolio Management. This book has been written as per the syllabus prescribed for the MBA (Finance), M.Com, C.S. C.A. MFA, PGDBF, PGDBM, PGDFM, CFA. MFC, MFM etc., We are confident that this book will help the students, faculty members, Executives in Finance area, NBFCs, stock brokers, registrars and fund managers of Mutual Funds as well as to those individuals who desire to up grade their knowledge on Investment Management.

This book is divided into Five Units. All the parts are organised into related chapters which should usually be read in the order presented. But these parts are fairly independent of each other.

Unit-1: Consists of three chapters and provides a broad view of the valuation of securities.

Unit-2: Contains 3 chapters and deals with capital markets.

Unit-3: It is devoted to cover the *Securities Analysis.* It considers economic industry and company analysis and helps to reach the estimates of risk and return on individual securities. The security analysis is an essential process for portfolio management.

Unit-4: It is devoted to cover portfolio analysis, selection and management. It deals systematically with the procedures involved in portfolio management. In the past several decades the fields of *Security Analysis and Portfolio Management* have changed from a completely descriptive institutional body of literature to a highly formalised quantitative area of study. We have attempted to blend the best and the most relevant pieces from the evolving field of endeavour into a meaningful analysis. The text starts with a view that the reader has no *knowledge* of investments but, expecting some knowledge of accounting and economics.

Unit-5: It covers Management of Financial Derivatives. It is the latest and modern type of financial engineering. Derivatives have been a very successful innovation in the Capital Market. With the help of financial derivatives the finance manager can create new instruments that have highly specialised and desirable risk and return characteristics. The spectacular growth of financial derivatives in the global financial markets has generated a demand for unfied economic theory of the effect of these on optimal allocation of resources.

Since, the book is synthesis, we are indebted to all authors who have contributed to the *World of Finance*. We hope that we have interpreted their views correctly. We have made acknowledgements of every idea whose sources, we have been able to identify. We are indebted to our colleagues both academic and professionals and to countless students. It would be impossible to list them all. Anyhow for evincing personal interest in under-taking a project of this magnitude and making invaluable suggestions from time to time, we would like to thank all those who have directly and indirectly encouraged and helped in the completion of this book. We wish to express our thanks to Mr. J.L. Kumar, Managing Director. Anmol Publications New Delhi for his whole-hearted support and co-operation for publishing the book. We sincerely acknowledge the help and encouragement given by Sri Gopal Gupta, M/s. Kalyani Publishers for the publication of this book.

We feel extremely obliged to readers who were thoughtful enough to offer constructive criticism along with useful suggestions for improvement.

Warangal

- Prof. V. Gangadhar

- Dr. G. Ramesh

Unit-I

1. *Investment Management*
2. *Valuation of Equity Shares*
3. *Valuation of Bonds*

1

INVESTMENT MANAGEMENT

INTRODUCTION

The emerging economic environment of competitive markets signifying customer's sovereignty has profound implications for the savings and their investment in India. Investment means a person's commitment of funds towards his future life. It is an economic activity. It refers to acquisition of assets which generates income. It means the diversification of money towards investment and thereby increasing productivity of a nation. Investment means parking of one's idle funds in income generating assets.

The term investment refers to funds invested in various securities, consisting of Government and Semi - Government securities, Loans, Debentures of Local authorities, such as *Port Trusts, Municipal Corporations* and debentures and shares of companies. Investments represent legal claims of various securities, such as *Bonds, shares, Debentures etc.,* and are assets of special nature. There are various forms of investments available with their relative merits and demerits. Investments are freely bought and sold in the stock exchange through banks and brokers, who charge a small amount of commission for their services. Investment means the use of money to earn more money by way of interest, dividend or capital appreciation. Well planned investment alone can ensure regular income, capital appreciation and can be used to meet the financial requirements of the investors. The dynamics of economic growth provide various opportunities for investors to invest their money in different types of securities.

The financial and economic meaning of investment is related to each other, because investment is a part of the savings of individuals, which flow into the capital market either directly or through institutions divided into new and secondary capital financing. Investors as suppliers and users of long term funds will find a meeting place in the capital market.

Investment will generally be used in its financial sense and as such, investment is the allocation of monetary resources to assets that are expected to yield some gain or positive return over a given period of time.

Investment is a commitment of a person's funds to derive future income in the form of interest, dividends, rent, premium, pension benefits or the appreciation of the value of his investment. In the process of investment the transfer of financial assets will be made from one person or institution to an investor. Investments will include various kinds of instruments or securities and institutional media into which savings are placed.

Definition of Investment

According to *F. Amling* "Investment may be defined as the purchase by an individual or institutional investor of a financial or real asset that produces a return proportional to the risk assumed over some future investment period."

Fisher and Jordan defined investment as "commitment of funds made in the expectation of some positive rate of return. If the investment is properly undertaken, the return will commensurate with the risk the investor assumes."

The term investment cannotes different concepts and meanings. The important three concepts of investments are explained below:

A) Economic Investment

B) Commitment Investment

C) Financial Investment

A) Economic Investment

Economic Investment means the net additions to the capital stock of the society which consists of goods and services that are used in the production of other goods and services. Addition to the capital stock means an increase in buildings, plants, equipments and inventories over the amount of goods and services that existed.

B) Commitment Investment

Commitment Investment refers to money commitment to satisfy personal desires, since no rate of return is involved in such investment nor capital growth is expected. *For ex:* a commitment of money to a new car is certainly an investment from an individual point of view.

C) Financial Investment

It involves the investment of funds in various assets, such as *Stock, Bonds, Real Estate, Mortgages etc.* Investment is the employment of funds with the aim of achieving additional income or growth in value. It involves the commitment of resources which have been saved or put away from current consumption in the hope some benefits will accrue in future. Investment involves long term commitment of funds and waiting for a *reward in the future.*

Elements of Investment

The following factors are to be considered as elements of investment.

1. Reward (Return)
2. Risk and Return
3. Time

1. Reward

Generally, the investors may buy and sell financial assets in order to earn return on them. The return better known as reward from investments includes both current income and capital gains or losses which arise by the increase or decrease of the security price.

2. Risk and Return

A good understanding of the working of financial markets requires the knowledge of the meaning and types of risk and return, their relationship and the process of valuation of securities. The value of financial assets depends among other things on their return and risk. Risk can be defined as the chance that the expected or prospective gains, or profit or return may not materialise, that the actual outcome of investment may be less than the expected outcome. The greater the variability or dispersion in the possible outcome, the greater will be the risk.

John J. Hampton defined risk as: "The chance of future that can be foreseen."[1]

Risk means, an estimation about the degree of happening of the loss. Risk is a measurable element. Risk and Return are inseparable. Return is an expected income from the investment. Risk can be quantified by using precise statistical techniques. The investment process must be considered in terms of both aspects of risks and return. The Return represents the benefits derived by an investor from his investments. The rate of return required by the investor to a great extent depends upon the risk involved in his investments. Higher the risk, greater is the return expected by the firm.

3. Time

The important factor in investment is the time which offers several different courses of action. Time period depends on the attitude of the investor who follows a buy and hold strategy. As time moves on, analysts believe that conditions change and investors revaluate expected return for each investment.

---

1. Hampton John J. "Financial Decision Making" P.No. 22.

NATURE OF INVESTMENT

Investment requires a continuous flow of decisions which cannot be avoided. All investment choices are made at points of time in respect to personal investments and in contemplation of an uncertain future. Investors in stock market will from time to time reappraise and revaluate their various investment commitments in the light of new information changed expectations and ends. Investment choices are found to be outcomes of the following different but related classes of factors.

The investment decisions are based on many streams of data which taken together, represent to an investor the observable environment and the general and particular of the securities and enterprises in which he may invest.

Investing has been an activity confined to the rich and business class in the past. This can be attributed to the fact that availability of investible funds is a pre-requisite to deployment of funds. But today, we find that investment has become a household word and is very popular with people from all walks of life. According to the quick estimates of the Central Statistical Organisation, the Gross Domestic Savings reached a new peak of 25.6% of GDP at current market prices which was an improvement over the previous peak of *24.9%* in 1994-95. Overall, the higher saving rate lead to phenomenal increase in investment activities.

Factors influencing for Investment

Increasing popularity of investments can be attributed to the following factors:

A. Increase in Investing Population

B. Availability of Tax Incentives

C. Tendency of people for Investment

D. Availability of Investment Opportunities

E. Increase in Investment related Information

A) Increase in investing population

The Indian Capital Market has been growing tremendously during the last decade. India is having the largest number of listed companies in the world. Investment in shares and debentures has become a major source of income at present days. The country boasts of entertaining a large number of shareholders *For Ex:* The largest number of Unit holders being *65 lakhs* in UTI's Master gain - 1992. After implementation of privatisation, liberalisation and globalisation policies, the investment habits increased among the Indian citizens. At present, the investors in

6. Investment Channels

The investor in selection of best investments will have to mix between high rate of return oriented and stability of return oriented securities to reap the benefits of both. Various schemes for investments are offered to the public by the Government of India, public Financial Institutions, PSUs, Public Companies, and Mutual Funds. Most of these schemes are absolutely safe investments, but yield low return. However, in some schemes the overall return may increase along with providing various tax benefits. There are various schemes designed specifically for retired persons or those who are close to their retirement, while others are general schemes aimed at providing investment opportunity to cross section of the public. Thus, the distinctive features of each scheme differ from one to other and no particular scheme can be preferred to the others in every circumstance. The schemes that prove most attractive to an individual, would depend on his objectives and the different circumstances at any specific time. The growth and development of the country coupled with the policy of liberalisation and globalisation lead to introduction of a vast array of investment outlets.

INVESTMENT ENVIRONMENT

The Investment environment must be favourable so that the investors can invest their savings properly. While making a decision regarding investment, the investor should observe the economic environment of the country. Generally, the following are the basic considerations which faster growth and bring opportunities for a sound investment strategy:

1. *Stable Government*
2. *Stable Currency*
3. *Prescience of public Financial Institutions*
4. *Development of Corporate Sector*

Stable Government

A stable Government of a country frames adequate level safeguards h encourages accumulation of savings and investments. In India the tors will be willing to invest their savings if they have the assurance e safety of principal and expected return. A strong government can provide this facility.

le Currency

proper monitary policy will give a better direction to the investment well systematised monitary policy is necessary to encourage the t among the people. The monitary policy should neither promote y pressures nor prepare for a deflation model. A reasonable stable attracts a huge amount of capital investment by both Indian and

India is about more than *1.25* crores. While comparing with the developed markets, India is still backward in investing population.

B) Availability of Tax Incentives

The investment in securities can not be made without considering the various provisions of the tax laws. The investor may find that most of his profits have eroded by the payment of taxes. A tax planning could lead to a substantial increase in the amount of savings. Various tax incentives offered by the government make this possible. Provisions of Income Tax Act, and the Wealth Tax Act are important to an investor in planning investments. According to the Income Tax Act, the gross total income of an individual is computed in the following heads:

a) Income from salaries.

b) Income from house property

c) Profits and gains of business or profession

d) Capital gains

e) Income from other sources.

The incidence of income tax depends on the residential status of an individual. Income by way of *Interest, Premium,* issued by the central government is exempt from income tax. There are so many exemptions and deductions available to the investors under Income Tax Act, and Wealth Tax Act.

C) Tendency of people for Investment

The emerging economic environment of competitive markets, signifying customer sovereignty, has profound implications for the savings investment market in India. As household's sector share is overwhelmingly large in the country's savings, after implementation of government policies since 1991. Household savings constitute around *82%* of India's gross domestic savings. Approximately half of this takes the form of financial saving. Rapid changes are occurring all over the financial landscape as a result of financial liberalisation.

D) Investment Opportunities

There are various schemes available to the investors which are offered by the *Government of India, Public Sector Financial Institutions, Public Limited Companies, Public Sector Enterprises* and other institutions. Most of these investment opportunities are absolutely safe but yield low returns. But in some schemes the over all returns increase as they also provide various tax benefits. The following are the best investment opportunities available to Indian investors.

1. Investment in post office savings bank.
2. Schemes offered by Unit Trust of India.
3. Schemes offered by Development Banks.
4. Schemes offered by P.S.Us.
5. Schemes offered by Mutual Funds (Private & Public Sector).
6. Schemes offered by LIC, GIC.
7. Investment opportunities in public limited companies.
8. Investment in immovable property.
9. Investment in Gold, bultion, antiqnes etc.

E) Increase in Investment related information

The investors now have better information of market conditions to reap more benefit. For taking a right investment decisions, investors generally need to know the best sources of information. The best sources of information to the intelligent investor is *''Financial Periodicals, Satellite Channels, Global Affairs, National Economic Affairs, Associations, Company Information Quotations, and Publications etc.,*

When the analysis passes from the stage of description to the higher stage of security selection, the investor's frame of reference widens. The Investment activity now considers not only securities, but security holders as well. The power of selection or rejection of an investment depends upon the forces that will meet the requirements of the mass of investors who make up market. The key to successful investing involves examination and analysis of three chronological segments of the business operations *''past performance, present condition, future prospects.''*

NEED FOR INVESTMENT

Investments are both important and useful in the context of present day conditions. The following factors have made investment decisions increasingly important.

1. Increase in life expectancy
2. Interest rates
3. Increasing rate of taxation
4. Income
5. Inflation
6. Investment channels.

1. Increase in Life Expectancy

A tremendous increase in working population, proper planning for life span and longevity have ensured the need for investment decisions. Investment decisions have become significant because working people retire

between the age of 55 and 60. The life expectancy has increased due to improved living conditions, medical facilities etc. Savings from the current earnings must be invested in a proper way so that principal and income thereon will be adequate to meet expenditure on them after their retirement.

2. Interest Rates

The level of interest rates is another factor for a sound investment plan. Interest rates may vary between one investment to other risky and non-risky investments. The investor has to decide whether he is getting an acceptable return on the investment commensurate with the risks that are faced by him because stability of interest is as important as receiving a high rate of Interest.

3. Increasing rate of taxation

Taxation is one of the crucial factors in a person's savings. Tax planning is an essential part of over all investment planning. If the investment or disinvestment in securities is made without considering the various provisions of the tax laws, the investor may find that most of his profits have been eroded by the payment of taxes. Proper planning coul lead to a substantial increase in the amount of tax to be paid. On the ot hand, good tax planning and investing in tax savings schemes not reduces the tax payable by the investor but also helps him to save ta other incomes. Various tax incentives offered by the governme relevant provisions of the Income Tax Act, the Wealth Tax important to an investor in planning investments.

4. Income

Income is also a factor in making a sound investment general increase in employment opportunities which gave level and avenues for investment, have lead to the abilit of working population to save and invest such savings.

5. Inflation

In the conditions of inflation, the prices wi power of rupee will decline. On account of this, th year to the extent of rise in the inflation. The should be regarded as positive, when such retu inflation. For maintaining purchasing powe carefully plan and invest their funds by ma

(a) The rate of expected return and i

(b) The possibilities of expected gai

(c) The limitations imposed by perso

foreign investors. Attracting of huge amount of investments are based on wise monitary and fiscal policies, proper government control, good governance, economic well being and a growth oriented market for protecting the investors.

3. Presence of Public Financial Institutions

The Public Financial Institutions encourage a good amount of savings and direct them to productive purpose which help the investment market to grow rapidly. U.T.I, LIC, IDBI, IFCI, NABARD, ICICI, GIC offer a wide variety of schemes for savings along with tax benefits. These organisations lend an element of strength to the capital market and promote discipline while encouraging growth.

4. Development of Corporate Sector

The public limited companies are popular for investment, rather than the sole proprietorship or partnership firms. The public limited companies are the best forms of organisation as the characteristics of them are very helpful for investors.

SCOPE FOR INVESTMENT

The ultimate objective of the investor is to derive a variety of investments that meet his preference for risk and expected return. The investor will select the portfolio which will maximise his utility. The temperament and psychology of the investor is the another important consideration in making an investment decision by the investors. It is not only the construction of a portfolio that will promise the highest expected return, but also the satisfaction of the investor for his return. Many types of investment media or channels for making investments are available. Securities ranging from risk free instruments to highly speculative shares and debentures are available for alternative investments.

INVESTMENT MEDIA

Many types of investment channels for making investments are available. A sound investment programme can be constructed if the investor familiarizes the various attractive investments available. Investment media are of several kinds. Some media are simple and direct, others are complex. Some are familiar, others are relatively new and unidentified. Some investments are appropriate for an type of investor and another suitable to another person.

The ultimate objective of the investor is to derive a variety of investment opportunities that meet his preference for risk and expected return. The investor will select the portfolio which will maximise his profitability or minimize loss. Securities present a wide range of risks, from risk free instruments to highly risk speculative shares and debentures. From this broad spectrum the investor will have to select those securities that minimise his risk. The investor has an optimisation problem. He has to choose the security which will maximize his expected return subject to certain considerations. The objectives of the investors are different from investor to investor. It is not only the construction of a portfolio that will promise the highest expected return but also it must fulfil the condition of liquidity and safety of investment. Some investors would not mind to face high risk, because they would like to achieve huge return. Such investors invest their savings in growth shares. Another important consideration for investment is the temperament and psychology of the investor. Some investors are prepared to take risks and some do not face risk and they do not invest in risky securities even if the return is high. Some investors may prefer government bonds as they offer safety and liquidity, whereas others may be willing to invest in blue chip equity shares of reputed companies.

There are many alternative investments exist for investors. Such alternatives are presented in a chart given below:

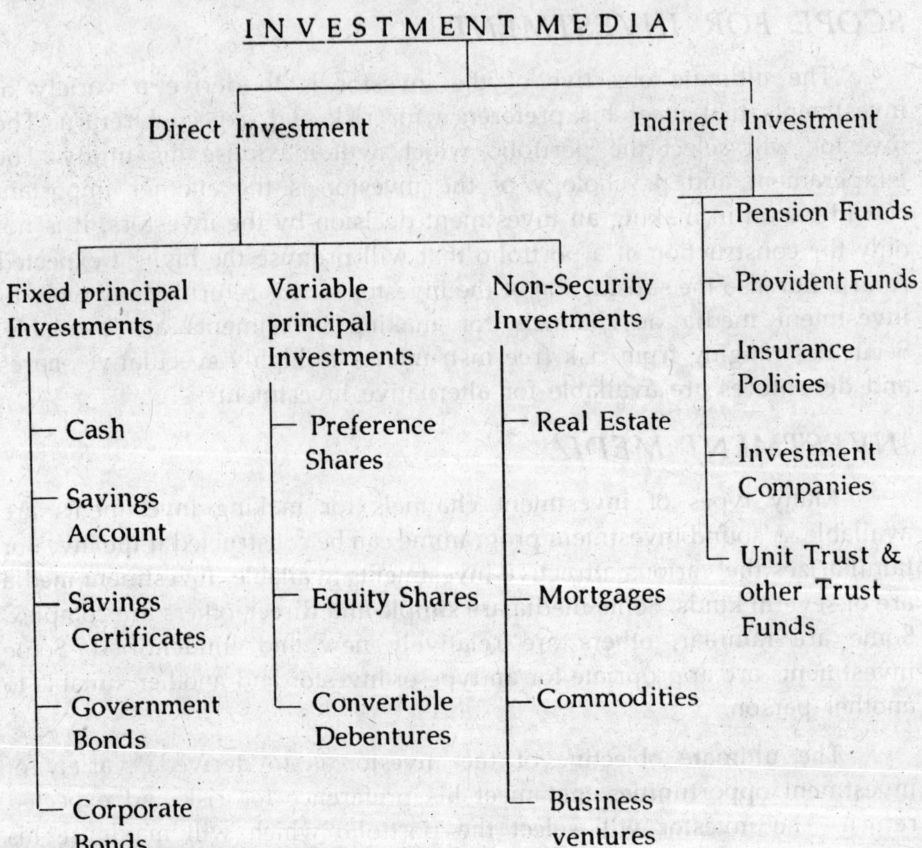

India is about more than *1.25* crores. While comparing with the developed markets, India is still backward in investing population.

B) Availability of Tax Incentives

The investment in securities can not be made without considering the various provisions of the tax laws. The investor may find that most of his profits have eroded by the payment of taxes. A tax planning could lead to a substantial increase in the amount of savings. Various tax incentives offered by the government make this possible. Provisions of Income Tax Act, and the Wealth Tax Act are important to an investor in planning investments. According to the Income Tax Act, the gross total income of an individual is computed in the following heads:

a) Income from salaries.

b) Income from house property

c) Profits and gains of business or profession

d) Capital gains

e) Income from other sources.

The incidence of income tax depends on the residential status of an individual. Income by way of *Interest*, *Premium*, issued by the central government is exempt from income tax. There are so many exemptions and deductions available to the investors under Income Tax Act, and Wealth Tax Act.

C) Tendency of people for Investment

The emerging economic environment of competitive markets, signifying customer sovereignty, has profound implications for the savings investment market in India. As household's sector share is overwhelmingly large in the country's savings, after implementation of government policies since 1991. Household savings constitute around *82%* of India's gross domestic savings. Approximately half of this takes the form of financial saving. Rapid changes are occurring all over the financial landscape as a result of financial liberalisation.

D) Investment Opportunities

There are various schemes available to the investors which are offered by the *Government of India, Public Sector Financial Institutions, Public Limited Companies, Public Sector Enterprises* and other institutions. Most of these investment opportunities are absolutely safe but yield low returns. But in some schemes the over all returns increase as they also provide various tax benefits. The following are the best investment opportunities available to Indian investors.

1. Investment in post office savings bank.
2. Schemes offered by Unit Trust of India.
3. Schemes offered by Development Banks.
4. Schemes offered by P.S.Us.
5. Schemes offered by Mutual Funds (Private & Public Sector).
6. Schemes offered by LIC, GIC.
7. Investment opportunities in public limited companies.
8. Investment in immovable property.
9. Investment in Gold, bultion, antiqnes etc.

E) Increase in Investment related information

The investors now have better information of market conditions to reap more benefit. For taking a right investment decisions, investors generally need to know the best sources of information. The best sources of information to the intelligent investor is *''Financial Periodicals, Satellite Channels, Global Affairs, National Economic Affairs, Associations, Company Information Quotations, and Publications etc.,*

When the analysis passes from the stage of description to the higher stage of security selection, the investor's frame of reference widens. The Investment activity now considers not only securities, but security holders as well. The power of selection or rejection of an investment depends upon the forces that will meet the requirements of the mass of investors who make up market. The key to successful investing involves examination and analysis of three chronological segments of the business operations *''past performance, present condition, future prospects."*

NEED FOR INVESTMENT

Investments are both important and useful in the context of present day conditions. The following factors have made investment decisions increasingly important.

1. Increase in life expectancy
2. Interest rates
3. Increasing rate of taxation
4. Income
5. Inflation
6. Investment channels.

1. Increase in Life Expectancy

A tremendous increase in working population, proper planning for life span and longevity have ensured the need for investment decisions. Investment decisions have become significant because working people retire between the age of 55 and 60. The life expectancy has increased due to improved living conditions, medical facilities etc. Savings from the current earnings must be invested in a proper way so that principal and income thereon will be adequate to meet expenditure on them after their retirement.

2. Interest Rates

The level of interest rates is another factor for a sound investment plan. Interest rates may vary between one investment to other risky and non-risky investments. The investor has to decide whether he is getting an acceptable return on the investment commensurate with the risks that are faced by him because stability of interest is as important as receiving a high rate of Interest.

3. Increasing rate of taxation

Taxation is one of the crucial factors in a person's savings. Tax planning is an essential part of over all investment planning. If the investment or disinvestment in securities is made without considering the various provisions of the tax laws, the investor may find that most of his profits have been eroded by the payment of taxes. Proper planning could lead to a substantial increase in the amount of tax to be paid. On the other hand, good tax planning and investing in tax savings schemes not only reduces the tax payable by the investor but also helps him to save taxes on other incomes. Various tax incentives offered by the government and relevant provisions of the Income Tax Act, the Wealth Tax Act, are important to an investor in planning investments.

4. Income

Income is also a factor in making a sound investment decision. The general increase in employment opportunities which gave rise to income level and avenues for investment, have lead to the ability and willingness of working population to save and invest such savings.

5. Inflation

In the conditions of inflation, the prices will rise and purchasing power of rupee will decline. On account of this, the capital is eroded every year to the extent of rise in the inflation. The return on any investment should be regarded as positive, when such return compensates the effect of inflation. For maintaining purchasing power stability, investors should carefully plan and invest their funds by making analysis

(a) The rate of expected return and inflation rate

(b) The possibilities of expected gain or loss on their investments and

(c) The limitations imposed by personal and family considerations.

6. Investment Channels

The investor in selection of best investments will have to mix between high rate of return oriented and stability of return oriented securities to reap the benefits of both. Various schemes for investments are offered to the public by the Government of India, public Financial Institutions, PSUs, Public Companies, and Mutual Funds. Most of these schemes are absolutely safe investments, but yield low return. However, in some schemes the overall return may increase along with providing various tax benefits. There are various schemes designed specifically for retired persons or those who are close to their retirement, while others are general schemes aimed at providing investment opportunity to cross section of the public. Thus, the distinctive features of each scheme differ from one to other and no particular scheme can be preferred to the others in every circumstance. The schemes that prove most attractive to an individual, would depend on his objectives and the different circumstances at any specific time. The growth and development of the country coupled with the policy of liberalisation and globalisation lead to introduction of a vast array of investment outlets.

INVESTMENT ENVIRONMENT

The Investment environment must be favourable so that the investors can invest their savings properly. While making a decision regarding investment, the investor should observe the economic environment of the country. Generally, the following are the basic considerations which faster growth and bring opportunities for a sound investment strategy:

1. *Stable Government*
2. *Stable Currency*
3. *Prescience of public Financial Institutions*
4. *Development of Corporate Sector*

1. Stable Government

A stable Government of a country frames adequate level safeguards which encourages accumulation of savings and investments. In India the investors will be willing to invest their savings if they have the assurance for the safety of principal and expected return. A strong government can alone provide this facility.

2. Stable Currency

A proper monitary policy will give a better direction to the investment outlets. A well systematised monitary policy is necessary to encourage the investment among the people. The monitary policy should neither promote inflationary pressures nor prepare for a deflation model. A reasonable stable price level attracts a huge amount of capital investment by both Indian and

foreign investors. Attracting of huge amount of investments are based on wise monitary and fiscal policies, proper government control, good governance, economic well being and a growth oriented market for protecting the investors.

3. Presence of Public Financial Institutions

The Public Financial Institutions encourage a good amount of savings and direct them to productive purpose which help the investment market to grow rapidly. U.T.I, LIC, IDBI, IFCI, NABARD, ICICI, GIC offer a wide variety of schemes for savings along with tax benefits. These organisations lend an element of strength to the capital market and promote discipline while encouraging growth.

4. Development of Corporate Sector

The public limited companies are popular for investment, rather than the sole proprietorship or partnership firms. The public limited companies are the best forms of organisation as the characteristics of them are very helpful for investors.

SCOPE FOR INVESTMENT

The ultimate objective of the investor is to derive a variety of investments that meet his preference for risk and expected return. The investor will select the portfolio which will maximise his utility. The temperament and psychology of the investor is the another important consideration in making an investment decision by the investors. It is not only the construction of a portfolio that will promise the highest expected return, but also the satisfaction of the investor for his return. Many types of investment media or channels for making investments are available. Securities ranging from risk free instruments to highly speculative shares and debentures are available for alternative investments.

INVESTMENT MEDIA

Many types of investment channels for making investments are available. A sound investment programme can be constructed if the investor familiarizes the various attractive investments available. Investment media are of several kinds. Some media are simple and direct, others are complex. Some are familiar, others are relatively new and unidentified. Some investments are appropriate for an type of investor and another suitable to another person.

The ultimate objective of the investor is to derive a variety of investment opportunities that meet his preference for risk and expected return. The investor will select the portfolio which will maximise his

profitability or minimize loss. Securities present a wide range of risks, from risk free instruments to highly risk speculative shares and debentures. From this broad spectrum the investor will have to select those securities that minimise his risk. The investor has an optimisation problem. He has to choose the security which will maximize his expected return subject to certain considerations. The objectives of the investors are different from investor to investor. It is not only the construction of a portfolio that will promise the highest expected return but also it must fulfil the condition of liquidity and safety of investment. Some investors would not mind to face high risk, because they would like to achieve huge return. Such investors invest their savings in growth shares. Another important consideration for investment is the temperament and psychology of the investor. Some investors are prepared to take risks and some do not face risk and they do not invest in risky securities even if the return is high. Some investors may prefer government bonds as they offer safety and liquidity, whereas others may be willing to invest in blue chip equity shares of reputed companies.

There are many alternative investments exist for investors. Such alternatives are presented in a chart given below:

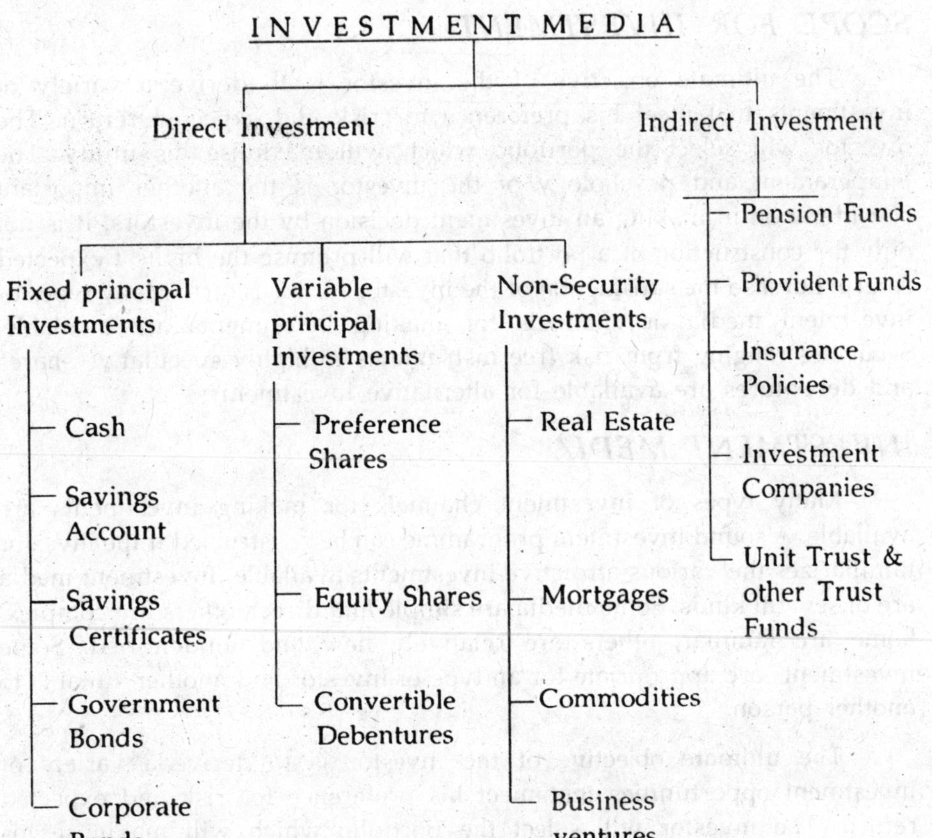

These media alternatives have basically been categorised as

A) Direct investment alternatives

B) Indirect investment alternatives

A) Direct Investment alternatives

Direct investments are those, where the individual makes his own choice and investment decision. Direct investments are again classified into

1. Fixed Principal Investments
2. Variable Principal Investments
3. Non-Security Investments

1. *Fixed Principal Investments*

These are those, whose principal amount and the terminal value are known with certainty. Cash has a constant rupee value. It does not earn any amount of return if it kept idle. Savings account have a fixed return, they differ only in terms of time period. Saving certificates are of a quite recent origin. They are available in the form of ''*National Saving Certificates, short-Term Deposit Certificates, Postal Saving Certificates, Government bonds, Debentures*'' have fixed maturity value and fixed rate of income over time.

2. *Variable Principal Securities*

These Securities terminal value are not known with certainity. Equity shares have no fixed return or maturity date. Their price is determined by demand and supply forces.

3. *Non-Security Investment*

These differ from securities in other aspects. Real estate such as Land, buildings and ownership of a house and its terminal value is uncertain. It is liquid than securities. Mortgage represents financing of real estate which has a periodic fixed income and the principal is recovered on a stated maturity date. Commodities are bought and sold in spot markets.

Contracts to buy and sell commodities at a future date are traded in future markets. Business ventures sell ownership securities to public, Art, Antiques and other valuables like gold, silver and jewellary are other types of specialised investments which possess aesthetic value.

B) Indirect Investment Alternatives

Indirect investments are those in which the individual has no direct hold on the amount he invests. He contributes his savings to certain organisations like '' *LIC or UTI*'' and depends upon them to make investment on his behalf. So there is no direct responsibility to hold the securities. An individual makes indirect investment for *"Retirement benefits"* in the form of *provident funds, pension funds, LIC policies, Investment in company securities, Units of U.T.I.* Individuals have no control on the investments. They are entrusted to the care of the particular organisation. Organisations like, *LIC, UTI, PSUs* are managed according to their investment policy by a group of trusts on behalf of the investors. While choosing specific investments, investors look for certain features which are suited to their needs and conveniences.

TABLE No.I (2)

Steps in selecting a portfolio

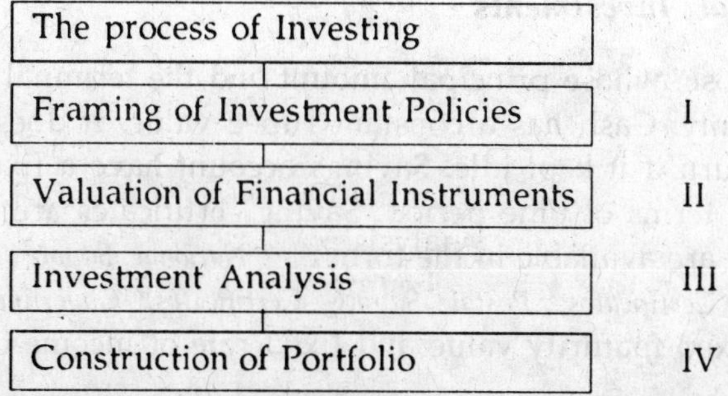

I. Framing of Investment policy: It includes the following:

a) Determination of Investing amount

b) Determination of portfolio objectives

c) Identification of potential investment assets.

d) Allocation of wealth to asset categories.

II. Valuation of Investment: It includes the following:

a) Valuation of stocks

b) Valuation of debentures

c) Valuation of bonds

d) Valuation of other assets

III. Investment Analysis: It include the following:

Table-I (3)

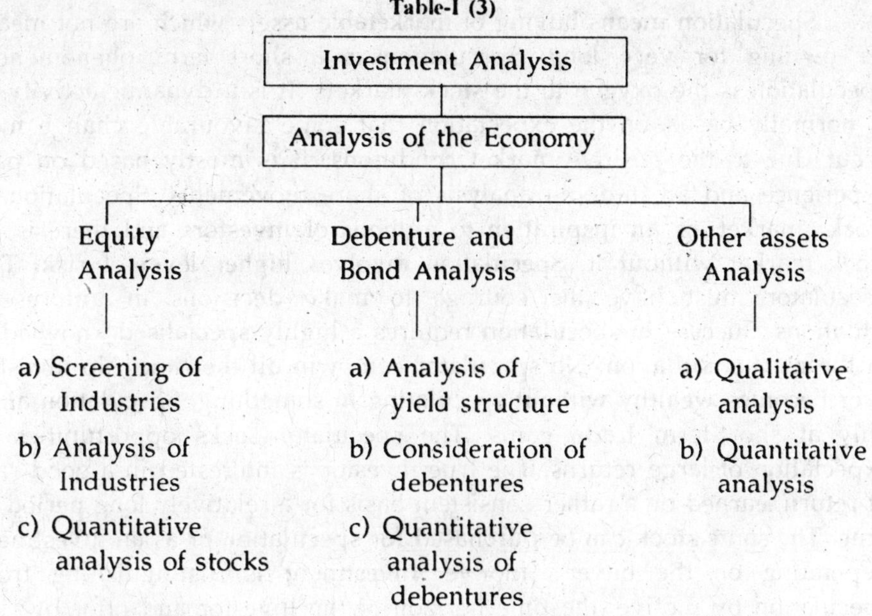

IV. Portfolio Construction (Basket of different kinds of Investment)

Table-I (4)

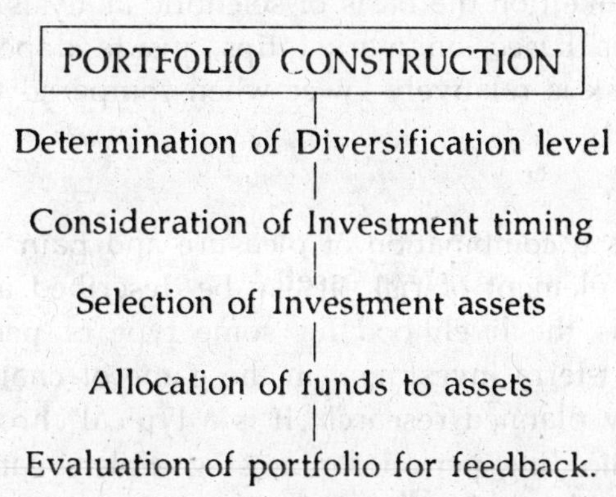

All investors are savers but all savers cannot be good investors. Investment is a science and an art. The growth of urbanisation and literacy have activated the cult of investment. Recently, the activity has become more popular with the change in Government policies towards liberalisation, globalisation and financial deregulation. Investment is of long-term nature. Savings and investments are the basis of capital formation and economic growth in the country. The economic performance is reflected in the growth of income. Growth refers to a rise in output and levels of income. The rate of investment, in a country depends upon the rate of saving made by the community.

SPECULATION

Speculation means buying of marketable assets which are not meant for owning for very long. Speculation is a short term phenomenon. Speculation is the oxygen to the stock markets. It is a dynamic activity. It is normally based on the expectation that some favourable change may occur due to the positive market conditions. It is mostly based on past experience and an in-depth analysis of share movements. Speculation in stock market is an inspiration to millions of investors and there is no stock market without it. Speculation involves higher level of risk. The speculator must have the courage to make decisions in unforeseen situations. Success in speculation requires a highly specialised knowledge in the market situation. No speculator can win all the time. No investor ever becomes wealthy without speculating in something. Speculation aims only at short-term trade gains. The speculator seeks opportunities in expectation of large returns. The true investor is interested in a good rate of return, earned on a rather consistent basis for a relatively long period of time. The same stock can be purchased for speculation or as an investment depending on the buyer's motive. Investment is distinguishing from speculation by motive, the time horizon of the investor and offer by risk return characteristics of the investment. Investment is based on long-term nature but speculation is short-term phenomenon. Investment decision will be taken on the basis of scientific analysis of intrinsic value, but speculation is based on market tips, inside dope, hunches etc. In investment the risk is relatively lower when compared to speculation.

GAMBLING

Gambling is a combination of pleasure and pain. It refers to an act involving pure element of risk. It can be described as easy money for lazy persons. It is the livelihood for some type of people. Gambling is usually very short-term investment in the game of chance. It is far away from the carefully planned research. It is a typical chronic and repetitive experience. The holding period for most gamblers can be measured in seconds. The gambler moves with due consideration for ''*hunches*'' and other tactics. In gambling artificial and unnecessary risks are created. Gambling has to do with acceptance of risks. The gambler never stops after winning the money, but he still continues to earn more and more. Gambling is the quite opposite of investment.

Ex: for gambling: "Horse riding"

"Game of cards"

"Lottery".

INVESTMENT PRINCIPLES

Before choosing specific investment plan, investor's will need to have definite ideas regarding expected return and risk for their investment. All investors want their investments to be safe and they would like to see that it must grow with an increased rate of growth. But money is a very fluid asset. Inflation erodes its value. Therefore, the money is to be properly invested to earn a rate of return or at least it must compensate the rate of inflation. Well planned investment can alone ensure that the value of the investment must increase alongwith enhanced monetary returns. The dynamics of economic growth provide various opportunities for investors. For choosing right investments, the investor must follow the principles of investment. Investment principles should be consistent with the investor's general objectives. The following are the investment principles for a successful selection of investment:

1. Safety
2. Liquidity
3. Profit
4. Taxation
5. Inflation
6. Government control
7. Legality
8. Transferability
9. Tangibility

Let us now discuss the principles of investment in detail.

1. Safety of Investment

Generally, every investor would be primarily concerned with safety of his investment. Adequate protection should exist against the risk of loss of capital. However, a highly safe investment will generate relatively low return. Apart from the safety, the investor must also take care of sound liquidity coupled with the marketability of the investments. Fixed income securities provide safety but their rate of return is very low. Alternatively, investor can invest in shares of diversified list of various growth oriented industries by properly selecting the companies in order to achieve the objective of safety and a satisfactory yield, because the risk is spread due to diversification among different scrips of companies.

2. Liquidity

Any investment is said to be liquid, if it can be converted into cash or sold as and when required. A liquid investment would enable the investor to encash his investment whenever the need arise. It would also permit to sell off an unremunerative investment, thereby minimising the losses, and switch over to a more promising investment. Thus, the liquidity of an investment offers flexibility in the face of changing economic and political environment.

3. Profit

The main reason we invest our idle funds is for earning a profit. Profit can be realized in either or both of the following forms.

a) Capital appreciation

b) Yield

Capital appreciation occurs when an investment is disposed of at a higher value as compared to the price for which it was purchased. The difference between the net selling price and the purchase price, when positive, denotes capital appreciation. Yield from an investment is derived in the form of interest or dividend. The rate of interest is usually fixed whereas the rate of dividend may fluctuate from year to year, depending on the profitability of the concern in which money has been invested.

4) Tax implications

While planning investment strategy, one should bear in mind the various provisions of tax laws vis-a-vis investment income and other incomes. Important taxation provisions and tax planning possibilities are to be kept in mind while planning an investment strategy.

5) Inflation

In our country, every year the purchasing power of the rupee declines as we suffer from a continuing inflation in prices. So our capital is eroded every year to the extent of the rate of inflation.

6) Government control

Various Government statutes and controls, the Gold Control Act and the Urban Land Ceiling Act, affect investment decisions and so need to be considered.

7) Legality

Law relating to Minors, Estates, Trusts, Shares and Insurance should be studied and all investments should be approved by law.

8) Transferability

Though the investor presumably buys high grade securities and holds for the long term, the securities must be easily and legally transferable both on monetary and non-monitory terms.

9) Tangibility

Tangible assets do not yield an income. Some investors prefer such investments because intangible assets may have lost their value due to price level changes, regulation of Law, or social collapse.

SOURCES OF INVESTMENT INFORMATION

For taking of a right investment decision, investors generally need to know the better sources of information to invest. In stock market, information about the corporate world plays an important role in making decisions. Investors should react to the tune of market environment. Analysis of the information requires an expertise. The investors who have better information use to reap more benefit. Following are the best sources of information to the intelligent investor.

a) Global affairs
b) National economic affairs
c) Associations
d) Company information
e) Financial periodicals
f) Quotations
g) Publications
h) Satellite channels

a) Global Affairs

Day to-day developments around globe are published in news papers like *''Indian Economist, Far Eastern Economic Review, Newyork Times, Washington Post, Economic Times, Financial Express, Business Standard, Business Lines'' etc,* world information is also available with IMF quarterly Journal, IMF News survey, News Letters of standard chartered bank, Times Magazine etc.

b) National Economic Affairs

These affairs are covered in all the leading financial news papers like *''The Economic Times, The Business Standard, Financial Express and Journals like Business India, Business World, Business Today, Southern Economist, Economic and Political Weekly, the Capital Market, Vikalpa, Finance India, Indian Management - Fortune India, Dalal Street, Intelligent Investor, Arthasasthra etc.''*

c) Associations

Almost many daily news papers bring out regularly the result of studies made on the working of industries and their prospects. In India there are various associations like "*Chamber of Commerce, FICCI, Trade Associations*" and other agencies publish knowledgeable, analytical data. The reports of Planning Commission, Government of India, RBI Bulletins, publications contain a good amount of information. *The Centre for Monitoring Indian Economy (CMIE)* is a research based organisation is involved in preparing the reports about Indian economy in all sectors. It also updates the information and renders expert advice to the needy business organisations on a fee charge basis. The monthly reports of various associations of industries give more upto date and timely information.

d) Company Information

At present the companies information is freely available in almost all the news papers, periodicals, journals and some pages are allotted for the reports about the business in general and company working results, performance of companies and other needful data. Besides news papers, the Journals of *Capital Market, Dalal Street, Business World, Money and Business India* contain a lot of information about the industries and companies listed on stock exchanges. Results of equity and market research are published in the journals. Annual reports, quarterly and half-yearly results also form important sources of information. The financial Journalists give write ups on various companies after interviewing the executives of the corporate sector.

e) Financial Periodicals

The big broker firms are sending news letters as market information with fundamental and technical analysis with the help of their equity research departments. The "*ICFAI*" publishes a monthly journal called "*Chartered Financial Analyst*". The Indian Institute of Finance publishes a Journal called "*Finance India.*" "*The Capital Market*" "*Wall Street Journal*" "*Dalal Street Journal*". "*The Banker*", "*The Management*" "*Management Accountant*" "*Artha vignanam*" "*Reports of Prime Data Base Management*" "*Reports of SEBI*". *RBI Bulletins* and publications also bringout useful information. The Economic Times especially established a department of "*Investor's Guide*", "*Equity Research Bureau*", "*Fund Monitor*" to carryout studies and to publish research based articles which are found to be more valuable in the taking of a right investment decisions.

Investment analysis is available to subscribers and to their own clients. Others can avail this facility at stipulated rates. The data is available about settlements, record dates, book-closures trade cycle, price of a particular scrip during a particular week, month, year, quantity of volume of business done in Stock Exchange, trading activities, analytical data, financial performance, trend in market etc,.

f) Quotations

Generally the news papers carry share price quotations in their daily editions, which are listed by National Stock Exchange, Mumbai stock exchange H S E, D S E, M S E, C S E etc., Every stock exchange is publishing its own daily quotations list with all the particulars of traded securities. ''*The Capital Market, Dalal Street, Intelligent Investor, Economic Times, Finance India and Indian Management give* company information regarding all financial barometers like'' *Gross profit margin, Net profit, Earning before depreciation, interest and tax, profit after tax, Profit before tax, Earning per share* and other important ratios, with the development of information technology sector, almost all the relevant data is available in a computer at the click of the Mouse. The B.S.E publishes all the required data for technical analysis and makes it also available in computer floppies in a fraction of a minute. In *Economic Times*, stock Indices like *Mindex, SEP ''NIFTY'' ''SENSEX''* etc., are published. All the indices, daily volumes, Advances, Declines, high, low, volume, carry forward transactions, depository services, top gainers, top losers, are also published.

g) Publications

The RBI will publish all the financial transactions which have occurred throughout the nation in the form of Bulletins. It contains a vast data about money market, Bullion market, Forex market, Current exchange rates, Gold and silver prices etc. All this information is also available in *''CMIE''* reports and *''NCAER''* publications. The data as *''FOREX MARKET'', ''ABROAD NEWS''* can be obtained from *''Wall Street Journal'', ''London Economist'', ''Far Eastern Economic Review''* etc., The information on forex market is also available with *''Foreign Exchange Dealers Association of India'' (FADAI)* and foreign banks. The *''SEBI''* reports also make available this data. Data on mutual funds are published in Economic Times. They publish the latest *''NAVs''* of all mutual funds in the country irrespective of private and public. The data provides details of current schemes, NAV of each scheme, market price of each scheme, repurchase/redemption price, entry cost, exit cost open ended schemes, close ended schemes etc. *''The Capital Market'', ''Bulls Eye'', ''Dalal Street'', ''Business World'', ''Economic Times'' ''Premium'', ''Capital'', ''Money'', ''Intelligent Investor'', ''Business India''*. etc. publish information about mutual funds.

h) Satellite Channels

Private T.V channels are providing information about the corporate affairs on day to-day basis. They also telecast the interviews of well known experts, professional analysts, the views of management consultants and other persons. Almost all national as well as local channels are covering business briefs after the news bulletins. Some channels like *''Jain TV'' ''CNBC'' ''CNN'' ''Star News'' ''Zee News''* devote more time for corporate news on global basis. Business News, Interviews with consultants, fund managers, portfolio managers, stock market analysts, managing directors of reputed organisations, trustees of mutual funds, finance directors of companies and their comments, are transmitted.

AVENUES OF INVESTMENTS

Investment refers to acquisition of some assets. It means the conversion of money into claims of money. Investment is the diversion of money from savings to production activity. Investment results in regular income/return and capital appreciation and capital gains.

The following table presents the data on preference of investment in various firms by the public. The findings of a survey conducted by RBI and published in "Business Line" are given below.

Investments in various Financial Instruments

A) LIC	-	32%
B) Fixed Deposits	-	31%
C) Mutual Funds	-	9%
D) Chit Funds	-	6%
E) Jewellry	-	6%
F) Gold	-	3%
G) Secondary Market	-	5%
H) Primary Market	-	5%
I) Others	-	3%

MODES OF INVESTMENT

The investment means use of funds for productive purposes. In India there are different types of securities available to the investors. The various avenues for investment, ranging from riskless to high risk investment opportunities. All financial instruments which are available in our country from time to time for potential investors are presented below:

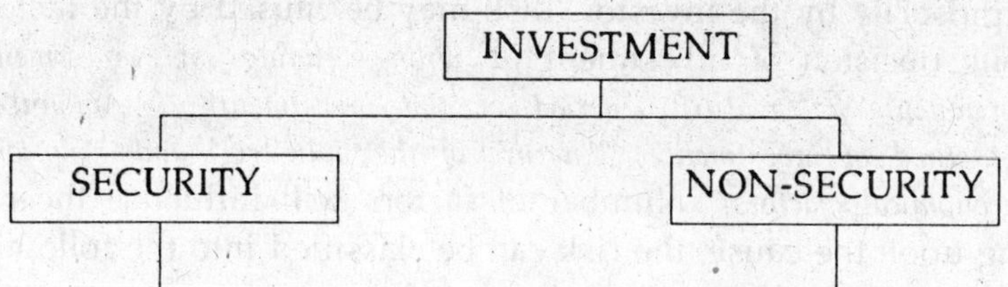

SECURITY

1. Equity shares
   (New issue, Rights, Bonus issue)
2. Preference Shares.
3. Public Sector Bonds
   (Taxable, Tax free)
4. Debentures
   (Convertible, partly convertible, optionally convertible and Non-convertible)

NON-SECURITY

1. National Savings Certificate.
2. Post Office Saving Bank Account.
3. L.I.C Policies
4. Provident Funds
5. Corporate Fixed Deposits
6. Unit Schemes of U.T.I.
7. Other schemes

Investment involves proper cash management and asset management. Investment in risky assets both marketable and non - marketable has to be planned. Management of investments requires a lot of expertise, dynamism, knowledge about the corporate sector, stock market skills and talent etc.

ANALYSIS OF RISK IN INVESTMENT

Savings are invested in various investment opportunities for earning better returns. The returns of the investment depends upon the risk of such investment. All investments involve some risk. The objective of any investor is to minimise the risk and maximise return. The value of financial assets depends on their return and risk pattern.

Risk may be defined as *''the chance of future loss that can be foreseen''*

Risk can be defined as *''the chance factor in trading in which expected or perspective advantage, gain, profit or return may not materialise.''*

The actual outcome of investment may be less than the expected outcome. The greater is the variability in the possible outcome, the greater is the risk. Generally, the variance and standard deviation of return are used as the alternative statistical measures of the risk of the financial asset. Similarly, co-variance measures the risk of the asset, relative to other asset in a portfolio. Risk free investment means only the certainity of the return of an investment and not free from all risks. Risk comprises all elements which cause for the variability in the return. Some risks can be controlled by the investors. Others cannot be controlled, and they are to be borne compulsorily by the investor. Risk may be caused by the factors, such as "wrong decision of investment", *''wrong timing of Investment", ''kinds of instruments", ''maturity period of the investment", ''Amount of investment" ''Method of investment", ''nature of the industry" and ''national, international economical factors."* Number of factors will influence the risk and depending upon the cause, the risk can be classified into the following major types:

1. Default Risk
2. Financial Risk
3. Business Risk
4. Liquidity Risk
5. Maturity Risk
6. Call Risk
7. Interest Rate Risk
8. Inflation Risk
9. Currency Risk

1. Default Risk

Default risk means, the failure of the borrower to pay the interest and principal amount within the stipulated period of time. The default risk has the capital risk and income risk as its components. It means not only failure to pay, but also delay in payment.

2. Financial Risk

Financial Risk refers to the risk on account of pattern of capital structure. It is usually measured by the debt equity mix of the firm. The higher the proportion of debt in the capital structure, greater is the variability of return and financial risk. Financial risk is an avoidable risk to the extent that managements have freedom. A firm with no debt financing has no financial risk. Financial risk is related to the debt and equity mix of financing in the firm. The reliance on debt financing is also called financial leverage. It has an important effect on shareholders return. Debt financing increases the variability of their returns.

3. Business Risk

Business risk arises due to the uncertainty of return which depends upon the nature of business. It will influence for the firm's operating income. It relates to the variability of the business,. sales, income, expenses, and profits. It depends upon the market conditions for the product mix, input supplies, strength of the competitor .etc. The business risk may be classified into two kinds viz., Internal risk and external risk. Internal risk is related to the operating efficiency of the firm. This is manageable within or by the firm. Internal business risk leads to fall in revenues and profit of the companies. External risk refers to the policies of Government or strategies of competitor or unforeseen situation in market. This risk may not be controlled and corrected by the firm.

4. Liquidity Risk

Liquidity risk refers to a situation wherein it may not possible to sell the asset. Liquidity risk refers to inability to meet the liabilities of creditors when they want to withdraw their money. Assets are disposed off at great inconvenience and cost in terms of money and time. Any asset that can be bought and sold quickly is said to be liquid. Failure of disposable of an asset is called liquidity risk. Liquidity risk has a different meaning from the point of view of banks and financial institutions.

5. Maturity Risk

Maturity risk will arise when the money was not received at the time of maturity of the security. It is on long-term basis. It will happen when the term of maturity, period of the security is longer. The longer the term to maturity, the greater is the risk, because forecasting the environment, for assessing conditions and situation, becomes more and more difficult.

6. Call Risk

It is associated with corporate bonds. The bonds are issued with call back provisions and the issues will have the right of redeeming the bonds. The bondholders face the risk of giving up higher coupon bonds. The reinvesting the proceeds at lower interest rates may arise and incurring the cost and inconvenience of investment.

7. Interest Rate Risk

It is the difference between the expected interest rates and the current market interest rate. The markets will have different interest rate fluctuations, according to market situation, supply and demand position of cash or credit. The degree of interest rate risk is related to the length of time to maturity of the security. If the maturity period is long, the market value of the security may fluctuate widely. Further, the market activity and investor perceptions change with the change in the interest rates and interest rates also depend upon the nature of instruments such as bonds, debentures, loans and maturity period, credit worthiness of the security issues.

8. Inflation Risk

Inflation risk is also called as purchasing power risk. It is closely related to interest rate risk since interest rates generally rise when inflation occurs. Inflation risk is more relevant in case of fixed income securities, shares are regarded as hedge against inflation. It is the risk that the real rate of return on security may be less than the nominal return. There is always a chance that the purchasing power of invested money will decline or that the real return will decline due to inflation. The return expected by investor will change due to change in real value of returns. Cost push inflation is caused by rise in the costs due to rise in the input costs. Push and pull forces operate to increase prices due to inadequate supplies and raising demand.

9. Currency Risk/Exchange Rate Risk

Exchange rate risk is also called as currency risk. It is associated with the exchange rate fluctuation of foreign exchange on international transactions. The risk is faced by the limited organisations which are involved in export or import business. This risk will arise due to changes in currency exchange rates, may have an unfavourable impact on costs or revenues. There is no exchange rate risk under the fixed exchange rate system. It refers to cashflow variability experienced by companies in international exchanges on account of uncertainty in exchange rates.

The following table shows components of risk:

Table No.I (7)

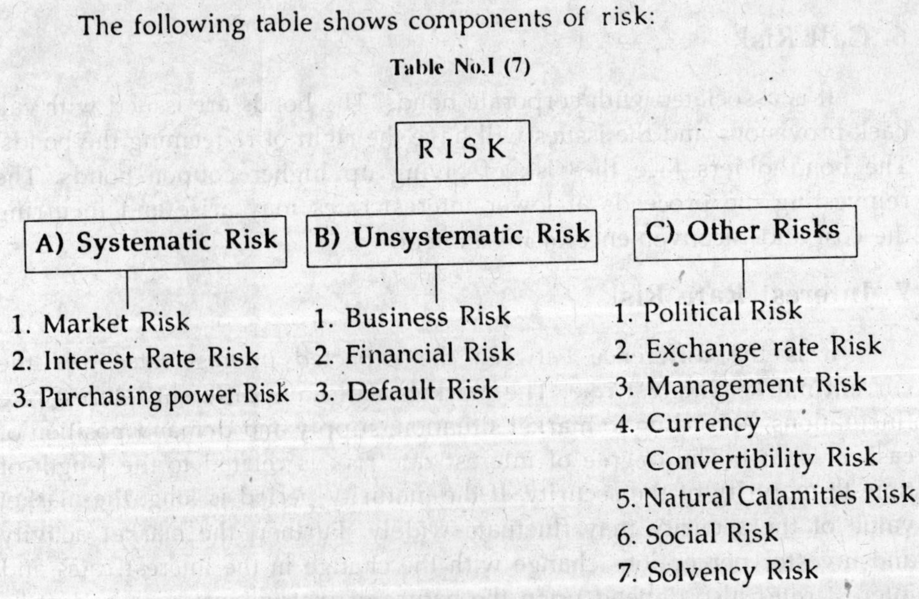

A) Systematic Risk

It is also called non-diversified risk. It is unavoidable. It may also be called as market risk. The variability in a securities total return is directly associated with the overall movements in the general market or economy is called systematic risk. This risk is inescapable from the investment. No matter how well the portfolio is diversified. It is caused by a wide range of factors exogenous to securities themselves viz., recession, war, and structural changes in the economy.

B) Unsystematic risk

Unsystematic risk is also called *''Diversifiable risk''* or *''Non-market risk''*. Unsystematic risk can be minimised or eliminated through diversification of security holding. The variability in a scrip's total return that is not related to the overall market variability is called unsystematic risk. It represents the portion of an investment risk that can be eliminated by holding diversified stocks. This risk is due to management changes in the company, labour problems, strikes etc.

C) Total Risk (Other risks)

It is the total variability in the return on the assets or the portfolio, whatever may be the source of the variability. It is the uncertainty or volatility in return due to both security - specific and economic factors. We can say that total risk is the combination of systematic and unsystematic risks.

Total Risk = Systematic risk + Unsystematic risk

***Beta* (β):**

Beta is a measure of relative risk of a security or its sensitivity to the movements in the market. It is a measure of volatility or the systematic risk faced by an asset or portfolio or project. It is calculated by using the covariance between returns of assets and returns of the market portfolio, divided by variance of return on the market portfolio. It shows how the price of a security responds to market factors. The more responsive is the price of a security to changes in the market, the higher will be its beta. β is also calculated by relating the return on security with the returns for the market. Market return is measured by the average return of a large sample of stocks.

The beta for the overall market is equal to 1.00 and other betas are viewed in relation to this value. Betas can be positive or negative. Many large brokerage firms, investment companies amd financial consultants provide beta data for a large number of stocks.

All investments are risky. The higher the risk taken, the higher is the return. But proper management of risk involves the right choice of investments whose risks are compensating. The total risks of two companies may be different and even lower than the risk of a group of two companies if their risks are offset by each other. Thus, if the risk of Reliance is represented by Beta of 1.90 and of Dr. Reddy's Lab at 0.70 the total of these two is 1.30, on average. But the actual Beta of the group of these two may be less than that due to the fact that covariances of these two may be negative or independent. It may be more than that if there is a strong positive covariance between them. The formula for calculation of beta can be given as follows:

$$R_S = a = \beta_S + R_M$$

R_S = Estimated return on the stock.

a = Estimated return when the market return is zero.

β_S = Measure of stocks sensitivity to the market Index.

R_M = Return on the market index.

CAPITAL ASSET PRICING MODEL

Under this theory, the return on each security is related to the total risk of the security. This risk is made up of systematic risk related to the market and unsystematic risk related to the company. In capital asset pricing model, the company risk is eliminated and only the market risk remains. The market should be a free market and the free flow of correct information. This information is digested by the market. Then the price of a share is determined as in action system and the market is the best performer. Stock risk and the market risk are related by variable called beta. The concept of beta is useful in portfolio management. The beta measures, the movement of one scrip in relation to the market trend, using beta as the measure of the nondiversifiable risk. The Capital Asset Pricing Model is used to define the required rate of return on a security according to the following equation:

$$R_S = Rf + \beta_S (R_M - Rf)$$

R_S = The rate of return required on the investment.

Rf = The rate of return that can be earned on risk free investment. [Treasury bills]

R_M = The average rate of return on all securities.

β_S = The security's beta risk [systematic]

Illustration (1):- A security with beta 1.4 is being purchased at a time when the risk free rate is 4 percent and the market return is expected to be 12%. Calculate the rate of return required on the investment.

$$R_S = Rf + B_S [R_M - Rf]$$

Rf = 4% R_M = 12% β_S = 1.4% R_S = 4% + 1.4 (12% - 4%)

R_S = 4% + 1.4% (8%)

R_S = 4% + 11.2

R_S = **15.2%**

The investor therefore require 15.2% return on his investment for a non-diversified risk of the security's beta of 1.4.

Illustration (2):- A security with a beta of 2 is being considered at a time when the risk free rate is 4% and the market return is expected to be 10%. Calculate the required rate of return on the investment.

$$R_S = Rf + \beta_S (R_M - Rf)$$

Rf = 4% β_S = 2% R_M = 10%

R_S = 4% + 2 (6%)

R_S = 4% + 12% = **16%.**

Illustration (3):- A security with a beta of 0.85 is being considered at a time when the risk free rate is 4% and the market return is expected to be 10%. Calculate the required rate of return on the investment.

$$R_S = Rf + \beta_S (R_M - Rf)$$

Rf = 4% β = 0.85 R_M = 10%

R_S = 4% + 1 (10% - 4%)

R_S = 4% + 1(6%)

R_S = 4% + 6% = **10%.**

Illustration (4):- A security with a beta of 0.25 is being considered at a time when the risk free rate is 4% and the market return is expected to be 10%. Calculate the required rate of return on the investment.

$$R_S = Rf + \beta_S (R_M - Rf)$$

$Rf = 4\%$; $\beta_S = 0.25$; $R_M = 10\%$

$R_s = 4\% + 0.25\ (10\text{-}4)$

$R_s = 4\% + 0.25(6)$

$R_s = 4\% + 1.5\%$

$R_s = \boxed{5.5\%.}$

RETURN

Return is a reward and motivating force behind every investment. Return is always haunted by investment. Return is the amount or rate of gain, profit which accrues to an investment. The return represents the benefits derived by a business firm from its operations. The rate of return required by a firm to a great extent depends upon the risk involved, higher the risk, greater is the return expected by the firm. Return on investment has two components, regular income in the form of interest or dividend and capital appreciation. The total return on investment can be defined as *''Income plus (minus) price appreciation (depreciation).''*

Types of Return

The following are the various kinds of return:

A) Internal rate of return

B) Coupon rate

C) Expected return

D) Holding period return

E) Basic yield

F) Current yield

G) Yield to Maturity

H) Dividend yield

I) Earning yield

J) Real and Nominal return

K) Gross and Net yield

L) Required rate of return.

A) Internal Rate of Return

This is also known as yield rate. It is the rate which discounts the cash flows to zero. Internal rate of return is that rate at which the sum of discounted cash inflows equals the sum of discounted cash outflows. The marginal IRR is the rate of discount which makes the present value of the marginal revenue from the additional investment equal to unity.

B) Bond Rate/Coupon Rate

Coupon rate means, the interest rate received on the face value or the par value of the bond. If a company or Government issues a 10 - year bond with Rs.100 as face value and 14 percent rate of interest, it would be described as 14% bond or debenture and may be said to have, a coupon rate of 14%.

C) Expected return/Realised Return

Return is not guaranteed. It is mostly expected and it may or may not be realised. Therefore the expected return is an anticipated or predicted, desired return by the investor which is subject to uncertainty. Realised return means actually earned and received.

D) Holding Period Yield/Return

Holding period yield (HPY) measures the total return from an investment during a given or designated time period in which the asset is held by the investor. It is to be noted that HPY does not mean that the security is actually sold and the gain or loss is actually realised by the investor. The concept of HPY is applicable whether one is measuring the realised return or estimating the future (expected) return. It can be calculated as follows:

$$\text{HPY} = \frac{\text{Any cash payments received + price change over the holding period}}{\text{Price at which the asset is purchased (beginning price)}}$$

E) Basic yield

Basic yield is associated with high grade bonds. It is the lowest yield actually attained the market. Basic yield can be understood by noting the concept of pure rate of interest, which is unique and absolutely riskless; it implies absolute safety and certainty of principal and income and also freedom from losses through changes in commodity prices, interest rates and taxes. The basic yield, however, does not imply either riskless or uniqueness.

F) Current Yield

Current yield is also known as the market yield/income yield/ running yield. Bonds are offered to the public with coupon rate. Current yield is the ratio of interest per year to the current market price of the bond. It does not take into account the return earned by the investor because of appreciation in the value of bond.

G) Yield to Maturity

It is also known as redemption yield. It is the promised rate of return an investor will receive from a bond purchased at the current market price and held till maturity.

$$YTM = \frac{\text{Annual interest} \pm \text{(Appreciation/Depreciation of the Asset)}}{\text{Redemption value or face value}}$$

H) Dividend Yield

Dividend yield is the ratio of per share expected dividends, gross of tax to the current market price of the share.

I) Earnings Yield

It is the ratio of expected EPS of the firm to the current market price of the share. There is no difference between dividend yield and earnings yield, if the firms dividend payout ratio is 100%.

J) Nominal and Real Return

Nominal return is the return in nominal rupees, the real return is equal to the nominal return adjusted for inflation.

K) Gross and Net Yield

The yield realised by the investor before paying taxes, is called as gross yield. The Net yield is gross yield less income tax paid.

Net yield = Gross yield [1-Tax rate]

L) Required Rate of Return

Required rate of return is an important factor to be considered for buying securities. The RRR is defined as the minimum expected rate of return needed to an investor to purchase the security, given its risk. The RRR has two components viz. The risk free rate of return or the time value of money. The second component of RRR is the risk premium. It is the return that an investor must get for facing the risk by investing his money in all those risk generating investments.

RRR = The time value of money + inflation premium + risk premium

[or]

RRR = Risk free rate of return + risk premium.

SUMMARY

This chapter provided a broad view about the nature of investment. It was noted that the process of investing and valuation of financial investments are the main focus of the Investment Management. In this chapter we have explored the investment avenues and characteristics of investment. Investors want to maximise expected return subject to their tolerance for risk. The risk is associated with holding of common stocks. Uncontrollable forces, called sources of systematic risk. The principal sources of unsystematic risk affecting the holding of common stocks are business risk and financial risk. The various sources of risk in holding common stocks must be quantified. A reasonable surrogate of risk is the variability of return. Total risk of an investment can be thought of as consisting of two components, diversified and non-diversifiable risks. Beta measures the risk and can be used to determine the appropriate required return on a security.

QUESTIONS

1. Define the term "Investment".
2. Explain the important factors which generally have a bearing on investment decisions.
3. What are the elements of Investment?
4. Explain the nature of Investment?
5. What are the factors influencing for investment?
6. Write an essay on need for investment?
7. Discuss about the factors of investment environment?
8. What do you mean by Investment media?
9. What are the differences between speculation and gambling?
10. Write an essay about the principles of Investment?
11. What do you mean by Investment information? What are the sources of Investment information?
12. Differentiate between risk and uncertainty?
13. What are the major types of risk?
14. What do you mean by Return ? How many types of Returns?
15. What is the Meaning of Beta?
16. Write an essay about capital asset pricing mode.

❀ ❀ ❀

2

VALUATION OF EQUITY SHARES

The security analyst will evaluate the past performance of a particular company's scrip when he faces with the problem of making a buy, hold, or sell decision. The evaluation result and then coupled with his personal experience, predict its future performance and relative market position. The detailed data available to the analyst for this task far exceeds his human capabilities of assimilation. The analyst will normally base his perdiction on several basic attributes of the security and modify these results in the light of his intuitive beliefs.

The valuation of equity shares will be quite difficult and different because the return on equity is uncertain and can change from time to time. The amount of the return and the degree of variability of return together will determine the value of a share. If the value of the share is lower than the infrinsic value, then share is undervalued and better to buy because, the same can be sold when it is overvalued in the market. There are different methods of valuation of equity shares. These are presented with the following chart:

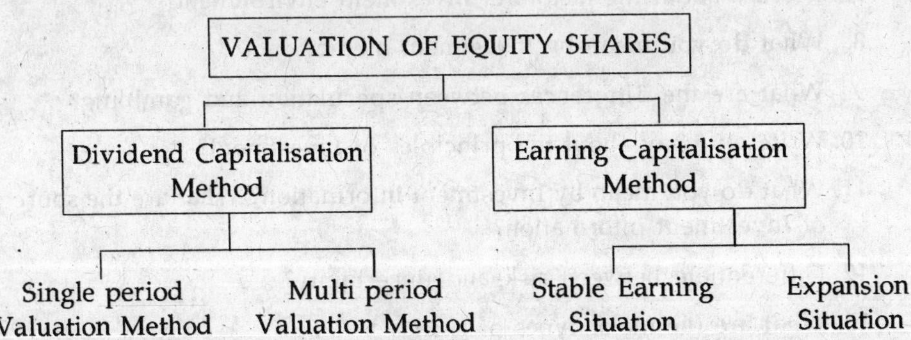

1. *DIVIDEND CAPITALISATION APPROACH*

This is conceptually a very sound approach. According to this approach, the value of an equity share is equivalent to the present value of future dividends plus the present value of the price expected to be realised on its sale.

This approach is based on following assumption:-

i) Dividends are paid annually.

ii) The dividend is received after the expiry of a year of purchase of equity share.

This approach is divided in to two types:

A) Single period Valuation Model

B) Multi period Valuation Model

A) Single period Valuation Model

In this approach, it is assumed that the investor expects to hold the equity share for a year. The following formula indicates the value of equity share.

$$CPE = \frac{D_1}{(1+ke)} + \frac{P_1}{(1+ke)}$$

CPE = Current price of equity share.

D_1 = Dividend per share expected at the end of the 1st year.

P_1 = Expected market price of the share at the end of first year.

ke = Cost of equity capital/capitalisation rate(or)discount rate.

Illustration No. 1: Mr.X holds an equity share, which pays an annual dividend of Rs.25. He expects to sell the share at Rs.200 at the end of a year. Calculate the value of the share, if the required rate of return is 15%.

D_1 = Rs.25 Ke = 25% P_1 = Rs.200.

$$CPE = \frac{D_1}{(1+ke)} + \frac{P_1}{(1+ke)}$$

$$CPE = \frac{25}{(1+0.15)} + \frac{200}{(1+0.15)}$$

CPE = Rs.196 approximately.

Illustration No. 2: Mr. Raju holds an equity share in Infosys.LTD. The annual dividend is Rs.15 per share. He expects to sell the share for Rs.140 at the end of a year. Calculate the value of the share, if the required rate of return is 16%.

D_1 = Rs.15 Ke = 16% P_1 = Rs.140.

$$CPE = \frac{D_1}{(1+ke)} + \frac{P_1}{(1+ke)}$$

$$CPE = \frac{15}{(1+16\%)} + \frac{140}{(1+16\%)}$$

CPE = Rs. 133.61

Illustration No. 3: Mrs. Anitha holds shares in ACC. The annual dividend is Rs.60. She expects to sell the share for Rs.200 at the end of a year. Calculate the value of the share if the required rate of return is 15%.

Solution: $CPE = \frac{D_1}{(1+ke)} + \frac{P_1}{(1+ke)}$

D_1 = Rs.60 Ke = 15% P_1 = Rs.200.

$$CPE = \frac{60}{(1+15\%)} + \frac{200}{(1+15\%)}$$

$$CPE = \frac{60}{(1.15)} + \frac{200}{(1.15)} = \text{Rs. } 226.08$$

Illustration No. 4: Smt. Aruna holds shares in Global Trust Bank. The annual dividend per share is Rs.25. She expects to sell the share for Rs.100 at the end of a year. Calculate the value of a share if the required rate of return is 20%.

Solution: $CPE = \frac{D_1}{(1+ke)} + \frac{P_1}{(1+ke)}$

D_1 = Rs.25 Ke = 20% P_1 = Rs.100.

$$CPE = \frac{25}{(1+20\%)} + \frac{100}{(1+20\%)}$$

$$CPE = \frac{25}{1.20} + \frac{100}{1.20}$$

CPE = Rs. 104 approximately

MULTI PERIOD VALUATION MODEL

The equity shares are perpetual. They do not have maturity period. An equity share holder in general expects cash inflows in the form of dividends not for a year but for an infinite period. Then the value of an equity share is equivalent to the present value of its future stream of dividends. In case, the dividend per share remains constant, the value of an equity share can also be determined on the basis of the valuation methods applied to value the debentures or bonds.

Symbolically it may be presented below:

$$CVE = \frac{Di}{ke}$$

CVE = Current Value of equity share.

Di = expected annual dividend per share.

ke = Capitalisation rate.

Illustration No. 5: Ballarpur Industries Limited currently paying a dividend of Rs.50 per share. It is expected that the company will not deviate from this rate in the future. The current capitalisation rate is 20%. Calculate the present value of an equity share.

Solution: $CVE = \frac{Di}{ke}$

Di = Rs. 50 Ke = 20%

$$CVE = \frac{50}{20} \times 100 = \text{Rs. } 250$$

CVE = Rs. 250.

Growth in Dividends

The earnings and dividends of most companies grow over a time, because of their earnings and retention policies. As a result of this, the company would have an increased earning per share year after year provided the number of shares does not change. The growth rate of dividends can be calculated by using the following formula.

$$\text{Growth in dividends} = \frac{\text{Dividends in 2nd year} - \text{Dividend in Ist year}}{\text{Dividends in year '1'}} \times 100$$

$$\text{Growth in dividends} = \frac{D_2 - D_1}{D_1} \times 100$$

Market Price per Share:

$$P_o = \left(\frac{D_1}{ke - g}\right)$$

P_o = Current Market price of an equity share.

D_1 = Dividend at the end of the year 1.

Ke = Capitalisation Rate.

g = Growth rate in dividends.

Illustration No. 6: Orchid Chemicals has a share capital of Rs. 10,00,000. The company has the policy of retaining 70% of its earnings. Calculate the growth rate in dividends, if the company earns 15% on its capital employed.

Solution:

1 year	*Rs.*
Total earnings (15% of Rs.10,00,000)	1,50,000
(-) Retained earnings (70% of Rs.1,50,000)	1,05,000
Dividends distributed	45,000
II year	
15% earnings on capital employed (i.e. 15% of 10,00,000+1,05,000)	1,65,750
Less: Retained earnings 70% of earnings of Rs.1,65,750	1,16,025
Dividends distributed	Rs.49,725

$$\text{Growth in dividends} = \frac{\text{Dividends in 2nd year - Dividends in 1st year}}{\text{Dividends in 1st year}} \times 100$$

$$= \frac{49{,}725 - 45{,}000}{45{,}000} \times 100$$

$$= \frac{4{,}725}{45{,}000} \times 100$$

$$= \boxed{10.5\%}$$

Illustration No. 7: Voltas Ltd., has a share capital of Rs. 50,00,000. The company has the policy of retaining 50% of its earnings. Calculate the growth rate in dividends if the company earns 20% of its capital employed.

Solution: *I year* *Rs.*

	Rs.
Total earnings (20% of Rs.50,00,000)	10,00,000
Less: Retained earnings 50% of earnings	5,00,000
Dividends distributed	5,00,000
II year	
Earnings on capital employed 20% of 50,00,000+5,00,000	11,00,000
Less: Retained earnings (50%)	5,50,000
Dividends distributed	Rs.5,50,000

$$\text{Growth in dividends} = \frac{\text{Dividends in 2nd year - Dividends in 1st year}}{\text{Dividends in 1st year}} \times 100$$

$$= \frac{\text{Rs.}5{,}50{,}000 - 5{,}00{,}000}{\text{Rs.}5{,}00{,}000} \times 100$$

$$= \boxed{10\%}$$

Illustration No.8: Cybertech Ltd. has a share capital of Rs.70,00,000. The company has the policy of retaining 60% of its earnings. Calculate the growth rate in dividends, if the company earns 15% on its capital employed.

Solution: *I year*

	Rs.
Total earnings (15% of Rs.70,00,000)	10,50,000
Less: Retained earnings (60% of earnings)	6,30,000
Dividends distributed	4,20,000
II year	
15% Earnings on capital employed (10,50,000+94,500)	11,44,500
Less: Retained earnings	6,86,700
Dividends distributed	Rs.4,57,800

$$\text{Growth in dividends} = \frac{\text{Dividends in 2nd year - Dividends in 1st year}}{\text{Dividends in 1st year}} \times 100$$

$$= \frac{\text{Rs.}4{,}57{,}800 - 4{,}20{,}000}{4{,}20{,}000} \times 100$$

$$= \boxed{9\%}$$

The formula for evaluation of the equity share with a growth rate of dividends can be as follows:

$$P_o = \frac{D_1}{(ke - g)}$$

P_o = Current market price of an equity share.

ke = Capitalisation rate

D_1 = Dividend at the end of the year

g = Growth rate in dividends.

Illustration No. 9: XYZ Ltd.,is expected to pay a dividend at Rs.50 per share. Dividends are expected to grow at 10%. You are required to calculate the market value of the share if capitalisation rate is 12%.

$$P_o = \frac{D_1}{(ke - g)}$$

D_1 = Rs. 50 ke = 12% g = 10%

$$P_o = \frac{50}{(0.12 - 0.10)} = 50.02 = \boxed{250.}$$

Illustration No. 10: India Cements Ltd., is expected to pay a dividend at Rs.80/- per share. Dividends are expected to grow at 12%. you are required to calculate the market value of the share at a capitalised rate of 14%.

$$P_o = \frac{D_1}{(ke - g)}$$

D_1 = Rs. 80 ke = 14% g = 12%

$$P_o = \frac{80}{(14 - 12)}$$

$$P_o = \frac{80}{0.2}$$

$$P_o = \boxed{\text{Rs. } 400}$$

II. EARNINGS CAPITALISATION APPROACH

The earnings capitalisation approach is classified in to two categories. Valuation of share, when the earnings of the firm are stable, valuation of share when the firm is in expansion stage, can be presented as follows:-

$$Po = \frac{E_1}{ke}$$

P_o = Current value of an equity share.

E_1 = Expected earning for share at the end of year 1.

Ke = Capitalisation rate.

Illustration No. 11: Calculate price of an equity share according to earning Capitalisation approch with the following particulars:

Earning per share	20
Capitalisation Rate	25%
Retained earnings	0

$$Po = \frac{E_1}{ke}$$

$E_1 = 20$ ke = 25%

$$P_o = \frac{2000}{25} = \frac{20}{25} \times 100$$

P_o = Rs. 80

Illustration No. 12: Calculate the price of an equity share according to earnings capitalisation approach with the following particulars:

A) Share Capital Rs.2,00,000 (20,000 shares of Rs.10 each)

B) Earnings available to equity share holders 40,000

C) Capitalisation Rate 20%

$$Po = \frac{E}{ke} \times 100$$

$$Po = \frac{2}{20} \times 100 = \frac{200}{20} = \text{Rs. } 10$$

$$\text{Earning per Share} = \frac{\text{Earnings avalable to shareholders}}{\text{Number of Equity Shares}}$$

$$\text{Earning per Share} = \frac{40,000}{20,000} = \boxed{\text{Rs. } 2}$$

Illustratian No. 13: "Uma" Ltd., is expected to pay a dividend of Rs.4/- per equity share. The dividend is expected to grow at 8%. The current capitalisation rate is 12%. You are required to find out the value of the equity share.

$$P_o = \frac{D_1}{(ke - g)}$$

D_1 = Rs. 2 ke = 12% g = 18%

$$Po = \frac{4}{(.12 - 0.8)} = \frac{4}{0.04}$$

$$Po = \frac{4}{0.04} = \frac{400}{4} = \frac{100}{1} = \boxed{\text{Rs. } 100}$$

Illustration No. 14: Raasi Cements Ltd,.is paying a dividend of Rs 5 per share. The market expects the dividend to grow at 10%. The market Capitalisation rate is 13% for earnings of similar companies. Calculate the share value of the company.

$$P_o = \frac{D_1}{(ke - g)}$$

D_1 = Rs. 5 ke = 13% g = 10%

$$Po = \frac{5}{(13\% - 10\%)}$$

$$Po = \frac{5}{.13 - .10}$$

$$Po = \frac{5}{0.03}$$

$$Po = \frac{500}{3}$$

$$Po = \boxed{\text{Rs. } 167.}$$

Illustration No. 15: A firm pays a dividend of 15% on the equity share of face value of Rs.100 each. Find out the value of the equity share given that the dividend rate is expected to remain the same and the required rate of return of the investor is 17%.

Solution: $P_O = \frac{D_1}{ke}$

P_o = Value of equity share
D_1 = Annual Dividend
ke = Required rate of return of equity investor

$D_1 = 15.$ Ke = 17%

$Po = \frac{15}{.17}$

Po = 1500/17

Po = Rs.88.24, approximately 88.

Illustration No. 16: Mrs. Devi invested in ABC Ltd. The capitalisation rate of company is 14% and the current dividend is Rs. 3.00 per share. Calculate the value of the company's equity share, if the company is slowly sinking with an annual decline rate of 5% as the dividend.

$$VE = \frac{D_1}{(ke - g)}$$

VE = Value of equity share
D_1 = Current dividend
ke = Capitalisation rate
g = Growth rate/decline rate

$D_1 = 3$ Ke = 14% g = -5%

$$VE = \frac{3(1 - 0.05)}{0.14 - (-0.05)}$$

$$VE = \frac{3(0.95)}{0.14 + 0.05}$$

$$VE = \frac{2.85}{0.19}$$

VE=285/19 = 15

VE= Rs. 15.

Illustration No. 17: Smt. Radhika invested in "XZ" Ltd. The Capitalisation rate of the company is 15% and the current dividend is

Rs.2.00 per share. Calculate the value of the company's equity share, if the company is slowly sinking with an annual decline rate of 5% in the dividend.

$$VE = \frac{D_1}{(ke - g)}$$

$$VE = \frac{2(1 - 0.05)}{0.15 - (-0.05)}$$

$$VE = \frac{1.90}{0.20}$$

$$VE = \boxed{\text{Rs. } 9.50}$$

Illustration No. 18: "ABC" Ltd. shares were purchased by Mr. Raju. The capitalisation rate is 15% and the current divident is Rs 2.00 per share. The dividend growth is at an average rate of 7%. Compute the value of equity share.

Solution: $VE = \dfrac{D_1}{(ke - g)}$

$D_1 = 2.00$ ke = 15% g = 7%

$$VE = \frac{2(1 + 0.07)}{15 - (-0.07)}$$

$$VE = \frac{2(1.07)}{15 - (-0.07)}$$

$$VE = \frac{2.14}{0.08}$$

$$VE = \boxed{\text{Rs. } 26.75}$$

Illustration No. 19: Mr. Anand has invested in XYZ Ltd. The capitalisation rate of the company is 18% and the current dividend is Rs.6.00 per share. The annual dividend growth is at an average rate of 10%. Compute the value of equity share.

Solution: $VE = \dfrac{D_1}{(ke - g)}$

$D_1 = 6$ ke = 18% g = 10%

$$VE = \frac{6(1+0.10)}{18\% - (-10\%)}$$

$$VE = \frac{6(1.10)}{.18 - (.10)}$$

$$VE = \frac{6.6}{0.08}$$

VE= Rs. 82.5

Illustration No. 20: Mr. Narayan has invested in a company which is growing at an above average rate, translated to an annual increase in dividends of 18 percent for 15 years. Thereafter dividend growth rate is an average rate of 7 percent. The capitalisation rate of the company is 9% and the current dividend per equity share is Rs. 1 per share. Determine the value of the equity share.

Ans:- All the necessary dividend computations are shown in following tables:

Year	Dividend 1 (1+0.20)		Discount factor $1(1+0.09)^t$	Dividend's present value $2\times3=4$
1.	$1(1+0.15)^1$	1.15	0.917	1.055
2.	$1(1+0.15)^2$	1.32	0.842	1.111
3.	$1(1+0.15)^3$	1.52	0.722	1.097
4.	$1(1+0.15)^4$	1.75	0.708	1.239
5.	$1(1+0.15)^5$	2.01	0.650	1.306
6.	$1(1+0.15)^6$	2.31	0.596	1.377
7.	$1(1+0.15)^7$	2.66	0.547	1.455
8.	$1(1+0.15)^8$	3.06	0.502	1.536
9.	$1(1+0.15)^9$	3.52	0.460	1.619
10.	$1(1+0.15)^{10}$	4.05	0.442	1.790
11.	$1(1+0.15)^{11}$	4.66	0.388	1.808
12.	$1(1+0.15)^{12}$	5.36	0.356	1.908
13.	$1(1+0.15)^{13}$	6.16	0.326	2.008
14.	$1(1+0.15)^{14}$	7.08	0.299	2.116
15.	$1(1+0.15)^{15}$	8.14	0.275	2.239
		54.75		23.66

The value of the equity share at the end of 15 years is = 23.66

$$V_{15} = \frac{D_{15}(1+0.07)}{(ke-g)}$$

D_{15} = Rs.8.14, g = 7%, Ke = 9%

$$V_{15} = \frac{8.14(1+0.07)}{9\%-7\%}$$

$$V_{15} = \frac{8.14(1.07)}{2\%}$$

$$V_{15} = \frac{8.709}{.02}$$

V_{15} = **Rs.435.45** or Say Rs.435

The present value of Rs. 435 to be recieved in 15 yeas discounted at I percent is Rs.120(435 × 0.275). This value with the present value of the expected dividend for the next 15 years(23 .66) an investor would be willing to pay is Rs. 144 per share (120+23.66)

Illustration No. 21: Vani Products curently pays a dividend of Rs. 3.00 per share and this dividend is expected to grow at a 12% annual rate for 3 years. Then at 10% rate for the next 3 years, after it is expected to grow at a 5 percent rate for ever.

(a) What value would you place on the equity if 9% rate of return was required?

(b) Would you calculate change if you expect to hold the equity only for 3 years.

Solution:

End of year	Dividend=$(1+g)^n$	Present value of dividends 9%
1.	$3.00(1+0.12)^1$=3.36	3.36 × 0.9174=3.082
2.	$3.00(1+.12)^2$=3.76	3.76 × 0.8417=3.167
3.	$3.00(1+.12)^3$=4.21	4.21 × 0.7722=3.251
4.	$4.21(1+.10)^1$=4.63	4.63 × 0.7084=3.279
5.	$4.21(1+.10)^2$=5.09	5.09 × 0.6499=3.309
6,	$4.21(1+.10)^3$=5.60	5.60 × 0.5963=3.339
		19.427

(a)

7-year dividend 5.60 (1.10) = 6.16

Market value at the end of year 6 = $P_0 = \frac{D_1}{(ke - g)}$

$= \frac{6.16}{(0.09 - 0.05)}$

$= \frac{6.16}{0.04}$

$= 154$

Present value of rupees
154 with 9% discount rate = 154×0.5963

= 91.83

valuation = 91.83 + 19.43

= **Rs. 111.26**

(b)

Present market value at
the end of the year 3 = 3.279+3.309+3.339+91.83
= 101.75

Present value of expected dividend to be recieved at the end of year 1, 2 and 3

= 3.082+3.167+3.251
= 9.5

Total value = 101.75+9.5

= **Rs.111.25**

Illustration No. 22: The market price for Max India Ltd. equity is Rs.75 per share. The price at the end of one year is expected to be Rs.100 and dividends for next year should be Rs.3.50. What is the expected rate of return.

Solution:

$$\text{ERR} = \frac{\text{Dividend in year 1} + \text{Price in year 1}}{\text{Current Price}} - 1$$

$$\therefore \text{Current Price} = \frac{\text{Dividend in year 1}}{(1 + \text{ERR})} + \frac{\text{Price in year 1}}{(1 + \text{ERR})}$$

Symbolically: $\frac{D_1 + P_1}{C_P} - 1$

$$C_P = \frac{D_1}{(1+ERR)} + \frac{P_1}{(1+ERR)}$$

$P_1 = 100$; $D_1 = 3.50$; $C_P = 75$

$$ERR = \frac{3.50+100}{75}$$

$$= \frac{103.50}{75} - 1$$

$$ERR = 1.38\text{-}1$$

$$= \boxed{0.38} \text{ (or) } \boxed{\text{Say } 38\%}$$

Illustration No. 23: Reliance Petro is expected to pay Rs.4.00 as dividend in the next year, and the market price is projected to be Rs. 90 by year end. If the investor's required rate of return is 18%, what is the current value of the share?

$$VE = \frac{\text{Dividend in year 1}}{(1 + \text{required rate})} + \frac{\text{Price in year 1}}{(1 + \text{required rate})}$$

$$VE = \frac{4}{(1+.18)} + \frac{90}{(1+.18)}$$

$$= \frac{4}{1.18} + \frac{90}{1.18}$$

$$= 3.389 + 76.27$$

$$= \boxed{79.66}$$

Illustration No. 24: An investor, holds an equity share giving him an annual dividend of Rs.32. He expects to sell the share for Rs.320 at the end of a year. Calculate the value of the share if the required rate of return is 10%.

Solution: $P_0 = \frac{D_1}{(1+i)} + \frac{P_1}{(1+i)}$ (or)

$$Po = \frac{D1 + P1}{(1+i)}$$

Where,

P_o = The current price of the share.

i = The required rate of return or the cost of equity.

D_1 = Dividend recieved at the end of the period.

P_1 = Market price of share at the end of the period.

Substituting the values, we get

$$Po = \frac{Rs.32 + Rs.320}{(1+0.10)}$$

$$= \frac{Rs.352}{1.10}$$

$$= \boxed{Rs.\ 320}$$

Illustration No. 25: Rajesh Textile's equity share currently sells for Rs.25 per share. The company's Finance Manager anticipates a constant growth rate of 11% and an end-of-year dividend of Rs.3.00.

a) What is the expected rate of return?

b) If the investor requires a 17% return, should he purchase the stock?

a) Expected rate of return $= \frac{\text{Dividend in year 1}}{\text{Market Price in year 1}} + \text{Growth Rate}$

$$= \frac{Rs.3.00}{Rs.25.00} + 0.11$$

$$= \boxed{0.23\ (or)\ 23\%.}$$

b) $$VE = \frac{Rs.3.00}{0.17 - 0.11}$$

$$= \boxed{Rs.50.}$$

Illustration No. 26: Ramesh's equity shares currently sells for Rs.25 per share. The Finance Manager of Ramesh anticipates a constant growth rate of 15% and dividend per share of Rs.3.00.

a) What is the expected rate of return if the share is sold for Rs.30?

b) If the required rate of return is at 20 percent, should you purchase the stock?

Solution:

a) Expected rate of return $= \frac{\text{Dividend in year 1}}{\text{Market Price in year 1}} + \text{Growth Rate}$

$$= \frac{D}{Po} + g$$

$$= \frac{Rs.3.00}{Rs.30} + 0.15$$

$= 0.25$ (or) 25%

b) $Po = \frac{D}{(ke - g)}$

$$VE = \frac{Rs.3.00}{(0.2 - 0.15)} = \frac{Rs.3.00}{0.05}$$

$= Rs.60.$

Illustration No. 27: A firm's current EPS is Rs.8. Its dividend pay out is 50 percent, and its growth rate of EPS is 12%. The normal P/E multipule is 17/1. What is the stock's value based on the capitalisation of earnings method? What is its value in 3 years?

Solution: PV = PE × EPS current

P/E × EPS Current = PV

PV = 17 × 8 = 136

EPS_3 = $8\ (1.120)^3$

= 8 (1.404)

= Rs.11.23

Value in 3 years = 17 × Rs. 11.23

= **Rs.190.19.**

Illustration No. 28: Given the following current dividend Rs.5; dividend payout 45%, normal capitalisation rate, 10%; actual capitalisation rate, 16%, what is the current value of the stock? If it increases its dividend pay out to 55%, how much will the current value go up or down?

Solution: VE = Rs. 5/(10%-16% × 55%)

VE = Rs. 5/(10%-8.3%)

VE = Rs. 5/(1.2%)

VE = Rs. 416.66

Change in dividend pay out Ratio and VE

VE = Rs.5.5/(10%-16% × 45%)

= Rs.196.4

Illustration No. 29: G.K Naidu is a conservative investor, who expects 10% return on his fixed investment, but 20% from his equity investments. He has been considering the purchase of an equity that pays Rs.3.00 in dividend this year and whose dividends are expected to grow at 10% per year for the next 3 years. Earnings in this year are Rs.6 per share and are exected to grow at 20% for the next seven years. Stocks growing at this rate generally sell at 40 times earnings. What price Naidu pays for this equity?

Solution: Using the 3 years valuation formula

$$Po = \frac{D(1+g)}{(1+k)} + \frac{D(1+g)^2}{(1+k)^2} + \frac{D(1+g)^3 + P_3}{(1+k)^3}$$

Where,

P_3 = (E) (P/E) $(1+g)^3$

P_3 = (Rs.4) (40) $(1+20\%)^3$

= Rs.276.48

$$Po = \frac{Rs.3.00(1+.10)}{(1+.20)} + \frac{Rs.3.00(1+.10)^2}{(1+.20)^2} + \frac{Rs.3.00(1+.10)^3 + Rs.276.48}{(1+.20)^3}$$

= Rs.2.75 + Rs.2.520 + Rs.162.310

= Rs. 167.58

Illustration No. 30: C.K. Rao can buy an equity that will pay Rs. 3.00 in dividends annually over the next 3 years. The earnings of the company are expected to grow and the equity is expected to reach a price of Rs.80 per share at the end of the 3 years. This is a conservative investement and Rao expects a yield of 18%. What price should Rao has to pay, for the equity if he wishes to earn 18%?

Solution:

$$\text{Yield:} \quad (Y) = \frac{\dfrac{D + (P_3 - P_o)}{3}}{\dfrac{P_3 + P_o}{2}}$$

$$\text{Solving for } P_o = \frac{(Y)(P_3 + P_o)}{2} + D + \frac{P_3 - P_o}{3}$$

$$(3)\ (Y)\ (P_3 + P_o) = (2)(3)(D) + (2)\ (P_3 - P_o)$$

$$3\ Y P_3 + 3YP_o = 6D + 2P_3 - 2P_o$$

$$3\ Y P_o + 2P_o = 6D + 2P_3 - 3YP_3$$

$$P_o = \frac{6D + P_3(2 - 3Y)}{3\quad + 2}$$

Substituting:

$$P_o = \frac{(9 \times Rs.3) + Rs.80[3 - (3)(0.18)]}{3(0.18) + 3}$$

$$P_o = \frac{223.8}{3 + 0.54}$$

$$= \text{Rs. } 63.2$$

Verification:

$$.18 = \frac{Rs.3.00 + \dfrac{(80 - 63.2)}{3}}{\dfrac{80 + 63.2}{2}}$$

$$= \frac{Rs.3.00 + 5.6}{71.6}$$

$$= 8.6/71.6$$

$$= \boxed{12.011\%}$$

Illustration No. 31: A firm pays a dividend of 25% on the equity shares of face value of Rs.100 each. Find out the value of the equity share given that the dividend rate is expected to remain the same and the required rate of return of the investor is 20%.

Solution: In this solution the following information is given:

Ke = 20%

D = 25 (25% of Rs.100)

$$\therefore P_o = \frac{25}{20}$$

$$= \boxed{125.}$$

Illustration No. 32: A firm is paying a dividend of Rs. 1.50 per share. The rate of dividend is expected to grow at 10% for next 3 years and 5% thereafter infinitely. Find out the value of the share given that the required rate of return of the investor is 15%.

Solution: For this situation the following information is available:

Ke = 15%

D_o = 1.50

g_1 = 10% (for 3 years)

g_2 = 5% (infinitely)

Now, the value may be calculated as follows:

End of year	Div.Ant (Rs)	PVF	Pr
1.	1.65	.870	1.44
2.	1.82	.756	1.38
3.	2.00	.658	1.32
			Rs. 4.14

Rs. 4.14 is the present value of dividends expected from the company for first 3 years. The value of the equity shares at the end of year three will be as follows:

$$P_3 = \frac{D3(1+g)}{(ke-g)}$$

$$P_3 = \frac{2(1.05)}{15-0.5}$$

$$= \boxed{Rs.21}$$

The value of the share at the end of the year 3 will be Rs 21. The percent value of Rs 21 is

$$Rs.21\left[PVF_{(15\%,3\%)}\right]$$

$$= Rs.\ 21\ (.658)$$

$$= \boxed{Rs.13.82}$$

The value of the share at present is Rs.4.14 + Rs.13.82 ie Rs.17.96.

Illustration No.33: A firm is not expected to pay any dividend for first 3 years but thereafter will be paying a dividend of Rs.2 growing at 10% p.a for ever. What is the value of the share, given the required rate of return is at 15%?

As per the constant growth rate model, the value of the share at the end of the year 3 will be

$$P_3 = \frac{D_4}{ke - g}$$

$$= \frac{2}{15 - .10}$$

$$= \boxed{Rs.40.}$$

Now, this is the value of the share at the end of year 3. This value should now be discounted at 15% to find out the present value

$$P_O = P_3\left[PVF_{(15\%,3\%)}\right]$$

$$= Rs.40\ (.658)$$

$$= \boxed{Rs.26.32.}$$

So, the value of the share is Rs.26.32.

Illustration No. 34: A firm pays a dividend of Rs 2.00 with a growth rate at 7%, the risk-free rate, is 9% and the market rate of return, Km is 13%, the firm has a, beta factor of 1.50. However, due to a decision of the Finance Manager, β is likely to increase to 1.75. Find out the present as well as the likely value of the share after the decision.

Solution: In order to find out the value of a share with constant growth model, the value of ke should be ascertained with the help of "CAPM" model is as follows:

The amount of Rs.824.50 is redeemable after 15 years. ore, the present value of this amount at 9% is Rs.226.74 (i.e. × .275)

Now, the value of the share is the sum of the (i) present value of dividend and (ii) present value of expected price of the end of the 5 i.e.

Value = Rs.34.96 + Rs.226.74

= **Rs.261.70.**

IMARY

This chapter is mainly focussed on finding out of "intrinsic value" share. The security analyst will evaluate the past performance of a cular company's scrip when he faces with the problem of making a hold or sell decision. The valuation of equity shares will be quite rent and difficult. There are different methods of valuation of equity es i.e. *Dividend capitalisation method, Earning capitalisation method.* ner the dividend capitalisation method is divided into *single period tion model and multiple valuation model. The earning capitalisation* *ach* is classified into two categories namely *''valuation of share when arnings of the firm are stable'', ''valuation of share when the firm is in nsion stage''.* The amount of the return and the degree of variability eturn together will determine the value of a share.

QUESTIONS

Explain the two approaches which are adopted for valuation of equity shares with appropriate model.

What do you understand by "Growth in dividends?" Explain with examples.

EXERCISE

. An equity share of Rs.10 is expected to earn an annual dividend of Rs.2 and the share will be sold for Rs.18 after a year. The required rate of return is 12%. Calculate the value of the equity share.

[Ans: Rs.17.86]

$$KE = R_f + B\,(K_m - I_F)$$

$$= 0.09 + 1.5\,(0.13 - 0.09)$$

$$= .15 \text{ OR } 15\%$$

and the value of the share as per constant growth model is

$$P_o = \frac{D_1}{(ke-g)}$$

$$P_o = \frac{2.00}{.15-.07}$$

$$= \boxed{\text{Rs.25.}}$$

However, if the financial decision is implemented, the beta (β) factor is likely to increase to 1.75 and therefore Ke would be

$$K_e = R_f + \beta\,(K_m - I_F)$$

$$= .09 + 1.75\,(.13 - .09)$$

$$= .16 \text{ (or) } 16\%$$

The value of the share is

$$P_o = \frac{D1}{(ke-g)}$$

$$P_o = \frac{2.00}{(.16-.07)}$$

$$= \boxed{\text{Rs } 22.22}$$

Illustration No. 35: Calculate the value of equity share from the following:

Equity share capital (Rs.20 each)	Rs.	25,00,000
Reserves and surplus	Rs.	2,50,000
15% secured loans	Rs.	12,50,000
12.5% unsecured loans	Rs.	5,00,000
Fixed assets	Rs.	15,00,000
Investments	Rs.	2,50,000
Operating profit	Rs.	12,50,000
Tax rate		50%
P/E Ratio (price - earnings)		6.25

Solution: In the given situation the value of the share can be ascertained on the basis of earnings of the firm and the price-earning multiple as follows.

Value = EPS × P/E Ratio

The P/E Ratio is given and the EPS may be ascertained as follows.

Operating profit i.e 'EBIT'		12,50,000
Less: Interest on 15% Secured loans	1,87,500	
Less: Interest on 12.5% unsecured loans	62,500	2,50,000
Profit before Tax (PBT)		10,00,000
Less: income tax (50%) =		5,00,000
Profit after tax		5,00,000

$$\text{Number of equity shares} = \frac{25{,}00{,}00}{20} = \quad 1{,}25{,}000$$

$$\therefore \text{ Earning per share} = \frac{5{,}00{,}000}{1{,}25{,}000} = \quad \text{Rs.}4$$

P.E Ratio is given 6.25

$\therefore$ The value of equity = EPS × PE Ratio

= 4 × 6.25

= **25.**

Illustration No. 36: An investor has invested his savings in a company from whom dividends are expected to grow at 20% for 15 years and thereafter at 7% forever. Find out the value of the equity share given that the current dividend per share is Rs. 1 and the required rate of return of the investor is 9%.

Solution: The dividends from the company are expected to grow at 20% P.A. for first 15 years and at 7% P.A thereafter for ever. Therefore, the value of the equity share is to be calculated in two stages as follows:

Stage-1: Calculation of present value of dividends for 15 years.

Year	Dividend (Rs.) (g=20%)	PVF at (9%)
1.	1.200	.917
2.	1.440	.842
3.	1.728	.722
4.	2.074	.708
5.	2.488	.650
6.	2.986	.596
7.	3.583	.547
8.	4.300	.502
9.	5.160	.460
10.	6.192	.442
11.	7.430	.388
12.	8.916	.356
13.	10.696	.326
14.	12.839	.299
15.	15.407	.275
Total:	86.442	

So, the total dividends of Rs.86.44 are expected from during next 15 years, whose present value @ 9% is Rs.34.96.

Stage-2: The value of the equity share at the end depends upon the dividend for the 16th year (D16), Ke and rate, g, as follows:

$$D_{16} = D_{15}(1+g) = \text{Rs.}16.49$$

$$\text{The share price is } P_{15} = \frac{D_{16}}{(ke - g)}$$

$$= \frac{\text{Rs.}16.49}{(.09 - .07)}$$

$$= \boxed{\text{Rs. } 824.50.}$$

Theref
824.50

future
year

SUM

of a
parti
buy,
diffe
shar
Furt
valu
appr
the
expa
of r

4. Calculate the value of equity share from the following data.

a) Equity share capital (10/-each)	Rs. 12,50,000
b) Reserves & surplus	Rs. 1,25,000
c) 15% secured loans	Rs. 6,25,000
d) 12.5% Unsecured loans.	Rs. 2,50,000
e) Fixed Assets	Rs. 7,50,000
f) Investment	Rs. 1,25,000
g) Oparating profit	Rs. 6,25,000
h) Tax Rate	50%
i) PE Ratio	3.15

[Ans.Rs.6.30]

5. A company pays a dividend of Rs. 4.00 with a growth rate at 14%, the risk free rate is 9% and the market rate of return, Km is 20%, presently, the firm has a beta factor of 3. However due to a decision of the Finance Manager, beta is likely to increase to 3.50. Findout the present as well as the likely value of the share after the decision.

[Ans: Rs.20]
[Ans. Rs.16]

6. Wokhard India Ltd., pays a dividend of 50% on the equity share face value of Rs.100 each. Findout the value of the equity share given that the dividend rate is expected to remain the same and the required rate of return of the investor is 25%.

[Ans. Rs.50]

7. An investor holds an equity share giving him an annual dividend of Rs. 64. He expects to sell the share for Rs.640 at the end of a year. Calculate the value of the share if the required rate of return is 20%.

[Ans. Rs.587]

8. Jaiprakash Industries Ltd., is expected to pay Rs.8.00 as dividend next year, and the market price is projected to be Rs.180 by the year end. If the investor's required rate of return is 20%, what is the current value of the share?

[Ans. Rs.157 approximately]

9. Jyothi Industries Ltd., is expected to declare dividend in the next year Rs.7.00. The market price of equity share is Rs.150. The price at the end of one year is expected to be Rs.200. What is the expected rate of return?

[Ans: 38%]

10. Smt. Anitha has invested in Essar Steels Ltd. The capitalisation rate of the company is 15% and the current dividend is Rs.12.00 per share. The dividends will grow at an average rate of 12%. Compute the value of equity share.

[Ans: Rs.448]

11. Mrs.Vani invested in Pfizer India Ltd. The capitalisation rate is 18% and the current dividend is Rs.2.00 per share. Calculate the value of the equity share if the dividends decline at a rate of 10%.

[Ans: Rs.8.26]

13. Calculate the price of an equity share according to earning capitalisation approach for the following data:

EPS.	Rs.28
Capitalisation Rate	20%
Retained earnings.	0

[Ans: Rs.140]

3

VALUATION OF BONDS

INTRODUCTION

Debt instruments are fixed income securities like bonds and debentures. Bonds and debentures are issued by public and private sector undertakings. A bond or a debenture is a debt security issued by a borrower and purchased by an investor. These are usual forms of long term financing issued by firms with a promise to make payment of interest and principal under clearly defined terms and conditions. Bond is an unsecured debt of the issuer, either in the Government sector or Corporate sector. Bond market in India is underdeveloped. The National Stock Exchange (NSE) is established to create liquidity for bonds in India. Basically, in practice both bonds and debentures are the same. Bonds and debentures are issued by public sector financial institutions, private and public sector undertakings and semi-Government bodies in India.

Debentures are one of the sources of raising borrowed capital to meet financial needs. The term debenture has come from Latin word "Debre" which means to owe. *Palmer* defines a debenture as an "Instrument under seal evidencing debt the essence of it being admission of indebtedness"

According to Tophan debentures can be defined as *''Document given by a company as evidence of debt to the holder, usually arising out of loan and most commonly secured by charge''.*

The bonds are instruments of debt. They represent the promise of a corporation to pay a fixed amount at a specified maturity date and interest at regular intervals, until then the payment of bonds is made either gradually as serial maturity dates or through a sinking fund arrangements under which a specified portion of earnings is regularly set a side and used for the retirement of bonds. In the U.S.A. the term debenture ordinarily refers to relatively long term unsecured obligation, while in India it is statutorily used as a synonym of the word bond. In common parlance in India, the term bond is associated with loanable instrument issued by public undertakings.

Corporate debentures are less liquid investments as compared to Government securities and actively traded equity shares. Debentures redeemable period generally is between 5 and 7 years. The nature of capital thus raised is called debt capital. These debentures have limited trading. The functioning of NSE which primarily deals in debt instruments, has in-creased liquidity in debt instruments.

Corporate debentures though less liquid investment medium but they are relatively more popular among institutional investors, such as Insurance Companies, U.T.I. Commercial Banks, and Mutual Funds than among individual investors. But convertible debentures with attractive terms in recent years have become more popular amongst individual investors.

In order to understand the valuation of bonds knowing the following basic terms is required. (a) Par value, (b) Coupon rate, (c) Maturity

a) Par Value

The par value of a bond is also called as face value. It is the principal amount of a bond and is stated on the face of the bond. The par value of a bond may be Rs.100, Rs.1000 or any amount.

b) Coupon Rate

This is the rate at which interest on the par value of the bond is payable as per the payment schedule. The interest may be paid annually, half-yearly or even monthly. The coupon rate is usually described as percent and is applied to the par value to find out the periodic interest amount.

c) Maturity

The maturity of a bond refers to the period from the date of issue, after the expiry of which the redemption repayment will be made to the investor by the borrower firm. Generally firms issue bonds with a maturity period up to 10 years only.

The Indian Companies Act does not provide rules for bonds, but only for debentures and warrants of various categories. The whosesale debt market on NSE comprises Bank bonds, certificates of deposit, commercial paper, Corporate bonds, Government and Semi-Government bonds and Institutional bonds including those of IDBI, UTI etc.

EVALUATION OF BONDS

Bond investment agencies evaluate the quality of bonds and rank them in categories according to relative probability of default. For the typical investor, this evaluation somewhat simplifies the process of assessing default risk. The principal rating agencies are *''Moody's Investors Service'' and ''Standard & Poor's Corporation''* CRISIL, ICRA etc.

Default risk is a matter of degree from the simple extension of time to make an interest payment to legal liquidation of the debtor to settle accumulated interest and principal. An extension occurs when creditors voluntarily allow extension of maturity and/or postponement of interest payments.

Liquidation may occur when a number of successive interest payments are missed owing to underlying problems of management. The borrower has no hope of turning the situation around, then liquidation proceedings are instituted. Creditors hope to recover some portion of the original principal advanced plus interest due.

Losses in high-grade bonds arise from either of two factors.

a) Changes in the level of interest rates.

b) Impairment in quality.

Market fluctuations due to interest rate changes may be short run or long run, but in any event the original principal is recovered at maturity and the only loss is an opportunity cost in maximising income. An impairment in quality causes a greater loss in market value, which may become permanent in case of default quality impairment arises principally from a decline in earning power.

Rating of Bonds/Debentures by Investment Agencies.

(i) MOODY'S INVESTOR'S SERVICE

Aaa	---	Best Quality
Aa	---	High Grade
A	---	Higher Medium Grade
Baa	---	Lower Medium Grade
Ba	---	Possess Speculative Elements
B	---	Generally lack characteristics of desirable investment
Caa	---	Poor Standing may be in default
Ca	---	Speculative to a high degree often in default
C	---	Lowest Grade

(ii) STANDARD & POOR'S CORP.

AAA	---	Highest Grade
AA	---	High Grade
A	---	Upper Medium Grade
BBB	---	Medium Grade
BB	---	Lower Medium Grade
B	---	Speculative
CCC-CC	---	Outright Speculation
C	---	Reserved for income bonds
DDD-D	---	In default

The bond categories are assigned by letter grade. The highest grade bonds, whose risk of default is felt to be negligible, are rated triple AAA (A) the rating agencies assign pluses or minuses when appropriate to show the relative standing within the major rating categories.

RISKS OF BONDS

The risks involved in Bonds to the investor are as follows:

a) Purchasing Power Risk.

b) Default Risk

c) Interest Rate Risk.

a) Purchasing Power Risk

It is associatedwith rising inflation rates. The bond redemption price being fixed, at the end of maturity of say 10 to 12 years, the real value of the redemption price will be completely wiped out by an inflation rate. The only way to protect from inflation is to have accounting for real rates or yields for calculating the present bond price or to have yields, which will give risk free return plus inflation adjusted return for the risk premium.

b) Default Risk

It is another risk, related to the company or agency, issuing the bonds. This is the risk of non-payment or delayed payments of interest and redemption value. For managing the default risk, the investor has to use the techniques of analysis of the financial statements of the company including the past ratios of debt to equity, finance charge, relative gross profits, debt/leverage ratios, and liquidity ratios.

c) Interest Rate Risk

If the bond has a coupon price, the risk of change in interest rates is high, the higher the maturity period, lower the coupon rate.

The bond will have following features:

1. They have risk in the form of purchasing power, default, interest rate etc.
2. They are fixed income earners, generally with a coupon rate of interest.
3. The lower is the maturity period of the bond, the greater is the risk and longer is the percentage change in its price relative to interest rate changes.

Types of Bonds

The following are the various kinds of bonds/debentures:

a) Convertible and Non-convertible bonds

b) Participation Bonds

c) Income Bonds

d) Assured Bonds

e) Redeemable and Irredeemable Bonds

f) Adjustment Bonds

g) Guaranteed Bonds

h) Joint Bonds

i) Mortgage (or) Secured Bonds

j) Sinking Fund Bonds

k) Serial Bonds

l) Collateral Bond

a) Convertible and Non-convertable Bonds

Convertible bonds are converted into equity shares on a date of conversion. They will fetch interest up to the date of conversion,

Then after the convention into equity, they will get the dividends and capital appreciation along with other equity shareholders. Some times there is provision for compulsory conversion of bonds into shares at specified date. The rate may also be left to be decided by the appropriate authority on the date of conversion.

b) Participating bonds

Generally, the companies which are in poor credit position issue participating bonds. They have a guaranteed rate of interest but may also participate in earnings up to an additional specified percentage.

c) Income bonds

On these bonds, the payment of interest is mandatory to the extent of current earnings. If earnings are sufficient to pay only a portion of the interest that portion usually is required to be paid, but if the corporation is able to pay the unearned balance out of its cash resources, it is of course free to do so.

d) Assured Bonds

Assured bonds are issued in respect of a company that has been acquired by another by way of merger or as a result of the reorganisation. In taking over the property of the original issuer, the debts of the issuer are assured by the successor company.

e) Redeemable and Irredeemable bonds

A redeemable bond is a bond which has been issued for a certain period on the expiry of which its holder will be repaid, the amount thereof with or without premium. A bond without the aforesaid redemption period is termed as an irredeemable debenture. These may be repaid either in the event of the winding up of company or the happening of certain specified uncertain or contingent events.

f) Adjustment Bonds

Adjustment bonds are issued in the re-organisation of companies in financial difficulties. In practice, interest is only payable on them, if earnings permit. These are a leading type of income bonds?

g) Guaranteed bonds

These types of bonds may be guaranteed by firm other than debtors. Some guarantors assure payment of both principle and interest whereas some assure interest only. In this case, lessor company agrees to pay a long term rent which is more than sufficient to service the lessor's bonds.

h) Joint bonds

Joint bonds are issued by two or more companies. Joint bonds are just loan certificates. Two companies that use a common facility and have raised money to finance it through the sale of debt.

i) Mortgage Secured Bonds

The term mortgage refers to a lien on real property or buildings. Mortgage bonds may be open-end or close-end or limited open-end. An open-end mortgage means that a corporation under the mortgage may issue additional bonds. But the open-end mortgage indenture usually provides that the corporation can issue more bonds only if the earnings or additional security obtained by selling the new securities to meet certain tests of earnings and asset coverage.

j) Sinking fund bonds

When the company decides to retire its bond issued systematically by setting aside certain amount in each year for sinking fund with a view to use the same to redeem the bonds at their time of maturity.

k) Serial Bonds

Serial Bonds means, the company will divide their issue of bonds into a different series. Each part of the series maturing at different times will be paid by the company. These bonds are not callable. The company pays each part of the series as and when it matures. Serial bonds are not any special types of bonds. Serial bonds are more useful to the companies where the refund of amount spread across a period of time. Repayment of serial bonds are more convenient to the corporate sector for better utilisation of funds with a little amount of interest cost.

l) Collateral Trust Bonds

Instead of being secured by a pledge of tangible property like mortgage bonds, collatoral trust bonds are issued to secure by a pledge of intangibles usually in the form of stocks and bonds of a corporation or a company.

INGREDIENTS IN ACTIVE BOND MANAGEMENT

Incremental returns to bond portfolio management derive essentially from correctly positioning the portfolio with maturity structure, coupon rate of interest along with benefit from changes in the general level of interest rates. This positioning calls for major strategy decisions or judgments regarding market rates and the shape of the yield curve.

A second source of incremental return results from weighing the bond portfolio in the more favourably situated bond sectors (Treasuries, corporates, utilities, municipalities). The third source involves substitutions, where similar bonds are substituted for one another when their yield get out of line. Sector and substitution, switching or swapping are more tactical in nature because they may be made independent of interest-rate forecast strategies and depend upon opportunities available.

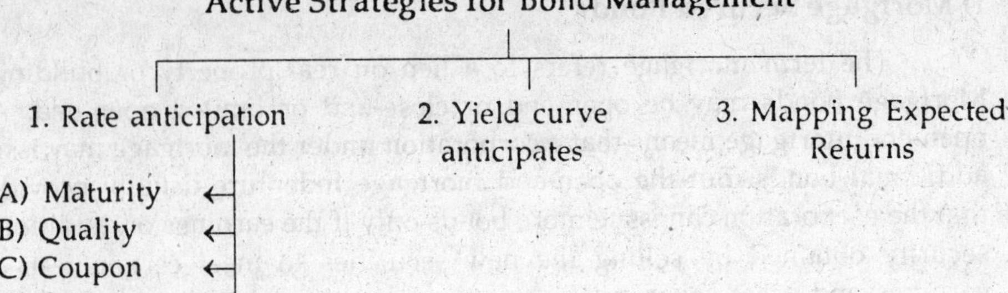

1. Active Strategies Anticipation

Switching bonds based upon rate forecasting can be the most productive bond portfolio action. It is also the riskiest. The types of portfolio decisions required, fall roughly into four categories.

a) Maturity
b) Quality
c) Coupon
d) Sector

a) Maturity

Interest-rate expectations are an important guideline for maturity selection. Maturities should be lengthened when interest rates are expected to fall and prices to rise, and maturities should be shortened when interest rates are expected to rise.

The maturity structure of a bond portfolio depends heavily upon cyclical forecasts of interest rates if an investor is going to engage in active bond portfolio management. Such forecasts should consider expected interest rates for various maturities and also the expected slope of the yield curve. Moreover, such forecasts should be reviewed frequently because expected interest rates may change significantly due to changing economic expectations.

b) Quality

Quality, diversification is another important consideration in constructing a bond portfolio. Ratings by Moody's and Standard & Poor's help the investor to differentiate between the borrower to pay interest and principal promptly when due. Uncritical acceptance of bord ratings is not advisable, however, these ratings have a tendency to lag behind changes in the financial characteristics of a company.

c) Coupon

The investor may select from high-coupon bonds ordinarily selling at a premium above par, current- coupon issues at par or about par, and low-coupon issues selling at discounts. High- coupon bonds trading at or above their redemption price are often called cushion bonds. Although their potential for future price appreciation is restricted regardless of further declines in long-term interest rates, in a subsequent period of rising interest rates, the high coupon provides appreciation in the value of the bond. Yield and price relationships between bonds of different coupons change because of factors such as the supply of new issues, sinking-fund activity, call features, dealer carrying costs and the general level and expected trend of interest rates.

d) Sector

Sector transactions attempt to increase total return by anticipating changes in yield differentials between different categories of bonds, such as Government, industrials, utilities, and the like. These relationships change because of factors such as the relative supply of new issues and the outlook for specific areas of the economy. For example, the economic effects of inflation have caused general widening of yield differentials between utility bonds and many other sectors in the past several years. However, improvement in 'utilities' ability to cope, with inflation through a more understanding regulatory for new construction may affect their outlook favourable and canbe yield differential to narrow.

2. Yield-Curve Anticipation

The preceding discussion placed the primary emphasis on effective rate anticipation. The downward movement from a peak inverted curve can lead to attractive returns from intermediate maturities. One should also note that in deteriorating markets, there can also be an upward movement effect with the result that intermediates perform worse than long. This can hurt investors who believe that intermediates offer reduced price volatility relative to long. On average, the intermediates, probably do have less price volatility than longs. However, strongly inverted or strongly positive yield curve shapes are not reflective of average conditions.

The prospects of yield curve reshaping can add an important refinement and balance to the rate-anticipation process. For example, suppose an investor with a defensive short-term posture anticipates that the long market rates are approaching a peak. He must then determine the correct time to begin deploying at least a portion of his short-term reserves. This action may be based either on the definite belief that the peak level of rates is actually at hand or simply as a counter balance to his uncertainty as to when and how that peak will occur. In any case once the decision has been made to commit some reserves, then the second decision must be to select the most appropriate maturity sector. If the investor believes that a good prospect exists for lower rates to be accompanied by a drop in the yield curve, then intermediate maturities should be explored as an interesting reentry vehicle on a risk-reward basis. If rates improve and the yield curve does move down to a more positive shape, then the right intermediate maturities can provide returns that are comparable to the long-term market. On the other hand, if long term rates continue to rise (without a significat increase in the degree of inversion), then the shorter maturity of the intermediates will provide a certain protection against the full deterioration that would be experienced in the long market.

3. Mapping Expected Returns

Today's yield reflects all information about supply and demand of a security, then an investor who buys a bond would expect his total return to reflect today's yield curve. Thus, total return could be equal to coupon income (c), amortization of premium or discount (A) and repricing (Roll). Because coupon income (C) and amortization (A) are the components of yield to maturity (YTM) then

$$\text{Total Return} = \text{YTM} + \text{Roll} = C + A + R$$

For ex: *A 30 years bond has a yield to maturity of 8.5% at the beginning of the period with 8.4% expected 3 months later. If the bond had an 8% coupon, calculate the total Return of the bond.*

Solution: The expected value of a bond over a horizon of one quarter.

Opening price at 8.5% for 30 years 94.60% Table-4.

Closing price at 8.5% for 29.75 years 94.59%. Compound value of an annuity of Re.1/-

Table No. (1)

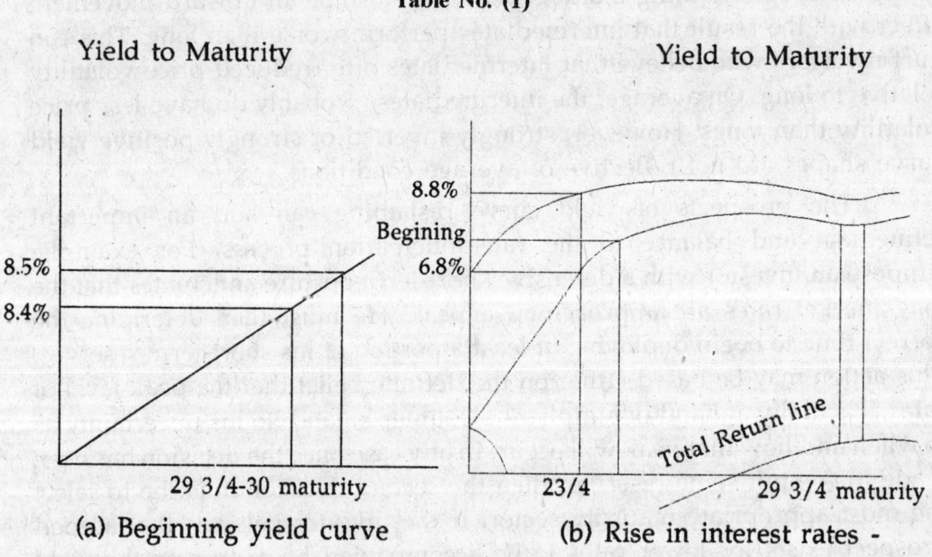

(a) Beginning yield curve

(b) Rise in interest rates - Forecasts.

Table 1 Closing price at 8.4% for 29.75 years = 95.63%
8% coupon payment accrued = 2.00%

Thus,

Total Return = C+A+R

C = Coupon Income
A = Amortization of premium/discount
R = Roll

$$C = \frac{\text{Coupon rate of interest earned}}{\text{Opening price of the bond}}$$

$$C = \frac{2.00}{94.60} = 0.0211416$$

$$A = \frac{\text{Price change as level yield curve}}{\text{Opening price}}$$

$$= \frac{-0.01}{94.60} = -.0001$$

$$= (95.63\% - 94.60\%) = \boxed{1.03}$$

$$R = \frac{\text{Price change}}{\text{Openingprice}} = \frac{1.03}{94.60} = 0.0110$$

$$\text{Total Return} = 0.0211 - 0.0001 + 0.0110$$

$$= 3.20\%$$

We know from our earlier discussion of bond price volatility that long - maturity, low - coupon bonds are the most volatile, knowledge of these facts plus a forecast of interest rates (z) is the basis for a strategy of interest - rate anticipation.

Assume that you forecast a rise in interest rates, as shown in the top two curves of figure. Further, let us assume that you make a comparison between the previously considered thirty - year, 8 percent bond versus a three-year 8 per cent bond. Thus, the total return of each bond can now be viewed as: Expected Forecast.

$$\text{Total return} = \frac{\text{Expected Forecast}}{C + A + R + I}$$

Where I for the three - years bond,

It is calculated as (98.06-102.95) - 102.66 = 0.0476 = 4.76%

Properties of Bonds and Bond Value

In India, bonds have a maturity period and companies, semi - Government and Government bodies are not issuing irredeemable bonds. They are redeemable in 5 to 9 years investment of bonds and 12 years for preference shares.

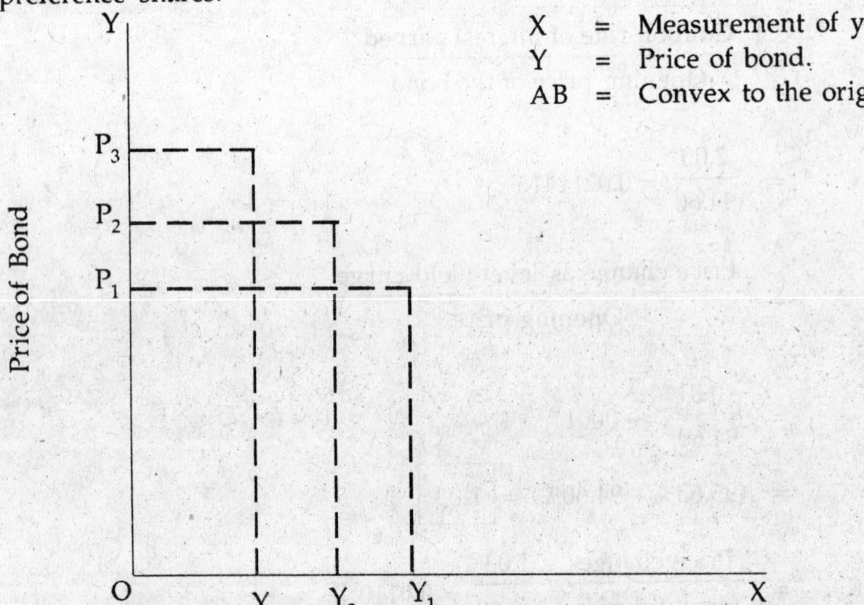

The properties of bonds can be described through the graph showing the price and yield relationship is revealed in the curve AB which is convex. 'X' axis measures the yield and Y axis the price of a Bond. The relationship of yield to price and to maturity periods can be set out in the following axioms:

1. Yield will decline with rise in price and vice versa
2. If required rate of return is the same as the coupon rate, bond price is the par value.
3. If required return is lower than the coupon rate, bond price is higher than face value and inverse is true.
4. Discount or premium on face value will fall as the bond approaches maturity.
5. Sensitivity of bond price changes to a given change in interest rates will be high, if the bond is of longer maturity, and the coupon rate is lower (Interest rate elasticity)

6. As the 'YTM' increases, the percentage change in price increases at a diminishing rate. The capital gains/losses on bonds will emerge on account of changes in price due to interest rate changes.

Yield Curves - Term Structure

The term structure of interest rates is the one of the major factors influencing the yields. For a given bond issuer, "the structure of yield for bonds with different terms to maturity (but no other differences)is called the term structure of interest rates." The market interest rate of the "i" the bond at the "t" the time period is effected by varing the bond issue term to maturity.

Market interest rate for a bond =

$$\begin{pmatrix}\text{Real rate of}\\ \text{Return}\end{pmatrix} + \begin{bmatrix}\text{Risk premium for}\\ \text{"i" at "t"}\end{bmatrix} + \begin{bmatrix}\text{Expected rate of}\\ \text{inflation at "t"}\end{bmatrix} + \begin{bmatrix}\text{Term structure of}\\ \text{interest rate for "i" at "t"}\end{bmatrix}$$

The term structure of interest rates is also called the yield curve and is defined as "the relationship of yields to maturities of bonds".

The following graph of yields curve can be given as an example:

CHART

Yield Curve

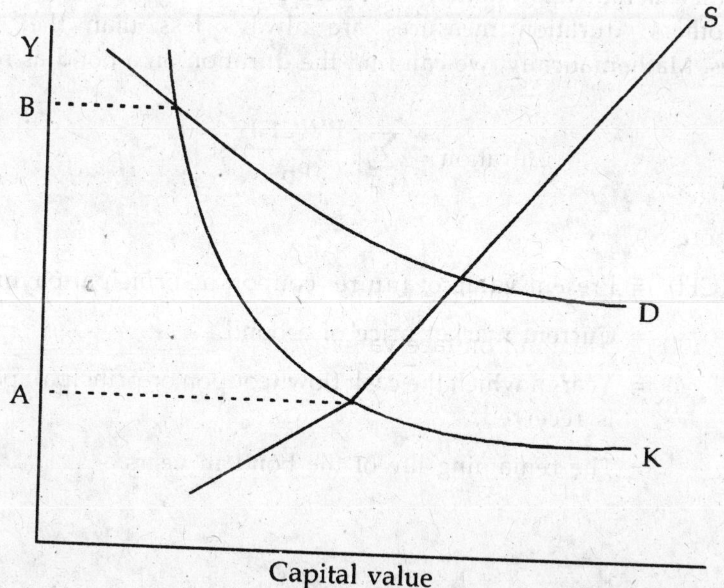

The above chart shows that higher the risk, the higher is the return. The larger is maturity, the higher is the return.

Duration: Duration is a measure of average time prior to receipt of payment. Duration is useful to make proper investment decision on bonds. Calculation of duration helps in investment decision making, revision of portfolio of bonds etc. Duration means the weighted average measure of time period of bond's life. It is valuable in understanding about the bond's prices changes in response to interest rate changes. The bond which has no coupon rate, the duration is equal to its maturity period.

$P_O = P_v$ (ct) for only are cash flow.

Usually, bond duration possesses the following properties

a) higher coupon rate results in shorter durations.

b) longer maturities mean longer duration.

c) Higher yields(YTM) lead to shorter duration.

Together, a bond's coupon, maturity and yield interact with one another to produce the issue's measure of duration. Knowing a bond's duration is helpful because it combines price and reinvestment risks in such a way that it captures the underlying volatility of a bond. A bond's duration and volatility are directly related; the shorter the duration, the less volatility in the bond prices.

Measuring Duration

Duration is a measure of the effective maturity of a fixed income as opposed to actual maturity. Only those bonds which promise a single payment to be received at maturity (i.e. No yearly coupon) have duration equal to their actual years to maturity. Zero coupon bonds are such bonds. For all others, duration measures are always less than their actual maturities. Mathematically, we can find the duration on a bond as follows:

$$\text{Duration} = \sum_{t=1}^{T}\left[\frac{PV(CF_t)}{Pb}\times t\right]$$

Where

P (CFt) = Present value of future coupon or principal payment

Pb = Current market price of a bond.

t = Year in which the cash flow (coupon or principal) payment is received.

T = The remaining life of the bond in years.

Illustration No.1: Calculate the duration value from the following data:

A bond with 12%, 10 years bond price at Rs.930 to yield 16%.

Solution:

Table No. (I)(14)

Duration Calculation for a 12%, 10 years bond priced at 16%

YEAR	Amount Cashflow (CFt)	Pv at 16%	Pv of annual cashflows Pv(CFt)	Pv(CFt) dividend by current market price of the bond (4) ÷ Rs.930	Time-weighted relative cashflow (1) × (5)
(1)	(2)	(3)	(4)=(2) × (3)	(5)	(6)
1	120	0.862	103.44	0.1112	0.1112
2	120	0.743	89.16	0.0958	0.1916
3	120	0.641	76.92	0.0837	0.2511
4	120	0.552	66.24	0.0712	0.2848
5	120	0.476	57.12	0.0614	0.307
6	120	0.410	49.20	0.0539	0.3234
7	120	0.354	42.48	0.0456	0.3192
8	120	0.305	36.60	0.0333	0.2664
9	120	0.263	31.56	0.0339	0.3051
10	1120	0.227	254.24	0.2733	2.733

Uses of Bond duration measures

Bond investors have many uses of duration analysis. Firstly, to measure the price volatility of a particular issue. Secondly, for structuring of bond portfolios, for example, if a bond investor, believes that interest rates are about to increase, he could calculate the expected percentage, decrease in the value of his portfolio, given a certain change, in the market interest rates, and the overall duration of the portfolio by selling higher-duration bonds and buying those of shorter duration. Such a strategy would prove quite profitable since short duration instruments do not decline in value to the same degree as longer bonds. Of course, if the investor believed that interest rates were about to decrease, the opposite strategy would be optimal.

Macaulay's Duration [MD]

Macaulay's Duration can be defined as the weighted average number of years, until the cash flows occur, where the relative present values of each cash payment are used as the weights. The formula for MD is as follows:

$$MD \sum_{t=1}^{N} \frac{ct}{(1+\text{YTM})t} + \frac{FT}{(1+\text{YTM})T}$$

$$\begin{bmatrix} \text{Weighted} \\ \text{average} \\ \text{maturity} \end{bmatrix} = \begin{bmatrix} \text{Maturities of} \\ \text{various time} \\ \text{periods to payment} \\ \text{“‘t’ \& ‘T’’’} \end{bmatrix} \times \begin{bmatrix} \text{Proportion of Bond's} \\ \text{value accounted for} \\ \text{by the payment in} \\ \text{square brackets} \end{bmatrix}$$

Immunisation

A bond holder faces the interest rate risk and fluctuations in rates will lead to changes in bond returns. A bond which is of longer period faces longer fluctuations with a given-change in interest rate than a short duration bond. Bond investor faces the interest rate risk between the time of investment and the future holding period. Interest rate risk is composed of two risks. Viz.,

a) Price Risk
b) Coupon Reinvestment Risk.

a) Price Risk and Coupon Reinvestment Risk

If interest rates rise in the meantime, the bond price will fall and there will be capital depreciation. Second risk is the coupon reinvestment risk as the yield to maturity computation implicitly assume that the coupon flows will be reinvested. Thus, if the interest income is reinvested at a higher rate, then the total end sum would be above that expected.

The above two effects are opposite to each other. While one increases the total bond return, the other decreases it, in the case of fall in interest rate. The reverse is true in the case of rise in interest rates. The elimination of these risks is called bond immunisation. If the realized return on investment in bonds is sure to be atleast as large as the appropriately computed yield to the time horizon, then the investment is immunised.

The maximisation is achieved by making the duration of the portfolio as equal to the desired holding period. Duration is the time period at which price risk and coupon reinvestment risk of a bond portfolio are of equal magnitude and opposite in direction.

1. Graded Illustrations

Illustration No. 1: A bond of Rs.1,000 bearing a coupon rate of 12% is redeemable at par after 10 years. Find out the value of the bond if;

i) Required rate of return is 12% or 10% or 14%

ii) Required rate of return is 14% and the maturity period is 8 years or 12 years.

iii) Required rate of return is 12% and redeemable at Rs 950 or at Rs.1050 after 10 years.

iv) Required rate of return is 14% and redeemable at par but the issue price is Rs.900 or Rs.1000

Solution: The value of the bond can be calculated by using the equation as follows:

$$Bo = \sum_{i=1}^{n} \frac{I_i}{(1+Kd)^i} + \frac{R_v}{(1+Kd)^n}$$

or

$$Bo = I\ (PVAF_{i,n}) + R_v\ (PVF_{i,n})$$

where,

$(PVAF_{i,n})$ = Present value of annuity factor at the rate of interest i, and number of years, n...

$(PVF_{i,n})$ = Present value factor for a given rate of interest i, and number of years, n,

These values may be found from the factor tables given at the end of text book.

Coupon rates 12%, 10%, 14%

Redeemable at par maturity period of 10 years.

If the required rate of return is 12%

the interest = $\frac{1000 \times 12}{100}$ = 120

Bo = 120(5.650) + 1000(.322)

= 678 + 322

= Rs 1000

If required rate of return is 10%

$$Bo = 120 (6.145) + 1,000 (.386)$$
$$= 737.4 + 386$$
$$= \boxed{\text{Rs. } 1,123.40}$$

If required rate of return is 14%

$$Bo = 120 (5.216) + 1,000 (.270)$$
$$= \text{Rs. } 625.92 + 270$$
$$= \boxed{\text{Rs. } 895.92}$$

Coupon rate is 12%.

Redeemable at par maturity 8 or 12 years.

Required rate of return is 14%

If maturity period is 8 years

$$Bo = 120 (4.639) + 1,000 (.351)$$
$$= 556.68 + 351$$
$$= \boxed{\text{Rs.} 907.68}$$

If maturity period is 12 years

$$Bo = 120 (5.660) + 1,000 (.208)$$
$$= 679.20 + 208$$
$$= \boxed{\text{Rs. } 887.20}$$

Coupon rate 12%

Required rate of return 12%

$$Bo = 120 (5.650) + 950 (.322)$$
$$= 678 + 305.90$$
$$= \boxed{\text{Rs. } 983.90}$$

If redeemable amount is Rs.1,050

$$Bo = 120 (5.650) + 1,050 (.322)$$
$$= 678 + 338.10$$
$$= \boxed{\text{Rs. } 1,016.10}$$

Illustration No. 2: A Bond of Rupees 1,000 bering a coupon rate of 8% is redeemable at par in 10 years. Find out the value of the bond if,

a) required rate of return is 8% or 10% or 12%

b) required rate of return is 12% and the maturity period is 8 years or 12 years.

c) required rate of return is 10%, redeemable at 920 or at rupees 1020 after 10 years.

Solution: $$Bo = \sum_{i=1}^{n} \frac{I_i}{(1+Kd)^i} + \frac{R_v}{(1+Kd)^n}$$

a) Coupon rate 8%, 10%, 12%

Redeemable at par maturity 10 years.

If the required rate of return is 8%

Bo = 80 (6.710) + 1000 (.463)

= 536.8 + 463

= 999.8

If the required rate of return is 10%

Bo = 80 (6.145) + 1000 (0.386)

= 491.6+ 386

= 877.6

If required rate of return is 12%

Bo = 80 (5.650) + 1000 (.322)

= 452 + 322

= 724

b) If the maturity period is 8 years

(required rate of return is 12%)

Bo = 80 (4.968) + 1000 (0.404)

= 397.44 + 404

= 801.44

If the maturity period is 12 years

(required rate of return is 12%)

B_o = 80 (6.194) + 1000 (0.257)

= 495.52 + 257

= **752.52**

c) If the redemption amount is rupees 920, required rate of return 10% maturity 10 years

B_o = 80 (6.145) + 920 (.386)

= 491.6 + 355.12

= **846.72**

If redemption amount is 1020

B_o = 80 (6.145) + 1020 (.386)

= 491.6 + 393.72

= **885.32**

Illustration No. 3: A bond of Rs. 1000 bearing a coupon rate of 10% p.a. payable half-yearly is redeemable after five years at par. Find out the value of the bond given that the required rate of return is 14%.

Solution:

Annual interest = Rs.100

Kd = 14%

n = 5 years

face value = 1000

Value of the bond = 50 $(PVAF_{7\%,\ 10\%})$ + 1000 $(PVF_{7\%,10\%})$

= 50 (7.024) + 1000 (.508)

= 351.2 + 508

= **859.2**

So, the value of a bond is Rs 859.2. In the same case, if the interest is payable on yearly interval, then the value of the bond is as follows:

= 100 $(PVAF_{14\%,\ 5\%})$ + 1000 $(PVF_{14\%,\ 5\%})$

= 100 (3.433) + 1000 (.519)

= 343.3 + 519

= **862.3**

Illustration No. 4: From the following information, calculate the present value, market price as per Macaulay's Duration Premium over face value = (1025.76 - 1000) = 25.76.

a) Face value Rs.1000

b) YTM = 8%

c) Coupon rate 9%

d) Number of year to maturity 3 years

Year (Na)	Cash flow (Ct)	I (Ytm)'	4=2×3 V_0=present values of Cash flow
(1)	(2)	(3)	(4)
(1)	90	$\frac{1000}{(1.08)^1}$ = 925.92	83.33
(2)	90	$\frac{1000}{(1.08)^2}$ = 857.33	77.16
(3)	1090	$\frac{1000}{(1.08)^3}$ = 793.83	865.27
			1025.76

Year	Present value of cashflow V_0	Present value as proportion of V_0	Columns 3×1=(4)
(1)	(2)	(3)	(4)
1.	83.33	0.0812	0.0812
2.	77.16	0.0752	0.1504
3.	865.27	0.8435	2.5305
	1025		2.7621

Illustration No. 5: From the following information, calculate market price of present value as per Macaulay's duration period.

a) Number of years to maturity = 3 years

b) Annual coupon rate = 7%

c) YTM = 6%

d) Par value 1000

$$V_0 \text{ or } P_0 = \sum_{1}^{T} \frac{Ct}{(1+YTM)^t} \quad \text{(Put the above values)}$$

Year (Na)	Cash flow (Ct)	I (YTM)^t	4=2×3 V_0=present values of Cash flows
(1)	(2)	(3)	(4)
1.	70	$\frac{1}{(1.06)^1} = 94.34$	66.04
2.	70	$\frac{1}{(1.06)^2} = 89.00$	62.30
3.	1070	$\frac{1}{(1.06)^3} = 83.96$	898.39
			V_0 = 1,026.73

Year	Present value of Cash flow	Present value proportion of V_0	Columns 3×1=(4)
(1)	(2)	(3)	(4)
1.	66.04	0.0643	0.0643
2.	62.30	0.0607	0.1214
3.	898.39	0.8750	2.6250
	1026.73	1.00	MD = 2.8107

Illustration No. 6: A Rs 1,000 bond matures in 20 years and offers a 8% coupon rate. The required rate of return is 12%. Compute the bond's value.

Solution: The annual interest payment is Rs.80. At the end of the year 20, the bondholder receives Rs.80. interest payment and Rs.1000 par value.

The present value of the interest payment is obtained by using the presentvalue annuity factor for 11% and 20 payments.

P_v = Interest $(PVAF_{11\%, 20\%})$

P_v = 80 (7.469) = 597.52

The present value of the Rs.1000 principal repayment is obtained by using the present value, single-payment factor for 12% and 20 years.

P_v = Amount (PVF 12%, 20%)

P_v = 1000 (.104)

= Rs.104

Therefore, the bond's value is

= 597.52 + 104

= **701.52**

Illustration No. 7: A Rs.5000 bond with a 12% coupon rate matures in 8 years and currently sells at 96%. Is this bond a desirable investement for an invertor whose required rate of return is 10%?

Solution:

PV = Interest $(PVAF_{10\%, 8\%})$ + face value $(PVAF_{10\%, 8\%})$

PV = 600(5.335)+5000 (.467)

= 3201 + 2335

= 5536

Current price = 5000(96%)

= **4,800**

Illustration No. 8: ABC Ltd., is contemplating a debenture issue on the following terms:

Face value = Rs 100 per Debenture

Term to maturity = 7 years

Coupon rate of interest:

Year 1-2 = 10% p.a

3-4 = 14% p.a

5-7 = 15% p.a

The current market rate of interest of similar debentures is 15% p.a. The company proposes its price issue so as to yield a return of 16% p.a to the investors. Determine the issue price. Assume the redemption of debenture at a premium of 5%.

(***Note:*** The present value interest factors at 16% p.a for years 1 to 7 are .862, .743, .641, .552, .476, .410 and .354 respectively).

Solution: The interest payments over the life of the debentures and the present values are given in the following table:

Year	Interest (Rs.)	PVF at the rate of 16%	Present value (Rs.)
1.	10	.862	8.62
2.	10	.743	7.43
3.	14	.641	8.97
4.	14	.552	7.72
5.	15	.476	7.14
6.	15	.410	6.15
7.	15	.354	5.31
			Total = 51.34

The present value of redemption amount of Rs.105 (100+5) at the rate of 16% per annum is $105 \times (.354) = 37.17$.

Therefore the present value of debenture is 51.34 + 37.17 = **88.51**

The company should issue the debentures at this value in order to yield a return of 16% to the investor.

Illustration No. 9: A bond of Rs.10,000 bearing coupon rate of 10% and redeemable in 8 years at par is being traded at Rs.10,400. Find out the YTM of the bond.

Solution: In order to find out the YTM is to be solved for the value of Kd. For this purpose, different values are to be assumed for Kd and the starting point can be the coupon rate itself.

At Kd = 10%

B_0 = 10,000 (Coupon rate = Kd)

$$\text{Approximate Yield} = \frac{I + \dfrac{R_v - B_0}{n}}{(R_v + B_0)/2}$$

$$\text{YTM} = \frac{(1{,}000 + 10{,}000 - 10{,}400)/8}{(10{,}000 + 10{,}400)/2}$$

$$= \frac{950}{10{,}200}$$

$$= 0.0931 \text{ or Say } \boxed{9.31\%}$$

Illustration No. 10: From the following information, calculate duration

a) Par value 1000

b) Market price 55

c) YTM = 10%

d) Coupon rate = 8%

e) Annual Coupon payment = 80

f) Maturity 3 years

Solution: $\text{Duration} = \dfrac{\sum P_v(ct) \times t}{P_0}$

P_o = Present value of all future cash flows.

Period	Cashflow amount	Present value factor Y	Present value of cashflows $P_v(ct)$	Present value of cashflow × Time (t)
1.	80	.9091	72.73	72.73
2.	80	.8264	.8264	132.23
3.	1080	.7513	.7513	2434.21
			950.25	2639.17

$$D = \frac{2639.17}{950.25}$$

$$= \boxed{2.78}$$

Illustration No. 11: If YTM of 10% coupon bond is 12% and it has 3 years to maturity, what is its present value.

Solution:

$$V_0 = \frac{Coupon_{i1}}{(1+YTM)^1} + \frac{Coupon_{i2}}{(1+YTM)^2} - - - - - - - + \frac{Coupon_{in}}{(1+YTM)^n}$$

Coupon is 10%, return on Rs.100

So the return is 10

$$V_0 = \frac{10}{(1+0.12)^1} + \frac{10}{(1+0.12)^2} + \frac{10+100}{(1+0.12)^3}$$

$$= \frac{10}{1.12} + \frac{10}{(1.12)^2} + \frac{110}{(1.12)^3}$$

$= 8.928 + 7.971 + 78.29$

$= \boxed{95.18}$

Illustration No. 12: The formula for Macaulay's duration is

$$MD = \frac{\sum \frac{ct}{(1+YTM)^t} + \frac{Ft}{(1+YTM)^T}}{V_0}$$

The rate of V_o, the market price is to be calculated

Year (1)	Cashflow (2)	$\frac{1}{(1+YTM)^t}$ (3)	Cashflow $\times \frac{1}{(1+YTM)^t}$ (2) × (3)=(4)
1.	100	$\frac{1}{(1.12)^1}=0.892$	89.2
2.	100	$\frac{1}{(1.12)^2}=0.797$	79.7
3.	100	$\frac{1}{(1.12)^3}=0.7117$	71.1
4.	1100	$\frac{1}{(1.12)^4}=0.635$	698.5
			Total=938.5

Year	Cashflow $\times \frac{1}{(1+YTM)^t}$	Present value percentage	(4)=3 × 1
(1)	(2)	(3)	(4)
1.	89.2	0.095	0.095
2.	79.7	0.0849	0.1698
3.	71.1	0.0757	0.2271
4.	698.5	0.7442	2.9768
	938.5	1.00	3.2039

$$MMD = \frac{MD}{(1+YTM)}$$

$$= \frac{3.2039}{1.12}$$

$$= 2.860$$

Illustration No. 13: Find out the Macaulay's duration of a bond that has a face value of Rs.1000, a coupon rate of 6% and a maturity period of 4 years the bond's YTM is 8%.

Solution: The formula for Macaulay's duration is

$$MD = \frac{\sum \frac{ct}{(1+YTM)^t} + \frac{Ft}{(1+YTM)^T}}{V_0}$$

The value of V_o the market price is to be calculated

Year	Cashflow	$\frac{1}{(1+YTM)^t}$	Cashflow $\times \frac{1}{(1+YTM)^t}$
(1)	(2)	(3)	(2) × (3)=(4)
1.	60	1/(1.06)1 = 0.925	55.5
2.	60	1/(1.06)1 = 0.8573	51.19
3.	60	1/(1.06)3 = 0.7938	47.62
4.	1060	1/(1.06)4 = 0.7350	779.1
			933.4

Year	Cashflow $\times \frac{1}{(1+YTM)^t}$	Present Value as a percentage	(3) × (1)=(4)
(1)	(2)	(3)	(4)
1.	55.5	0.0594	0.0594
2.	51.19	0.0548	0.1096
3.	47.62	0.0510	0.153
4.	779.1	0.8346	3.338
			Total = 3.66

$$MMD = \frac{MD}{(1+YTM)}$$

$$= \frac{3.66}{(1+0.08}$$

$$= \frac{3.66}{1.08}$$

$$= \boxed{3.38}$$

Illustration No. 14: If "XY" Company pays an amount of Rs.30 per year during the next year on bonds currently yielding 12%, calculate the weighted average of MD.

Solution:

Year (1)	Outflow (2)	Present value of 2 at 12% (3)	3 as % of total (4)	Liability M.D. (1) × (4)=(5)
1.	30	$\frac{1}{(1+0.12)} \times 30 = 26.78$	53%	0.53
2.	30	$\frac{1}{(1+0.12)^2} \times 30 = 23.92$	47%	0.94
		50.7	100%	1.47

Weighted average M.D = $\boxed{1.47}$

In order to minimise this portfolio, a 12% zero coupon bond with a maturity of 1.47 years should be used. It is to be noted that the duration of a zero coupon bond is its maturity.

Illustration No. 15: If "AB" Company has an amount of Rs.90 lakhs to be paid out every year for the next 4 years, what is its MD for this liability? If the company immunises by investing in zero coupon bonds of 2 years and 5 years maturity, what proportion in each will immunise the liability YTM = 11%

Solution:

Year (1)	Payout (2)	Present value of column 2 (3)	Column 3% of total (4)	Liability of M.D. (1) × (4)=(5)
1.	40	$40 \times \frac{1}{(1+0.11)} = 36.03$	0.29	0.29
2.	40	$40 \times \frac{1}{(1+0.11)^2} = 32.46$	0.26	0.52
3.	40	$40 \times \frac{1}{(1+0.11)^3} = 29.26$	0.24	0.72
4.	40	$40 \times \frac{1}{(1+0.11)^4} = 26.35$	0.21	0.84
		124.1		MD=2.37

The immunisation of the above portfolio liability may be assumed to have 'X' percent in 2 years bond and (1-x) percent in 5 year bond, so that the weights are equal to unity.

MD of 2 years bonds (x) + Md of 5 years bonds (1-x) = 2.37 years

$$\text{Thus, } 2x + 5(1-x) = 2.37$$

$$2x + 5 - 5x = 2.37$$

$$5 - 2.37 = 3x$$

$$2.63 = 3x$$

$$x = \frac{2.63}{3}$$

$$x = 0.876$$

Investment in 2 years bond should be 88% and investment in 5 years bond should be 12%.

Illustration No. 16: If Rs.1000 zero coupon bonds have a YTM= 14% and maturity of 10 years, what is its price,

Solution: $P_0 = \frac{\text{MV face value}}{(1 + \text{YTM})^{10}}$

$$= \frac{1000}{(1+.14)^{10}}$$

$$= \frac{1000}{4.22}$$

$$= 236.966$$

What is YTM of this bond if its price is zero

$$\text{YTM} = \left[\frac{\text{MV face value}}{\text{Market value}}\right] - 1$$

$$\text{YTM} = \left[\frac{1000}{200}\right]^{1/10} - 1$$

$$= (5)^{1/10}\text{-}1$$

$$= 1.746\text{-}1$$

$$= \boxed{17.46\%}$$

Illustration No. 17: If Rs.1000 zero coupon bond has a YTM 12% and maturity of 5 years, what is its price?

Solution: $P_0 = \frac{\text{MV face value}}{(1 + \text{YTM})^{10}}$

$$= \frac{1000}{(1+0.12)^5}$$

$$= \frac{1000}{(1.12)^5}$$

$$= \frac{1000}{1.7623}$$

$$= 567.44$$

$$P_0 = \boxed{567.44}$$

Illustration No. 18: Suppose that 'X' corporation must make a Rs.40 lakh pension fund payment each year for the next 4 years. Determine the average Macaulay's duration (MD) for this four year payment liability. Suppose that 'X' corporation decided to immunise the payments by currently investing in zero coupon bond with 2-year and 5-year maturities. What percent should 'X' corporation allocate to each zero coupon bonds, what will be the accumulated face value of the bonds? Assume the Yield curve is float at 11%?

Solution: The duration of the payments can be determined for treating each payment like a zero coupon bond with a maturity date equal to the maturity date of the payment.

Year (1)	Paymet (2)	PV of 11% (3)	Percent of Total (4)	Payments (MD) (1)(4)=(5)
1	Rs.40 Lakhs	40×0.9009=36.03	0.2903	0.29
2.	Rs.40 Lakhs	$40\times .812$=32.48	0.2617	0.52
3.	Rs.40 Lakhs	$40\times .731$=29.34	0.2355	0.70
4.	Rs.40 Lakhs	$40\times .659$=26.36	0.2133	0.86
		124.11	1.00	2.37

To determine the immunising asset allocation, let 'X' equal the percent of the 2 year bonds that are needed. This implies that (1-x) will be the percent of 5 year bonds because the two weights must sum to 1.

(MD of 2 year bonds) (x) + [MD of 5 year bonds] (1-x) = 2.37

= (2 years)(x) + (5 years)(1-x) = 2.37

= 2x+5-5x = 2.37

= 3x+5 = 2.37

= 3x = 2.63

$$x = \frac{2.63}{3}$$

= .88 (or) 88%

1-x = 1-88

= 12%

∴ 88 percent of the portfolio will be 2 year bonds and 12 percent will be 5 year bonds. The duration for a zero coupon bonds is equal to its time to maturity.

(A) present value of bonds : total PV = 62.05

(a) 2-year bond $.88 \times 62.05 = 54.6$

(b) 5-year bond $0.12 \times 62.05 =$ 7.45

Total = 62.05

(B) face value of bonds: (Yield is 11%)

(a) 2-year bond is

$$54.6 \times (1.11)2 = 54.6 \times 1.2321$$
$$= 67.27$$

(b) 5-year bond is

$$= 7.45 \times (1.11)5$$
$$= 7.45 \times 1.6851$$
$$= 12.54$$

Macaulay's Duration:

Illustration No. 19: Determine Macaulay's duration of a bond which has a face value of Rs.1000 and 10% annual coupon rate, and 4-year to go for maturity, the bond's YTM is 12% ?

Solution:

$$\sum_{t=1}^{+} \frac{[C,t/(\bar{1}+YTM)]+Ft/(\bar{1}+YTM)^{T}}{V_0}$$

C, is the coupon to be received at time t

I, is the face value of the bond

$V_{0'}$ is the present/market value of the bond

$$\sum_{t=1}^{+} \frac{[100\ t/1+12]+1000T/(1.12)^{4}}{V_0}$$

The value V_0 is equal to

Year (1)	Cashflow (2)	$1(1+YTM)^t$ (3)	$(2)\times(3)=4$
1.	100	$.893=1(1.12)^1$	89.3
2.	100	$.797=1(1.12)^2$	79.7
3.	100	$.712=1(1.12)^3$	71.2
4.	100+1000	$.636=1(1.12)^4$	699.6
			939.8

Year (1)	PV of C.t (2)	PV of Cf as proportion (3)	$(3)\times(1)=4$
1.	89.3	0.095	0.095
2.	79.7	0.084	0.168
3.	71.2	0.075	0.225
4.	699.6	0.744	0.976
	939.8	0.998	3.464

Duration: 3.464

SUMMARY

In this chapter we discussed the valuation of bonds in different situations. Changes in interest rates are the most powerful forces affecting prices of fixed income securities. The systematic risk factor is really two dimensional i.e., the level of interest rates and the level of rates changes. Forecasting the level of interest rates requires insight into business activity, prices and employment for the period ahead. Along with predicting the economic environment and price and employment prospects. Monetary and fiscal policy must be predicted as a force that will augment or upset projections of business activity prices and employment. As the level of interest rates is forecast to move up or down, the shape of the yield curve may change. Yields differ on various kinds of bonds. Investors are guided in assessing relative risks of default by established independent rating agencies. Non-risk factors influence yields as the result of tax laws, various features of security contracts and the way in which the securities market functions. The management of Bond was mostly a passive exercise. In recent years active bond management has taken centre stage. Presently the Investors have begun to concentrate on correctly positioning their portfolios maturity structure, coupons, and quality to benefit from changes in general level of interest rates.

We have concentrated on bond management strategies which plays an important role in portfolio management. The bond management strategies constitute the "Rate anticipation, yield, curve anticipation, mapping expected return" etc., The rate anticipation occupies an important role in determination of bond value. The value of bond depends upon "Maturity, Quality, Coupon and Sector".

In this chapter, we also concentrated about the problems on bond management. Valuation of bond is the main occupant in construction of portfolio, which requires a constant observation about the price change, interest rates and market situation. Therefore, the valuation of bond is more important on par with the equity market. The bond market is more popular in USA, UK markets. In the developed capital market, bonds occupies 70% of trading activity and creates a high liquidity to the bonds.

QUESTIONS

1. Explain the term "Bond." What are the differences between Debenture and Bond ?
2. Explain the concept of "Coupon Rate, Maturity".
3. What are the differences between purchasing power risk and default risk ?
4. Write an essay on different types of bonds.
5. What are the ingredients in Active Bond Management ?
6. What do you mean by "Duration"?
7. Explain the concepts of Macaulay's Duration ? How it will be measured ?
8. What is meant by Yield to Maturity (YTM)?
9. Describe the process of bond portfolio Immunisation.
10. Explain why interest rates are important to constrictive and aggressive bond investors.

11. What are the limitations of using duration as a measure of bond's price sensitivity to interest rate changes ?

EXERCISE

1. A bond of Rs.1000 bearing a coupon rate of 12% p.a. payable half-yearly is redeemable after 5 years at par. Find out the value of the bond given the required rate of return is 16%.

[Ans: Rs.865.60]

2. ABC Ltd., issued debentures last year. The debentures face value is Rs.100 and it carries an interest of 12% p.a. It will mature after 8 years. The required rate of return is 14%. Calculate the value of debenture.

[Ans: Rs.90.77]

3. Reliance Industries Ltd., raised the funds through issue of debentures. The debenture face value is Rs.1000, and it carries a coupon rate of 14%. The required rate of return is 13%. Compute the value of debenture, if its maturity period is 5 years.

[Ans: Rs.1035.40]

4. Voltas Ltd., approached the capital market for raising of funds by issue of debentures. The debenture face value is of Rs.1000, it carries an interest rate of 13%. The company's required rate of return is 15%. Calculate the debenture value if (a) the maturity period is 7 years (b) the period of maturity is 8 years.

[Ans: (a) Rs.916.80; (b) Rs.910.30]

❀ ❀ ❀

Unit-II

1. *Money Market*
2. *Capital Market-I*
3. *Capital Market-II*

1

MONEY MARKET

INTRODUCTION

Finance is the basic foundation of all kinds of economic activities. Business needs money to make more money. The business concern's efficiency is closely linked with efficient management of its finance. Finance involves, raising of funds and their effective utilisation. Finance is required by all individuals, households, commercial enterprises and the Government. Individuals and households need funds in order to meet their routine expenses and to acquire capital goods. Commercial enterprises need funds for smooth functioning of their business activities. The central and state governments need sufficient funds to meet their normal expenditure for their development programmes. The corporate and government sectors of the economy are borrowers and individuals and households are savers. The business concerns borrow the fund to meet their long-term needs of funds for new projects, modernization, diversification and expansion or to meet their operating expenses. Government also borrows funds to meet its deficit. Financial wealth of a nation will be built by individuals and organisations. The wealth of a country is stored in the form of financial assets such as equity shares and bonds. These are subject to the risk of loss of capital, if such wealth is liquidated. The financial assets owners always demand a better return on investment. Usually they require a better interest or in the form of dividend as a reward for their risk in capital.

The Indian financial system has undergone a dramatic change after implementation of liberalisation policy in 1991. It has witnessed a commendable progress and diversification of money and capital market.

Capital Market can be defined as "A complex of institutions investment and practices with established links between the demand for and supply of different types of capital gains".[1]

Capital Market is the centre or arrangement that provides facilities for buying and selling of financial instruments such as shares and debentures. It deals only with buying and selling of secondary securities.

---

1. *Arun, K. Datta*, Government Finance & Capital Market, P.G. Book Mart, P.No. 17, Kolkata - 1963.

F. Livingston defined the capital market as "In developing economy, it is the business of the capital market to facilitate the main stream of command over capital to the point of the highest yield. By doing so it enables control over resources to pass into hands of those who can employ them most effectively there by increasing productive capacity and spreading the national dividend."[1]

"Capital Market is a place wherein funds are raised for companies for meeting their long term requirements. Capital market is a market for long term capital. It refers to all the facilities and the institutional arrangements for borrowing and lending long term capital. The development of capital market depends upon the economy. The entire Indian economy was influenced by agricultural performance. The performance of agriculture sector is based on the rain fall."

Capital market consists of gilt-edged market and the industrial securities market. The gilt-edged market refers to the market for Government and semi-government securities backed by the RBI. The securities traded in this market are stable in value and are much sought after by banks and other institutions. The industrial securities market refers to the market for equities and debentures of old and new companies. The industrial securities market is further divided by the new issues market and further capital issue market. The new issue capital market (N.I.M) refers to the rising of capital by new companies in the form of shares and debentures, while the further issue capital market (F.I.M) deals with securities issued by existing companies. Both markets are equally important. But often the NIM is much more important from the point of view of economic growth. However, the functioning of the NIM will be facilitated only when there are facilities for transfer of existing securities.

Financial market deals in financial securities or instruments and financial services. It provides a mechanism for an investor to sell a financial asset. The markets provide liquidity to the investors, the individuals, the corporations, financial institutions and government. Trading in financial products in these markets is done either directly or through brokers. The participants are agents, brokers, borrowers lenders, financial institutions dealers etc., Financial markets are said to be perfect in the following situations.

1. A large number of savers and investors will have to operate in the market.
2. There are no taxes.
3. The savers and investors are rational.
4. The information is freely available to all market operators.

---

1. *F. Livingston*, The English Capital Market, Metheuir, Landon 1929.

5. There are no transaction costs.

Financial Markets are classified into following two types;

A) Money Market

B) Capital Market

A) Money Market

Money Market is a market for short term funds. In money market the funds which are available for less than one year. The money market is dominated by the central bank. The central bank is the watch dog of the monetary system. The money market provides a channel for exchange of financial assets for money. The money market is the mechanism through which holders of temporary cash surplus meet the holders of temporary cash deficit. Money market is of very great help in financing industry and commerce for their working capital requirements. The existence of a capital market is dependent upon the existence of a well organised money market and the two markets together play an important role in the economic development of a country. The money market offers the commercial banks a very good means of temporary employment of funds in liquid or near money investments and constitute a reservoir from which funds are obtained when demand arise. There is a strong reason behind non development of money market in under developed countries because they do not have very efficient and strong banking system.

Central bank acts as a promotional and development banker in money market. The short term sources of funds are available through organised sector and unorganised sectors. Unorganised sector is consisting of indigenous bankers and village money lenders. The organised sector consisting of RBI, SBI, Mutual Funds, companies, cooperative societies and financial institutions. The RBI has the full authority over money market. It can regulate, issue directions, frame rules and regulations, to participants.

Definition of Money Market

J.S.W. Wilson defined the money market as "The centre in which financial institutions congregate for the purpose of dealing impersonally in monetary assets."[1]

RBI defines the money market as "The money market is a market for short term financial assets that are close substitutes for money, facilitates the exchange of money for new financial claims in the primary market as also for financial claims, already issued, in the secondary market."[2]

1. *V.A. Avadhani*, Capital Market Management, Himalaya Publishing House, 1997)
2. *I.M. Panday*, Financial Management, P.No.964, Vikas Publishing House (P) Ltd, 1999.

Geographically the money market may be located or associated with a particular place, like Indian Money Market, New York Money Market, Mumbai Money Market etc., In the Mumbai Money Market, short-term loanable funds are attracted and are quickly borrowed and lent. London money market is the market for international importance. It is known as international money market. It attracts term funds from all over the world for redistribution among the borrowers. The demand for short period comes primarily from the Government, business concerns and private individuals. The government has become probably the biggest borrower to meet the current deficit. Industrial and commercial concerns borrow funds for working capital needs. Some times they borrow to enable them to carry additional inventories. Other important private borrowers include stock exchange brokers, dealers in government and other security merchants, manufactures, farmers and others. Banks themselves may require additional funds and may borrow from the central bank or from each other. The supply of loanable funds in the money market comes mostly from the central bank of the country, the commercial banks and other finance companies. The central bank is the source of credit to commercial banks while the latter constitute the most important source of short-term credit to both individual and business houses and the brokers.

Characteristics of Money Market

The following are the characteristics of money market.

1. It involves in arrangement of short-term funds.
2. It is a tool for preparation of monetary policy and fiscal management.
3. It deals in high liquid instruments.
4. The players in this market is RBI and commercial banks and companies.
5. It is subject to RBI regulations.
6. It tells about the trends in liquidity and interest rates.
7. It provides funds at low transaction cost
8. It suits the requirements of borrowers for short term funds.
9. It encourages open market operations.

Different sub markets of a developed money market help in the proper functioning of the central bank. The money market and short-term rates of interest serve as a good barometer of monetary and banking system in the country and thus provide a valuable guide to the determination of central banking policy. The developed money market being a highly integrated structure, enables the central bank to deal with the most sensitive of the sub markets also.

nature. Call money markets are highly liquid. Generally, in our country commercial banks give loans to discount houses on the call basis. The call loans are normally repayable when demanded. They are mostly secured loans. The call loans are secured against treasury bills. The call money màrket provides funds to *bill market, inter bank uses, operators in Bullion market, dealers in stock exchange, cash credit and over draft facilities* to industrialists. The seasonal ups and downs are believed to be reflected in the volume of money at call and short notice. The call money market rates are different and fluctuated on daily basis. The demand for call money is the highest in the month of March of every year. Because it is the time to meet year end and tax payments and withdrawals of funds by financial institutions to meet their statutory obligations. Usually, the call money borrowing will increase where there is an increase in the *''Cash Reserve Ratio''*. The participants in the call money market are;

1. Scheduled Commercial banks and RBI
2. Non-Scheduled Commercial Banks
3. Foreign Banks
4. Co-operative Banks
5. Discount and Finance House of India (DFHI)
6. Securities Trading Corporation of India. (STCI)

The DFHI and STCI are active players in the call money market. They will borrow as well as lend like banks. At present the small banks and non-scheduled banks also actively participating in this market. SBI is a major lender but a small borrower in the call market. In 1970 a new development occurred in the call market, the All India Financial Institutions like *IDBI, ICICI, IFCI, UTI, LIC, GIC* entered in the market. The supply of call loans on the money market by these institutions has been advantageous in many ways. Continuous participation in th call market will help to the economy. The Vaghul Working Group (1987) has been appointed by RBI to study about the market. The committee has recommended that the call market should be

1. preserve participation of commercial banks without any ceiling on call rates.
2. LIC, UTI and others may be allowed temporarily in market with ceiling of interest rate of 10% per annum.
3. the committee further recommended that no ceiling on call rate for all the participants.

According to the latest RBI policy *LIC, UTI, GIC, IDBI and NABARD* are allowed to participate in the call market as lenders, many dealers to

participate in this market as both borrowers and lenders. Some mutual funds are also allowed to act as lenders.

The call money market in India, Pakistan and U.S.A are examples of a sub market dealing with overnight money. The demand for the funds in the call market comes from commercial banks who fall short of reserves overnight or a few days, and the supply also comes from banks. These transactions are called as *Inter bank call markets.* In this market the funds are transferred and book adjustments will be made between banks to meet the statutory cash reserves requirements. Among some banks there is regular arrangement without the payment of interest, for other banks the price of overnight money is 2 *paise* per hundred rupees per night. The turnover in the call market has been growing exponentially.[1] On an average the daily turnover in the call market has been around **Rs.6000** crores during 1991-1997. The call money rate remained around 7% during the April-Oct 2001. The volatility of the call rate can be attributed to factors such as the following;

1. CRR - requirement
2. Occasional factors (disruption in banking industry)
3. Call money interest rates
4. Taxation - will influence the call rates. Demand comes from corporate sector
5. The liquidity crisis in money market.
6. No matching between liabilities and assets of the banks.
7. The link between forex market and call market.
8. Windo dressing by banks.
9. The tactics of 31st March by commercial banks

2. Treasury Bills

A treasury bill is a promissory note issued by Government. A treasury bill is a kind of finance bill. A bill which does not arise from any genuine transaction in goods is called a finance bill. The treasury bills were introduced in India in 1937. The finance raised by the central government through these bills replenish government cash balances. The treasury bills are issued for a period of *91 days, 182 days, and 364 days.* The bills are issued by tender or on tap system. The treasury bills transactions are carried out by RBI on behalf of central government. The interest rate is administered and fixed by the RBI. Treasury bills in India

1. Economic Times Midterm Review of Monetary & Credit Policy 2001-2002 Oct. 23 2001. P.No.6

is available in two kinds. *a) Ordinary Treasury bills, b) Ad-hoc treasury bills.* Ordinary treasury bills are issued by RBI. These bills provide short-term finance to the central government. The adhoc treasury bills are issued by state governments, semi-governments, and foreign central banks. The ad-hoc bills were financed by the created money. These ad-hoc bills were quickly replaced by borrowing against dated securities from the market. The ad-hoc bills became the device for automatic monetisation of the budget deficit. The RBI gave an assurance to remove the adhoc treasury bills from the market from April 1997 onwards. The adhoc treasury bills system is replaced by Ways and Means Advance (WMA) method. The *ways and means advance* introduced by RBI from 1-4-1997 to accommodate temporary mismatches of the central government in receipts and payments. WMA is not a source of financing budget deficit. Ways and Means are becoming a sources of funds to the state governments.

Treasury bills are sold in auction system. The date of auction, and the notified amount are announced by the RBI from time to time. The state governments, state run pension funds, provident funds were permitted to participate in auction on a non-competitive basis from August 1994 onwards. These organisations are not allowed to bid. They have to apply to the RBI and the RBI will decide the cut-off rate for the competitive bills of banks. These bills are taken into consideration for the purpose of SLR for banks. The treasury bill market in India is limited and is active. This market is yet to be developed in our country. The important factor for non development of this market in India is ''*extremely low rate of return on investment in treasury bills.* In U.K. the treasury bill market was well developed. In India the treasury bill market can be developed exponentially by providing a reasonable rate of return on investment in treasury bills. Treasury bill rate is the rate of interest of the bill sold by RBI. The treasury bill rate has now become a money market reference rate. The treasury bill rate became market determind. Treasury bills constitute a separate segment of the market there are 4 kinds of treasury bills available in India.

i) 14 days treasury bills

ii) 91 days treasury bills

iii) 182 days treasury bills

iv) 364 days treasury bills

91 days treasury bills are available through auction system. This system was introduced from 1-1-'93. The auctions are held on weekly basis and the amount for auction will be notified by the RBI. After introduction of auction system, interest rates are being determined by the market forces. The important features of treasury bills are presented below;

Features

1. Highly liquid
2. Do not have risk of default
3. Ready availability
4. Assured yield
5. Low transaction cost
6. Eligibility for the purpose of SLR for banks
7. Negligible capital depreciation

i) 14 days treasury bills

The authorities have introduced recently two types of *14 day treasury bills* i.e., a) *Intermediate Treasury Bill* (ITB), b) 14 day treasury bill. ITB introduced on 1-4-1997 and the second one was on 20-5-1997. The *ITB* has replaced by 91 day treasury bill. The ITB has been sold to State Governments, Foreign Central Banks and other specified bodies. The ITB is issued in a book entry form. It is not transferable. It can be repaid at par on the expiration of 14 days from the date of issue.

ii) 91 days treasury bills

The 91 days treasury bills total yearly turnover has increased enormously over time. The bills are purchased by *RBI, Commercial Banks, LIC, UTI, State Governments, Other approved bodies.* The RBI and commercial banks are active participants in this market. They are involved in 90% of sales in every year.

iii) 182 days treasury bills

182 days treasury bills had introduced in India in November 1986. It is a major financial innovation in money market. It provides funds for short-term nature. This type of treasury bills are developed towards short-term money market. It is a tool, the government to raise financial resources for its budgetary expenditure. These bills are sold in auction by RBI the auction for this instrument will be conducted at the beginning of every month. Now, they were made available fortnightly. The bills were normally issued at a discount for a minimum of *Rs. One lakh* and its multiples. These bills also eligible for the purpose of *SLR* to the banking sector. The 182 days bills may be purchased by *an Indian Resident, Firms, Companies, Banks & Financial institutions.* It should be remembered that RBI did not purchase these bills. The regular participants can quote the rate of discount through auction. The return usually available quite high and it had tended to rise over the year. These treasury bills are more liquid because of refinancing facility. The yield on treasury bill was freely determined by market forces. The bill had become a popular instrument for *banks, financial institutions, corporate financemanagers* to invest their short term liquid funds. Generally, the level of yield on this instrument is *8 to 10 percent.*

iv) 364 days treasury bills

The authorities introduced a new money market instrument known as "364 days treasury bill" with effect from April 1992. The bills will be sold by auction. The auction will be held fortnightly. The treasury bills have the same features like *184 day treasury bill.* The RBI does not purchase and rediscount this bill. This instrument has attracted more investors in the market at each and every time of auction. There is a good response from the investors. The response is reflected in terms of number of bids and the amount tendered. The response from investors will depend on the following factors;

1. Uncertainty in the government securities market
2. Fluctuations in SLR position
3. The yield available on this instrument

This treasury bills yield has been quite attractive and it has been higher than the yield on the other bills. The yield on this instrument is ranging from *10.10% to 13.12%.** The interest rate is emerging as the bench mark in the financial sector. The turnover of this instrument is around Rs.8000 crores during 1996-97, The bid and offer price of this bill is 5.81% and 7.81%. The volume of turnover in IV th week of Sept.2001 was *Rs.1407 crores.*

3. Commercial Bill Market

Commercial bills of exchange was an important segment of the money market. In this market, bill of exchanges are bought and sold, the commercial bills are transferable and are eligible for rediscount. RBI has permitted the financial institutions, mutual funds, commercial banks and co-operative banks to enter in this market. Bill of exchange means the liability to make the payment on a specified date when goods are bought and sold.

A bill of exchange is ''*An instrument in writing containing an unconditional order signed by the maker directing a certain person to pay a certain sum of money only to or the order of a certain person or to the bearer of the instrument.*"

- Section 5 of the Negotiable Instrument Act, 1881.

* Source: RBI, Annual Report 1996-97. P.No.208-209.

In a broad bill finance is one of the major type of finance provided by banks. The bill is used for financing a transaction in goods. The bills will be treated as a negotiable instrument. The operators in the money market regard bills as a self liquidating paper. The liquidity position of the bill is often only *to cash, call loan, and treasury bill*. The bill carries a low degree of risk of loss. There are two main categories of bills i.e., demand bill and usance bill. A demand bill is payable immediately on presentation or at sight to the drawee. Demand bill some times may not have specific time. *Usance bill* is also called as time bill. It is payable at a specified later date. Similarly bills can be categorised as *''documentary bills and clean bills.''* Documentary bill means, the drafts are accompanied by documents of title to goods. *For ex: Railway receipts, bills of lading*. These bills further can be classified as *''Documents against acceptance (D/A) and Documents against payment (D/P).''* DA bill is deliverable against acceptance by the drawee. The DA bill becomes a clean bill after delivery of documents. DP bill is accepted by the drawee, the documents of title are held by the banker till the bill of exchange is mature.

The bills further may be classified as *inland bills and foreign bills.* Inland bills mean the amount of bill must be payable in India. The bill must be drawn on resident in India. An inland bill may be endorsed in a foreign country and remain in circulation there. *Foreign bill* is a bill which is drawn outside India and payable anywhere in abroad. Further it may be classified as *export bill and import bill.* Export bills are drawn by exporters on any country outside India. Import bills are drawn on importers in India by exporters outside India.

Commercial bills are occupying an important role in foreign countries. But In U.S. and U.K. the bills are used for international trade. In India the use of bill of exchange is very limited in *Agricultural Sector, Cottage and Small Scale Industries etc.* For financing the movement of agricultural produce a variety of bill of exchange is used and which is known as *''hundi''*. Hundi has a long tradition of use in India. It is used to raise money or to finance domestic trade by bankers. There are two kinds of hundis. *(a) darshani (b) muddati.* Darshini hundi is again categorised such as *1. shahjog 2. namjog 3. dekharnar jog 4. femanijog 5. jokhami 6. Dhanijog.* Darshini hundi is used for payment of goods originating from up country places and transmitting to different party's places. Muddati hundi is used in local markets. Its maturity period varies between *30 days to 120 days.*

The SBI has since 1965 stopped providing discounting facilities. But other commercial banks continue to extend such facilities. Banks discount hundis on the basis of the personal standing of the indigenous bankers. The present arrangements should be taken advantage for developing the bill market in India. The experience in this market reveals an increasing *bad debts, delay in recoveries, increasing administrative expenses, low profitability etc.* These problems may overcome if efforts are made by the Government to correct them. The SBI should restart the discounting facility and earn profits. The Government should adopt a better policy of discounting hundies as a regular business.

There are other bills which are known to the money market as *Accommodation bill and supply bill.* Accommodation bill is also called as wind bill. An accommodation bill is defined as "One in which a person, called an accommodation party, puts his name to accommodate another person without receiving any consideration." The *supply bill* is a "Bill drawn by the supplier country on the Government on account of supplies of goods made under contract to the concerned. The supplier of the material can obtain advance from a commercial bank against such bills. These bills do not have the status of negotiable instrument. Banks advances against supply bills are clean advances. The process of bill finance is very simple. However, in practice it is quite complex and varies a great deal. The financing of bill requires a lot of process. At the first instance a bill may pass through many parties before its maturity. The second step is willingness of acceptance services by commercial bank or a specialised financial institution on behalf of the debtor. In this process "services of acceptance" is the most important factor in financing of bills of exchange. Acceptance service is a guarantee service provided for commission for trade bills. It does not involve either borrowing or lending. The acceptance services business is not well developed in India. The services are provided by commercial banks on a commission basis. The commercial banks and indigenous banks should take the responsibility for providing this service.

The maturity period of a bill is generally ranging from 30 days to 120 days. 90 days bills are become very popular in India. Import trade from abroad is financed by 60 days bills. Usually the domestic bills may have a maturity period of *90 days* from the date of purchase or discount. Export bills may have a maturity period of *180 days.* A bill for agricultural finance may have a maturity period of *15 months.* The bill for financing cottage and SSI may have maturity period of *12 months.* Bills are an important financial instrument which provide high liquidity. Bill financing provides the efficient system of payments. Because payment is assured on a due date. Bill financing promotes efficient use of credit. Bill financing ensures the liquidity of the banks. The maturity of bills are determined by commercial banks preferences for particular assignments. RBI has the ultimate authority in deciding the maturity period of bills.

Characteristics of Bill Market

The following are the characteristics of the Bill market;

1. The supply of bills would be continous and quite large.

2. An instrument providing credit to customers.

3. The market offers facilities to rediscount the bills.

4. RBI's willingness to rediscount bills throughout the year.

5. Ready availability of facilities for acceptance at low cost.

Limitations

The bill market will have following limitations;

1. The bill market in India must be judged as an underdeveloped.
2. There is no developed market in India for bills of exchange.
3. Large part of the bills discounted by banks are not genuine bills.
4. The facilities for discounting bills in India is very limited while comparing with *U.K. and U.S.*
5. RBI acts in the market as a lender of the first resort rather than as a lender of last resort.
6. *The acceptance services* in this market is very much restricted.

RBI has taken the innovative steps of permitting scheduled commercial banks to rediscount genuine trade bills. RBI has been attempting to develop the bill market by offering rediscounting facilities. RBI has been taking efforts to develop this market by *(a) 1952 Scheme (b) 1970 Scheme.* The 1952 Scheme facilitates the scheduled banks to get advances by way of demand loans on the security of eligible promissory notes of their constituents. The scheme provides lodgement of bills as security for loans from the RBI and not for their being rediscounted by it. Further, the scheme gets advances from RBI at concessional interest rate. The scheme also covers export bills to provide the credit facilities to the exporters.

According to the scheme of 1970 all licensed scheduled commercial banks are eligible for rediscounting of their bills with RBI. The scheme covers only genuine trade bills. The guidelines issued by *RBI* are presented below.

1. There must be an evidence of sale of goods.
2. These are to be drawn on and accepted by the purchaser's bank and where the latter is not a licensed schedule bank, the bill should in addition bear the endorsement of a licensed scheduled bank.

3. The scheme provides refinance facility throughout the year.
4. The bill should have usance of 90 days.
5. The bill should bear atleast two good signatures.

The schemes aimed at increasing the availability of adequate rediscounting facilities with the central bank. The practice of discounting and rediscounting of bills is yet to take root in India. 1970 scheme is a slight modified than the 1952 scheme. The 1970 scheme tried to arrange credit facilities to only genuine bills. RBI has also permitting them for rediscounting. The RBI has also felt that there is a strong need to promote the bill market with continuation of rediscounting facility. The RBI has appointed many committees to study the bill market in India such as *''The Tandon Committee, Chore Committee, Chakravarthy Committee and Vaghul Working Group''*. As a result of the recommendations of the committees, the RBI has been endeavoring to develop the bill market in India. The recent measures of RBI are presented below:

1. The Committees have advised banks to fix minimum of 25% of their inland credit purchases as bill acceptance limit.
2. It has been recommended to the GOI for remission of stamp duty on bills and the Government has accepted it.
3. Introduction of a derivative usage promissory notes for not more than 90 days. The derivative promissory note has been exempted from stamp duty.
4. In May 1990 the following institutions are permitted to participate in bills rediscounting scheme.
    1. All Scheduled Commercial Banks.
    2. LIC and its subsidiaries
    3. GIC and its subsidiaries
    4. ICICI
    5. IRBI
    6. UTI
    7. DHFI (Discount and Finance House of India)
    8. NABARD
    9. SCICI
    10. Exim bank
    11. LIC Mutual Fund
    12. SBI Mutual Fund
    13. MSCB

14. SIDBI
15. ECGC
16. Select U.C.Bs
17. Canbank Mutual Fund.
18. IFCI
19. IDBI
20. NHB
21. TFCI.

The Bill market rates in India, will determine the cost of bill finance as per the following:

a) Bank rate
b) SBI hundi rate
c) Bazaar bill rate
d) Commercial banks bill finance rate
e) SBI discount rate.

Usually the bill discounting rates varied between *9.75% to 22%* in the market.

4. Certificates of Deposit Market (CD)

Certificates of Deposit are a new instrument in money market. It is a short term negotiable instrument. It is introduced by RBI in 1989. It represents bank deposit account which is transferable from one party to another. CD is a bearer form of instrument, issued by commercial banks and financial institutions for a minimum period of 3 months and maximum period of one year. The minimum amount of issue could be Rs.25 lakhs. C.D's are technically part of bank's time deposits. They can be sold anywhere to any one. Liquidity and marketability are said to be hallmarks of CDs. CDs are riskless in terms of default of payment of interest and principal. They are issued at a face value. The interest rate on CD will depend upon market conditions. The RBI has permitted to deal with C.Ds in 1992 to several non bank public financial institutions such as *IDBI, SIDBI, IRBI, IFCI, ICICI, Exim bank, TFCI and SCICI.* CDs are the obligations of banks. Commercial Banks can issue or sell either directly to the investors or through the dealers. CDs are quit flexible in respect of maturity period. The Commercial banks can issue CDs at a rate which is lower than the rates for deposits of the similar maturity. The yield on CDs is higher than that of treasury bills. CDs are involved in interest rate risk. The participants in CDs market are *''State Governments, Local Governments, Foreign Governments, Central Bank, Non-Bank Financial institutions individuals and Mutual Funds.* Banks themselves may buy and sell CDs in the secondary market. When CDs issued in global markets are called as **"Euro Certificates of Deposit"**. The banks are interested to capture the advantages of over the time deposits by issuing CDs. CDs are also a major source of resources mobilised by banks. The banks have introduced CDs as a weapon to counter the competition from financial institutions. Since 1980s a serious assessment efforts were made to introduce CDs in India. The Vaghul Working Group made has following recommendations in 1982 regarding CDs are presented below:

a) There was no secondary money market in India.

b) The CDs may be given to rise fictitious transactions.

c) The interest rates are always controlled at every moment.

The Vaghul Working Group has been appointed to study about the development of CDs in India. They submitted the report in 1987 and recommended for introducing CDs provided with short term deposit rates. Ultimately RBI launched a scheme in June 1989 permitting the banks to issue CDs with a view to develop the money market.

Certificates of Deposit Market in India (CDs)

The CDs market is yet to be developed. RBI has been taking several steps to develop this market. The CDs in Indian money market have the following *characteristics:*

1. The CDs had the maturity period of 3 months to 1 year.
2. CDs are freely transferable, endorsed and delivered only after the lock in period of 45 days after the date of issue.
3. All schedules banks are eligible to issue CDs.
4. CDs issued by banks should not exceed 1% of fortnightly average deposits.
5. All CDs must be subject to CRR and SLR requirements.
6. Banks are not permitted to buy back their CDs before their maturity date..
7. CDs will have to bear stamp duty at the prevailing rates in markets.
8. The CDs may be subscribed by NRIs on a repatriation basis.

The RBI has modified its original scheme from time to time. The Discount and Finance House of India (DFHI) plays an important role in this segment. The DFHI fully involved in developing the secondary market in CDs. There will be a potential for the growth of primary and secondary markets for CDs. CDs can get support from various sources. For ex: Large PSUs and private corporate bodies are interested towards this market. The funds for CDs are coming from the current accounts.

5. Money Market Mutual Funds

The Money Market Mutual Fund is a fund which mobilises funds from the general public. The resources will be deployed in money market instruments. The instruments are with short-term maturities with high yield benefits as these investments to the unit holders. MMMFs are regulated by the Ministry of Finance and RBI. The MMMFs were permitted to invest in rated corporate bonds and debentures with a maturity period of one year. These were made more attractive to investors by reducing the lock in period from 46 to 30 days with effect from 1-7-96. The MMMFs were originated in the U.S. in 1972. Investors are using MMMFs as a parking place. MMMFs have not really developed. The first MMMF set up by *Kothari Pioneer* in 1997 but did not succeed. The *UTI MMF* opened on 23-04-97 had collected about Rs.30 crores. The scheme is open to *Resident Individuals, HUFs, Trusts, Societies and Corporates*. The minimum required investment is Rs.10,000. The investor can with draw any amount after the lock in period of 30 days. The MMMFs will repurchase the units after the lock in period, NAV is to be calculated on daily basis. The MMMFs help to stabilize the volatile interest rates when the liquidity is high.

The RBI has issued following guidelines on MMMFs:

1. All MMMFs should get permission of RBI.
2. MMMFs units are available only to individuals.
3. Mutual Funds, Public Financial Institutions, Scheduled Commercial Banks are permitted to start MMMFs.
4. The private sector MMMFs are required to get clearance from SEBI.

The MMMFs were intended to be invested in money market instruments for the benefit of individual investors. Investment in MMMF are considered highly safe, self liquidating assets having a low risk like *Treasury bills, Gift-edged securities, Call money, Certificate of deposits of commercial banks and financial institutions, derivative usance of bills, commercial papers and securitised debts of banks.*

Limitations

1. MMMFs involve heavy stamp duty.
2. High cost of floatation expenses.
3. Lack of investors education.
4. Lack of fully developed secondary market for trading.

The resources mobilised by MMMFs is required to be invested in call money, CDs, Commercial bills and Treasury bills. The exposure of MMMFs to CPs should not exceed 3% of the resources of MMMFs. MMFs cannot make any investment in privately placed securities issued by associated companies of the spansor. The *Discount and Finance House of India (DFHI)* is making efforts to activate the secondary market for money market instruments and for integrating various segments of market. RBI has also taken steps to widen the scope of market by allowing more participants.

MMMFs cannot deploy their funds in capital market. The MMMFs will not have insurance cover from any organisation. MMMFs cannot be offered for a guaranteed return to the holders. The NAV calculation and other formalities of MMMFs should be followed by SEBI rules and regulations. NAV is calculated on daily basis.

6. Commercial Paper Market

Commercial paper is a short-term unsecured promissory note, issued by corporations mostly on a discount basis. Commercial paper is a new instrument in the money market. Commercial Papers are issued mostly by leading, *nationally reputed, credit worthy and highly rated large corporations.* The Commercial paper is also called as *Industrial paper or Financial paper or Corporate paper.* Commercial papers are issued in domestic market and in global market. In global market they are called as *"Euro Commercial Paper".* Commercial papers are not secured and they are backed by the credit worthiness of the issuing companies. CPs are negotiable by endorsement and delivery. They are highly liquid instruments. The CPs normally have a buy back facility. Generally, CPs are issued in bearer form on discount basis. The CPs are mostly in large denominations. The CPs will be issued through banks or merchant bankers or dealers or brokers in the open market. Sometimes they may be issued directly to the investors. CPs are mostly issued by *transportation companies, public utilities, insurance companies and finance companies.* The CPs will be purchased by mostly the *Commercial banks, Non-Banking Finance Companies, Liquid business concerns* CPs have a very flexible maturity. The maturity period of CPs have different periods in different countries throughout the globe.

For ex: The maturity period in USA not more than 270 days.

The maturity period in UK between 7 to 364 days.

The maturity period in France 10 days to 7 years.

The maturity period in Canada 30 days to 365 days.

The maturity period in Australia up to 185 days.

The yield on CPs is slightly higher than the yield an Treasury bills. It is also slightly lower than the prime lending rate of banks. The yield on CPs is also more than bank deposit rate. CPs are better and cheap sources of finance than bank. The CPs market was well developed in advanced countries. But in India primary market for CPs is developed but the secondary market is not active. The CPs will be issued to meet the need of current transactions and seasonal needs of the funds. They are not suitable to finance either the fixed assets or permanent working capital. The CPs are mostly suitable as a means of interim finance.

The RBI announced in March,1989 regarding its decision to introduce a scheme for issue of commercial paper programme by the participants. Registered corporate bodies, banks, unincorporated bodies, any person can invest in CPs. CPs finance is not an additional finance, it is just a substitute for bank finance. If the commercial paper market develops, the fund of the intercorporate resources will be diverted to this segment and same unhealthy practices may arise. Therefore, *the Vaghul Committee* strongly supported the introduction and development of CP in the Indian Money Market and suggested the following;

1. CP should be issued to investors directly or through banks.
2. The CP issuing company must have a networth of not less than Rs.5 crores.
3. The issuing company shares must be listed in stock exchange.
4. The minimum amount of issue should be Rs.1 Crore and the minimum denomination of Rs.5 lakhs.
5. The CPs issuing cost should not exceed 1% of the amount raised.
6. The RBI is the sole authority to decide the size of issue and timing of issue.
7. The instrument should not be subject to stamp duty at the time of issue and there should not be any tax deduction at sources.
8. The interest on commercial paper shall be a market determined.
9. The issuing companies should get certification of credit rating for every six months and "A" grading enterprises may be permitted to enter the market.
10. Some legislative amendments or necessary to develop this market.

In 1988-89, the RBI has implemented various recommendations of the Vaghul Committee. The RBI initially gave the permission to the companies where its tangible networth is Rs.10 crores. The working capital limit of the concern be not less than Rs. 25 crores. The Companies also required to get a minimum credit rating of *p1+* from *CRISIL* and that the maximum amount of CP would be limited to *20%* of the maximum permissible bank finance. Most of CPs outstanding has been held by commercial banks in India.

The Need for a Money Market

1. The Money Market is a coordinator between borrowers and lenders of short term funds.
2. It provides transmission of funds from surplus concerns to concerns which are short of funds.
3. MM is a device to the Government to balance its cash inflows and outflows.
4. MM is a weapon to business firms to meet their short-term funds.
5. MM creates a minimum rate of return on idle fund lying at the disposal of corporate sector and banking sectors.
6. MM is a tool to the Finance Manager inorder to utilise surplus funds to enhance the shareholders wealth.

The Goals of Money Market Investor

1. Investors main objective is to achieve the safety and liquidity of the principal amount along with some gains.
2. Money Market is a parking place of idle fund.
3. The investors will escape squarely from long-term market risks.
4. Money Market instruments generally offer more protection against political risk and inflation risk.
5. In Money Market the investor never face default risk.

On overall evaluation of the Money Market we can find that, it is entirely dominated by RBI. All the policy matters of the sector will be finalised by the India's Central Bank. SEBI and other statutory organisations are also playing an import role for smooth functioning of the Money Market. The Money Market is a powerful weapon in the hands of Central Government and it should be handled skilfully by the *Ministry of Finance.* Therefore, the development of Money Market can boost the wealth of a nation and encourages the Capital Market.

Recent developments in Money Market

The annual statement on monetary and credit policy released on April 19, 2001 projected a GDP growth rate of 6 to 6.5% for 2000-2001. This projection is based on the assumptions of a *reasonable monsoon, good performance of exports and a revival of the industrial sector.*

The annual policy statement had indicated that under normal circumstances and barging emergence of any adverse and unexpected developments in domestic or external sectors, the overall monetary policy for 2001-02 will be:

a) The average call money rate comedown sharply from 8.6% in early April to 7% in mid oct.,2001. During this period, the repo rate also comedown from 7% to 6.5%. The CRR was reduced by 50 basis points to 7.5% effective from May19,2001, augmenting lendable resources of the banking system by Rs.4,500 crores. Responding to these operations, the interest rates on other money market instruments also showed a declining trend. The primary yield on 91 *day* treasury bills declined by 150 basis points from 8.5% to 7%, between April and mid Oct.,2001. During the same period, primary yield on 364 day treasury bills fell by 168 basis points from 8.85% to 7.17%. The discount rates on CP also showed a similar trend. At the long end of the market, the secondary market yield on government paper in the range of 10-20 years have softened from 10.08% - 10.70% in April to 9.12% - 9.92% by mid-October 2001.

b) RBI issued fresh guidelines for issuance of commercial paper in Oct.,2000 relaxing the terms and conditions and streamlining the procedures. As indicated in the annual policy statement of April 2001, *Banks, FIs, PDs, Satellite Dealers (SDs)* are now permitted to make fresh investments and hold CPs only in dematerialised form, effective from *June 30, 2001*. In this context Fixed Income Money Market and Derivatives Association of India circulated a "Report as FIMMAD working Group as primary relating to market conventions and guidelines for CPs. FIMMADA in consultation with market participants, depositories, and RBI, prepared the related guidelines and made them public on October3, 2001. These guidelines seen to be working reasonably well, and no changes are being proposed at present."

c) As announced in the annual policy statement, 14days and 182 days Treasury Bills (TBs) have been withdrawn from the week beginning May 14,2001. The notified amount of 91 *days* TBs has been simultaneously increased to Rs.250 *crores*. It has also been ensured that both the 91 *days* & 364 *days* TBs mature on the same day inorder to facilitate the availability of adequate fungible stocks of TBs varying maturities in the secondary market. Increased attractiveness of TBs is evident from the fact that no development as the RBI has taken place in TB questions and the bid-coverage ratio, particularly with respect to 364 *day* TBs, has also improved.

d) *A Negotiable Dealing System (NDS)* is being introduced with a view to facilitating electronic bidding in auctions and secondary market transactions in government securities and dissemination of information. The technology infrastructure related to *NDS* has been tested with the involvement of all market participants in *LAN* and *WAN* environments.

e) *The clearing Corporation of India Ltd.,(CCIL)* was registered as on April 30, 2001 under the Companies Act, 1956 with the SBI as the chief promoter. Initially, the CCIL will be clearing all transactions and on reported on the NDS of RBI and also US/rupee/dollar forex spot and forward deals. The operations of CCIL linked to the NDS is expected to commence with a test run in Nov.2001. Necessary amendments to notification were issued by the Government for introduction of uniform price auction format for auctions of dated securities. With the approval of the Government, the new auction format will be introduced as an experimental basis.

f) A scheme of retail participation including the middle segment encompassing PFs, Trusts in the primary market for government securities as Non-competitive basis has been finalised in consultation with market participants and the Technical Advisory Committee on Money Market and Government Securities Market. The details of the scheme are yet to be finalised by RBI.

g) *The Satellite System Dealership* was launches in 1996 to serve as a second tier to primary dealers in retailing of G-Secs. The RBI in its midterm monetary and credit policy has tacitly accepted that the concept of satellite dealers as not taken off as an efficient medium for retailing of government securities The Central Bank has decided to review the entire system of satellite dealers in the fixed income market. RBI has decided to allow players such as provident funds, trusts to participate in government bond auctions, on a non-competitive basis. This review will consider the role carved out for satellite dealers in the development of retail market. The review would focus on building linkages between primary and satellite dealers and improving the satellite dealership system.

h) An overall review of the present environment in the market, the RBI had decided to undertake a review of the SD system in close consultation with SDs, PDs, and TAC. The review will consider the role carred out for SDs in the development of retail market, particularly in the context of the expanding role of PDs, emerging alternative mechanism of retailing government securities as the screen based trading in exchanges, and the supervisory concerns in monitoring SD's operations. The review will examine the scope for establishing a better linkage between SDs and PDs and thereby improving the SD system as an effective distribution channel at a retail level for government securities.

i) *Call Money Market* with average daily gross lending improved to *Rs.19,600 crore* in May-September 2001 from *Rs.10,900 crores* during the corresponding period of the previous year. Therefore the central bank feels that the planned phasing out of non-banking participants from the call money market has not caused any strain on the market.

SUMMARY

Financial Market deals in Financial Securities or instruments and financial services. Financial instruments differ in their investments characteristics such as *liquidity, risk, maturity, tax status, rate of return etc.* Financial Markets can be classified as *Money Market and Capital Market.* Money Market provides a channel for the exchange of financial assets for money. Money market is a market where the short-term funds are available. Money Market deals in highly liquid instruments. Money market is subject to RBI regulations. The main borrowers of short term funds in the money market are *Commercial Banks, Central Government, State Government, Corporate Sector, and Local Bodies.* Money Market is to provide liquidity position to the market. The MM is involved in buying and selling of short term instruments. The instruments are *call money, Treasury bills, Commercial papers, Certificate of Deposits, Bills and MMMFs.* If money is lent for a day it is called as call money. A treasury bill is a promissory note issued by Government. The bills are issued for 14 days, 91 days, 182 days, 364 days. Treasury bills are sold in auction system. A bill of exchange is bought and sold in commercial bill market. There are several types of bills in the market. Certificate of deposits is a short-term negotiable instrument. It represents bank deposit. It may be issued for 3 months to 1 year period of time. Money Market Mutual Fund is a fund which mobilises funds from the general public. The MMMFs are controlled by RBI. Commercial paper means, a short-term unsecured promissory note issued by companies for discounted values. The yield on CPs is slightly higher than the yield on treasury bills. CPs are highly liquid instruments. The CPs normally have a buy back facility. Usually they are issued in bearer form on discount basis. The CPs are mostly on large denominations. CPs are issued by Public Utilities, Transport Companies, Insurance Companies, and Finance Companies. The CPs will be mostly purchased by Banks, NBFCs, Liquid Business Concerns. CPs have a flexible maturity period.

QUESTIONS

1. What do you understand by Financial Market?
2. Define Money Market.
3. What are the characteristics of a Money Market?

4. Explain the different kinds of money market instruments.
5. Define call money market.
6. What is a Treasury bill? Explain the different types of bills available in the market
7. Write an essay on commercial bill market.
8. What do you understand by commercial papers?
9. What are the features of commercial paper?
10. Explain the concept of certificate of deposits.
11. What do you mean by MMMF? Explain their features and functions.
12. What are the guidelines issued by RBI on MMMFs?
13. What are the recent developments in Money Market?
14. Discuss the Role of RBI in Money Market.
15. What are the institutions involved in Money Market?

Annexure-I

Average Daily Turnover in Call Money Market

(Rs. in Crores)

Fortnight ended	Turnover per day
May 5, 2000	Rs.48,056
May 19, 2000	Rs.39,214
June 2, 2000	Rs.40,056
June 16, 2000	Rs.38,300
June 30, 2000	Rs.38,357
July 14, 2000	Rs.42,465
July 28, 2000	Rs.39,797
Aug. 11, 2000	Rs.39,275
Aug. 25, 2000	Rs.35,973
Sept. 8, 2000	Rs.41,797
Sept. 22, 2000	Rs.42,933
Oct. 6, 2000	Rs.44,635
Oct. 20, 2000	Rs.45,776
Nov. 3, 2000	Rs.47,321
Nov. 17, 2000	Rs.46,805
Dec 1, 2000	Rs.47,310

Dec 15, 2000	Rs.46,747
Dec 29, 2000	Rs.43,568
Jan 12, 2001	Rs.50,396
Jan 26, 2001	Rs.49,039
Feb. 9, 2001	Rs.50,675
Feb. 23, 2001	Rs.45,987
March 9, 2001	Rs.51,550
March 23, 2001	Rs.50,314
April 6, 2001	Rs.44,630
April 20, 2001	Rs.50,957
May 4, 2001	Rs.48,008
May 18, 2001	Rs.41,395
June 1, 2001	Rs.46,156
June 15, 2001	Rs.44,790
June 29, 2001	Rs.47,052
July 13, 2001	Rs.47,071
July 27, 2001	Rs.44,597

Sources: RBI Bulletin, Oct., 2001. Page No. 997.

Annexure - II

Daily Call Money Rates from 01-08-2001 to Sept.12-09-2001.

As on.	Range of Borrowings	Rates of Lending (%)	Weighted average rate of Borrowing	Lending
Aug. 1, 2001	5.47-7.10	4.92-7.50	6.90	6.92
Aug. 2, 2001	5.89-7.10	4.89-7.40	6.86	6.88
Aug. 3, 2001	5.85-7.10	4.85-7.00	6.92	6.87
Aug. 4, 2001	6.15-7.05	5.39-7.05	6.82	6.96
Aug. 6, 2001	5.80-7.05	4.80-7.10	6.78	6.80
Aug. 7, 2001	5.45-7.20	4.90-7.10	6.88	6.89
Aug. 8, 2001	5.70-7.65	5.10-7.90	7.11	7.12
Aug. 9, 2001	5.79-7.60	5.20-7.60	7.18	7.26
Aug. 10, 2001	5.94-7.50	6.25-7.50	6.93	6.97
Aug. 11, 2001	5.90-7.25	5.54-7.25	6.97	6.97
Aug. 13, 2001	5.21-7.25	4.97-7.90	6.92	6.99

Aug. 14, 2001	6.00-8.30	5.11-8.30	7.05	7.06
Aug. 16, 2001	5.59-7.30	5.09-7.30	7.04	7.08
Aug. 17, 2001	5.55-7.30	5.03-7.30	7.02	7.01
Aug. 18, 2001	5.96-7.15	6.50-7.25	6.97	7.00
Aug. 20, 2001	5.59-7.34	5.06-7.90	7.04	7.04
Aug. 23, 2001	5.61-7.25	5.06-7.25	7.04	7.04
Aug. 24, 2001	6.00-7.50	5.75-7.25	7.04	7.08
Aug. 25, 2001	5.86-7.20	5.42-7.80	6.86	6.88
Aug. 27, 2001	5.85-7.05	4.85-7.05	6.84	6.85
Aug. 28, 2001	5.30-7.30	4.75-7.10	6.74	6.75
Aug. 29, 2001	5.26-7.30	4.75-7.80	6.73	6.78
Aug. 30, 2001	5.44-7.40	4.89-7.10	6.90	6.93
Aug. 31, 2001	5.53-7.55	4.96-7.55	6.95	6.98
Sept. 1, 2001	5.92-7.10	6.10-7.15	6.91	6.92
Sept. 3, 2001	5.45-7.45	4.90-7.50	6.89	6.91
Sept. 4, 2001	5.85-7.00	6.00-7.15	6.85	6.86
Sept. 5, 2001	5.43-7.25	4.89-7.25	6.98	6.90
Sept. 7, 2001	6.00-7.95	5.89-7.95	7.14	7.17
Sept. 8, 2001	6.08-7.40	6.60-7.40	7.08	7.08
Sept. 10, 2001	6.05-7.75	5.05-7.75	7.02	7.15
Sept. 11, 2001	6.10-7.80	5.10-7.50	7.06	7.06

Sources: RBI Bulletin Oct., 2001.P.No. 996.

2

CAPITAL MARKET-I

INTRODUCTION

Capital Market deals with long-term funds. It supplies long term and medium term funds. Capital market deals with ordinary shares, stocks, debentures and bonds of corporations and securities of the government. The funds which flow into the capital market comes from savers. Further, there are various institutions, which operate in the capital market give quantitative and qualitative direction to the flow of funds and bring rational allocation of resources. They do so by converting financial assets into productive physical assets. This leads to the development of industries.

Capital market provides a market mechanism for those who have savings and to those who need funds for productive investments. It diverts resources from wasteful and unproductive channels to productive investments.

Since 1951, the Indian capital market has been broadening slowly. The volume of savings and investments, have started showing steady improvement. Many types of encouragement and tax relief exit in the country to promote savings. Several steps have been taken to protect the interest of investors. An important indicator in the growth of capital market is the growth of joint stock companies and corporate enterprises. In 1951 there were 28,500 companies with a paid up capital of nearly Rs.775 crores and as on *31-3-98* there were more than *2,00,000* companies with a paid up capital of nearly Rs.**1,37,959 crores**. The growth of investment has been quite phenomenal in recent years in keeping with the accelerated tempo of development of the Indian economy under the impetus of the 5 years plans, introduction of liberalisation and globalisation policies in India. The growth of public borrowings for investment purpose is also an indicator of the growth of the capital market.

Indian financial system has undergone revolutionary changes in the recent past. Besides, there has been an explosive growth of financial

innovation. New methods of finance have gained prominence in the financial market.

Considerable deregulation of financial markets has taken place in India favouring unbridled growth of financial service companies. Reforms undertaken have increased competitiveness within the financial sector by means of free interest rates, allowing new financial institutions and instruments. As a consequence, the scope and activities of banks and non-banking finance companies have expanded rapidly due to liberalisation drive, more particularly since 1991. The non-banking finance companies have been competing and complementing the services of commercial banks. It has been observed that the growth of non-banking finance companies is more pronounced than banking companies.

The Growth of the capital market:

Today the Indian financial system is both developed and integrated. Integration has been through a participatory approach to the granting of loans as well as saving schemes. The expansion in size and number of institutions has led to a considerable degree of diversification and increase in types of financial instruments.

The development banks in the Indian financial system have witnessed vast changes in the planning periods. Now, the development banks constitute the backbone of the Indian capital market. The relevance of the development banks in the industrial financial system is not merely quantitative, but they have over whelmingly qualitative dimensions in terms of their promotional and innovational functions. The growth of the capital market is determined by the following factors.

a) Economic development

b) Rapid industrialisation

c) Level of savings and investment of the household sector

d) Technology advances

e) Corporate performance

f) Regulatory frame work

g) participation of FIIs in the capital market

h) Development of financial services

i) Liquidity factors

j) Political stability

k) Globalisation

l) Financial innovation

m) Economic and financial sector reforms

n) International developments

o) Agency costs

p) Emergence of financial intermediaries

q) Sophistication among investment managers

r) Tax incentives

s) Speed in acquiring, processing and acting upon information

t) NRIs investment

STRUCTURE OF CAPITAL MARKET IN INDIA

The structure of the capital market has undergone a remarkable transformation. Now, the capital market comprises as an impressive network of financial institutions and new financial instruments. The term capital market covers both the primary market and the secondary market. The primary market or New Issue Market is one in which long-term capital is raised by corporations directly from the public. The secondary market refers to the stock market where the financial instruments which are used for raising long-term capital are traded. The secondary market has become more sophisticated in response to the varied needs of the investors. Provision of long-term credit is entrusted with specialised financial institutions.

There are various sub-markets in the capital market in India. The structure has undergone vast changes in recent years. New instruments and new institutions have emerged on the scene. The sub markets are as follows;

a) Equity Market

b) Debt Market

c) Government Securities Market

d) Mutual Funds.

Structure of Capital Market

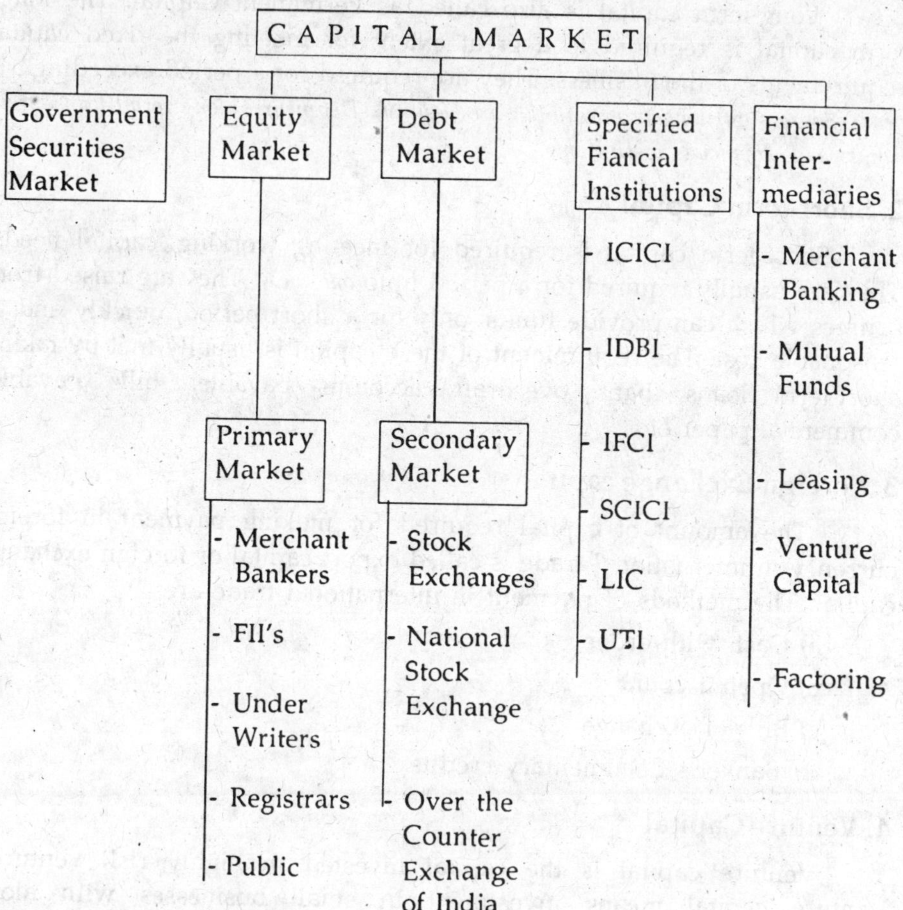

Categories of Capital

Capital Market depends on the available savings and investment in the economy and the performance of the industry in general. Among others the monsoon and agriculture, industrial growth and performance of the corporate sector in particular, reflecting the fundamentals in the economy would influence the tone of capital and stock market. The following are the different categories of capital:

1. Long-term Capital
2. Short-term Capital
3. Foreign Exchange Capital
4. Venture Capital

1. Long-term Capital

Long-term capital is also called as Permanent Capital. The long-term capital is required to a great extent for meeting the fixed capital requirements of the business. They are required for a period exceeding *one year. Sources of long-term capital are Equity, Debentures long-term loans from banks and financial institutions.*

2. Short-term Capital

Short-term capital is required for meeting working capital needs. They are usually required for a period upto *one year*. They are raised from sources which can provide funds only for a short period, quickly and at reasonable cost. The requirement of these capital is usually met by taking short-term loans, bank overdraft, accounts payable, bills payable, commercial paper etc.

3. Foreign Exchange capital

The amount of capital required for making payment in foreign currency in international trade is called export capital or foreign exchange capital. The methods of payment in international trade are:

a) Cash with order

b) Open account

c) Bills of exchange

d) Banker's documentary credits

4. Venture Capital

Venture capital is the capital invested in highly risk ventures. Venture capital means investment in small businesses with along gestation, start up and early stages, such financing involves long-term commitments. Venture capital is regarded as "pre public" financing. In the *United States* approximately 60% of the companies get financed through pre-public financing and they eventually go public. In *Western European* countries a minimum rate of return of *30%* per year is considered as normal on the venture capital investment.

The venture capital assistance is made available in 3 forms; a) equity b) Conditional Loans C) Income notes. In India the venture capital industry is presently having 13 active players. The major players operate at *Mumbay, Delhi, Calcutta and Bangalore*. Broadly they can be classified in the following four categories;

a) Companies set up by financial institutions

b) Companies set up by state level financial institutions

c) Companies set up by Commercial banks and

d) Companies set up by the private sector.

The following are some of the institutions / funds which are offering venture capital Finance:

1. IDBI's Venture Capital Fund.
2. Technology Development and Information Company of India Ltd. (TDICI).
3. Risk Capital and Technology Finance Corporation Ltd. (RCTC)
4. Can Bank Venture Capital Fund.
5. 20th Century Venture Capital Fund.
6. Industrial Venture Capital Fund.
7. A.P.I.D.C Venture Capital Ltd.

PLAYERS IN THE CAPITAL MARKET

Capital Market plays a vital role in mobilising savings and channelising them into productive investments for the development of trade, commerce, and industry. The capital market helps in capital formation and economic development of the country.

Capital market facilitates the movement of stream of capital to be used more effectively, efficiently and profitably to increase the national income. Capital market acts as an important link between those who save and those who need such savings for investing in projects. Funds flow into the capital market from individuals, financial institutions. Companies and financial institutions, companies and financial intermediaries will collects new funds to be used by companies engaged in the industrial activities and Government.

The capital market provides return to the savers in the form of interest or dividend and transfers funds to investors. Capital market diverts resources from wasteful and unproductive channels to productive investments. A well developed capital market helps to integrate the national economy with the global economy by allowing foreign investment in the national economy.

The players in the capital market are broadly divided into three categories.

A) Companies Issuing Securities

B) Financial Intermediaries

C) Investors

A) Companies Issuing Securities

As per SEBI Guidelines, companies intending to issue securities are divided into three categories, Viz.,

a) New companies
b) Existing unlisted companies
c) Existing listed companies.

A company is a new company if it satisfies all the following three conditions:

a) It has not completed 12 months of commercial operations.
b) Its audited operative results are not available.
c) It is set up by entrepreneurs with or without track record.

A company is said to be an existing listed company if its shares are listed in any one of the recognised stock exchanges. Existing closely held or private companies are called as existing unlisted companies.

b) Financial Intermediaries

Intermediaries are institutional or individual agencies who assist in the process of transforming savings into investment. The major intermediaries in the capital market are:

i) Merchant bankers
ii) Under-writers
iii) Registrars
iv) Brokers
v) Depositories
vi) Collection agents
vii) Advertising agencies
viii) Agents
ix) Stock brokers and sub-brokers
x) Mutual funds

C) Investors

Investors comprising of financial and investment companies and the general public; these are employing funds in the hope of receiving future benefits. All rational investors prefer return, but most investors are risk averse, and attempt to maximise capital gains. Their preference for dividends or capital gains depends on their economic status and the effect of tax differential on dividends and capital gains. The institutions and companies raising capital from investors frame the schemes in such a way that these are suitable to all type of investors. The main objectives of investments are: *''Safety''; ''Profitability''; ''Liquidity''; ''Capital appreciation'' and ''Minimum risk.''*

COMPONENTS OF THE CAPITAL MARKET

In a capital market, banks and financial institutions are important components. They act as catalysts in the economic development of any country. These institutions mobilise financial savings from household, corporate and other sectors of the economy and channalise them into productive investments. They act as a reservoir of resources and form the backbone of the economic and financial system. The banking industry has undergone a sea chang during the last three decades, after the nationalization of banks. They not only lend for social and económic causes but also participate in the development programmes of the central

Government, State Government. The main components of capital market in India are:

a) Primary Market

b) Secondary Market

A) Primary Market

Primary Market is also called as New-Issue Market. The New Issue Market creates financial claims. The New Issue Market deals with those securities which have been made available to the public for the first time. Another factor which makes the role of the new issue market and stock exchange complimentary to each other is the infrastructure facilities provided for sale and purchase of securities. The new issues of shares are subscribed to the corporate sector through the application forms before the closing date of the issue. The amount of resources mobilised through public issues after liberalisation policy was presented in table No.II (1). The data reveals that the primary market has not been quite encouraging since 1997-98.

Table No.II (1)

Capital Raised through Public Issues 1991-2001.

(Rs. in Crores)

Year	PUBLIC ISSUES		RIGHT ISSUES		GRAND TOTAL	
	No. of Issues	Amount	No. of Issues	Amount	No. of Issues	Amount
1991-92	196	1711	316	3851	512	5562
1992-93	527	6059	488	12630	1015	18689
1993-94	770	12544	384	9306	1154	21850
1994-95	1342	21044	324	6577	1666	27621
1995-96	1426	14240	299	6564	1725	20804
1996-97	730	7761	112	2663	842	10424
1997-98	62	2862	49	1708	111	4570
1998-99	24	2602	24	2411	48	5013
1999-2000	55	4028	24	1125	79	5153
2000-2001	38	356	05	160	43	516
2001-2002 (June)	02	410	-	-	02	410

Sources: 1. RBI Bulletin, Oct. 2001, Page No. S 1017.

2. RBI Bulletin, July 2000, Page No.s 681

3. RBI Bulletin, March 99, Page No.s 277.

4. Prime Annual Report, 1991-94.

Public equity issues are not very active at present. According to Prime database,* the public issues for debt and equity issues just Rs.1,101 Crores and Rs. 6 crores respectively in the *first half of the current fiscal 2001-02* period. The first half of the current year witnessed *118* institutions and corporate enterprises mobilised an amount of *Rs. 22673 crore* through the private placement of debt. The amount raised by the private sector recorded a *31%* gain to reach *Rs.6234 crore* compared to *Rs. 4812 crores* raised in the first half of 2001-2002.

Mega Issues

During the current fiscal year 2001-2002 the leading mobilisers was *Reliance petroleum* with Rs.1,061 crores, followed by *GE capital with Rs.520 crores. Tisco, Rs.350 crores* and *Tata power Rs.300 crores.* The increasing mobilisation by the private sector can be partly explained by the near demise of the IPO route.

The amount raised by PSUs too saw a *34%* improvement with *Rs.4816 crore* being garnered led by major mobilisers like. *REC Rs. 869 crores, power Grid corpn. Rs.761 crores, SAIL Rs.700 crores, NTPC Rs.575 crores and BPCL Rs.445 crores.* On the other hand the mobilisation by state level under takings (SLU) is rose by 51% from Rs.5,858 crore to Rs.2,891 crore in the relevant periods 2000-2001 & 2001-2002 respectively. According to new RBI guidelines the commercial banks can invest in state government papers. It is found that the most of the funds raised by SLUs have been for the infrastructure sector, mainly power, roads, and water resources. The leader in mobilisation during the 6 month (2001-2002) (upto Oct. 30, 2001) was Krishna Bhagya Jala Nigam. *Rs. 356 crore,* followed by *GEB Rs.300 crores, Maharashtra Vikrikar Rs.244 crores J K SPDC Rs.200 crores* and GSRTC Rs.200 crores.

Significantly a total of Rs.12,272 crores was raised by AAA rated paper. On the other hand Rs.2,025 crores of paper was not rated at all during the 2000-2001 year. On an industry wise analysis it was found that the financial services sector including banking and term lending, continued to dominate the market, collectively raising Rs.10,736 crores, power sector ranked second with Rs.3,765 crores. The analysis of public issues during 2000-2001 further revealed that Maharashtra lead the resources mobilisation activity at Rs.9,877 crores, followed by Delhi at Rs. 6,778 crores and Karnataka at Rs.1,940 crores.

B) Secondary Markets

The stock exchanges, are the secondary markets. They serve not only the private sector but also the joint and public sectors by providing a

---

* Economic Times, Dt. 1-10-2001, P.No. 13.

ORGANISATION AND MANAGEMENT OF STOCK EXCHANGES

Stock exchanges are regulated and organised under the Securities Contracts (Regulation) Act, 1956. Under the Act, 23 stock Exchanges have been recognised by the Government. They have been formed either as voluntary nonprofit making associations or joint stock companies limited by shares or companies limited by guarantee. SEBI perscribes and approves the rules, regulations and bye-laws of all recognised stock exchanges. Their articles, amendments are also subject to the approval of SEBI.

Every stock exchange has a governing body (board of directors) and it is vested with various administrative and financial powers. Membership of the stock exchange is as per the provisions of the Securities Contracts (Regulations) Rules 1975; the members of the stock exchange can do their business as an individual/sole proprietor in partnership or also as representative members. The main function of active members of the stock exchange is to do the business of purchase and sale of securities in the market. All active members can appoint authorised assistants or clerks to do business on behalf of members. In some cases remisiers are also appointed. Members of stock exchange have acquired various functional specialisation such as acting as a commission broker, a floor broker, jobber or 'taravaniwala', dealer in non-cleared securities, dealer in odd lots, badla financiers or 'badiwala', acting as an arbitrator, dealer in Government securities and acting as and underwriter, in case of new issues.

Stock exchanges also appoint various committees, to deal with defaults, arbitration, disciplinary matters, market operations, floor Governors, purchase, administration, building, library, computerisation etc.

The governing council is the supreme body and it manages the stock exchange activities in accordance with the rules, bye-laws and regulations prescribed. The day to-day administration is looked after by the executive director. The executive director reports to the council of management and also to the central Government SEBI. The qualifications for membership of a recognised stock exchange are provided vide Reg. 8 of the Securities Contracts (Regulation) Rules 1957. Amendments have been made to regulation and accordingly a company as defined in the Companies Act 1956 is also eligible to the elected as a member of the stock exchange, subject to the conditions detailed in the regulation. Further, where the Government makes a recommendation for the governing body of a stock exchange is also required to admit corporations companies like the Industrial Finance Corporation, the Industrial Development Bank of India etc., sub-rule (4-A) allows companies formed in compliance with the provisions of sec 12 of the

facility for the transferability of shares held by the public. The stock exchanges not only effect purchases and sale of securities but also make a continuous valuation of securities traded in the market. Another important role played by the stock exchanges and generally not known is, relating the securities issued by the central and state Governments, Municipalities, Investment Trusts port trusts and various other public bodies. The new issues market and stock exchanges are inter linked and work in conjunction with each other. They cannot be described as two separate markets because of their functions they perform. Thus the stock exchange is a medium of transfer of resources for those securities which have already been issued. It also plays an important role in the transfer of securities with the companies whose shares are being dealt with, as the process the registration of shares must be done when they are transferred. In the secondary market securities issued in primary markets are bought and sold. In this market the public can buy and sell securities. Secondary market does not create financial claims. In this market funds do not flow between sellers of and buyers of securities. The brokers, the investors, mutual funds, and the financial institutions are the important constituents of the secondary market. By providing liquidity to lenders, the secondary market assists the operations associated with the primary market. The secondary market consisting of regional stock exchanges, BSE, NSE, OTCEI etc.

STOCK EXCHANGE

Definitions

Stock exchange represents an organised market in trading of securities. Stock exchange is established with the main purpose of providing a market place for the members to deal in securities. Stock exchanges are indispensable for the proper functioning of corporate enterprises. Stock exchange helps the investors, ready and continuous market, negotiability, liquidity and safety of investments.

According to Securities Contract (Regulation) Act 1956, the stock exchange can be defined as "An association, organisation or body of individuals, whether incorporated or not, established for the purpose of assisting, regulating and controlling business in buying, selling and dealing in securities."

Hastrong defined it as "stock exchange or securities market comprises of all the places where buyers and sellers of stock and bonds or their representatives under take transactions involving the sale of securities".

According to *Husband & Dockery* "Securities or stock exchanges are privately organised markets which used to facilitate trading securities".

J.E. *Payle* defined the stock exchange as the "Security exchanges are market places where securities that have been listed there on may be bought and sold for either investment or speculation".

Orgin and Growth of Stock Exchange

The organised stock exchanges in India are of comparatively not recent origin. The First Stock Exchange was set up in India under the name of 'Native share and stock brokers association of Bombay" now, known as Bombay stock Exchange in 1875. The enactment of companies act and the introduction of the principal of limited liability followed by the development in the means of communication and transport were gave impetus to the stock business in India. The stock exchanges in India have made a phenomenal growth since world war-II. During this period numerous stock Exchanges were set up at ''*Ahmedabad, Kanpur, Hyderabad and at Delhi*". In 1951 the Government prepared a draft bill for stock exchange regulation and referred it to an expert committee under the chairmanship of A.D Gorwala, and on the recommendations of the committee, the Government passed the Securities Contracts (Regulation) Act 1956. The main objectives of this act are as follows:

a) To regulate stock market practices

b) To create efficient securities market

c) To ensure fair dealing and protection to investors

d) To improve the working of stock exchange

e) To control the undesirable speculative practices.

At present, there are 23 stock exchanges recognised under the Securities Contracts (Regulation) Act. All of them operate under the rules, bye-laws and regulations, duly approved by Government. Statutes which are applicable to stock exchanges involve the following.

a) The Companies Act, 1956

b) The Income Tax Act, 1961

c) Foreign Exchange Regulation Act 1973.

Beside, to ensure the self regulatory role in 1988, SEBI was established by the Government of India.

Out of 23 stock exchanges, recognition to the Bombay Stock Exchange was granted on a permanent basis, while others are recognised for a period of 5 years. There is no uniformity in respect of the organisation pattern of the stock exchanges in India. Some are public limited companies, while others are limited by Guarantee or as voluntary

Nonprofit marketing organisations. Table portrays the organisatio stock exchanges in India.

Table -II (6)

Organisation Pattern of Recognised Stock Exchanges in India

Sl. No.	Name of Stock Exchange	Year of Establishment	Type of Association
1.	Bombay	1875	Voluntary nonprofit association of persons.
2.	Ahmedabad	1894	Voluntary nonprofit maki association of persons.
3.	Calcutta	1908	Public limited company.
4.	Madras	1908	Public limited company
5.	Indore	1930	Voluntary nonprofit mak association of persons.
6.	Hyderabad	1943	Company limited by Guara
7.	Delhi	1947	Public limited company
8.	Bangalore	1957	Public limited company.
9.	Cochin	1978	Public limited company.
10.	Kanpur	1982	Public limited company.
11.	Pune	1982	Company limited by guarar
12.	Ludhiana	1983	Public limited company.
13.	Gauhati	1983	Public limited company.
14.	Kanara	1985	Public limited company.
15.	Magadh	1986	Company limited by guaran
16.	Jaipur	1984	Public limited company
17.	Bhuvaneswar	1989	Company limited by guaran
18.	Sourashtra	1989	Company limited by guaran
19.	OTC Exchange	1989	Public limited company.
20.	Vadodara (Baroda)	1990	Public limited company.
21.	Coimbatore	1991	Public limited company.
22.	Meerut	1991	Public limited company.
23.	National Stock Exchange	1992	Public limited company.

Securities and Exchange Board of India Act,1992, to be eligible to be elected as a member of a stock exchange. The various conditions and stipulations for such eligibility have been detailed in the sub-rule (4A).

As a measure to improve the functioning of stock exchanges, these were required to broad-base, their governing bodies in such a manner that the ratio of elected stock-broker directors on the hand and outsiders, viz. Nominees of the Government and public representatives on the other to be 50:50, vide circular F.No 4/16/se/92 dated 19th August, 1991 issued by SEBI. This measure was taken so that the management of the affairs of the stock exchanges were carried on in an objective manner in the general interest of investors. Rule 10 of the Securities Contracts (Regulation) Rules 1957 permitted nomination by the Government, nominees on the bodies of recognised stock exchanges and through amendment, this power has since been delegated to the Securities and Exchange Board of India. Pursuant to this SEBI has appointed a joint secretary 3 Regional Directors and 12 Registrars of companies as its nominees on the board of 19 recognised stock exchanges, on 5th January 1995.

The executive director is appointed by the governing boards of stock exchanges; however this is subject to approval by SEBI and Central Government. His functions and duties engulf a wide area spreading across investors, companies, members and governing bodies of stock exchanges, SEBI, Central Government, Public, press etc., Considering such a variety of segments to be made by a standing committee, consisting of representatives of interests involved, so that he can discharge his onerous functions without fear or favour.

The regulations of the stock exchange cover the entire gamut of the operations, from enrolment of members and their authorised assistant, enlistment of securities, disciplining members activities, besides control over trading etc., stock exchanges are empowered to subject its members to various forms of disciplinary action like warning, reprimand, censure, fine withdrawal of all or any of membership rights. Contravention of provisions and actions may arise when there are evasion of payment of margins, breaching of various trading restrictions such as limits on carry - forward and jobbing prohibition of future dealing except for delivery compulsory liquidation of outstanding business etc., Kerb trading failure to attend to investor's complaints etc., The exchange through its monitoring and inspection departments are required to keep a close watch on the activities of its members. To secure that trading is conducted in an orderly and systematic manner and settlements take place in time without any problem governing councils are ceiling prices, prohibition of speculative transactions, closing the market, trading on account and circuit breakers.

FUNCTIONS

Stock exchange is established with the main purpose of providing a market place for the members to deal in securities under well laid down regulations and to protect the interests of the investors. Thus, the functions of the exchanges are the following:

1. Bring companies and investors together, so that.
   i) Investors can put risk capital into companies;
   ii) Companies can use the capital.
2. Provide an orderly regulated market for securities.
3. Facilitate continuous, ready and open market for selling and buying securities.
4. Promote saving and investment in the economy by attracting funds from the investors.
5. Facilitate take overs by means of acquiring majority of shares traded on the stock market.
6. Act as clearing house of business information.
7. Extend liquidity to securities.
8. Facilitate marketability and transparency of securities.
9. Allow companies to float their shares on the market.
10. Ensure wider ownership of securities.
11. Enable investors to evaluate the net worth of their holding.
12. Provide capital to profitable sectors.
13. Ensure safety and fair dealings to all.
14. Motivate managers of well reputed companies, to retain their share in "A" group, to improve performance.
15. Induce managers to improve performance for converting non-specified shares into specified shares in the exchange.

MEMBERSHIP

Constituents of the stock market are the companies issuing securities, intermediaries and brokers who match buying selling orders and the investors in the securities. But, only members of the exchange are allowed to do the business of selling and buying of securities at the floor of stock exchange. To be a member a person has to confirm to certain rules and regulations stated under the Securities Contract (Regulation) Rules 1957. The following are the important provisions as per Rule 8 of the Securities Contract (Regulation) Rules 1957.

1. No. Person shall be eligible to be elected as a member if:
   a) he is less than 21 years of age;
   b) he is not a citizen of India;

c) he has been adjudged bankrupt or proved to be insolvent;

d) he has compounded with his creditors;

e) he has been convicted of an offence involving fraud or dishonesty;

f) he is engaged as principal or employee in any business other than that of securities;

g) he is associated with or a member or subscriber or share holder or debenture holder or connected through a partner or employee with any other organisation, institution, association company or corporation in India, where dealings in securities are carried unless he undertakes admission to serve such association or connection;

h) he has been at any time expelled or declared as a defaulter by any other stock exchange;

i) he has been previously refused admission to membership unless a period of one year has elapsed since the date of such rejection.

2. No person is eligible for admission as a member under sub rule shall be admitted as a member unless;

   a) he has worked for not less than two years as a partner with, or as an authorised assistant or authorised clerk or apprentice to a member or

   b) he agrees to work for a minimum period of two years as a partner or representative member with another member and to enter into bargains on the floor of the stock exchange not in his own name but in the name of such other member or

   c) he succeeds to the established business of a deceased or retiring member who is his father, uncle, brothers or any other person who is in the opinion of the governing body, a close relative

3. A company as defined in the Companies Act, 1956 shall be eligible to be elected as a member of a stock exchange, if:

   a) such company is formed in compliance with the provisions of section 322 of the said act.

   b) a majority of the directors of such company are shareholders of such company and also members of that stock exchange; and

   c) the directors of such company, who are members of that stock exchange, have unlimited liability in such company.

Types of members and operators

The various types of the members of stock exchange are explained below;

1. Jobbers

Jobbers are dealers in securities in a stock exchange. They cannot deal on behalf of public. Jobbers buy and sell at securities at lower quotation higher ones. The difference between the buying and two selling prices is the Jobbers profit called Jobbers turn.

2. Brokers

Brokers are commission agents and/or floor agents who transact business in securities either for their customers or for other members. In the former case they are called commission brokers and in the latter case they are called floor brokers. Commission brokers act on behalf of clients, who wish to buy or sell some of their shares or debentures. Brokers charge commission from both the parties for their services. The investors who do not know the techniques of stock exchanges are greatly benefited by the expertise of brokers. Floor brokers execute orders of other members.

3. Tarawani walas

Tarawani walas are like jobbers and often handle transactions on a commission basis for other brokers. They make transactions on their own account and may act as brokers on behalf of the public.

4. Budliwalas

Budliwala is an intermediary who provides the necessary finance for taking delivery of shares or lends the required shares for making delivery at the end of clearing. They usually give fully secured loan for a short period of two to three weeks. The budliwalas charge fees, called cantago or "Seedhabadla" and backwardation or "Undabadla", for granting credit facilities to the buyers and the sellers.

5. Arbitrageurs

Arbitrageur is a broker, purchases security in one market and sells the same in another market to get opportunitic profit. The dealers who enter the dealings with securities in different stock exchange centers at the same time are called arbitragers. They make simultaneous or same or equivalent securities in an attempt to take advantage of price differences in the same or different markets.

6. Odd Lot Dealers

Only standard trading units i.e., prescribed round lots are traded on the floor of the stock exchange. Most of the companies have fixed market lot as 100 or 50. Anything less than the round lot (market lot) is odd lot. The broker who specialises in handling odd lots is called odd lot dealer. Odd lots arise from the issue of bouns or rights shares. For instance, if HLL Ltd. declares a bonus issue in the ratio of 1:3 (Assume that market lot of the company is 50), a shareholder who is holding 50 shares gets 17 shares which is less than the market lot and treated as an odd lot. If he holds 150 shares he will get 50 bonus shares which is clearly a market lot. If he holds 250 shares he can avail 83 shares, out of which, 50 is market lot and the rest of 33 shares is an odd lot. Stock exchanges are now making alternative arrangements for dealing with odd lots.

Non-Members Acting for Members

1. Authorised clerks

They are employees of a member of the stock exchange. The members of the exchange are empowered to appoint a fixed number of authorised clerks. Authorised clerks have authorisation to transact business on behalf of their employers.

2. Remisiers

They are sub brokers employed by a member to secure business. They obtain business for their principal. They get their remuneration in the form of a commission for the business secured by them.

Listing of Securities

Listing means admission of the securities of a company on a recognised stock exchange which provides a common forum for dealing of securities. Securities of the company are said to be listed when they have been included in the official list of the stock exchange for the purpose of trading.

Prior to the Companies (Amendment) Act, 1988, listing of securities offered to the public for subscription was not compulsory. According to section 73 of the Companies (Amendment) Act, 1988, every company intending to offer shares or debentures to the public for subscription by the issue of a prospectus shall, before such issue make an application to one or more recognised stock exchanges for permission for the shares and debentures intending to be offered, to be dealt with in the stock exchanges.

If a prospectus states that an application has been made for permission for the shares or debentures offered, there by to be dealt in one or more stock exchanges, then any allotment made on an application shall be void; if the permission by the stock exchanges is not granted before the expiry of ten weeks from the date of closure of subscription list.

Advantages of Listing

Following are the advantages of listing;

1. It provides liquidity to the securities of the company.
2. Improves public image of the company.
3. The listed companies enjoy concessional rates of income tax under the Income tax Act, because they are treated as widely held companies.
4. It enables the company to market the securities.
5. It facilitates the company to mobilise the savings from all over the country.
6. It provides greatest collateral value to the securities.
7. The investing public gets regular information about the worth of the securities since the transactions of listed companies are reported in daily newspapers.
8. It ensures free transferability of securities.
9. Forced disclosure of vital information is beneficial for investors.

Disadvantages of Listing

Following are the disadvantages of listing:

1. Once the shares are listed the companies subjected for various regulatory measures of stock exchanges and SEBI.
2. Listed companies must submit and disclose vital information to the stock exchanges.
3. The company has to send notices of Annual General Meetings, Annual Reports etc., to a large number of share holders, resulting in unnecessary expenditure.
4. Companies have to spend heavily in the process of placing the securities with public.

Requirements of Listing:

1. The minimum issued capital of a company shall be Rs. 3 crores
2. The minimum public offer of equity capital shall be Rs. 1.8 crores.
3. Prospectus shall be scrutinised by the stock exchange and SEBI.
4. Applications should be for minimum trading lots of securities.
5. Memorandum and Articles of Association must contain prescribed provisions.
6. Allotment should be fair and unconditional and on equitable basis.
7. Listing of securities on more than one stock exchange is obligatory for any company if the paid-up capital of the company is above Rs. 5 crores.

8. There should be atleast 3 years locking period for promoters contribution.
9. Minimum shareholders of at least 10 for every Rs. One lac. of fresh issue of capital.
10. Minimum share holders of 20 for every Rs. One lac of sale of existing capital.
11. Incase of over subscription allotment has to be finalised in consultation with the Regional Stock Exchange.
12. In all public issues of advertisements, equal treatment shall be given to the risk factors and high lights.

Classification of Listed securities in stock exchange

The securities listed for trading in Bombay Stock Exchange are grouped into the following categories;

Group A Shares

Listed securities are classified as cleared or specified or Group A securities and non - cleared or unspecified or Group B or cash securities. The securities in which forward trading is allowed are called as specified securities or group A shares. Group A shares on a given exchange are those that are included in the cleared list of that exchange after the shares have satisfied the following conditions:

i) The shares should be fully paid up.
ii) The company's paid up capital should be at least Rs.5 crores.
iii) The shares should have been actively traded while on the cash list.
iv) The number of shareholders must be more than 20,000.
v) The company's shares should have market capitalisation of at least Rs.10 crores.
vi) The company should have a growth potential.
vii) The company should be a dividend paying one.

Group B shares

The shares which are traded on cash basis are called Group B shares. They are also called as cash shares. The carry forward facility is not available to group B shares.

Permitted Securities

The securities which are listed with some of the recognised stock exchanges, when permitted to be traded by those stock exchanges where they are not listed are called permitted securities. Such permission is granted as per the rules and regulations of the stock exchange.

Cleared Securities

The securities which are traded for fortnightly settlement. The payment and delivery will be completed in the third week following fortnightly clearing. The cleared securities are also called as specified securities. Speculation activity is permitted only for those shares which are included in cleared securities list. The governing board of the concerned stock exchange has the power to pass special resolutions specifying the securities which may from time to time be included in the specified securities list.

Non-cleared securities

The securities which are traded between brokers is called as non-cleared securities, these securities are not cleared through the stock exchange clearing house. Therefore the securities are not permitted for carry over facilities.

Stock exchange transactions

Transactions on stock exchange are carried out on either cash basis or carry over basis. Carry over is permitted only in respect of Group-A securities. The types of transactions on cash basis according to arrangement for delivery are:

a) **Spot delivery:** In case of spot delivery transaction, the delivery and payment are completed on the same day of contract or on the next day.

b) **Hand delivery:** When a transaction is settled by delivery and payment on the day fixed at the time of entering into contract or within 14 days from the date of the contract.

c) **Special delivery:** In this method delivery and payment are made beyond 14 days.

The Group-A securities are settled through clearing houses in addition to the above methods of settlement. At the end of the settlement date, the investor in specified shares has three options.

i) He can complete the transaction by actual delivery of securities.

ii) He can complete the transaction by revising the transaction through a neutralising purchase or sale.

iii) He can carry over the transaction to the next settlement day.

Sensex

The equity shares of 30 companies from both specified and non-specified groups have been selected on the basis of market activity with due representation to the major industries. The shares selected and the industrial concern to which they belong for the purpose of compiling the index are presented below:

Sl.No.	*Name of the company*	*Industry Group*
1.	H.L.L	FMCG
2.	Reliance Industries.	Textiles
3.	I.T.C	Cigar Industry
4.	InfosysTechnologies.	Computer Software
5.	Reliance Petroleum.	Petroleum
6.	SBI	Banking
7.	MTNL	Telecom
8.	Ranbaxy Labs	Pharmaceuticals
9.	Dr. Reddy's Lab	Pharmaceuticals
10.	Cipla	Pharmaceuticals
11.	Nestle	FMCG.
12.	HPCL	Petroleum
13.	L and T	General engineering
14.	Hindalco Industries	Aluminium
15.	ICICI	Banking.
16.	Satyam	Computer Software
17.	Zee Telefilm	Entertainment
18.	Castrol	Lubricant
19.	BHEL	Electrical
20.	TISCO	Iron & Steel
21.	Bajaj Auto	Automobiles
22.	BSES	Electric supply
23.	Grasim Industries	Textiles
24.	Gujarath Ambuja	Cement
25.	Colgate Palmolive	FMCH.
26.	ACC	Cement
27.	TELCO	Automobiles
28.	Glaxo	Pharmaceuticals
29.	Mahindra & Mahindra	Automobiles
30.	NIIT	ComputerSoftwaretraining

Sources: The Economic Times, Dt: 4/10/2001. P.No. 3.

The method of compilation of the BSE sensitive index of equity prices is the same as used by Standard Proof of, U.S.A. in construction of share price indices. The index for a day is calculated as the percentage of the aggregate market value of the equity shares of all the companies in the sample on that day to the average market value of the equity shares of the same companies during the base period. The formula for calculation of sensex is as follows.

$$S \& P_i = \frac{\sum Pit \sum Qit}{\sum Pio \sum Qio} \times 100$$

$S\&P_i$ = Standard and Poor Index

P_{it} = Price of the stock "i" in period "t"

Q_{it} = Number of shares outstanding for stock "i" in period "t"

P_{io} = Price of the stock "i" in the base period "o" and.

Q_{io} = No. of shares outstanding for stock in the base period "o" and the base period is 1978-79.

The sensex has high volatile during 1995-2001. The average yearly sensex were presented below.

SENSEX

Year	Average	High	Low
1995-96	3288.68	3598.37	2826.08
1996-97	3469.24	4096.26	2745.06
1997-98	3812.86	4548.02	3209.55
1998-99	3294.76	4280.96	2764.16
1999-2000	4658.63	5933.56	3245.27
2000-2001	4269.69	5541.54	3540.65
2001-2002			
April 2001	3487.44	3605.01	3183.77
May 2001	3613.84	3742.07	3494.48
June 2001	3439.01	3557.64	3318.67

Sources: RBI, August 2001. P.No.5796

BADLA CHARGES

The third option i,e, the transaction is carry over to the next settlement day is called carry over or *badla*. This can be made by paying premium called *badla charges.* Badla charges are the interest payable for carry over transactions from one settlement to the other for the amount of transaction. When the badla charges are paid by buyers to the sellers it is called *''seedabadla''* or *''cantango''* and when it is payable by sellers to buyers it is called *''backwardation''* or *''Undhbadla''* The SEBI has imposed ban on badla in all stock exchanges from 14 th may 2001 and introduced in its place the derivates-options, Futures trading as per the rules. SEBI has permitted 31 companies scrips for future standing in stock exchanges.

SPECULATION

Speculation means buying and selling of *''financial instruments''* in the hope of a profit from anticipated changes in the price of securities. It assumes *risk of loss* with a view to making profit. Speculation calls for full information about the capital market and its detailed analysis and interpretation. It requires a lot of expertise on the part of the speculator. It is a trading method for the quick return *i.e. the motive of speculation is to achieve profits through Price changes.* Speculation may be in the form of

a) Constructive Speculation

b) Destructive Speculation

Constructive speculation is based on rational forecasting of future trend of prices. It demands an intelligent analysis of security market. While destructive speculation is hardly based on the proper evaluation of the security market.

Advantages

1. It helps to undertake forward trading.
2. It expedites trading of derivative instruments.
3. It makes demand and supply functions on continuous basis so that they can produce a smooth security price curve.
4. It helps to build a large volume of trade which imparts liquidity to the market.
5. It lends stability in prices by enabling arbitrage process.
6. It helps in buying and selling of securities through out the year.

Disadvantages:

Speculation is an intelligent activity which requires expertise and perfect knowledge of capital market trends. Though it is good for the growth of business but it can create problems if not practiced properly. Some of the speculative dealings and its disadvantages are given below:

1. Manipulation

Manipulation means the purchase and sale of securities by a group of speculators to give an impression that such transactions are the result of natural forces. It involves the creation of false opinion, spreading of rumours and trusting artificially the price structure.

2. Wash Sales

A sale or purchase of shares at the same time by the same speculator, to create an illusion of great activity in the share, with the objective of increasing the price. This gives a misleading and incorrect position about the value of the security in the market.

3. Rigging

The speculator gives different orders to different brokers, some for buying, some for selling. This is done to artificially stir up the market. This prompts brokers to indulge in real transactions. It will affect the normal interplay of demand and supply of securities.

4. Cornering

Sometimes speculators make large acquisition of shares to create a scarcity for delivery against the existing contracts. In this situation those who have dealt with short sales will be squeezed. This is an unhealthy practice of trading.

5. Arbitrage

Arbitrage transactions are carried on by speculators to earn profit on the different price conditions existing in different markets. The speculator buys in the cheaper market and sells it in the dearer market. This will create artificial ups and downs in the prices of the securities.

6. Kerb deals

Speculator may promote unofficial deals i.e., purchase and sale of securities before or after the official hours of business. Trading on the stock exchange is officially done through "On Line Trading System" from 10.00 a.m. to 4.00 p.m. Trading before or after official hours is called kerb trading. This is an unfair practice of dealing.

Types of Speculators

1. Bull

A bull or Tejiwala is a person who believes that current prices are too low and will rise in the future. In anticipation of price rise, he makes purchase of securities with the intention to sell at higher prices in future. If his expectation comes true he sells securities at a higher prices and makes a profit. He buy's securities with the intention of not taking delivery of securities and sells it when the price rises.

***Example* of a** Bull deal;

Suppose, a bull asks his broker to buy 1000 shares of X Ltd. at Rs. 10 each. The broker executes the deal. When the time comes for settlement of transaction the market price of shares of X Ltd. is Rs.25 each. Bull would instruct his broker to sell the shares of X Ltd. and takes the difference in prices i.e.

Sales proceeds of 1000 shares of X Ltd. @ Rs.25 each	Rs.25,000
Purchase of 1000 shares of X Ltd. @ Rs.10 each	Rs.10,000
Bull's profit out of bull deal	Rs.15,000

2. Bear

A bear or Mandiwala is a person who expects a fall in prices of securities in the future. In expectation of price fall, he makes sale of securities with the intention to buy at lower prices in future. He will make a profit if prices decline as expected.

Example of Bear deal.

Suppose a bear asks his broker to sell 1000 shares of M LTD. at Rs. 100 each. When the time comes for settlement of transaction, the actual price of the shares of M Ltd. is Rs. 80 each. He would instruct his broker to purchase the shares of M Ltd. and take the difference in prices i.e.

Sale proceeds of 1000 shares of M Ltd. @ Rs.100 each	Rs.1,00,000
Purchase price of 1000 shares of M LTD. @ Rs.80 each	Rs. 80,000
Bear's profit out of bear deal	Rs. 20,000

3. Lame Duck

When a bear speculator is unable to fulfil his commitment he is called struggling like a lame duck.

4. Stag

Stag or premium hunter is a cautious speculator in the stock exchange he applies for shares in the new issue market and expects to sell them at a premium if he gets allotment.

Blank Transfer

Under this system, the transferer hands over to the transferee the share certificates with a transfer form completely blank except for the signature of the transferer in such case shares may further be transferred merely by delivering the blank transfer form. The evils associated with a blank transfer are:

a) Concealment of the identify of the real owner

b) Evasion of tax

c) Encourages speculation

d) Non-payment of transfer fee.

SERVICES OF STOCK EXCHANGE

There is a strong need for the growth of capital market and stock exchanges in any country. The stock exchange operations in India have shown an increasing tendency during the period under the review. The growth in number of stock exchanges and other related activities is shown in the following table. The data of the table reveals that during the period, the number of the stock exchanges have increased in India to provide valuable services to the community. The services investing are provided by the stock exchanges are presented below:

A) Services to the nation

B) Services to investors

C) Services to corporate Sector

A) Services to the nation

The services are provided by stock exchanges to the nation are described below:

1. The development of corporate sector has been possible only with the help of stock exchanges. It is inturn helps in the process of economic development of the nation.
2. Stock exchanges serve as an agency of capital formation.
3. Stock exchanges divert the savings towards productive channels.
4. Stock exchanges help in better utilisation of the country's financial resources.
5. Stock exchanges provide liquidity and continuous market facility.
6. Stock exchanges provide a forum for raising public debt for national important projects.
7. Stock exchange activities reflects the state of industrial development in the country.

B) Services to the Investors

The following services are provided by the stock exchange to the investors;

1. It provides ready marketability of securities.
2. It ensures safe and fair dealings in securities.
3. Listed securities in stock exchanges are negotiable instruments which are useful as collateral security for raising loans.
4. Stock exchange provides the facilities for quick disposal of securities.
5. Stock exchanges help to educate the public by various methods.
6. Some stock exchanges publish data, reports and they serve as a clearing house of business information and provide advice and guidance to investors.

C) Services to Corporate Sector

Stock exchange has a great value for corporate sector. The companies which are listed in stock exchange enjoy the following benefits;

1. Stock exchange helps to minimise fluctuations in the prices of securities.
2. Stock exchange help the corporate sector for raising of capital from the public.
3. Listing of securities in stock exchange is a symbol of credit worthiness of a corporate entity.
4. Active trading in market and entering into a sensex component is a prestigious and status symbol for corporate corridors.

In India close supervision and control over stock exchanges is exercised by the central Government under the Securities Contracts (Regulation) Act 1956. The Securities Act provides for the procedure to be followed for recognition of stock exchanges, submission of annual report, and periodical returns by recognised stock exchanges, requirements for listing of securities and procedure for inquiry into the affairs of any stock exchange and its members. These rules constitute a code of standardised regulations for uniform application to all the recognised stock exchanges in the country.

FINANCIAL INSTRUMENTS IN CAPITAL MARKET

The major financial instruments in the Indian stock market are *Equity Shares, Debentures, Bonds and Government Securities.* With the growth of the capital market, new financial instruments are being introduced to suit the requirements of the companies as well as the investors. Keeping in view the yield expected by investors, price and credit risks, liquidity of funds etc., the merchant bankers and fund managers design new instruments to cater to changing needs of companies and the investors. The following are the usual instruments of capital mobilisation in a capital market:

1. Equity Shares
2. Preference Shares
3. Debentures
4. Bonds

1. Equity Shares

Equity shares are usually regarded as corner stone of corporate financial resources. The ordinary shares provide a cushion of safety against temporary unfavourable developments as the payment of dividends is not compulsory and is depend on the discretion of management.

The reason for wide public interest in these securities is the possibility of trading in stock exchange, free transferability, and marketability. Equity shares constitute the ownership capital of a company and the equity holders have the right of voting and sharing in profits and assets in proportion to his holding in the total net assets of the company. He is entitled to all rights and obligations as a owner and to residual profits. The dividend distributed to them may be uncertain, variable and fluctuating. The equity holder gets his return in the form of dividends distributed plus capital appreciation on his shares. The dividends distributed depend upon the net earnings of the company after meeting all expenses. This would influence the share prices in the market, which may lead to fluctuations in prices either upward or downward and in turn capital appreciation or depreciation.

Definition of a Share

According to *section 2 (46)* of the Indian Companies Act a share can be defined as "The capital of a company and includes stock except where a distinction between stock and share is expressed or implied."

Forwell says that "The interest of a shareholder in the company is measured by a sum of money, for the purpose of liability in the first place, and of interest in the second but also consisting of a series of mutual convenient entered into by all the shareholders interest."

MERITS OF EQUITY SHARES

The merits of equity shares are summarised as follows;

i) Financing through equity shares does not impose any burden on the company, since payment of dividend on these shares depends on the availability of profits and the discretion of the directors.

ii) Capital raised through equity shares is perpetual source for the company since it is not repayable during the life time of the company. It is repayable only in the event of company's winding up and that too only after the claims of preference shareholders have been met in full.

iii) Equity shares do not carry any charge against the assets of the company hence the capacity of the company to raise additional funds through borrowings on the security of its assets is in no way diminished.

iv) Financing through equity shares also provides the company with sufficient flexibility in the utilisation of its profits and funds, since neither the payment of dividend is compulsory nor any provision is to be made for repayment of capital.

DEMERITS OF EQUITY SHARES

Following are the disadvantages of equity shares:

i) Financing through equity shares is costly as compared to financing through preference shares or debentures, on account of greater risk expectation of the equity shareholders is also high as compared to preference shares or debentures. Moreover, the dividend on equity shares is not deductible as an expense out of profits for taxation purpose.

ii) The control of the company can be easily manipulated through converting of shares by a group of shareholders for their personal advantage at the cost of company's interest.

iii) Conservative management often avoids issue of additional equity shares to raise additional funds. Since the new shareholders are entitled to vote at par with the existing shareholders, this increases the possibility of transferring of control from the existing holder to new holders of equity shares.

iv) Excessive reliance on financing through equity shares reduces the capacity of the company to trading on equity. This may ultimately result in over capitalisation of the company.

v) The cost of underwriting and distributing the equity share capital is generally higher than preference share capital or debentures.

Methods of Issue of Shares

Shares can be issued at par or premium or discount. There are no restrictions regarding issue of shares at par. However, for issue of shares at premium or discount, a company has to follow the restrictions imposed by the companies act 1956. Now, let us discuss various methods of issue of shares.

A) Issue of shares at par.

B) Issue of shares at premium

C) Issue of shares at discount.

A) Issue of shares at par

Shares are said to be issued at par when a shareholder is required to pay the face value of the shares to the company. The issue of share price can be received in one instalment or it can be spread over different instalments. One of the major developments in our securities market has been the removal of control over the issue of securities and the introduction of free pricing of issues. With the introduction of free pricing regime SEBI had issued its disclosure and investor protection guidelines and brought out a number of clarification from time to time.

B) Issue of shares at premium

A company can always issue shares at a premium i,e., for a value higher than the face value of shares, whether for cash or consideration, other than cash. According to section 78 of the Companies Act, the amount of such premium shall have to be transferred by the company to the share premium account. The share premium can be used by the company only for the following purposes;

a) Issue of fully paid bonus shares to the members of the company.

b) Writing off preliminary expenses of the company.

c) Writing off the expenses of or the commission paid or discount allowed on any issue of shares or debentures of the company and

d) Providing premium payable on the redemption of any redeemable preference shares or debentures of the company.

2. Issue of Shares at Discount

A company can issue shares at a discount (i.e., for a consideration less than the nominal value of the shares) subject to the following conditions laid down by section 79 of the Companies Act.

1. Shares to be issued at a discount must be of a class already issued.
2. Issue of shares at a discount must be authorised by an ordinary resolution of the company.
3. Issue must be sanctionad by the Company Law Board and SEBI.
4. Resolution must specify the maximum rate of discount.
5. One year must have passed since the date on which the company was allowed to commence business.
6. Issue must take place within two months after the date of the sanction of the Company Law Board unless the time is further extended.
7. Every prospectus relating to the issue of shares shall disclose particulars of the discount allowed on the issue of shares or that amount which has not been written off at the date of the issue of prospectus.

PREFERENCE SHARES

The preference shares enjoy the preferential rights as to dividend and repayment of capital in the event of winding up of the company, over the equity shares. The preference shares will get a fixed rate of dividend. These can be dividend into the following types;

a) Cumulative preference shares

b) Non-cumulative preference shares

c) Redeemable or Irredeemable preference shares

d) Participating or Non-participating preference shares.

A) Cumulative Preference Shares

In any year if the company does not pay the dividend due to inadequate profit such dividends foregone on preference shares is carried forward and paid in the future years profits are called cumulative preference shares. The unpaid dividends are treated as arrears and carried forward to subsequent years. Such unpaid dividend on these shares go on accumulating and become payable out of the profits of the company, in subsequent years. Only after such arrears have been paid off, any dividend can be paid on the equity shares. Thus a cumulative preference shareholder is sure to receive dividend on his shares for all the years out of the earnings of the company.

B) Non-cumulative Preference Shares

The holders of non-cumulative preference shares will get a preferential right in getting a fixed dividend before it is distributed to equity shareholders. The fixed percentage of dividend is to be paid only out of the divisible profits of that year, if in a particular year there is no profit for payment of preference dividend, such foregone dividends cannot be claimed by the shareholders from the next year profit of the company. Such dividends foregone in any year shall not be forwarded for payment from future years profits. However, these shares will be treated on the same footing as other preference shareholders as regards payment of capital is concerned.

C) Redeemable and Irredeemable Preference Shares

The capital raised through the issue of redeemable preference shares is to be paid back by the company to such shareholders after the expiry of a stipulated period. The date of redemption and terms of redemption are to be announced by the company in its prospectus only. Irredeemable shares means, the capital raised through this instrument will not be redeemed forever. The amount will be lying as a permanent capital.

D) Participating & Non-participating Preference Shares

The preference shares which are not entitled to share in the surplus profit of the company in addition to the fixed rate of dividend are know as participating preference shares. After the payment of the dividend a part of surplus is distributed as dividend among the equity shareholders at a particular rate. The balance may be shared both by equity and participating preference shareholders. Thus participating preference shareholders obtain return on their capital in two forms:

i) Fixed dividend

ii) Share in excess of profits.

Those preference shares which do not carry the right of share in excess profits are known as non-participating preference shares.

Advantages of Preference Shares

The following are the advantage of preference shares;

1. Rate of return is guaranteed and investors who prefer safety of their capital and want to earn income with greater certainty always prefer to invest in preference shares.
2. Helpfull in raising long term capital for a company.
3. Control of the company is not diluted by issuing the preference shares to outsiders, as preference shareholders have restricted voting rights.
4. Redeemable preference shares have the added advantage of repayment of capital, whenever there is surplus in the company.

5. There is no need to mortgage property for sharing security for these shares.

Preference share capital involves fixed cost and does not dilute the control of the company. Such capital can be used to adopt trading on equity.

Disadvantages of Preference Shares

The disadvantages of preference share capital are given below:

1. Permanent burden on the company to pay a fixed rate of dividend before paying anything on anther shares.
2. Preference share holders do not enjoy the voting rights.
3. Normally cost of raising preference capital will be higher compared to other fixed interest bearing securities such as debentures, bonds and loans.

DEBENTURES

A debenture is an acknowledgement of a debt. Debenture holders are paid interest on debentures. A fixed rate of interest is paid on debentures irrespective of profit or loss. Interest on debentures is a charge against profit. Debenture holders are only creditors of the company. They have no voice in the management of the company. Debentures can be redeemed after a certain period. Debenture holders claim priority over share holders for getting their amount.

Definition of Debenture

According to *Thomas Evelyn* debentures can be defined as "A document under the company's seal which provides for the payment of principal sum and interest there on at regular interval, which is usually secured by a fixed or floating charge on the company's property or undertaking and which acknowledges a loan to the company."

The Indian Companies Act, 1956 defines the term "Debenture, stock, bonds and any other securities of a company whether constituting a charge of the assets of the company or not."

Types of debentures

Debentures may be classified as follows.

1. Naked or Mortgage Debenture.
2. Redeemable or Irredeemable Debentures
3. First and Second Debentures
4. Bearer or Registered debentures
5. Convertible debentures and non convertible debentures.

1. Naked or Mortgage Debentures

Naked Debentures are the debentures, which do not carry any security in respect of repayment of interest or the principal. Mortgage Debentures are the debentures which are secured by a charge on the assets or properties of the company.

2. Redeemable or Irredeembale Debentures

Redeemable Debentures provide for the payment of principal amount on the expiry of a certain period. Redeemable debentures can be reissued even after they have been redeemed until they have been cancelled. Irredeemable Debentures are retained as a part of the capital structure of the company. They are also known as perpetual debentures. They are not refundable during the life time of the company.

3. First or Second Debentures

First Debentures, are those debentures which are paid first before any payment is made to another type of debentures. Second, Debentures are those debentures which are paid after making the payment of first debentures.

4. Bearer or Registered Debentures

Bearer Debentures are transferable by means of delivery and they are just like bearer cheques or government currency notes. They are treated as negotiable instruments. Registered debentures are issued specifically on the name of a particular person, who is registered by the company as a holder and are transferable in the same way as shares. The payment of interest and repayment of capital is made to those whose names are registered with the company and duly entered in the register of debenture holders.

5. Convertible or Non-convertible Debentures

Convertible debentures give an option to the debenture holders to convert them into equity or preference shares at a stated rate of exchange, after a certain period. Non-Convertible debentures are not convertible into equity or preference shares afterwards. Convertible debentures are very popular at present.

The composition of public issues in terms of equity at par, premium and debentures is presented for the period *1991-2001* in table No. II (2). During the period the number of issues were high in 1995-96 but in terms of amount it was the 1996-97. An over all analysis of the data reveals that debt is dominated by 50% throughout period. The data further reveals that the premium issues occupy next position.

Table No.II (2)

PUBLIC ISSUES

(Rs.in Crores)

Year	Instrument	No. of issues	Total Public issues	Percentage
1991-92				
	a) Equity at par	143	506.05	29.6
	b) Equity at premium	16	46.72	2.7
	c) Debentures and others	52	1158.59	67.7
		210	**1711.36**	**100.00**
1992-93				
	a) Equity at par	379	1378.32	22.7
	b) Equity at premium	108	1384.22	22.8
	c) Debentures & others	40	3296.09	55.5
		527	**6058.63**	**100**
1993-94				
	a) Equity at par	851	2830.00	21.25
	b) Equity at premium	453	6115.79	45.94
	c) Debentures	57	6356.35	50.6
		770	**12544.04**	**100**
1994-95				
	a) Equity at par	851	2830.00	21.25
	b) Equity at premium	453	6115.79	45.94
	c) Debentures	60	4365.81	32.81
		1364	**13.311.60**	**100**
1995-96				
	a) Equity at par	1104	3075.34	28.0
	b) Equity at premium	302	4679.00	42.6
	c) Debentures	22	3227.37	29.4
		1428	**10981.71**	**100**

Sources:

1. RBI Bulletin, Oct. 2001. P.No. S 1017, March 1999 P.No. S 257.
2. Prime Annual Reports 1991-95.

(Rs.in Crores)

Year	Instrument	No. of issues	Total Public issues	Percentage
1996-97				
	a) Equity at par	679	4654	44.64
	b) Equity at premium	126	1462	14.02
	c) Debentures & others	37	4308	41.32
	Total	**842**	**10424**	**100**
1997-98				
	a) Equity at par	60	508.9	16.21
	b) Equity at premium	29	653.5	20.82
	c) Debentures & others	13	1975.9	62.94
	Total	**102**	**3138.30**	**100**
1998-99				
	a) Equity shares	14	1237	24.67
	b) Equity at premium	48	2169	42.09
	c) Debentures & others	15	2450	48.88
	Total	**48**	**5013**	**100**
1999-2000				
	a) Equity at par	21	583	11.31
	b) Equity at premium	48	2169	42.09
	c) Debentures & others	10	2401	46.59
	Total	**79**	**5153**	**100**
2000-2001				
	a) Equity at par	77	1399	28.26
	b) Equity at premium	57	1267	25.60
	c) Debentures & other	11	2283	46.13
	Total	**145**	**4949**	**100**
2001-2002 (upto June)				
	a) Equity at par	1	5.00	1.21
	b) Equity at premium	1	5.00	1.21
	c) Debentures & others	01	400	97.56
	Total	**03**	**410**	**100**

NEW FINANCIAL INSTRUMENTS IN THE CAPITAL MARKET

The Indian capital market is very wide and large with more than 8000 companies listed, 2000 of whose scrips are actively traded. Number of investors is estimated to be more than 25 million. The market capitalisation of equity and debt is estimated at Rs. 5,00,000 crores and Rs. 10,00,000 crores respectively. This is more than one and half times of banking system deposits, which are serviced by over 65,000 branches.

With the evolution of the capital market, new financial instruments are being introduced to suit the requirements of the companies, keeping in view, the yield expected by the investors, price and credit risk, liquidity, quantum of funds etc. The merchant bankers and fund managers designed new instruments to cater the needs. Some of the new financial instruments introduced in recent years are as follow:

a) Zero Coupon Bonds

b) Warrants

c) Secured Premium Notes

d) Stock Investment Instrument

e) Deep Discount Bonds

f) Option Bonds

a) Zero Coupon Bonds

These are debt instruments with a zero rate of interest. It has no fixed coupon rate. The genesis of zero coupon bonds can be traced to U.S. security market. In India zero interest convertible bonds have also been issued by companies. These bonds do not carry any interest for a fixed period. Since, the investor is not entitled to any interest on the bonds, the conversion price is suitably adjusted to take care of the interest loss of the investor. The main advantage to the company is that there is no burden of servicing the debentures during the gestation of the project.

Advantages to the Company

The main advantage to the company is that there is no burden of servicing the debentures during the gestation of the project. By linking the redemption/ conversion period with the commissioning of the project, the company can ensure that there are considerable savings in project cost and has no cash out flow for servicing of the debentures during the implementation stage of the project.

Advantages to the Investors

From the investors view point, the interest is only notional and is not subject to tax. The gain on sale of shares after conversion is taxable as capital gain. Zero coupon bonds are attractive to investors if interest rates decline.

b) Warrants

A share warrant is an option to the investor to buy a specified number of equity shares at a specified price over a specified period of time. The warrant holder has to surrender the warrant and pay some cash known as the 'exercise price' of the warrant to purchase the shares. An exercise of the option, the warrant holder becomes a share holders. Warrant is a popular means of raising finance in developed countries. In India warrants are commonly used as a sweetener with NCD. Gradually the trends are changing and detachable warrants are issued with convertible debentures and equity shares too. The pricing of the warrant is an important factor. However warrants can be issued only by existing dividend paying companies. Warrant is yet to gain popularity in India, owing to the complex nature of the instrument.

Advantages to the Company

Growth oriented companies with a good track record will be in a position to issue Non-convertible debentures (NCD's) with an attractive equity warrant directly to the public and reduce their dependence on the financial institutions and mutual funds to take up the NCD's. Warrants provide a mechanism for raising additional capital depending on the cash - flow requirements of the company.

Advantages to the Investors

The warrant acts as a sweetener and ensures a better subscription to the NCD's, especially for companies with good track record. NCD with warrant option may also he offered to the investors with an offer of buy back of NCD's so that the investor is required to retain only the equity warrant and is not required to retain the NCD. NCD with warrant expect steady rate of return and capital appreciation on the NCD's.

c) Secured Premium Notes

These are the instruments issued by companies for raising debt, which can be converted into equity or reduced at a premium after 3 to 5 years. No coupon rate of interest is fixed on these instruments. Secured premium notes are issued at a nominal value and do not carry any interest. The note is reduced by repayment in several instalments at a premium over the face value. The premium amount is distributed equally over the period of maturity of the instalment. These notes may carry a detachable warrants, which will give the holder a right to claim allotment of one share for cash at a certain price. This right can be exercised by the holder after a certain period from the date of allotment of secured premium notes. It is suitable for companies with good track record and have highly capital intensive projects as there is no out flow on account of interest during the period of project. The secured premium notes are traded on the stock exchanges and have an easy liquidity. The investor can dispose of the notes on allotment at a premium, if the shares of the company command a high premium in the market, without even exercising the warrant option, or the investor can dispose of the right from itself as a premium in a right issue of secured premium notes.

Advantages to the Company

It is suited for companies with good track record with highly capital intensive projects as there is no out go of cash on account of interest during the period of the project.

Advantages to the Investor

The warrant option acts as a sweetener and ensures reasonable subscription to the SPN's,especially issued by companies with good track records.

d) Stock Investment Instrument

A new financial instrument called **"STOCK INVEST"** was introduced, which is to be used by the investors to enclose with a share / debenture application for application money. The amount will remain credited to the investors account in his bank but underlies with the banker till the allotment is made and will carry interest. The issuing company will be able to encash the instrument only when the shares are allotted to the investor. This will reduce the hardship suffered by the investors through loss of interest especially in the case of non-allotment of shares, this can be returned to investors and it avoids the delay in refunds. The stock investment scheme has already been started by many public sector and private sector banks and it was popular for couple of years. At present its use is not much popular, because of no public issues.

Advantages

1. The investor has to part with his funds only if he has allotted shares.
2. Since the account gets debited only after the allotment, he will continue to earn interest till that date.

e) Deep Discount Bonds

These bonds are sold to the investors at discount, while issuing them. The discount rate depends on the amount of discount and the number of years to maturity. These bonds were offered by **IDBI**. The main advantage to the issuing company is that there is no interest payment burden during the gestation period of the project. The advantage to the investor is that the initial investment is low as compared to other instruments. The bonds are advantageous to the investors when long-term interest rates are expected to fall.

f) Option Bonds

Option bonds may be cumulative or non-cumulative. In case of cumulative bonds the interest is accumulated and is payable at maturity, while in the case of non cumulative bonds it is payable at periodic intervals. These types, of bonds were issued by IDBI and ICIC were well received by the investors. These bonds will be converted into equity or preference shares at the option of the investor as per the conditions stated in the prospectus.

PUBLIC ISSUES

Public issue is essentially an exercise involving active participation of a number of agencies. With the growth of the number of public issues and the complexities in the efforts involved, today it has become necessary to enlist the active participation and support of number of agencies in making any public issue a success. A promoter as a principal representative of a company which is making the public issue should be clear about the number of agencies involved and their respective roles in the entire exercise. Initial issues are those floated by new companies for the first time, while further issues are subsequent issues floated by the existing companies. Issues can also be classified as those given for cash, for exchange of technical know how, exchange of shares of another company or exchange for any other services rendered by the agencies of promoters.

The placement of issues may be through;

a) Prospectus issues

b) Offer for Sale

c) Private placement

d) Rights issues

e) Bought out deales

The changing face of industry is rapidly influencing the way a merchant banking firm operates. "Merchant bank refers to an organization that under writes securities and advises such clients on issues like corporate mergers, involving in the ownership of commercial ventures." They also involved in project counselling, preparation of feasibility reports, selection of under writers, brokers and bankers. They are responsible for making applications on behalf of corporate clients to obtain requisite permissions from statutory bodies like SEBI for making public issues.

Merchant banking originated through the entering of London merchants in financing of foreign trade through acceptance of bills. Later the merchants also assisted the governments of undeveloped countries in raising long-term funds through floatation of bonds in the London market and obtaining their quotation on the London Stock Exchange. Over a period of time merchant banks extended their activities to domestic business of syndication of short-term and long-term finance, underwriting of new issues, acting as registrars and share transfer agents, debenture trustees, portfolio managers, negotiating agents for mergers and take-overs etc.

As per rule 2 (e) of SEBI the merchant banker can be defined as "Any person who is engaged in the business of issue management either by making arrangements regarding selling, buying or subscribing to securities as manager, consultant, advisor or rendering corporate advisory services in relation to such management."

Functions of Merchant Banker

The merchant bankers perform following functions:

1. Issue Management.
2. Underwriting of issues.
3. Project appraisal.
4. Handling stock exchange business on behalf of clients.
5. Dealing in foreign exchange.
6. Floatation of commercial paper.
7. Acting as trustees.
8. Share registration.
9. Helping financial engineering activities of the firm.
10. Undertaking cost audit and recruitment of executives.
11. Providing venture capital.
12. Arranging bridge loans.
13. Advising business customers i.e.; take-overs and mergers.

a) Prospectus

Public issues with prospectus is the most popular method of raising funds by the public limited companies. This involves inviting subscription from the public through issue of prospectus. This method of raising funds accounts for the bulk of capital raised and is necessary for listing of shares on stock exchanges. The price at which the securities are offered for sale is at the face value of the share in case of new companies and may be at a premium or discount in the case of existing companies.

b) Offer for Sale

The method of offer for sale consists of out right sale by the company instead of offering shares to public or through inter mediaries. In this case the company sells shares enabloc at an agreed price to brokers, who inturn resells them to the investing public. The issuing houses may act as agents of the company in such cases. Offer for sale of shares takes place in the case of existing shareholders purchasing enbloc and then reselling them to the public. Similarly, foreign collaborators or promoters may sell their shares to the Indian public through offer or sale which may be either through brokers or through prospectus.

c) Private Placement

The third method of issue of shares is private placement which is defined as sale by the issuing house or broker to his own clients of securities previously purchased by him. Under this method, the issuing houses or financial intermediataries buy them out rightly with the intention of placing them with their client afterwards. Here, the brokers are wholesalers and sell them in retail to the public. These brokers make their profits in the process of reselling to the public. This method of private placing is also made by bargaining with the financial institutions for their share of finance. In public issue, 10% of the issue amount goes as expenditure. Arrangement of public issue will take a lot of time. But in private placement with in short period, the company can raise its target amount from the market.

d) Rights Issue

The rights issue is an offer to the shareholders of existing companies to contribute to the share capital or its debt capital in the form of debentures. An existing company can issue rights to augment its equity base, if necessary. These are offered to the existing shareholders in a proportion to their existing share ownership. The ratio in which the new shares or debentures are offered to the existing shareholders of the company would depend on their requirement of capital. The rights are transferable and saleable in the market. No new company can issue rights shares. Under the companies act, where a company can increase its subscribed capital by the issue of new shares either after two years of its formation or after one year of the first issue of shares which ever is earlier. These have to be first offered to the existing shareholders with the right to reserve them in favour of a nominee. Rights shares are usually offered on terms advantageous to the shareholders. A company issuing rights is required to send a circular to all existing shareholders. The company limit of atleast one month to two months to shareholders to exercise their right before it is offered to the public. Rights may also be offered through under writers. If a company is doing well, rights will be received well by the share holders and the need for underwriting may not be felt.

e) Bought out Deals

In a bought out deal the company places securities with the spansor/co investor who inturn off-loads to the public through an offer for sale document after the project has commenced. Bought out is a process through which investment is made in the company by the spansor or a syndicate of investors directly. There is explicit understanding of taking the company public in a mutually agreed time frame. At the time of public offer the spansor syndicate of spansors dilute their holding to the requisite statutory minimum or may be even beyond. Bought out deals are becoming very popular for the following reasons;

1. Reducing the preliminary expenses.
2. More funds at short period of time.
3. New companies can raise premium issues.

The following advantages are available through bough out deals;

A) advantages to the corporate sector.

B) advantages to the investors.

A) Advantages to the Corporate Sector

1. wide geographical trading
2. Investor's Credibility.
3. low issue expenses.

B) Advantages to the Investors

1. Liquidity.
2. Transparency.
3. Safety of investment.
4. Fast transfer.
5. Single window access.
6. Easy exit.

RECOMMENDATIONS OF THE PHERWANI STUDY GROUP ON NEW FINANCIAL INSTRUMENTS

The Study Group constituted by the Government on 27th Marc 1991 with M.J. Pherwani as Chairman to formulate guidelines for issue o new instruments, recommended the following instruments. Some of th instruments have already been issued in the market.

1. Non-voting shares.
2. Detachable equity coupons/warrants.
3. Participating preference shares.
4. Participating debentures.
5. Convertible debentures with options.
6. Third party convertible debentures.
7. Mortgage backed securities.
8. Convertible debentures redeemable at premium.
9. Debt for equity swap.
10. Zero coupon convertible bonds.

INTERMEDIARIES OF CAPITAL MARKET

In the Capital Market, Banks and Financial Institutions are important intermediaries. They act as catalysts in the economic development of any country. These institutions mobilise financial savings from households, corporate and other sectors of the economy and channalise them into productive investments. They act as a reservoir of resources and form the backbone of the economic and financial systems. The banking industry has undergone a sea change during the last three decades, after the nationalization of banks. They not only lend for social and economic causes, but also participate in the development programmes of the Central Government, State Government. The main components of capital market in India are:

a) Merchant Bankers

b) Bankers

c) Underwriters

d) Brokers

e) Registrars

a) Merchant Banker

Every year, huge amounts of money is tapped from the capita market to finance various industrial projects. In attracting public money t capital issues, merchant bankers play a vital role as specialized agencie

14. Undertaking management of NRI investments.
15. Large - scale term-lending to corporate borrowers.
16. Providing corporate counselling and advisory services.
17. Managing investments on behalf of clients.
18. Acting as a stock-broker.

Merchant Banking Objectives

The following are the main objectives of merchant banking in India;

1. The objective of merchant banking is to help for capital formation.
2. It creates a secondary market to boost the industrial activities in the nation.
3. It assists and promote economic endeavor.
4. It prepares project reports, conducts market research pre-investment surverys.
5. It provides financial assistance to venture capital
6. It builds a data bank as human resources
7. Providing housing finance.
8. They provide seed capital to new concerns.
9. Merchant bankers are mainly involved in issue management
10. Merchant bankers act as underwriters
11. It identifies new projects and renderservices to getting clearance from government.
12. Provides financial clearance.
13. Merchant bankers help to mobilise funds from public.
14. They divert the savings of the nation towards productive channel.
15. They conduct investors conferences.
16. They obtain consent of stock exchange for listing.
17. Obtain the daily report of application money collected at various branches of banks.
18. MBs appoint bankers, brokers, underwriters etc.,
19. MBs supervise the process on behalf of NRIs for their ventures.
20. MBs provide service on fund based activities.
21. MBs assist in arrangement of loan syndication.

22. MBs may act as an acceptance house.

23. MBs assist and arrange mergers & acquisitions.

The need for merchant banking agencies is felt in context of a major chunk of public savings lying untapped. Merchant banks have been playing a useful role in procuring the funds for capital market for the corporate sector for financing their operations. The trends in the primary market in India further suggest that merchant bankers have played a very significant role in the corporate sector's drive for mobilizing funds from the public with the increase in the number of issues and amount raised, the number of merchant bankers have also increased.

According to clause 18(1) of the **SEBI** (Merchant Bankers) Regulations, 1992 requires that every public issue should necessarily be managed by atleast one authorized merchant banker (category I) as the lead merchant bankers to the issue. But not essential in an issue or offer of rights to the existing members with or without the rights of remuneration to the size of which does not exceed Rs.50 lakhs. Maximum number of lead merchant bankers for an issue has been prescribed by the clause 19 of the regulation which depends upon the size of the issue.

Table No.II (20)

Size of Issue	*Number of Merchant Bankers*
a) Less than Rs.50 crores.	Not more than 2
b) Rs.50 crores or more but. less than Rs.100 crores.	Not more than 3
c) Rs.100 crores - Rs.200 crores.	Not more than 4
d) Rs.400 crores or more.	5 or more as agreed by the board.

Being specialized in managing public issues, merchant bankers under the existing scenario associate themselves with a project, right from its inception and thus provide the expertise in determining the project size, capital structure, quantum of resources to be raised, sources of funds and provide inputs as and when to raise the resources. They are offering wide range of services from drafting to listing of securities in stock exchange.

Organizing merchant banking has been in use with reference to the time, since SEBI took upon itself the task of licensing merchant bankers on the basis of licensing and the permitted range of activities.

Merchant Bankers are classified into four categories according to the SEBI (Merchant Banking) Regulations 1992. These are as follows:

Category-I:

To carry on any activity relating to issue management and act as adviser, consultant manager, underwriter and portfolio manager for capital issues.

Category-II:

To act as adviser, consultant, co-manager, underwriter and portfolio manager for capital issues.

Category-III:

To act as underwriter, adviser consultant to an issue.

Category-IV:

To act only as adviser or consultant to an issue.

With over 1100 merchant bankers operating in the country, the primary market activity is picking up; there is bound to be some furious innovation on the part of managers of the primary stage of the capital market. Merchant banking services have assumed greater importance in the present capital market scenario. With the investor becoming more cautions and discerning, the role of merchant banker has gained more prominence. And he has to be in constant touch with the ever changing economic environment and the market trends to develop better marketing strategies; targeting specific investor groups and to constantly innovate new instruments catering to varying requirements like that of floating rate notes which are ideal for a blue chip company, raising debt resources under the falling interest rate scenario. An important task before the merchant banker today is the careful screening of the issues which are raising funds from the public. This involves a microscopic analysis of a company's financial performance, evaluation of pricing of the issues and above all filtering only genuine issues to prevent money being collected from innocent public. With the abolition of the office of the CCI, it has become the responsibility of the merchant banker to optimally price the issues of securities that gives the maximum benefit of premium to the issues, and at the same time is attractive and offers reasonable scope for capital appreciation, to the investor. The merchant banker also exercises due diligence independently to scrutinize meticulously a prospectus before issuing due diligence certificate. As each issue is different from the others there can be no single parameter for judging all issues. Each issue has to be assessed differently requiring original and conventional thinking on the part of the merchant banker to provide value addition to the issues at all stages in the resource raising process. Recently SEBI has announced its consideration of shifting the responsibility of vetting of prospectus, which is either to be done by SEBI or the merchant bankers. But this will lead to the problems of merchant bankers being blamed for any inconsistencies and non disclosures; if the data provided are not completely transparent.

The involvement of merchant banker in an issue should continue atleast till the completion of essential follow up steps are coming to amend. Which must include listing of the instrument and despatch of certificates or refunds. It shall also make available to **SEBI** such information, documents returns and reports as may be prescribed and called for.

Several ancillary services including provision of bridge loans and promoters funding for highly valued clients are offered by merchant bankers. But the credit policy of RBI has withdrawn the bridge loans. They also syndicate commercial loan from overseas banks, as the cost of borrowing in the international market is much lower. When unable to finance the clients, they take up the responsibility of syndicating loans from others.

Statement showing the mobilisation of resources from the primary market by Merchant Bankers

(Rs. in Crores)

Year	*No. of issues*	*Amount*
1991-92	210	1711
1992-93	527	6059
1993-94	770	12544
1994-95	1364	13312
1995-96	1428	10982
1996-97	842	10424
1997-98	102	3138
1998-99	48	5013
1999-2000	79	5153
2000-2001	145	4949
2001-2002 (up to June)	03	410

Sources: 1. RBI Bulletin Oct. 2001 P.No.s 1017.

2. Prime Annual Reports 1991-95.

3. RBI Bulletin March 1999 5257.

The data reveals that the public issues were declining in number and amount also in amount. At present no investor is interested towards NIM. Therefore, three merchant bankers shall move from fee based services to fund based services.

C) UNDER WRITING

Underwriting was originated to face the uncertainties of capital market when the company approaches for public issues. In new issue market, if the issue remains unsubscribed the company cannot proceed to allotment of shares. The company is required to return the money to the applicants. Consequently the project will fail. To overcome this situation the companies are taking precautions about the public issue for successful completion. Underwriting is the arrangement where the investment bankers to undertake for ensuring the full success of the issue of securities. The under writers agree to take a specified number of shares or debentures offered to the public in the event of non subscription by the investors. In this situation underwriters have to contribute the share capital for his assurance part. If the company gets success in public issues, the underwriter is entitled to get a commission for this assignment, it is called as ''*underwriting commission.*''

The amount of commission payable to the underwriters is statutorily regulated. It also depends upon market conditions, and the attractiveness of the investment to the public. The maximum commission is 5% of the issue price in case of shares, and 2.5% in case of debentures. The under writers are entitled to their commission even if they are not required to subscribe for any shares or debentures unconditionally to hold them as investment or other wise, it is called as "firm underwriting." The underwriters may sub contract their obligations with them.

Importance of Underwriting

In the new issue market the role of underwriters is a prominent and highly recognised for the success of the public issues of the corporate enterprises. The importance of the underwriting is mentioned below:

1. Investors feel secured about the viability of the project underwritten by underwriters.
2. Underwriters render yeoman's service to the cause of industrial development.
3. Successful floation of shares is sin-quo-non for rapid industrialisation programme.
4. Underwriters help in the wider disposal of ownership of security issue all over the country.
5. Issues backed by well known underwriters generally create confidence to investing public.
6. The cost of raising funds is minimised to the business entrepreneurs.
7. Underwriters perform combined functions of risk bearing and marketing of securities.

8. The society stepping towards the goal of prosperity by way of new projects.

Objectives of Underwriting

The following are the main objectives of underwriting:

1. Assurance
2. Refunding
3. Encouragement
4. Reorganisation

1. **Assurance:** The underwriters guarantee the sale of securities at a given price and by a specified time and assure the companies the necessary funds so that the company confidently proceed.

2. **Refunding:** When replacing the maturing securities through the offer of new securities or cash, the underwriters act as intermediaries who could guarantee to pay cash for all the new securities not subscribed by the old security holders.

3. **Encouragement:** During financial crisis if reputed intermediaries agree to underwrite the new issues it may be easier for the company to make the issue success.

4. **Reorganisation:** The underwriters agree to pay the security holders of the old company and take over their holding of the new company during reorganisation of a company.

Types of Underwriters

The underwriters in India are of the following types:

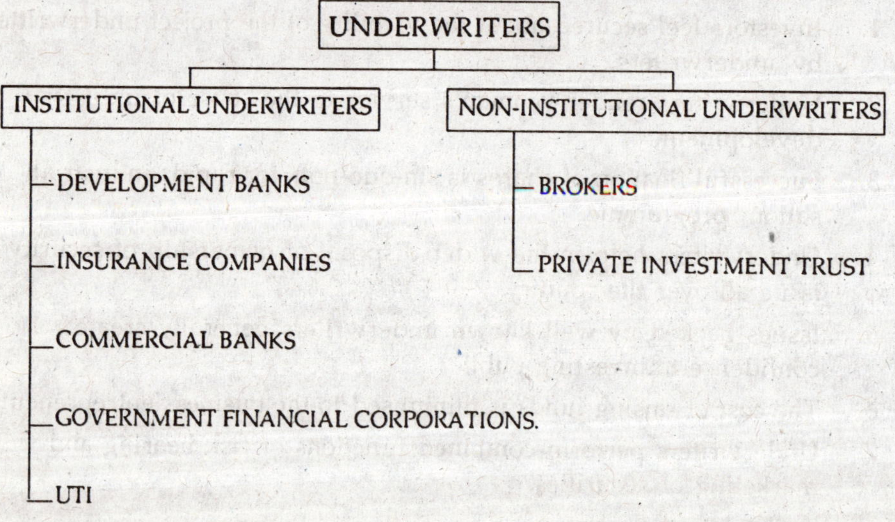

Institutional Underwriters

There are five types of underwriters in India.

1. Development Banks.
2. Insurance companies.
3. Commercial Banks.
4. Government Financial Corporations.
5. UTI.

1. Development Banks

Public Financial Institutions like, IDBI, IFCI, ICICI are also involved in underwriting business in India. These institutions are utilising the savings of investor's towards the growth of corporate sector. Development banks cover both commercial and public interest.

2. Insurance Companies

The LIC is basically involved in insurance business. India's premier institutions in insurance sector are LIC and GIC. They are basically investment institutions and not a development banks. These two investment institutions supply funds to provide liquidity in three forms.

a) Purchase of securities from stock market.

b) Subscribing shares and bonds.

c) Direct lending to industry.

3. Commercial Banks

Some commercial banks are also rendering the service as syndicaton's of loan's and managers to the issue. Banks normally act as passive agents supplying forms only on the request rather than on their own initiative and earn brokerage.

4. Government Financial Corporations

Government financial corporations are also involved in underwriting business. Government corporations like State Financial Corporations, State Industrial Development Corporations render their services to boost the capital market and specific development objectives.

5. U.T.I.

Another conventional investment institution is the Unit Trust of India. It is one type of open-ended investment company which enjoys a superiority as an organisational device due to certain features given below;

a) Continuous sale of units coupled with aggressive selling.

b) Redemption of units at asset value at any time with liquidity facility.

c) Convenience to the small investors.

d) Buying and selling of units requires no direct operations in the stock exchanges.

Non-institutional Underwriters

There are two types of non-institutional underwriters.

1. Brokers
2. Private Investment Companies

1. Brokers

Stock Brokers play a very crucial role in the area of underwriting. The professional expertism keeps them fully informed of the latest trends in the capital market. They can shape the issue in the most benefiting manner. They can influence their clients by persuasion or propaganda.

2. Private Investment Companies

Private investment companies are also called as financial institutions. Financial institutions obtain funds from a large number of investors through the selling of shares. These funds are then placed in a pool under professional management and securities (Financial assets) are purchased for the benefit of all the shareholders.

Underwriting is mandatory for the public issue. The company may appoint any one or more of the following parties as underwriters in consultation with the managers to the issue;

1. Financial Institutions
2. Bankers
3. Members of Stock Exchanges
4. Investment Companies
5. Trusts

The appointment of underwriters could be based on the following criteria:

1. Financial Soundness
2. Experience and Past Performance
3. Outstanding Underwriting Commitments
4. Guidelines of SEBI

Above all, underwriters would need to have a minimum net worth of Rs.20 lakhs and the total underwriting obligations at a point of time shall not exceed 20 times of underwriters networth. Underwriters are also required to abide by a code of conduct.

a) STOCK BROKERS

In a capital market another important component is stock brokers, who are simply known as brokers; who act as intermediaries in purchase and sale of securities in the primary and secondary markets. These persons have a network of sub brokers spread through out the length and breadth of the country. They are known as sub-brokers. These people spread message and give publicity of various issues in the offing. They readily supply application forms or even go to the extent of collecting money from the investors and remit on behalf of them. Thus small savings of small investors are mobilized through brokers in the capital market.

There are about 5500 main brokers operating in different stock exchanges in the country. Some of them are even corporate entities. They have unlimited number of sub-brokers. Though the requirement to become a member is a nominal monetary security deposit. The amount of deposit in the case of Bombay Stock Exchange is Rs. 2 crores, to safeguard the investors in the case of manipulative brokers. The brokers support the stock exchanges performing the following useful economic services;

a) Ready marketability and price continuity for listed shares and securities.

b) Contributing to the spread of investment habit by diverting savings from conventional investments to long term financial resources for industries and Government.

c) Facilitating for flow of distribution of savings into different classes of competitive investments.

d) Ensuring reasonable measure of safety in buying and selling of shares or securities.

e) Helping in the evaluation of securities on the basis of demand and supply and guiding the direction where savings could be invested.

b) BANKERS

Yet another important component of capital market is the commercial banks. They have wide network of branches throughout the country spread even in remote villages. Some bankers act as merchant bankers. Some are brokers, while some others are collecting agents. Companies usually entrust the task of collection and safe custody of the money mobilized to commercial banks; which play an inevitable role in transfer, transmission and safe custody of funds even from a remote village. The bankers to an issue are important intermediaries in the securities market and are engaged in activities such as acceptance of applications along with the application money from investors in respect of issue of capital, refund of application money and payment of dividends. They play a crucial role in the primary market. A banker to an issue shall be a scheduled bank. The bankers to an issue are usually decide in consultation with the lead managers to the issue. This is done with the object of having a wide network of collection centres throughout the country.

The mainstray of Finance, Stock Exchange division had originally prescribed 57 statutory centres for acceptance of new applications. Where reservation has been for NRI in the public issue, it is necessary to make arrangements for collection of subscription from NRI investors. In such cases, according to government institutions, the stock exchange centres are to be made as collection centres for NRI application money. Where arrangements are desired for opening of collection accounts and bank branches abroad, RBI approval is required and necessary action should be taken for the purpose.

The banker to an issue is required to maintain books of accounts, records, and other documents for a minimum period of three years, in respect of interalia, the number of applications received were forwarded to the registrars to an issue and the dates and amount of refund monies paid to the investors. The regulations impose certain obligations on the bankers to an issue to furnish information to SEBI on their activities. SEBI has been empowered to suspend or cancel the registration.

Obligation and Responsibility of Bankers to the Issue

1. Without SEBI's permission no banker can act banker to the public issue.
2. A Banker who have permitted by SEBI to act as banker, shall make an agreement with the issuing company.
3. Thc banker to issue shall maintain the records like, the number of applications received, the names of the investors etc.,
4. A banker to an issue shall submit required information to SEBI.
5. A banker to an issue must observe highest standards of integrity.

QUESTIONS

1. What is Capital Market?
2. Explanin the Structure of the Capital Market
3. What are a players in capital market? Explain their role in capital market operations.
4. Define and distingnish between Primary and Secodary markets.
5. Explain the role, the functions and duties of various member in the capital market.
6. What is meant by listing of Securities? Critically evaluate listing requirements and usefulness.
7. How do you clossify the shares in Stock Exchange?
8. What is sensex and how it will be computed?
9. What is a badla change?
10. What is a speculation? Explain different methods of speculation.
11. What are the different types of securities? Explain their main feautres
12. What do you understand by new financial instruments? Explain various new instruments issued in India.
13. What is a New Issue Market? Explain the different components of NIM.
14. What are the different intermediaries in the Capital Market? Explain their role.
15. What is a merchant banker? Discuss their functions, objectives and role in the Capital Market.
16. What is under writing? Discuss the nature, functions of under writers in Indian Capital Market.
17. Discuss the role of stock brokers in the stock exchange.

* * *

3

CAPITAL MARKET-II

INTRODUCTION

Investors confidence is precondition for the growth and development of the securities market. This confidence is a function of several factors in the primary and secondary markets. In the primary market the investors confidence depends, on a large measures, such as efficiency of issue management, which covers several aspects beginning from the consent for the issue, drafting and issue of prospectus or letter of offer, timely despatch or refund orders, certificates, etc., In the secondary market, among other things timely transfer of holdings, their registration and timely receipt of dividend and interest warrants can help to sustain the investor confidence.

REGISTRARS TO THE ISSUE (RTI)

The Registrars to the Issue (RTI) and Securities Transfer Agents (STA) are two of the intermediaries, who are involved in the primary and secondary markets. They provide several important services to the issuers of securities, companies and investors. The former by speedy processing of applications and the later primarily by quick processing of the transfers. This proceed can contribute to the efficiency of the securities market and building up investor confidence.

The Registrars to the Issue (RTI) undertake for and on behalf of an issuer of securities various activities ranging form designing of application forms to processing and despatch of refund orders/allotment letters/ certificates and several other issue related such activities.

The Securities Transfer Agents **(STA)** undertake for and on behalf of the company various activities ranging from transfer of holdings to despatch of documents, notices, annual reports, etc., and other related activities.

Functions

"Registrar to an issue" means the person appointed by a corporate enterprise or any person or group of persons to carry on the following activities on its or his or their behalf namely:

i) Collecting applications from investors in respect of an issue;

ii) Keeping proper record of applications and money received from investors are paid to the seller of the securities; and

iii) Assisting body corporate or person or group of person in:

   a) Determining the basis of allotment of securities in consultation with the stock exchange;

   b) Finalising the list of persons entitle to allotment of securities;

   c) Processing and despatching allotment letters, refund orders or certificates and other related documents in respect of the issue:

Recent Developments in Capital Market

The structure of capital market in India has gone under a vast change due to the liberalisation process initiated by the Government, specifically after 1991. The major functions performed by a capital market are as follows:

a) Mobilisation of financial resources

b) Securing the Foreign Capital

c) Promote balanced economic development.

The Indian financial system has been fast changing in accordance with the global financial system. The physical location of institutions and markets have now become less important, technology is having a powerful impact in the process of deregulation. The following are the recent developments in the Indian capital market:

1. Over the Counter Exchange of India (OTCEI)
2. National Stock Exchange (NSE)
3. Depository Services
4. Stock Holding Corporation of India Ltd. (SHCIL)
5. Securities and Exchange Board of India (SEBI)
6. Mutual Funds (MF)
7. Margin Trading

8. Capital Market Reforms
9. Credit Rating
10. GDRs/ADRs.

1. *OVER THE COUNTER EXCHANGE OF INDIA (OTCEI)*

The OTC Exchange of India (OTCEI) is a company incorporated under section 25 of the Indian Companies Act, 1956. It is a recognised stock exchange under sec.4 of the Securities Contracts (Regulation) Act, 1956. The computerised, fully transparent, single window exchange commenced live trading in september 1992. Its principal objective is to setup and operate an 'over-the-counter' exchange in India. The exchange is based on "NASDAQ" *(National Association of Securities Dealers Automated Quotation)*, the OTC Exchange in USA. The OTCEI has been promoted by the following financial Institutions and bank subsidiaries;

Unit Trust of India (UTI)

Industrial Credit and Investment Corporation of India (ICICI)

Industrial Development Bank of India (IDBI)

Industrial Finance Corporation of India (IFCI)

Life Insurance Corporation of India (LIC)

General Insurance Corporation of India (GIC) and its subsidiaries;

SBI Capital Markets.

Canbank Financial Services.

Companies listed on the OTC Exchange enjoy the same status as companies listed on other stock exchanges like Mumbai, Delhi, Calcutta etc., The exchange has setup new quality standards by attempting to popularise new concepts like sponsorship, screen based trading and continuous T+4 settlements. Over-the-counter implies trading across the counter in shares and securities which are listed on the OTCEI exchange. It was setup as an exchange, specially to list the small sized companies, with an issue size, as small as 30 lakhs. The comparative features of **BSE, NSE** and **OTCEI** are as included in the annexure. **OTCEI** is having a screen based trading system using telecommunication link.

The screen based trading system provides complete transparency to the transactions. **OTCEI** distinguishes itself with other exchange in some of the operations, such as providing market for spot deals (no speculation) net exposure by members/dealers being restricted to fixed percent of net worth.

The system provides for monitoring of transactions on a continuous basis. As the **OTC** exchange is meant for over-the-counter deals, forward buying and selling is expressly prohibited. However, investors investment will never suffer from lack of liquidity, for absence of any buyer. The buying and selling transactions by a market maker is called a direct deal and the market maker would not be able to charge any brokerage on such deals. The counter will charge brokerage on the put-through deal. It may be noted that deals outside the OTC system, that is between two investors, similarly deals between market makers are not permitted. One counter party has to be an investor.

In order to obtain listing on the OTCEI, companies are subjected to a thorough screening by the sponsors. The sponsor takes the responsibility to analyse and appraise projects, establish their viability, company's financial worth, evaluating the performance of management and most important, determining the market for company's products. The sponsor will also have to ensure that the project is in line with the latest policy of the Government laws and regulations. After establishing the financial, management, marketing, technical, commercial and economic viability and also fixing the value of the scrip to be listed, he sponsors the scrip to other members and dealers. The sponsorship is intended to screen companies before listing and to make it difficult for fly by night operators who take investors for a ride, to approach the public. This process provides guaranteed liquidity. The market making is done for at least one and a half year from the date of the scrips are offered for public trading compulsorily and the sponsor also arranges for at least one more member.

In view of the importance attached to market making and sponsorship activities, only financial institutions, mutual funds, banking subsidiaries, merchant-banks, venture capital funds approved by SEBI and other non-banking financial companies having a minimum net worth of Rs.2.5 crores are allowed and made eligible to be admitted as members at OTCEI. They normally have the standing and status to be able to carry the confidence of members and dealers. Further, the new entrants are allowed to enter the market only after they are screened by the OTCEI committee. A corporate body, firm and individual having a networth of Rs.5 lakhs can be admitted as dealer at the OTCEI to participate in investment, market making and OTC counter management activities. The dealers should have sound knowledge of trading, stock valuation, share transfer rules and laws. The dealers are expected to posses adequate financial resources; they should have the prescribed computers and electronic equipment at their counters to facilitate their operation.

Primary and Secondary Market Operations

Members and dealers also participate in primary market activities and secondary market operations in addition to trading and market making functions. In the primary issues, companies directly offer their share to the public. The sponsor handles the issue management and he may choose to subwrite his liability with a syndicate of members and dealers. A new company can get listing of its scrips at **OTCEI** only through a sponsor. In the event of any portion of the issue remaining unsubscribed the sponsor will have to subscribe the unsubscribed portion on the terms agreed upon between the sponsor and the company. The sponsor is responsible for fair allotment of shares and he is regulated by the guidelines prescribed by the **OTCEI.** In case a direct offer for sale is made, it must be accompanied with a prospectus. The prospectus should be in accordance with the regulations prescribed by the **OTCEI.** The companies and sponsors complete the process of allotment, compile the list of allottees and refundees, mail refunds and share certificate within the time prescribed by the **OTCEI.**

In the case of secondary issue, companies off load shares to the sponsor at the earlier date. The sponsor holds these shares till ready for public participation and he may then carry out the offer for sale. The sponsor makes the market by offering two way quotes for buying and selling of the security and the compulsory market making is performed for all such time as the scrips are listed. The market making function may be withdrawn after a period of two years from the commencement of public trading. The sponsor arranges some other member/dealer of the **OTCEI** for market making compulsorily in the security for a period of one year from the date of commencement of public trading. The securities at **OTCEI** are traded in standard lots of 100-securities and prices are also quoted for the standard lots.

Listing on the OTCEI

The following guidelines regarding listing on the **OTCEI** may be noted:

Companies with issued capital from Rs.30 lakhs to Rs.25 crores are eligible for listing subject to the following conditions:

i) Companies should make a minimum public offer of 25% of their capital or Rs.20 lakhs which ever is higher.

ii) Companies which are listed in other stock exchange will not be simultaneously eligible for listing on the **OTCEI.** The reason is while forward trading can be done on other stock exchanges, the **OTCEI** operations are on cash down basis and this would not result in investors buying on credit and realising sales in cash. This may lead to selling pressure on the **OTCEI.**

2. *NATIONAL STOCK EXCHANGE (NSE)*

The Indian Stock Exchanges had witnessed growth during 1980's in terms of the number of stock exchanges, listing companies. *market capitalisation trading volume, daily turnover, introduction of new financial instruments, liberalisation* reforms. This growth had not been evenly spread across the stock exchanges and there ''*intense*'' were variations. There was a tremendous increase in the investor base in terms of *geographical distribution* servicing of the investor was *still poor* and small investors in smaller exchanges were not able to participate effectively in the secondary market operations. In view of this situation the *Government of India* constituted a high power study group headed by *Sri M.T. Pherwani* to examine the need for establishment of new stock exchanges in India. The study group submitted its report in June, *1991* and its major recommendation was setting up of National Stock Exchange (NSE).

National Stock Exchange (NSE) was established with participation in capital by *IDBI* and other Public Financial Institutions in *Mumbai* in Nov. 1992. It was incorporated with a paid up capital of *Rs.25 crores.* It was registered as a limited company under the companies act, 1956. It is managed by its board of directors. It has appointed several committees, consisting of industrial professionals, trading members and exchange staff. It commenced the operations in ''*whole sale debt market (WDM) and Capital Market segment.*''

Objectives of NSE

Following are the objectives of NSE:

1. To cover wide area of geographical location for wide trading facilities.
2. To provide fast settlement process.
3. To check insider trading.
4. To provide efficient market facility.
5. To ensure transparency.
6. To reduce the default risk.

Trading System

1. Fair deal, automatic, transparent.
2. Matches buy order with sell order.
3. Unmatched orders remain in the system.
4. Provides full information.
5. Order driven system.

Characteristics

The Pheriwani group also recommended the setting up of NSE at New Mumbai. It will develop the national market system in the country. The infrastructure for National Market to be provided by NSE i.e. telecommunications facility computerisation, online processing system; library; research facilities, publicity department etc., The characteristics of National Stock Exchange system are as follows:

1. The National Stock Exchange system will have completely automated system.
2. PSUs and Medium sized companies are to be listed.
3. The NSE will have a separate trading time for debt instruments and capital market instruments.
4. National Market system provides liquidity and ready market.

The M.J. Pherwani Committee has suggested a three-tier stock Market system as follows:

a) Principal Stock Exchanges comprising of five major exchanges currently functioning in the metropolitan centres of *MUMBAI, DELHI, CALCUTTA, MADRAS and AHMEDABAD.*

b) Regional Stock Exchanges comprising of exchanges established in smaller metros and urban centres i.e., comprising of all other existing Stock Exchange.

c) Additional Trading Floors **(ATFs)** sponsored and managed by either a principal or a Regional Stock Exchange.

Features of NSE

1. The Exchange is completely automated.
2. It allows potential investors and professionals from other investment centres of the country.
3. It ensures liquidity in all scrips listed on the NSE.
4. It provides active secondary market for debt instruments.
5. The NSE got extensive library and research facilities.
6. Its capital out lay is Rs.30 crores.

The National Stock Exchange will provide nation wide stock trading facilities and equal access to investors from all over the country. It will also provide equal access to members of the wholesale debt market segment from all over the country. This service provided to investors would be of high quality due to an efficient, transparent and fair trading system.

There will be no trading floor in the exchange. Instead, each trading member will have a computer at his own office any where in India which will be connected to the central computer system at the NSE through leased lines or *VSAT (Very Small Aperture Terminals)*, for an interim transition period of six months and subsequently by satellite link. VSATs are relatively small dishes similar to a dish antenna for cable TVs and have the benefit of not being all over the country. This service provided to investor would be of high quality due to an efficient transparent and fair trading system.

A satellite network makes it possible to connect almost all parts of the nation quickly as it is easy to install, as against the ground lines such as up modems, leased lines etc., which are prone to disruption. Satellite links on the other hand, ensure high speed, availability and quality of the connection.

The trading at the NSE will be fully automated throughout the trading period, the trading member can enter his orders to buy or sell securities or to borrow/lend funds. When trading member executes an order, the order is immediately transmitted to the exchange computer system and stored in its memory, and maintained as an order book. The system checks to find a matching counter order. For example, if an order is placed to buy 100 shares of X Ltd., the order is transmitted to the computer, it would check whether anyone wants to sell 100 shares of X Ltd. and as soon as it finds a match the deal is struck. The buyers and sellers are informed accordingly. If a suitable match is not found, the order gets stocked in the system till a suitable counter order emerges and the transaction is closed at that point of time. At the end of each trading day the exchange system will generate a complete list of transactions done by the member for each trading member.

The following are the benefits of NSE:

a) Benefits to Investors.

b) Benefits to Trading Members.

c) Benefits to Issuers.

a) Benefits to Investors

The National Stock Exchange system provides following benefits to the investors:

1. A fair deal to investors.
2. More liquidity.
3. Best price availablity.
4. No problems of bad delivery/loss/theft.
5. Transperancy.
6. Date and time of trading are indicated.

b) Benefits to Trading Members

1. Reduces establishment costs.
2. Quick and efficient services.
3. Higher liquidity.
4. Full back office support for trading.
5. Automated trading system.
6. Very fast settlement.
7. Best Price to participants in the market.
8. Growth opportunities will also available.

c) Benefits to Issuers

1. Listing costs are reduced
2. High visibility.

3. *DEPOSITARY SERVICES*

The Indian Capital Market has been growing by leaps and bounds with India having the largest number of listed companies in the world as on today. The country also boasts of entertaiming a large number of shareholders, with the largest number of unit holders being in UTIs *Master gain 1992*, with a record holding of *65 lakhs* folio holders. The large number of participants in the Capital Market have given rise to large amounts of paper work, bringing with it several associated problems the increase in the volumes of trading has been simultaneous increase in the number of *bad deliveries*. There by introducing increased incidence of *risks* in settlement of trade disputes. As such the *threats of wrong/forged signatures, stolen shares, forged/fake* certificates, etc., have to be necessarily contained. If the investors were not step away from trading and investing in the Indian Markets. Huge volume of paper work related to processing of share certificates have encountered the clearing and settlement mechanism.

In this present *scenario*, it was found that the setting up of a Depository and the introduction of *''scripless''* trading and settlement would improve the efficiency of the markets, thereby eliminating the various problems brought about by dealing in physical certificates. The *Government of India* promulgated the *''Depositories Ordinance''* in september 1995. Thus paying the way for setting up of the depositories in the country. *The National Securities Depository Ltd.*, was registered on 7th June 1996. It was registered with *''Securities and Exchange Board of India''* as the first Depository in the country and called as National Securities Depository Ltd., a company promoted by leading financial institutions and banks have been set up with the *''state of the art''* systems to provide securities depository services in the country. NSDL is a professionally managed organisation with established practices of *''International Standards''* having employed the latest information technology.

It is observed that the total transactions of transfer of these instruments on normal business per day reaches *75,000* and above transactions, which further add misery to the investors redress. As a boon to the investors dealing in the capital market instruments most simplified, convenient and transparent system of transfer is enabled in a Depository system that has been introduced by the *Depository (Ordinance) Act 1996.*

A Depository system is a system of computerised book entry of securities and their transfers in the Capital Market transactions. A transfer of shares through a book entry, than a physical movement of certificates. In this method. The physical movement of security would be replaced by a computerised book entry system. The ownership of securities would pass by a computer entry on the basis of *Delivery vs Payment (DVP)* in which there is a simultaneous flow of shares and money in opposite direction. The present system involves physical movement of securities from one hand to another during the settlement. Major weakness of Indian Stock Market operations will be rationalised with the introduction of depository system.

Operations

Any Company/Financial Institution/Bank can apply for registration as a depository under the section *12 (1A)* of the *SEBI Act 1992*. After the necessary conditions fulfilled by the applicant of the depository, SEBI will grant a certificate of registration, thus the company will commence its operations as a *''Depository''*. The depository will in turn appoint agents called as *''participants''* who directly deal with the investors on behalf of depository. An investor who is interested in opening a depository account has to surrender the securities. Then the shares are *''dematerialised''* and recorded the investors as a owner of the security. This is the service of the account depository to keep a record of the investors. A depository performs the function of *''holding, transferring, withdrawal of securities.''*

Categories

The SEBI regulations have classified the depositories into the following categories:

a) Public Financial Institutions (PFCs)

b) Scheduled Banks.

c) State Finance Corporations (SFCs)

d) Non-Banking Financial Companies (NBFCs)

e) Registered Stock Brokers.

f) RBI approved Foreign Banks.

NSDL Services

The following services are offered by NSDL;

1. Maintaining beneficial holdings.
2. Providing for dematerialisation and rematerialisation.
3. Effecting Account transfers for settlement of trades.
4. Allowing for receipt of allotment in the electronic form.
5. Providing pledging facilities for deposited stocks.
6. Providing stock lending.
7. Receiving and disbursing corporate accounts.

Advantages of Depository System

The following are the advantages of depository system;

1. No risk of loss/theft/fraud of shares.
2. No risk of receiving Fake/Forged/Stolen certificates.
3. No stamp duty on transfer.
4. Low custodial charges.
5. Reduced transaction cost.
6. Fast and speedy transactions.
7. Very few Bad deliveries.
8. Reduced paper work.
9. No delay in transfers.
10. No problems of odd lots.

Depositories have come to stay in India. They are legally and technically safe. The following *statistics* of *NSDL (as on 20-3-1999)* are presented.

1. Number of companies availing depository services 361.
2. Number of beneficial owners above 3,75,000
3. Number of cities/towns covered 1533/Abroad 41
4. Number of depository participants 84.
5. Number of locations from where DP services offered 730
6. Number of stock exchanges which deal indent scrips 9
7. Number of brokers - deal in Demat scrips 2490
8. Market capitalisation - Demat scrips Rs.3,97,156 crores.
9. Number of shares demeterialised 680 crores.

4. *STOCK HOLDING CORPORATION OF INDIA LTD.(SHCIL)*

The Infrastructural facilities for servicing the millions of investors have not increased with the growth in the capital market. The financial institutions have taken initiative steps in establishing the *''Stock Holding Corporation of India Ltd."* It is a company which in corporated under the companies act, 1956. The company was established in July 1986. The company has been incorporated with authorised capital of *Rs.250* million and paid up capital of *Rs.105* million fully subscribed by the following Indian financial institutions.

1. Industrial Development Bank of India.
2. General Insurance Corporation
3. Life Insurance Corporation
4. Unit Trust of India
5. Industrial Finance Corporation of India
6. Industrial Credit and Investment Corporation of India
7. Industrial Reconstruction Bank of India

Functions

SHCIL is a board managed company. The operations of the corporation are fully computerised. SHCIL eliminates the paper and paper related work by introducing the book entry system for transfer of scrips. It is making efforts for immobilisation and dematerialisation of securities. The corporation was incorporated to provide comprehensive custodial services and fully automated infrastructural facilities for *trade, clearances, settlement and depository* services for securities and monetary instruments. It offers services mainly to various financial institutions. The corporation has recently formulated the frame work of National Clearing System. This system will comprise of;

1. National Trading Reporting System
2. National Clearing System
3. National Depository System

The services offered by the corporation can be broadly classified into 5 areas.

1. Clearing Services
2. Registration
3. Transferring Process
4. Depository Services
5. Corporate Actions & Benefits
6. Online Trading System

5. SECURITIES AND EXCHANGE BOARD OF INDIA (SEBI)

The duty of the Government is to control stock market operations through *legislative and administrative* measures for better and efficient working of the stock market. For this purpose the Government of India has passed a bill in Parliament on 4-4-1956 known as *''Securities Contracts (Regulation) Act, 1956."* It was a landmark in Indian Securities Market, The objectives of this legislation are as follows:

1. The act empowered the Central Government to control Securities Market operations.
2. The Government has full authority in protecting the investor's interest.
3. Create a well organised and efficient market.
4. Reform and improve the working of stock exchanges in the country.
5. Control and check the malpractices in the securities market.
6. Restrict excessive and undesirable speculative activities.
7. Create liquidity in stock exchanges, that makes flow of savings into investments.

Objectives of SEBI

a) To regulate the securities market,

b) To protect the interests of investors,

c) To promote the development of securities market.

Functions of the SEBI

1. To register and regulate the working of stock brokers.
2. To register and regulate the working of bankers to an issue.
3. To control and regulate securities market.
4. To exercise the powers under Securities Contracts (Regulations) Act.
5. To regulate the working of mutual funds.
6. To perform such other functions as may be prescribed.
7. To control fraudulent and unfair trade practices relating to securities market.
8. To conduct research for the above purposes.
9. To control investment business.

10. To regulate issue of securities.
11. To regulate take overs.
12. To prohibit insiders trading in securities.

Powers of SEBI

Following powers have been given to SEBI.

1. Power to conduct research and other functions.
2. Power to call for periodical returns from recognised stock exchanges.
3. Power to levy fees.
4. Power to call for any information or explanation from recognised stock exchanges of its members.
5. Power to regulate substantial acquisition of shares and take over of companies.
6. Power to direct inquires to be made in relation to affairs of stock exchanges or its members.
7. Power to promote investors education and trading of intermediaries in capital market.
8. Power to grant approval to bye-laws of recognised exchanges.
9. Power to prohibit insider trading.
10. Power to make or amend bye-laws of recognised exchanges.
11. Power to prohibit fraudulent and unfair trade practices relating to securities.
12. Power to declare applicability of section 17 of the Securities Contracts (Regulation) Act in any state or area and to grant licenses to dealers in securities.
13. Power to promote and regulate self-regulatory bodies.
14. Power to compel listing of securities by public companies.
15. Power to control and regulate stock exchanges.
16. Power to register and regulate working of collective investment schemes including mutual funds.
17. Power to grant registration to market intermediaries.

6. MUTUAL FUNDS

Definition

"MUTUAL FUND" is a non-depository, non-banking financial intermediary which acts an important vehicle for bringing wealth of holders and deficit units together indirectly."

Weston J. Fred and *Brigham* defined mutual fund as "a corporation which accepts money from investors and uses the same to buy stocks, long- term bonds, short-term debt instruments issued by issuers."

Objectives

1. To mobalise savings of Non-resident savers.
2. To offer a convenient way for the small investors to enter the capital and the money market.
3. To tap domestic savings and channelise them for profitable investment.
4. To enable the investors to share the prosperity of the capital market.
5. To act as agents for growth and stability of the capital market.
6. To attract investments from the risk aversers
7. To provide a measure of downward risk protection in a falling market.
8. To facilitate the orderly development of the capital market.

Advantages of Mutual Funds

1. Provides opportunity to the small investors to enjoy the cream of capital market.
2. Portfolio management service to the investors.
3. Creates awareness among small investors about the benefit of investment in capital markets.
4. Best timing of investments through professional approach.
5. Encourage saving habit.
6. No tax on capital gains.
7. Tax shelters.
8. Investment flexibility i.e., the investor can switch from one fund to another fund.
9. Liquidity of investment.

10. Safety of the investment.
11. Steady return to the investment.
12. Availability of various schemes at a reduced risk.
13. Capital appreciation to the investment.
14. Low investment is required to purchase units/shares of funds.
15. Automatic re-investment facilities of dividends and capital gains.

7. MARGIN TRADING

Margin Trading basically enables an investor to get an exposure against which he can buy or sell in lieu of his cash or shares that are with the broker or in his demat account.

In case an investor thinks that particular scrip is going to move he puts in a margin with his broker and then buys or sells up to the exposure given to him by the broker.

"Margin trading is a useful tool for a day trader, and is bound to increase the retail participation in the cash equity markets of the country."

Margin trading is a global phenomenon, in the US almost all online brokers have the facility of a Margin Account. The way it works on a portal like *Charles Schwab,* (Schwab account means, it is an account which may be operated on online network.) is that, if a customer has marginable securities in their Schwab Account, they can borrow funds from Schwab to buy additional securities or to make purchases. The securities serve as an automatic collateral for low cost margin loans.

Marginable securities are general securities traded on the major **US** exchanges. Typically a customer can borrow a maximum of 50% of the current value of the marginable securities. The interest rates vary from broker to broker. The interest charges are a function of the Broker Call Rate **(BCR)** also known as the Call Money Rate with the current charge being $\frac{3}{4}$% above the **BCR** for a value of **$ 50,000** and above and $1\frac{1}{4}$% above BCR for below **$ 50,000.** At Schwab a customer is charged 2% above their base rate.

From a broker's perspective, Margin Trading is a very useful tool for the day trader. Therefore, margin trading tends to make the business of the broker more profitable as turnover increases. But the flip side is the attached risk, especially on the Internet. In the traditional off line medium, risk was hedged through personal relationships.

But in the age of the faceless customer, trading with a broker in thousands of numbers with all-India spread technology is the only back up for the broker. A broker needs to closely monitor his position on a minute-by-minute basis. In case the market erodes the margin, the escape mechanism needs to be well defined in the form of either a automatic square up or giving the customer a call and asking for his next move.

Margin trading is surely going to increase the retail participation in the cash equity markets of the country. It enables a customer to leverage his cash and securities and helps broaden the market beyond cash rich individuals or corporates.

Online trading and Margin trading together will further strengthen the cause of empowering the retail investor, but the investor will need to be extremely cautious. In India, most of the online brokers are taking margins to a 25-50 per cent, thus giving tremendous flexibility. The underlying premise is that scrip prices can plunge a maximum of 16% a day, thus the clients loss will never exceed the margin. This methodology covers the risk of a broker to quite a large extent. But in this game, the investor wili need to take his day trading investing decision very carefully.

Most of the investors in the traditional mode had the privilege of the stock broker guiding them through the ups and downs of the market, therefore Margin Trading as a concept thrived. But the customers were a privileged lot with capacity to absorb losses.

But as the concept of online trading picks up and margin trading helps to increase. The participation and turnover a sense of caution will need to be installed in all such players.

A long teem player in the e-broking space will need to give the customer the choice of doing margin trading or not. Also, the customer will need to get access to almost all the information that a broker gets for a level playing field to prevail.

An online broker should have a short-term perspective of increasing turnover and thereby earnings, through the provision of margin trading. The most critical service to be provided by an online broker is execution quality coupled with real time information, which enables financial upside to a reasonable level for the customer.

10. CAPITAL MARKET REFORMS

The Capital Market in India has shown tremendous growth during 1990. The number of investing population has gone upto 26 millions. Important Capital Market reforms are stated as follows:

1. Abolition of CCI and introduction of **SEBI.**
2. Indian companies are permitted to access international Capital Markets through Euro issues.

3. *Empowered SEBI* with full powers for regulation and reforming Capital Market.

4. *Foreign Institutional Investors have been* permitted to invest in Indian Capital Market.

5. Control over premium and price of shares removed.

6. Investment norms for NRI's liberalised.

7. SEBI introduced new reforms in primary market.

8. Companies required to disclose all material facts.

9. Establishment of OTCEI

10. SEBI notified several regulations for intermediaries in the secondary market.

11. Permission to PSUs to sell bonds to NRIs

12. **RBI** has announced the setting up of the Securities Trading Corporation of India to develop a secondary market in Government dated securities and public sector bonds.

13. The Government has amended the law to enable nationalised banks to access the capital market.

14. The *''Mumbay Stock Exchange''* introduced circuit - breaker system to regulate trading in shares.

15. **SEBI** introduced a number of measures for streamlining the functioning of the secondary market, such as reconstitution of the governing boards of the stock exchanges, capital adequacy norms for brokers, and providing transparency in client/broker relationships.

16. **SEBI** introduced a code of advertisement for public issues for ensuring fair and truthful disclosures.

17. Private mutual funds are permitted and a few already setup.

18. Access to capital market tightened to improve the quality of paper.

19. A norm prescribed of 5 shareholders for every Rs.1.00 lakh of fresh issue of capital and 10 shareholders for every Rs.1.00 lakh of offer for sale prescribed as an initial and continuing listing requirement.

20. No entry restriction for public sector banks to access capital market.

21. The banks have been allowed to fix the premium on issue early after a two year profitability record.

22. Debt issues permitted to be sold entirely through book building process subject to sec 19(2) (b) of securities contract rules.
23. The promoters are allowed to bring their contribution in a phased manner, If their contribution exceeds Rs.100 crores.
24. A listed company required to meet the entry norm only, if the post issue networth becomes more than five times of the pre-issue network.
25. Unlisted companies are allowed to freely price its securities if they show net profit in the immediately preceding 3 years.
26. Only body of corporates to be allowed to function as Merchant Bankers.
27. Multiple categories of merchant bankers to be abolished and there shall be only one entity i.e., MB.
28. Listing requirement of stock exchanges to be made more stringent to get investor's confidence.
29. There should be phased introduction of derivative products with the stock index futures as the starting point.
30. Mutual funds permitted to underwrite public issues.
31. Banks, Mutual funds, and IDBI are allowed to dematerialise their scrips.
32. Foreign Exchange Management Act replaces the FERA Act.
33. FIIs allowed access to Indian capital market as registration with SEBI. They are permitted to invest upto 10% in equity of any company.
34. RBI established a single window agency for receipt and disposal of proposals for overseas investments by Indian companies.
35. Companies permitted to retain euro-issue proceeds as foreign currency deposits with banks and public financial institutions in India.
36. FIIs are permitted to access capital market and there is no lock in period for their investments.
37. The general permission from RBI shall also enable to;
    a) Open foreign currency denominated accounts in designated bank
    b) Open a special non-resident rupee account to business transactions
    c) They can transfer repatriable proceeds from the rupee account to the foreign currency accounts.

d) They can transfer sums from the foreign currency accounts to the rupee account or rupee accounts to the foreign currency accounts.

38. Portfolio investments in primary or secondary markets will be subject to a cieling of 30% of issued share capital for the total holdings of all registered FIIs in any company.

39. A registered FII can appoint a custodian, an agency approved by SEBI.

40. FIIs are required to submit any information required by the RBI at any time.

41. FIIs will avail the benefit from a concessional tax rate of a flat rate of 20% as dividend and interest income at 10% on long-term gains and @ 30% as short-term capital gains.

42. Every custodian shall appoint a compliance officer who will interact with SEBI for compliance and reporting issues.

43. Investors are provided for payment of interest after the disclosure of a public issue from the 30th day.

44. All exchanges shall follow the buying or auction procedure.

45. Stock exchanges have been asked to set up a clearing corporation

46. The stock exchanges are allowed to expand their trading terminals

47. Restrictions on OTCEI removed and OTCEI permitted to move to a five day accounting period settlement.

48. All short and long sales will have to be disclosed to the exchange at the end of each day.

49. Stock lending scheme has been introduced

50. Public Financial Institutions, Banks or Stock Exchanges can promo a depository in India.

51. Any purchases or sales above 1% of the paid up capital of a comp have to be publised and shall inform the concerned stock excha

52. The time gap between any two issues of banks has been redu from 24 to 12 months in all companies.

53. Companies now allowed to issue shares with differential vot rights including non-voting shares to the extend of 25% of t share capital issued, according to the notification issued by Department of Company Affairs (Rule 2000)

54. The companies which have defaulted in filing annual returns during the preceding 3 years or failed to repay their deposits or interest there on the due date, have redeemed debentures on the due date will not be eligible to issue shares with differential rights*.

55. Stock exchanges have been disallowed from renewing contracts in cash group of shares from one settlement to another.

56. A time limit of 11 months have been prescribed for the disposal of arbitration cases by the exchanges.

57. SEBI guidelines for *mutual funds* are presented below:

   i) Mutual funds shall be authorised for business by the SEBI.

   ii) Every mutual fund shall be established in the form of a trust.

   iii) Every mutual fund should be operated only by a separately established Asset Management Company (AMC)

   iv) The Directors of AMC should be persons of high repute, understanding, having at least 10years of professional experience in the relevant field.

   v) The AMC and the Trustee should be two separate legal entities.

   vi) AMC should not be permitted to undertake any other business activity than management of mutual funds.

   vii) No person should be a Director for more than one AMC.

   viii) No person should hold at a time either director of AMC or director in a trust.

   xi) The 50 per cent of the board of trustees shall be from outside members

   xii) The AMC should submit a quarterly report to the trustees, the trustees in turn shall submit a six monthly report to the SEBI

   xi) Each scheme of the mutual fund should have a permission from SEBI

   xii) Any mutual fund be allowed to start and operate both close end and open-end schemes.

   xiii) For each close-end scheme the minimum amount to be raised *Rs.20 crores* and for open-ended scheme *Rs.50 crores*. If fails the norms the amount should be returned by the fund to the investors.

---

* Economic Times, Dt: 21-03-2001.

xiv) Mutual funds should provide continuous liquidity, close-ended schemes should be listed units on exchanges and open ended scheme's can be sold or purchased based on NAV.

xv) MFs will be allowed to invest only in transferable securities either in the money market or in the capital market.

xvi) MFs should not be allowed to give term loans for any purpose.

xvii) MFs are not permitted to invest in more than **5%** of its corpus fund in any one company's shares.

xviii) Funds transferring between two schemes of the same AMC are not allowed.

xix) Each close end scheme should be extended with the permission of SEBI

xx) The total of all the expenses (except initial issue expenses) should not exceed **3%** of the weekly average net assets outstanding during the current year.

xxi) All mutual funds should distribute a minimum of **90%** of their profits.

xxii) SEBI will have the full authority to call any information regarding the operations of mutual funds.

xxiii) Every mutual fund shall submit the following periodic reports to SEBI

1. Copies of the duly audited annual statements of accounts.
2. Six monthly unaudited accounts
3. Quarterly statements regarding each scheme for their movement of net assets.
4. A portfolio statement including changes from the previous periods.

xxiv) SEBI has the authority to impose penalties on mutual funds for violating the guidelines.

xxv) Any appeals against decisions of SEBI, to be referred to the Department of Economic Affairs, Ministry of Finance.

xxvi) The MF should not invest more than **15%** of its funds in the shares and debentures of any specific industry.

xxvii) The initial issue expenses should not exceed **6%** of the funds raised under each scheme.

xxviii) MF should not make investments in any other unit trust.

58. **RBI guidelines** on mutual funds are presented below:

1. RBI permitted the commercial banks to enter into mutual fund sector.
2. The sponsoring bank should appoint a board of trustees to manage the fund.
3. The board of trustees should have at least two outside members.
4. The routine activities of the fund should be looked after by full time executive
5. Any clash of interest between sponsor bank and mutual fund shall be avoided;
6. The sponsor bank contribution to corpus fund is Rs.25 lakhs.
7. The MFs may invest their funds in money market for a period not exceeding 6 months.
8. MFs shall create a dividend equalisation fund for each scheme with surplus income
9. MFs shall maintain separate accounts for each scheme.
10. MFs are not allowed for switching of assets between two schemes operated by the same mutual fund.

59. The main objectives of New Economic Policy 1991 are presented below:

a) To develop a market oriented, competitive, world integrated diversified, autonomous, transparent financial system.

b) To increase the rate of return on real investment

c) To ensure that the rationalisation of interest rates.

d) To build a financial infrastructure.

e) To modernise the instruments of monetary control in a market economy.

f) To increase the effectiveness, accountability viability, profitability, balanced growth, operational efficiency in the financial sector.

60. The major reforms from 1991 onwards are presented below:

1. The reforms have been concentrated in operational matters, banking, primary and secondary markets, government securities market, external sector policies, etc.,

2. The major reforms are listed below in terms of certain categories
   a) Systematic and policy reforms
   b) Banking reforms.
   c) Primary & Secondary market reforms.

61. A listed company will be permitted to enter only if the post issue networth becomes more than 5 times the pre-issue networth.
62. Companies before making a public/right issue, make their partly paid up shares into fully paid up or forfeit the same.
63. The promoter's contribution for public issues made uniform at 20% irrespective of the issue size.
64. Appointment of Registrar to a rights issue made mandatory.
65. Private placements could be restricted to qualified institutional investors or high networth individuals.
66. Derivative market should have a separate governing council with representation of trading members of the derivative segment limited to 40%
67. Initial margin requirements related to the risk of loss as the position and capital adequacy norms shall be prescribed.
68. Every member of the derivative segment will be inspected annually by the stock exchanges.
69. In derivative trade segment corporate clients, financial institutions mutual funds are allowed.
70. SEBI plans to make it mandatory for all distributors to pass a certification test, commencing from November 1, 2001 "NSE-AMFI" test.
71. The players in the derivative market should follow the accounting norms according to the Institute of Chartered Accountants of India.

CREDIT RATING

The Indian capital market has achieved a tremendous growth. As the consequences of "*Liberalisation*" more and more companies have approached the market. Taking this movement as advantage, some scupulous promoters/*fly by night operators* have floated new companies without having a credible project in hand. Their aim is to cheat the investors. The reforms have brought some radical changes to check and control the bogus promoters. In this junctures a proper information regarding the quality of capital instruments is essential. To overcome this situation the "*Credit Rating*" system has emerged. The importance and need for a proper information system especially the credit rating system to ensure the market forces to play a *fair game necessary*.

Credit Rating is the process of evaluating the risk associated with a credit instrument. It is a technique of rating the borrower's expected capability and worth or reputation of solvency credit ability and probability of timely repayment of *principal* along with interest on due dates. It is not a general evaluation of the issuing organisation but instrument specific. Different instruments of the same company may carry different ratings. It is not just one time evaluation of credit risk of security but involves on going appraisal and evaluation by the rating agency whereby an instrument may be graded or down graded. The ratings should be useful to both the investors and companies.

"A current assessment of the credit worthiness of an obligator with respect to specific obligation."

- Standard & Poor.

"A corporate credit rating provides lenders with a simple system of gradation by which the relative capacities of companies make timely repayment of interest and principal on a particular type of debt."

- Australian Rating

Types of Credit Rating

Credit ratings are of different types. It depends upon the requirements of the rates and the rated instruments. The following are the common types of rating securities:

1. Bond Rating
2. Equity Rating
3. Commercial Paper Rating
4. Sovereign Rating

Credit Rating Agencies

There are 3 credit rating agencies in India. They are:

1. The Credit Rating Information Services of India (CRISIL)
2. Investment Information and Credit Rating Agency (ICRA)
3. Credit Analysis and Research (CARE)

Credit Rating Information Services of India Limited(CRISIL)

The CRISIL was established in 1988 jointly by the ICICI, UTI, GIC, SBI, ADB along with other financial institutions. It has been promoted as a public limited company. The CRISIL was the first rating agency in India to rate commercial paper programme in 1989. It was rated debt instruments of financial institutions and banks in 1992. It also undertakes credit rating of all securities i.e., fixed deposits, commercial papers, equity and preference shares and real estate projects. It analyses five factors in assessing a financial product. The five elements are as follows.

1. **Business analysis**
   (Industry risk, Market share, Operating efficiency)

2. **Financial analysis**
   (Valuation of Balance sheet, Earning potential, Cash flows)

3. **Management performance**
   (Management philosophy, Managerial talents)

4. **Competitive Environment**
   (Impact of government policies)

5. **Fundamental analysis**
   (Asset's quality, profitability)

The process of credit ratings can be described as follows.

1. The desired company may approach the CRISIL.
2. The CRISIL will assign the job to analyst team.
3. The team commences their job to compile the data from the company.
4. The team will analyse the data, the findings are presented to Rating Committee
5. The Rating Committee will grant the rating and communicates the information.
6. After issue of rating, the instrument will be kept in observation for modifications, if any needs.

Investment Information and Credit Rating Agency of India (ICRA)

Investment Information and Credit Rating Agency of India has been promoted by ICICI. Its headquarters was located in New-Delhi. It was established to provide rating facility to corporate sector for long term instruments. It works with two separate departments *(1) Information Service (2) Advisory Services.* The information services provide the services for intermediaries, financial institutions, banks, asset managers, institutional investors, and individual investors and others.

Credit Analysis and Research (CARE)

CARE was established in April 1993. It has started its operations in November 1993. It was established for the purpose of credit analysis and rating. It was promoted by IDBI jointly with investment institutions, banks and finance companies. The CARE offers the following services to its clients;

a) Credit Rating

b) Equity Research

c) Information Services

d) Ratings of Petro Products.

The following chart will explain about the process of rating of CARE.

Client requests and submits information

↓

Assignment to rating team and analyse the information

↓

Team interaction with company

↓

The client interacts with team

↓

Rating team submits report to Internal Committee.

↓

Internal committee communicates the rating to its client

↓

CARE will put the instrument in a periodic surveillance.

Rating Symbols of CARE

The CARE undertakes the following instruments for rating of the financial products:

A) Long-term and Medium-term instrument

B) Short-term instruments (promissory notes)

Rating of debt instruments issued by power, telecom and infrastructure companies. It also rates term credit instruments and long-term financial products. Advisory services department offers a wide range of services like strategic counselling, restructuring solutions, client need based activities in the financial services and banking sectors. ICRA rating methodology involves a detailed analysis of the past data of the client company. The factors rating methodology includes *industry analysis, competitive position of the client, operational efficiency, quality of management policies, commitments to new projects.*

The following system is adopted by ICRA in rating process;

Client company Request
↓
Assignment to Rating team
↓
collection of required data by team
↓
Industry experts advises
↓
Meeting with company management
↓
preview meeting
↓
Rating committee meeting
↓
Rating communication
↓
Rating Reviews
↓
Monitoring of grading

Rating by CRISIL

Debentures	FDRs	Remarks
A A A	F A A A	Highest Safety
A A	F A A	High Safety
A	F A	Adequate Safety
B B B	-	Sufficient Safety
B B	F B	Inadequate Safety
B	F C	High Risk
C	-	Substantial Risk
D	F D	In default

Rating by ICRA

LONG-TERM		MEDIUM-TERM	
LAAA	- Highest Safety	MAAA	- Highest Safety
LAA	- High Safety	MAA	- High Safety
LA	- Adequate Safety	MA	- Adequate Safety
LBBB	- Moderate Safety	MB	- Inadequate Safety
LBB	- Inadequate Safety	MC	- Risk Prone
LB	- Risk Prone	MD	- Default
LC	- Substantial Risk		
LD	- Default		

Credit Rating Benefits

Credit rating benefits for all classes of investors, viz., corporate borrowers, financial intermediaries, business counter parts and the regulators are highlighted;

i) **Investor:** They get information at a very low cost from an impartial agency. They can draw credit risk policies and assess the adequacy or otherwise of the risk premium offered by the borrower; they may be able to safeguard against bankruptcy, easy understandability of the investment proposal/credibility of the issuer.

ii) **Corporate Borrowers:** They can raise funds at relatively cheaper rates, use it as a marketing tool and enter foreign collaborations; it also encourages discipline in the borrowers. Apart from extensive mobilisation of resources, companies may be able to cut down their public issue expenses.

iii) **Merchant Bankers; Banks:** Investment advisers and other financial intermediaries, it provides useful inputs in taking decisions relating to lending and investments. It helps opening letters ofcredit; awarding contracts, establishing business relations etc. The Regulators are able to monitor the eligibility criteria, the entry barriers for the new securities and the efficiency of the debt instruments.

Global Depository Receipts (GDRs)

After implementation of Globalisation Policy in 1991, the trends in capital market have been grown tremendously. The new policy towards euro issues specifies an end use of the money raised and also stipulates Foreign Investment Promotion Board clearance in certain cases. The new guidelines for issue of GDRs envisaged that EURO issues will be treated as direct foreign investment. "GDR is an instrument governed by international laws, but not on the Indian laws. It is a dollar denominated instrument, which is tradeable on stock exchanges in *Europe or U.S.A.*" It represents a certain number of equity shares and equity comprised in such GDR are denominated in rupees, at the rate of exchange prevailing at the time of issue. The investors holding GDRs are not entitled to any voting rights. The securities are issued by the issuer to an intermediary called ''*Depository*''. The shares are registered in the name of the depository who inturn issues the *GDRs* to the investors. An agreement is made between the issuer and the depository. The shares are kept is physical possession of another intermediary named ''*Custodian*'' The custodian operates as an agent of the depository. GDRs were introduced in late 1990s. The investor making investment in such GDRs are FIIs, comprising mutual funds, pension funds. GDRs are investor friendly and quoted in US dollars. They are liquid and exchangeable with underlying securities. India companies are tapping the Euro market through GDRs or a convertible bond issues. GDRs are cheapest sources of foreign funds. Samsung Electronics of korea became the first developing company to tap the GDR market. *Reliance Industries* was the first Indian company to raise the GDRs with a great success. It was followed Grasim Industries. The following companies were successfully raised GDRs from Global Capital Market;

a) Hindalco Industries.
b) TELCO
c) Finolex Cables
d) Century Textiles
e) A.C.C.
f) Ashok Leyland
g) Bajaj Auto

Salient features

1. The company prefers to raise money through equity rather than debt because, it can help to reduce debt servicing ratio.
2. Competition through global level reduces the cost of funds. Hence the companies can reap the benefits from the market.
3. Global recognition with institutional investors may reliable sources rather than depending upon domestic capital market.
4. The pricing of issues are depends on basic determinants like market capitalisation, turnover, market depth and liquidity. In the case of companies with large capitalisation, liquidity can attract more funds from the market.

5. International investors invest only after thoroughly analysing the corporate prospects and fundamentals, they tend to be long term players and therefore, the foreign currency may not be withdrawn from the country in a short period.

The process of GDRs issue is presented below:

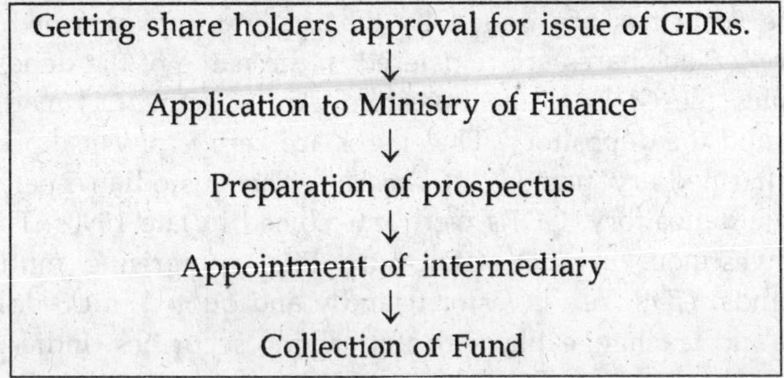

American Depository Receipts (ADRs)

An American Depository Receipt represents an ownership interest in foreign securities. ADR is a negotiable instrument. It is issued by an American Depository Bank. ADRs could be listed on the Newyork Stock Exchange, the American Stock Exchange and the National Association of Securities Dealers Automatic Quotation. ADRs are an ideal way for foreign companies to raise funds. ADRs expand the international capital base and get name and product exposure in the U.S.

The shares are not directly issued to the investor. First the shares will be issue by Indian company to a US intermediary with registration. The Depositary inturn issues the ADRs. The physical possession of shares is with custodian, he is also an intermediary. The dividend outflow from the company is in rupees. However, the depositary pays the dividend in dollars to the investors. There are very specific benefits to companies which access the global equity market through ADRs.

a) Developing countries can get the funds at a low cost.

b) International reputation leads further financing made easy.

ADRs will become increasingly popular. ADRs will have lower management fees and lower execution costs in buying foreign stocks. U.S. investors often prefer ADRs to the foreign securities because;

1. They trade & settle in the U.S.
2. The Convenience of buying & selling
3. Settlement will be within 5 days.
4. No settlement problems

Professional investors have many alternative to invest their savings. There are 50 countries with interest in securities markets and over 10,000 companies can match the investment criteria, professional equity investors are thinking about companies rather than countries. The general criteria the business concerns have to meet to be able to sell equity issues are presented below:

a) The aspiring companies should have current equity market capitalisation of at least **US $ 100 mn** equivalent.

b) The business concern's market turnover should at least **US $ 1 mn** a week in the domestic market.

c) The corporate entity must have a conservative debt.

d) The company shall have a significant and growing share of export earnings.

e) The company will have domestic market dominance in the market.

f) The companies should have to meet international accounting standards.

g) Financial disclossure arrangements to the international investor's community.

h) The companies will have to meet global competitiveness, therefore the concern have to concentrate **Research and Development.**

The inflow of **GDR/ADRs** are presented below;

Year	*GDR/ADRs inflow* (US $ million)
1992-1993	240
1993-1994	1520
1994-1995	2082
1995-1996	683
1996-1997	1366
1997-1998	645
1998-1999	270
1999-2000	768
2000-2001	831

Sources: 1. RBI Bulletin, March, 1999 P.No. S 294

2. RBI Bulletin, August, 2001 P.No. S 826

SUMMARY

Financial Market deals with financial securities or instruments and financial services. It provides a mechanism for an investor to sell a financial asset. Financial markets are classified into two categories viz., *(1) Money Market (2) Capital Market.* Money Market is for short-term funds. Money market provide the funds for less than one year. Money Market is dominated by central bank. Central bank acts as a promotional and development banker in money market. Money market is consisting of organised and unorganised sectors. The organised sector consist of *RBI, SBI, MFs, Companies, Co-operative Societies, and Financial institutions.* The unorganised sector consist of Money lenders, Indigenous banks. The main borrowers of short-term funds in the money market are *Commercial banks, Central Government, State Government, Corporate Sector and Local Bodies.* The money market is involved in buying and selling of short-term instruments. The instruments are call money, Treasury bills, commercial papers certificate of deposits, commercial bills and money market mutual funds. The money market provides funds to bill market, inter bank uses, operators in bullian market, dealers in stock exchange, cash credit and overdraft facilities.

Capital Market deals with long-term funds, capital market deals with ordinary shares, stocks, debentures and bonds of corporations and securities of the government. The development banks in the Indian financial system have witnessed vast changes in the planning periods. The development banks constitute the backbone of the Indian capital market. The structure of the capital market has undergone a remarkable transformation. The submarkets of capital markets are *Equity market, Debt market, Government securities market and Mutual funds.* There are different categories of capital like *long term capital, short-term capital, Foreign exchange and venture capital.* The players in the capital market are broadly divided into 3 categories companies, intermediaries and investors. The main components of the capital market in India are primary market and secondary market. Primary market is also called as new issue market. NIM deals with the companies which are going to issue the shares to the public at the first time. Stock exchanges are the secondary markets. These not only serve the private sector but also the joint and public sectors by providing a forum for the transferability of shares held by the public. The main objectives of the stock exchanges are to regulate stock market practices, to create efficient securities market, to ensure fair dealing and protection to the investors, to improve the working of stock exchanges, to control the undesirable speculative practices. At present there are 23 stock exchange recognised under the Securities Contract (Regulation) Act. There are various types of members and operators in the stock exchange i. e., jobbers, brokers, tarawaniwalas, budliwala, Arbitrageurs, odd lot dealers. The securities listed for trading in BSE are grouped as Group A shares, Group B shares, permitted securities, cleared securities, non-cleared securities etc., Speculation is the oxygen to the stock market. Speculation is an intelligent activity. It is based on expertise and perfect knowledge of capital market trends. Manipulation involves buying and selling of securities by a group of speculators. There are 4 types of speculators (a) Bull (b) Bear (c) Lame duck (d) Stag. The major financial instruments in the Indian stock market are Equity shares, Debentures, Bonds and Government securities.

New financial instruments in capital market are available to the investors. They can be described as (a) zero coupon bonds (b) warrants (c) secured premium notes (d) stock investment instrument (e) deep discount bonds (f) option bonds. The public issue is essentially an exercise involving active participation of a number of agencies. The placement of issues may be through prospectus, offer for sale, private placement, rights issue and bought out deals. The Pherwani Committee Recommended the instruments that have already been issued in the market, such as non voting shares, stockable equity coupons, participating preference shares, participating debentures etc., The main financial intermediaries of capital market in India are merchant bankers, underwriters, brokers, bankers and registrars. The recent developments found in the capital markets are OTCEI, NSE, Depository Services, SEBI, Credit Rating, MFs, Venture Capital, Capital market reforms etc.

QUESTIONS

1. What do you mean by Capital Market?
2. Discuss the nature of Indian Capital Market.
3. Define Capital Market and discuss its importance.
4. What are the objectives of Capital Market?
5. What are different components of Capital Market?
6. What do you mean by Money Market?
7. What are the financial instruments available in money market?
8. What do you mean by call money? What are its features?
9. Discuss the nature of treasury bill market in India.
10. Write the structure of money market in India.
11. What is a commercial paper?

12. Write the functioning of money market mutual funds.
13. What is Certificate of Deposits?
14. Write an essay on recent developments in money market
15. What factors will determine the growth of the capital market in India
16. Write an essay on the structure of the capital market in India
17. Discuss the role of different players in capital market
18. What is stock exchange? What are its functions?
19. Discuss the organisation and management of stock exchanges in India?
20. Write an essay on the different types of members and operators in stock exchange?
21. What do you mean by listing of securities? Critically examine the procedure for listing of securities in India
22. Write an essay on the classification of listed securities in stock exchanges
23. What is a speculation? Explain different types of peculators in stock exchange?
24. What are the financial instruments available in the capital market?
25. Discuss the introduction of new financial instruments in the capital market.
26. Disucss the recommendations of Pherwani study group on new financial instruments in the capital market.
27. Describe the different components of capital market in India.
28. Write brief notes on the following;
    a) OTCEI
    b) N.S.E.
    c) Sensex
    d) Development banks
    e) Depositary system
    f) Derivatives
    g) GDRs/ADRs
29. What is Credit Rating? Explain the process of Credit Rating in India.

30. Discuss the role and functions of CRISIL, ICRA and CARE organisations in credit rating in India.
31. What is a merchant banking? How does it differ from commercial banking?
32. What is underwriting? Critically examine the under writing in India
33. Discuss the broker's role in stock market? How he can influence the prices of different scrips?
34. What is a badla? Do you think that banning of badla is justified?
35. What is margin trading? Explain the Margin Trading System in India.

* * *

Unit-III

1. *Securities Analysis*

1

SECURITIES ANALYSIS

INTRODUCTION

The aim of the security analysis is to find out intrinsic value of a security. The intrinsic value is also called as the real value of a security is the true economic worth of a financial asset. The real value of the security indicates whether the present market price is *over priced* or *under priced* in order to make a right investment decision. The actual price of the security is considered to be a function of a set of anticipated capitalisation rate. Price changes, as anticipation risk and return change, which in turn change as a result of *latest information.*

Security analysis refers to analysing the securities from the point of view of the scrip prices, return and risks. The analysis will help in understanding the behaviour of security prices in the market for investment decision making. If it is an analysis of securities and referred to as a macro analysis of the behaviour of the market. Security analysis entails in arriving at investment decisions after collection and analysis of the requisite relevant information. To find out intrinsic value of a security "the potential price of that security and the future stream of cash inflows are to be forecast and then discounted back to the present value." The intrinsic value of the security is to be compared with the current market price and a decision may be taken for buying or selling the security. If the intrinsic value is lower than the market price, then the security is in the over bought position, hence it is to be sold. On the other hand, if the intrinsic value is higher than the market price the security's worth is not fully recognised by the market and it is in under bought position, hence it is to be purchased to gain profit in the future.

The Fundamentalists attempts to assess the real worth of a security by analysing the un explored earning potential of a firm, which in turn will depend on investment environment factors such as *''State of economy, economic growth, monetary policies, corporate laws, social and political environment, firms competitiveness, its quality of management, operational efficiency, financial capabilities, market tactics, profitability, cost reduction programmes, capital structure and dividend policy etc.,* Fundamentalists *John Burr Williams, Meader, BenJamin Graham and David Dodd,* who have contributed this approach are of the opinion that importance should be given to *earnings, dividends, and asset value of enterprises.*

The efficient management of investments, security price and evaluation are actually based on the following schools of thought.

1. Fundamental Analysis
2. Technical Analysis
3. Efficient Market Theory/Hypothesis

FUNDAMENTAL ANALYSIS

The fundamental analysis allows for selection of securities of different sectors of the economy that appear to offer profitable opportunities. The security analysis will help to establish what type of investment should be undertaken among various alternatives *i.e., real estate, bonds, debentures, equity shares, fixed deposits, gold, jewellery etc.,* Neither all industries grow at same rate nor do all companies. The growth rate of a company depends basically on its ability to satisfy human desires through production of goods or performance is important to analyse the national economy. It is very important to predict the course of national economy because economic activity substantially affects corporate profits, investors attitudes, expectations and ultimately security prices. An outlook of slagging economic growth can lead to lower corporate profits, investor's pessimism and lower security prices. Some industries might be expected to perform better and their stock prices may not decline as much as securities in general. The analyst should note that overall economic activity manifests itself in the behaviour of stocks in general or the stock market in particular.

If the economy is *booming*, incomes are rising and the demand will rise then the industries and companies in general may prosper. The following factors are considered to be essential for the better performance of the corporate sector:

a) The behaviour of monsoon.

b) The performance of agriculture sector.

c) The economic system of the country.

d) Monetary Policy of the government

e) Trends in money supply

f) The business cycles.

g) The economic and political stability

There are different business cycles and causing for movements in the economy such as ''*Boom, Depression, Recession*'' *etc.*, The performance of the economy depends basically on the monsoon and the growth rate of agriculture. The most important factor is the ''*Fiscal Policy*'', which incorporates government expenditure, taxation, borrowing, deficit financing and which influences both public and private sector in the economy. the industrial growth in general and of infrastructural industries in particular influence the corporate performance.

The security analysis is to be made by the investor, before making an investment decision. Such analysis will be useful to identify the potential industry/company/type of investment in order to maximise the expected return and minimise the risk. For this purpose the investor has to scan thoroughly the investment climate. The total analysis of the investment environment can be grouped into the following three types viz.,

1. Economic Analysis
2. Industry Analysis
3. Company Analysis

The total analysis of investment is also called as "EIC" analysis and can be presented in a following diagramme;

Diagramme. III (1)

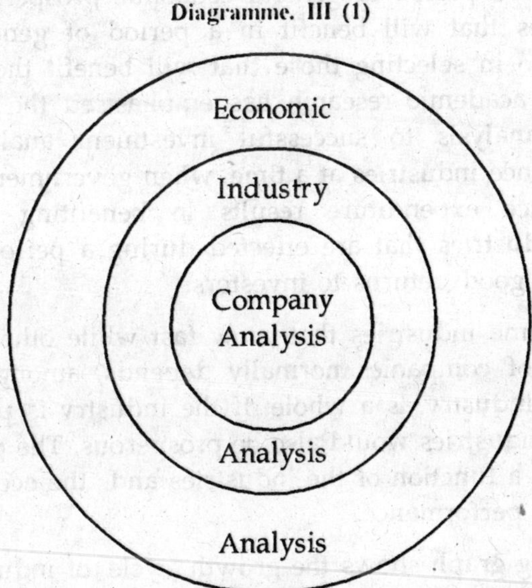

Now, let us discuss them in detail:

1. Economic Analysis

Investment climate in an economy can be observed from the *Gross National Product* and its components. The gross national product presents the aggregate amount of goods and services produced in the economy for a period of one year. Economists, Financial Analysts, Security Analysts, and investors deal in terms of the *GNP*. *GNP* is a measure of economic activity. If GNP grows, un employment rate relatively declines. An economic forecast would probably show increasingly high levels of expenditure on consumer durables, inventory, plant and equipment etc., as business appears to be buoyant and it is generally expected that such trend continues. Businessmen accumulate inventory in anticipation of further higher sales levels and they also increase their capacity through plant and equipment expenditure. At the same time, from the point of view as consumers, individual households experience a high level of personal discretionary income and they are free to spend some of their savings on residential housing, automobiles and other consumer durables. Indeed if prior economic periods had been far less booming than those just described expenditures on various durables having postponed would now become exaggerated.

It would be desirable at such a time to buy securities of firms in industries most likely to benefit from these patterns. The forecaster would arrive at specific estimates of the broad categories. It is easy to see how such an economic forecast can be helpful not only in selecting industries that will benefit in a period of general economic prosperity but also in selecting industries that will benefit in a period of general, economic prosperity but also in selecting those that will benefit the economy are expanding. Much academic research has emphasised the importance of sound industry analysis to successful investment analysis. *For ex:* investment in defence industries at a time, when government's thrust area is national defence expenditure results in benefiting the investors. Similarly food industries that are effected during a period of economic downsizing yields good returns to investors.

There are some industries that grow fast while others are decline. The performance of companies normally depends, among other things, upon the state of industry as a whole. If the industry is prosperous, the firms within that industries would also be prosperous. The performance of a company is thus a function of the industries and the economy, besides its own individual performance.

The following graph shows the growth cycle of industries;

Chart III (2)

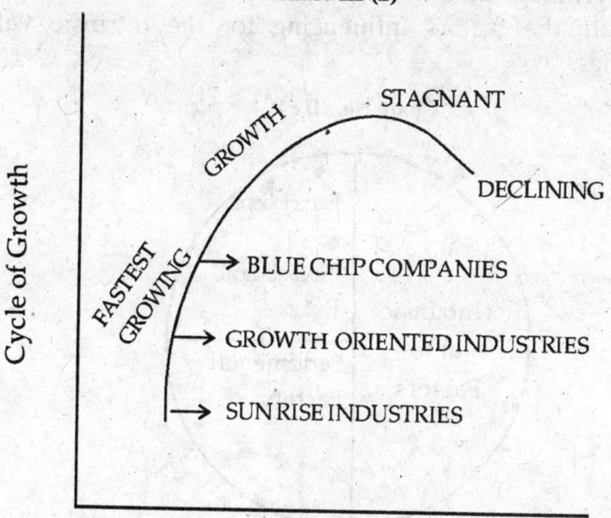

As referred earlier, the share price of the company is empirically found to depend up to 50% on the performance of the industry and economy. The economic and political situation in the country has thus a bearing on the prospects of the company. The industries in different stages of growth are shown below;

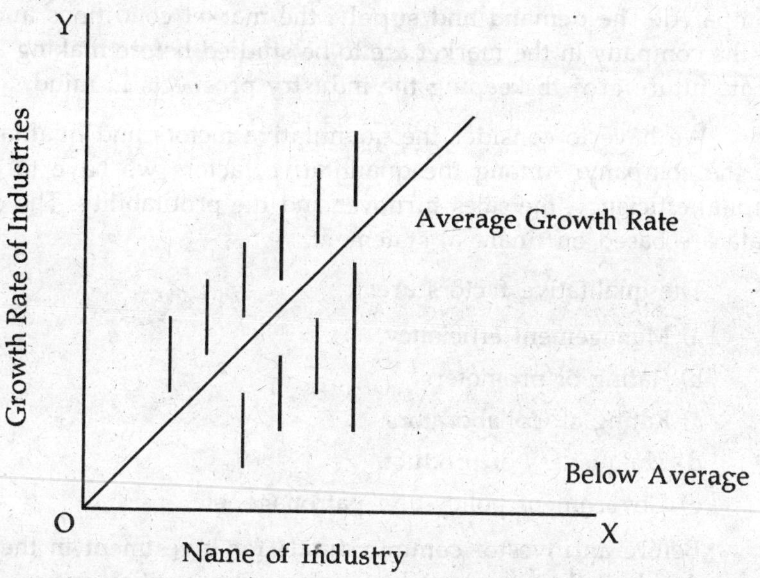

Even in the case of industries above average growth, there may be some companies of poor growth or no growth at all. The fundamental analysts of a company will explain, the market price (MP) is a function of intrinsic factors to the extent of about 50% and the rest is accounted by the expectations, psychological and sentimental factors. The following pie chart will indicate the factors influencing for the intrinsic value of a compay's securities.

Chart No. III (4)

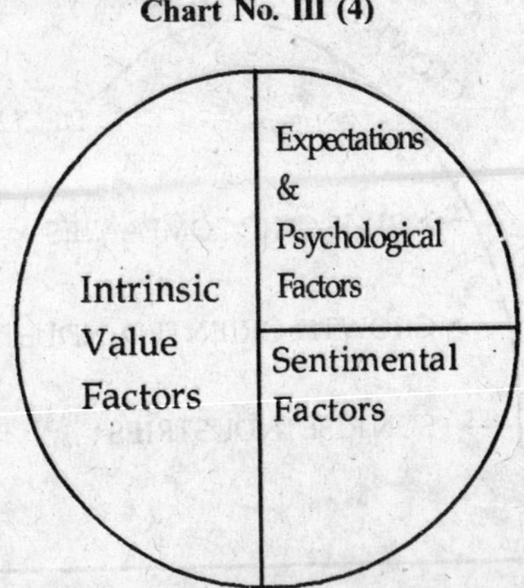

In the above context a particular industry can be studied with a view to assess the problems, prospects etc., of the company. The industry data are to be examined from the point of view of the product mix, raw material components, pricing, cost ot production etc., profit margins and related data of the company. The capacity utilisation of the industry in general and of the company in question within industry are to be compared. The demand and supply, the market conditions and the share of the company in the market are to be studied before making a projection of its future growth keeping the industry prospects in mind.

We have to consider the quantitative factors and qualitative factors of the company. Among the quantitative factors we have to analyse the capital efficiency, the sales turnover and the profitability. The quantitative data are based on financial statement.

The qualitative factors are:

a) Management efficiency.

b) Rating of promoters.

c) Rating of Collaborators.

d) Uniqueness of product.

e) Government policy and patronage, etc.,

Before an investor commits funds for investment in the market, he must decide if the time is right to invest in securities or not and if so, he must then decide which type of security is to be purchased under the circumstances. Thus, he must decide whether to purchase common stocks, options, preferred stocks, bonds, or some combination thereof. We will explore the relevance of broad economic variables such as national income and defence expenditure to the investor or analyst considering the purchase of common stocks. In the process, we will place major emphasis on the techniques most frequently employed by business economists as they go about their business of short-term economic forecasting. These are important for the security analyst or investor to know because he will be utilizing much of the output of-the economists' efforts as a basis for his own opinion about the impending economic environment. In this respect, the analyst can better evaluate economic forecasts if he has at least some knowledge of alternative economic forecasting tools-not only the techniques but also their advantages and short comings. For example: If an investor purchases the stock of an automobile manufacturing company that is selling near an all-time high, and shortly there after the automobile workers go on strike for a long period of time, the investor will surely suffer a large paper loss in his investment. Certainly, if the investor had waited until the strike was over other things being equal, his purchase price would have been considerably lower and his potential capital gains greatly enhanced. In analysing the economy, a careful analyst would have considered the potential impact of an impending automobile worker's strike.

However, there is yet another important reason for considering the economic environment before taking an investment action.

The matter of business forecasting is rather complex and quite specialised. As a result it is not likely that the security analyst or investor will be called upon to make his own complete forecast of the entire economy, or for that matter a complete forecast of any individual sector in the economy. Nonetheless, it will undoubtedly, be necessary for him to use, in his decision - making process concerning securities, economic forecasts or information that a business forecaster uses as a starting point; and thus, it is a prerequisite to knowledgeable and successful investing that he be able to understand and evaluate economic inputs and forecasts that are furnished to him.

ECONOMIC INDICATORS

Composite Index of Leading Indicators;

1. Average weekly hours of production of workers (manufacturing)
2. Average weekly initial claims for unemployment insurance.
3. Manufacturers new orders (Consumer goods and materials industries)
4. Vendor performance - slower deliveries diffusion index.
5. Contracts and orders for plant and equipment.

6. New-private housing units authorised.
7. Money supply (M_2)
8. Change in sensitive material prices
9. Stock prices of *500 common stocks*
10. Change in manufacturer's unfilled orders.
11. Index of consumer expectations.

Composite Index of Coincident Indicators

1. Employees payrolls of Non-Agricultural Sectors
2. Industrial production
3. Manufacturing and trade sales
4. Personal income less transfer payments

Composite Index of logging Indicators;

1. Average duration of unemployment
2. Ratio of trade inventories to sales.
3. Change in index of labour cost per unit of output
4. Commercial and industrial loans outstanding.
5. Average prime rate charged by banks
6. Rise of consumer installment credit outstanding to personal income.
7. Change in consumer price index for services.

Significance and Interpretation of the economic Indicators;

The investor makes an analysis of the economy primarily to determine an investment strategy. It is not necessary to make their own economic forecasts. The primary responsibility is to identify the trends in the economy and adjust the investment position accordingly. Many of the published forecasts are excellent and provide the necessary perspective.

Inflation will effect the real value of equity shares. Therefore, a real growth of GNP without inflation is always favourable and desirable. Higher rates of inflation is unfavourable for investment in both bonds and equities because which will bring down the real income for over of such investments.

Business investment is a key economic variable to watch. The expectation of an increase in business investment is an optimistic condition for the stock market and the economy.

The economy and market indicators are very useful to understand the situation of bullish or bearish indicator is in the economy and the stock market. A high level of construction activity is a good indicator of business conditions. A high level of automobile production and the expectation of growth are favourable indicators.

An increase in investment of inventories is good for the economy under conditions of inflation. But it also reflects that the accumulation of inventories is the economic slow down, which would be unfavourable. An increase in employment is favourable condition, whereas an increase in unemployment is unfavourable for the economy. An increase in personal income, coupled with substantial consumer confidence, is a favourable economic indicator. An increase in savings is a negative indicator in depress times, but positive under inflationary conditions. A deficit is positive for a depressed economy, but negative for an inflationary economy.

A high level of corporate profits and the expectation for increased corporate profits are favourable for the economy and the stock market. Generally, corporate profits are low when the GNP in real terms is low and vice versa.

A rising stock market suggests that the gloomy economy, a declining stock market suggests, the economy will not grow substantially in the year ahead.

An examination of these variables will give an investor a useful reference in interpreting the direction of the economy and the stock market. This, coupled with professional economic, opinion should lead to the establishment of a sound investment policy.

2. *INDUSTRY ANALYSIS*

The term industry is referred in a general way as a group of firms producing same product for the same market. Products of the firm cannot be termed same but have to be considered identical to constitute an industry. The term industry also refers to that part of business activity which concerns itself with the raising production, processing or fabrication of products. The products of an industry may be used either by the final consumers or by another industrial undertaking for further production. The industry may be defined as ''*a group of firms producing one type of product with slight differences but with greater scope for stabilisation*''. Firms which have a common bond like same type of inputs or the use of same processes of manufacturing also regarded as a single industry. The broad characteristic features of industry are given below;

a) Homogeneous Products

b) Common Raw Material

c) Processes of Production is similar

d) Similar Trade & Services.

The industries that contribute to the output of the major segments of the economy vary in their growth rate and in their overall contribution to economic activity. We can find successful companies in industries that are not growing. Investment success is more likely to be found in growing and strongly competitive industries.

The Industry Growth Cycle

An industry might be considered a community of interests. The growth of an industry usually begins with a major technological change. In recent years, Robots, personal computers, electronic equipment and communication devices, office equipment, automated control equipment have created new industries and rapid technological change, resulting in rapid industrial growth. As an industry expands, the following growth pattern emerges, according to *Simon Kunzets* in the beginning, rapid growth takes place at extremely high rates. As the industry expands over long period of time, the percentage rate of growth diminishes. Industries never experience, unrelated or accelerated growth for long periods of time. The growth of an industry depends upon industry's productivity. The productivity of an industry is an indicator of growth. The productivity naturally depends upon the extent of capacity utilisation of an industry. The importance of utilising the productive capacity created by investment can hardly be over emphasized. The extent of capacity utilisation is linked to efficient management and efficient use of resources. The industry's profitability depends on capacity utilisation. The volume of huge idle capacity in industries indicate, the extent to which the Indian economy is failing to use scarce resources. Therefore, full capacity utilisation has been one of the important objectives of industrial development in India. Growth industries are usually characterised by high rates of earnings. The growth of an industry is divided into 3 stages. The industry life cycle plays an important role in selecting a particular industry's scrip.

1. Pioneering Stage
2. Expansion Stage
3. Stagnation Stage

1. Pioneering Stage

The pioneering stage is mainly depends upon the technological development. The stage primary characteristics is rapid increase in

production and rapidly expanding demand for the product. Many companies enter the market to produce the product, and the market is extremely competitive. Profits are large for those firms that first introduce the product, but as competition increases, prices decline rapidly and profits fall. This tends to force out the less efficient firms. There is little price stability in the pioneering stage, and risk capital is supplied more by speculators and promoters than by investors, for the selection of the potential growth industry, its competitiveness with the other industries for its share of GNP, the stage of the industry and its stability of sales at the time of economic recession are the three important factors that need to be analysed. Demand for the firm's output can be anticipated to grow and even if more companies enter the market itself will permit the firm to maintain its profits in the face of increased competition. However, it is very difficult to identify such industries. At a point of time, one industry may be growth oriented but it may not be continuously in growth stage.

2. Expansion Stage

In this stage, the growth cycle is characterised by an expanding demand for the product, but the rate of growth is less than in pioneering stage. There is greater stability of prices, and production during this phase. Competition is keen, and a small number of larger firms dominate the industry.

3. The Stagnation Stage

In the later phase of the growth cycle of an industry, the rate of growth will slowdown. For some industries there is no growth at all in this phase, output actually declines. In this phase, the industry simply loses its power to expand. when the national economy shows economic strength, the growth of an industry in the stagnation stage does not keep pace, and its out put falls faster than the economy increases. The transition from the expansion to the stagnation stage comes about gradually to and unless investors are aware of the changes taking place in the industry, they will be taken by surprise.

Reasons for Decline in the Competitive Position of an Industry

In the stagnation stage, demand for the product is reduced by competition from other products or by factors that influence the profits of the industry by increasing costs. Grodinsky refers to these as factors of latent obsolescence that tend to destroy the competitive position of an industry. In this category increasing high labour costs, changes in social habits, changes in government regulations and improved technology or automation are included.

COMPANY ANALYSIS

The specific market and economic environment may enhance the performance of a company for a period of time, it is ultimately the firms own capabilities that will judge its performance over a long period of time. For this reason, the firms in the same industry are compared one another to ascertain which one is the best performer, i.e., which firm earns the most and out performs it competitors. The following chart shows the elements of the company analysis.

Chart No. III (5)

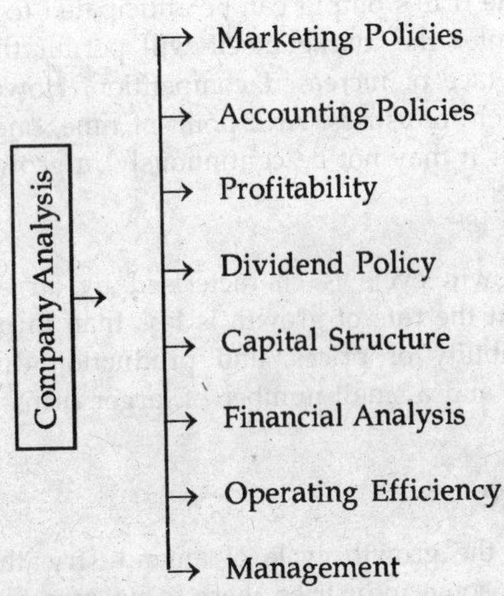

a) Marketing Polcies

This is the most important variable, it influences future earning in terms of both quality and quantity. This in turn is determined by the share of the company in the industry, growth of its sales strong competitive position will provide greater earnings, with more certainty than a company with a poor competitive position. The company with diversified activity should be competitive in all areas of its production sales with increased growth rate coupled with stability.

b) Accounting Policies

There is a risk of faulty interpretation of corporate earnings and consequently wrong judgement in purchasing, storing and selling stock. The accounting variations in reporting cost, expenses and extraordinary items could change earnings to a great extent, the accounting policies which will influence the following;

1. Inventory pricing
2. Depreciation methods
3. Non-operating income
4. Tax-carry overs

The inventory pricing method affects profitability and inventory costs. The depreciation for wear and tear of the machinery and other assets will reduce the value of assets and treated as fixed expense. Higher depreciation will reduce income and under value the fixed assets of the firm. While analysing the company's profitability non-operating income must also taken into consideration. The incidence of corporate tax and tax carryovers should also be analysed and taken into account.

c) Profitability

When we buy a security we are buying the right to future earnings. We are interested in income stability and growth of these earnings. To study the relationship between expenses and sales one needs to study the trends of the profitability ratios; namely, gross profit margin, net profit margin, earning power return on equity and earning per share.

1. Gross profit margin = Gross profit/Net sales
2. Net profit margin = Net profit/Net sales
3. Earning capability = EBIT/ Net total assets
4. Return on equity = Profits after tax/Net worth
5. Earning per share = Profit after tax/No. of equity shares
6. Cash earning per share = Cash earnings/No. of equity shares.

d) Dividend Policy

It is observed that the management tries to maintain a stable dividend policy with increased dividends. This can possible only when the company expects increased rate of earnings in the future.

e) Capital Structure

Return on the equity holder's investment can be magnified by using financial leverage, i.e., use of debt financing along with equity, instead of using equity financing only.

The mixing of fixed cost of funds such as debt and preference capital will maximise the earnings available to equity share holders.

f) Financial Analysis

It is the process of analysing the financial strengths and weaknesses of a company through various techniques of analysis. Financial analysis can be classified into two different categories based on the following;

a) The materials used.

b) The modus operandi of analysis.

On the basis of materials used

According to this method financial analysis can be of two types:

1. External Analysis
2. Internal Analysis

1. External Analysis

This analysis is done by out siders of the company. The term out siders includes *investors, credit rating agencies, governmental agencies, stock brokers, equity analysts etc.*, the position of these analyses have improved in recent times on account of increased governmental regulations requiring more disclosur norms of information for their financial statements. The out siders have no access to the internal records of the company.

2. Internal Analysis

This analysis is done by persons who have access to the books of account and other information related to the business. This analysis is done by *executives and employees* of the organisation or by officers appointed for this purpose by the government or the court under powers vested with them. The analysis is done depending upon the objective of the analysis.

On the basis of Modus Operandi

According to this classification financial analysis can also be divided into two types:

a) Horizontal Analysis

b) Vertical Analysis

a) Horizontal Analysis

In this type of analysis, financial statements for a number of years are reviewed and analysed. The current year's data is compared with the standard or base year. The statement contains data for *two or more* years and the changes are shown regarding each item from the base year in the form of *percentage*. This analysis gives a clear picture about the *strength and weaknesses* of the company. This analysis is also called as *''Dynamic*

Analysis". This analysis is based on the data from year to year rather than on any particular date.

b) Vertical Analysis

This analysis, is made to study the *quantitative relationship* of the various items in the financial statements on a particular date. *For ex:* the ratio's of different items of costs for a particular period may be calculated with the sales for that period.

This analysis is useful in comparing the performance of several companies in the same group or divisions or departments in the same company. Since this analysis depends on the data for a period, this is not very conductive to a proper analysis of the company's financial position. It is also called as *''Static Analysis"*. It is frequently used for referring to ratios developed on one particular date or for one accounting period. A financial analyst can adopt one or more of the following techniques/tools of financial analysis:

a) Comparative analysis

b) Common size analysis

c) Ratio analysis

a) Comparative Analysis

Comparative financial statements analysis is designed in such a way so as to provide time perspective to the consideration of various elements of financial position. In this analysis figures for two or more periods are taken to facilitate a meaningful comparison. In this analysis both income statement and balance sheet will be prepared.

b) Common Size Analysis

In common size analysis the figures reported in the financial statements are converted into percentages to some common base. The comparative common size financial statement shows the percentage of each item to the total.

c) Ratio Analysis

This is the most important tool available to financial analysts for their analysis. An accounting ratio is the relationship in mathematical terms between two inter related accounting figures.

g) Operating Efficiency

The operating efficiency is directly influencing the profitability of the company. A company with the *stable operating efficiency* will have more stable *revenues*. The efficiency in the operations can be achieved through efficient use of capital assets combined with raw material, labour and *other costs*. The following elements have the impact on company's profitability;

a) Profit margin rate and

b) Assets turnover

h) Management

The company's capabilities will depend on the efficiency of the management. The functions of management are to plan, organise, direct, control and coordinate the activities of the company to accomplish stated *objectives* by the use of human and other resources. The successful management should possess the following traits;

i) Intelligence,

ii) Initiative,

iii) Energy or drive,

iv) Emotional maturity,

v) Persuasive,

vi) Communicative skill,

vii) Self-assurance,

viii) Perception,

ix) Creativity and

x) Social participation.

The ability of the management is to be judged on the basis of the post record of the management in terms of the following abilities;

i) Ability to maintain the competitiveness of the firm.

ii) Ability to expand the firm.

iii) Ability of maintaining profit margins by controlling costs.

iv) Ability to maintain efficient production by proper utilisation of plant and machinery and by suitable inventory management, planning and scheduling.

v) Ability to finance the company adequately for execution of its expansion plans.

vi) Ability to work with employees and union.

ANALYSIS OF FINANCIAL POSITION

The following financial parameters can be used for judging the company's performance.

Financial Ratios	*Significance*
Equity to Networth	Share of equity to the owners funds.
Equity to capital employed	Share of equity funds in total assets financing
Equity to sales	Capital use/equity turnover
Rights and Bonus	Expansion prospects
Market price to book value	Over/under valuation
Market price to earning per share	Over/under valuation
Price/Earnings multiple	Comparison with industry average
Gross profit margin and net profit margin	Profitability of sales
Return on investment	Ability of company to generate profits
Dividend pay-out ratio	The share of distribution of after tax profits as dividends

Tips for Selecting a Growth Share

A growth share is the share of a company whose sales and profits are increasing rapidly. Important characteristics of a growth company are as follows:

- A rising trend in sales, profits and earnings.
- Growth in share holders funds.
- Frequent and generous bonus issues.
- High ratios of earnings to equity and returns on capital employed.
- Successful research and product development.
- Enjoys a distinct advantage over other competitors.
- Has a diversified business.
- A high dividend coverage.

The following points can be used to select the growth share;

1. Experienced and dynamic management.
2. Market share of the company must be at least 1/3rd.

3. The company must be in diversification.
4. The company must be in expansion stage.
5. The company must have a good earning capability.
6. The company must maintain good relations with investors.
7. High operating efficiency.
8. The company has to adopt scientific management techniques to cut down avoidable costs.
9. Ability of the management to maintain harmony with the government.
10. Innovation, research and development activities are given due weightage to maintain technical competence.
11. The management should lay right emphasis on training and development including development of its executives.
12. Ability of management to maintain harmonious relations with its customers and community.

Measuring Earnings

The most immediately recognisable effect of economic and industry influences on a specific company is probably the impact on revenues. the sales of some industries tend to more positive with the business cycle; others are relatively immune to the cycle; still other (such as housing) move counter cyclically. From the view point of the individual company, adjustments to changes in the general business cycle can be different from those of the industry in general. Product mix and pricing peculiar to specific firms can cause total revenues to respond more or less to broad economic and industry impact. Diversified product lines, for example, allow a company to spread cyclical effects.

Variety of information will influence the investment decisions. Investors need to know the characteristics of various investment alternatives and must keep informed on the institutions and markets where they are available. Up-to-date information is required on the status of and trends in the economy, particular industries, and firms.

Financial Statements

Three major financial statements are essential to provide financial information relating to the various financial aspects of a company. The statement of income and retained earnings, the balance sheet, and the statement of cash flows. Accompanying notes to these statements are also crucial and are less important that the statements themselves.

Income-Statement Format

The Accounting Principles Board (APB) has suggested a format for a statement of income, and a statement of retained earnings. The statement of retained earnings bridges the gap between the income statement and the position statement (balance sheet), in the sense that the net income on the income statement is reflected in the retained - earnings part of the stock holder's equity on the balance sheet. The usual changes in retained earnings are the net income or loss for the period, dividends declared and corrections of net income for prior periods.

The income statement is a key financial statement through which an analysts get insight into the managements performance. It is used perhaps more than any other statement in attempting to assess the future earnings. Past earnings reported in the income statement are very often used as a base for predicting future earnings. Thus a major job for the analyst is to probe important areas of the income-statement to assess their impact on earnings.

COMPARATIVE STATEMENT OF INCOME AND RETAINED EARNINGS

STATEMENT OF INCOME
for the Years Ended March. 31, 2001 and March. 31, 2002
(2001-2002)

Net sales (net of trade discounts, returns, and allowances)		x x x
Add: Other income (e.g., rents, interest, dividends, royalties)		x x x
Less: Costs and expenses:		x x x
Costs of goods sold (cost of merchandise sold during the period)	x x	
Less: Selling expenses (creating sales, storing goods and delivery, including depreciation)	x x x	
Administration and general expenses. (administering overall activities, including depreciation)	x x x	
Financial charges. (Interest on borrowed money)	x x x	
Other deductions (items extraneous to primary operations)	x x x	
Income tax (federal, state and local)	x x x	
Income before extra ordinary items.		x x x
Extra ordinary items, less applicable income tax (per share: 2K1 and 2K2)		x x x
Casually, nonrecurring and not related to primary operating activity of the business)		x x x
Net income (per share: 2K1 and 2K2)		x x x

STATEMENT OF RETAINED EARNINGS
Years Ended March. 31, 2001 and March. 31, 2002
(2001-2002)

Retained earning at the beginning of the year:	x x x
Adjustments (corrections of income reported in prior periods; e.g., settlements of law and tax suits, and for carelessness or imprudence involving assets at the end of earlier periods)	x x x
	x x x
As restated.	x x x
Net income (last line of statement of income)	x x x
Cash dividends on common and preferred stock (shown separately)	x x x
Retained earnings at end of year.	x x x

Calculation of Earning per share

	Sales	x x x
(-)	Variable Cost	x x
	Contribution	x x x
(-)	Fixed cost	x x
	Operating profit	x x x
(-)	Interest charges	x
	Profit before tax (PBT)	x x x
(-)	Income tax	x x
	Profit after tax	x x x
(-)	Preference Dividend	x x
	Earnings available to Equity share holders.	x x x

$$EPS = \frac{\text{Earnings available to equity shareholders}}{\text{Number of Equity Shares}}$$

A textile company has operating profit of Rs.1,60,000. Its capital structure consists of the following securities;

a) 10% Debentures Rs.5,00,000

b) 12% Preference shares Rs.1,00,000

c) Equity shares of Rs.100. Rs.4,00,000

d) The company is in 55% Tax bracket

You are required to find out the following:

1. EPS
2. The percent change in EPS associated with 30% increase or 30% decrease in EBIT.

Solution:

Particulars	*Amount (Rs.)*
Operating Profit	1,60,000
(-) 10% Interest	50,000
Profit Before Tax	1,10,000
(-) Income Tax (55%)	60,500
PAT	49,500
(-) Preference Dividend	12,000
Earnings available to equity Shareholders	37,500

$$EPS = \frac{\text{Earnings available to equity shareholders}}{\text{Number of equity shares}}$$

$$EPS = \frac{Rs.37,500}{Rs.4,000} = \boxed{Rs.9.37}$$

Working Notes:

a) 30% increase in EBIT =

$$= 30\% \text{ of } 1,60,000 = Rs.1,60,000 \times \frac{30}{100} = 48,000$$

$$EBIT = 1,60,000 + 48,000 = Rs.2,08,000$$

b) 30% decrease in EBIT =

$$= 30\% \text{ of } 1,60,000 = Rs.1,60,000 \times \frac{30}{100} = 48,000$$

$$EBIT = 1,60,000 - 48,000 = Rs.1,12,000.$$

B. Calculation of percentage change in EPS at 30% increase in EBIT.

Particulars	*Amount (Rs.)*
Operating Profit + EBIT	2,08,000
(-) 10% Interest	50,000
Profit Before Tax	1,58,000
(-) Income Tax (55%)	86,900
PAT	71,100
(-) Preference Dividend	12,000
Earnings available to equity Shareholders	59,100

$$EPS = \frac{\text{Earnings available to equity shareholders}}{\text{Number of equity shares}}$$

$$EPS = \frac{Rs.59,100}{Rs.4,000} = \boxed{Rs.14.78}$$

C. Calculation of percentage change in EPS at 30% decrease in EBIT.

Particulars	*Amount (Rs.)*
Operating Profit + EBIT	1,12,000
(-) 10% Interest (Debt.)	50,000
Profit Before Tax	62,000
(-) Income Tax (55%)	34,100
PAT	27,900
(-) Preference Dividend	12,000
Earnings available to equity Shareholders	15,900

$$EPS = \frac{\text{Earnings available to equity shareholders}}{\text{Number of equity shares}}$$

$$EPS = \frac{Rs.15,900}{Rs.4,000} = \boxed{Rs.3.97}$$

CASH FLOW ANALYSIS

Cash flow analysis is another important technique of financial analysis. It involves preparation of cash flow statement by identifying sources and applications of cash. Cash flow statement may be prepared on the basis of actual or estimated cash flows.

Meaning of Cashflow Statement

The cash is a broad term. It includes, cash, cheques, bank balances etc., A cash flow statement is a statement depicting change in cash position from one period to another. The cash flow statement explains the reasons for such inflows or outflows of cash, as the case may be. It also helps management in making plans for the immideate future. A projected cash flow statement or a cash budjet will help the management in ascertaining how much cash will be available to meet obligations of trade creditors payment of bank loans and dividend to the shareholders. A proper planning of the cash resources will enable management to have cash availability when ever needed and put it to some profitable or productive use if there is surplus cash.

Preparation of Cashflow Statement

Cash flow statement can be prepared by taking into consideration of various items. The following steps may be applied for calculation of cash flow analysis.

Step:	1)	Take the latest year's profit.		x x x
	2)	Add any changes in current.		x x x
		Assets variables (Decreases) to given profit.		x x x
	3)	Add any changes in current.		x x x
		liabilities variable (Increases) to given profit.		x x x
	4)	Substract from given profit for any change incurrent assets variables (Increase).	x x x	
	5)	Substract from given profit for any change incurrent liabilities variables (Decrease).	x x x	x x x
	6)	After making additions and substractions we can found cash from operations.		x x x
	7)	Cash from operations will be one of the sources of element for cash flow statement.		
	8)	Take opening cash balance for preparation of cash flow statement.		
	9)	Add all the sources of cash inflows to the opening cash balance.		
	10)	Substract the application of cash outflows to the opening cash balance.		
	11)	After making all adjustment we may find the closing cash balance.		

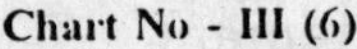

Chart No - III (6)

SOURCES OF CASH

1. Internal Sources

a) Depreciation on various assets

b) Ammortisation of intangible assets

c) Sale of fixed assets

d) Gains from sale of fixed assets

e) Creation of Reserves.

2. External Sources

a) Issue of new shares

b) Raising long-term loans

c) Short-term borrowings

For the sake of conveneince computation of cash from operations can be studied by taking two different situations.

When transactions are cash transactions.

When transactions are not cash transactions.

+ Increase in outstanding expenses.

+ Increase in Income received in advance.

Cash from Operations = Net Profit

(-) Decrease in outstanding expenses.

(-) Decrease in income received in advance.

Cash from Operations = Net Profit

+ Decrease in Debtors

+ Decrease in stock

+ Decrease in prepaid exp

+ Decrease in Accrued income

+ Increase in creditors

+ Increase in outstanding expenses.

- Increase in Debtors

- Increase in Stock

- Increase in prepaid exp

- Increase in accrued income

- Decrease in creditors

USES OF CASH

Application of Cash

Application of cash may take any of the following forms:

i) Purchase of fixed assets.

ii) Payment of long-term loans.

iii) Decrease in deferred payment liabilities.

iv) Loss on account of business operations.

v) Payment of tax.

vi) Payment of dividend.

vii) Decrease in unsecured loans, deposits etc.,

i) **Purchase of fixed assets:** Cash may be utilised for additional fixed assets or renewal or replacement of existing fixed assets.

ii) **Payment of long-term loans:** The payment of long-term loans such as loans from financial institutions or debentures results in decrease in cash. It is therefore, an application of cash.

iii) **Decrease in deferred payment liabilities:** Payments for plant and machinery purchased on deferred payment basis has to be made as per the agreement. It is there fore, an application of cash.

iv) **Loss on account of business operations:** Loss suffered on account of business operations will result in outflow of cash.

v) **Payment of tax:** Payment of tax will result in decrease of cash and hence, it is an application of cash.

vi) **Payment of dividend:** This decreases the cash balances for business and hence, it is an application of cash.

vii) **Decrease in unsecured loans, deposits etc:** Decrease in these liabilities denotes that they have been paid off to that extent. It results, in outflow of cash.

CASH FLOW STATEMENT

Opening balance on 1-1-2001

	Cash balance	....
	Bank balance	....
Add:	Sources of cash	....
	Issue of shares	....
	Raising of long-term loans	....
	Sale of fixed assets	....
	Short term borrowings	....
	Cash from operations	....
	Profit as per profit and loss account	....
Add/Less:	Adjustment for non-cash items;	....
Add:	Increase in current liabilities	....
	Decrease in current assets	....
Less:	Increase in current assets	....
	Decrease in current liabilities	....
	Total cash available (I)	....
Less:	Applications of cash	
	a) Redemption of redeemable preference shares	....
	b) Redemption of long-term loans	....
	c) Purchase of fixed assets	....
	d) Decrease in deferred payment liabilities	....
	e) Cash flow on account of operations	....
	f) Tax paid	....
	g) Dividend paid	....
	h) Decrease in unsecured loans, deposits etc.,	....
	Total application	....
	Closing balances on 1-1-2002	
	Cash balance	....
	Bank balance	....
		....

Utility of Cash Flow Analysis

A cash flow statement is useful for short-term planning. A business enterprise needs sufficient cash to meet its various obligations in the future, such as payment for purchase of fixed assets payment of debt, maturing, expenses of the business, etc., A statistical analysis of the different sources and applications of cash will enable the management to make reliable cash flow projections for the immediate future. If there is a surplus cash it can be used for investment or if it is deficit it can be recouped. A cash flow analysis is an important financial tool for the management. The advantages of cash flow-statements are given below;

1. Helps in efficient cash management.
2. Helps in cash control.
3. Discloses the movement of cash.
4. Indicates success or failure of cash planning.

Illustration: From the following balances you are required to calculate cash from operations:

	31-3-2001	*31-3-2002*
Debtors	Rs.50,000	Rs.47,000
Bills receivable	10,000	12,500
Creditors	20,000	25,000
Bills payble	8,000	6,000
Outstanding expenses	1,000	1,200
Prepaid expenses	800	700
Accured income	600	750
Income recieved in advance	300	250
Profit made during the year	---	1,30,000

Solution:

Cash from Operations

Profit for the year 2002			Rs.1,30,000
Add: Decrease in debtors		Rs.3,000	
Increase in creditors		Rs.5,000	
Increase in outstanding expenses		Rs. 200	
Decrease in prepaid exp.		Rs.100	8,300
			Rs.1,38,300
Less: Increase in B/R	Rs.2,500		
Decrease in B/P	Rs.2,000		
Increase in income received in advance	Rs.50		
Increase in accrued income	Rs. 150		Rs. 4,700
Cash from Operations			Rs.1,33,600

Factors Affecting Market Price

Some times the market price of a share may fluctuate widely because of seemingly unrelated factors. The every-day price of an equity share is subject to the influence of a statement of factors. When the share market is sensitive, such factors, together go to determine the price of a particular equity share. These may be listed as follows:

Factors

A) VIs-a-Vis the company.

B) Vis-a-vis industry.

C) Determinants of the market sentiments.

A) Factors vis-a-Vis the Company

★ The general frame work of the company: Whether it is a well established with adequate installed capacity, and its capacity utilisation against the industry norm etc.,

★ The quality of its management.

★ The market share of its product.

★ The present and future competition.

★ Its foreign tie-ups, if any

★ The diversified product range of a company would not be affected much to the recession in a particular class of industry.

★ The demand for the products of the company.

★ The financial ratios of the company like **EPS, PE Ratio etc.,**

★ The reserves held by the company.

★ The dividend policy of the company.

★ The raw materials required by the company and their availability and cost.

★ The availability of power.

★ The Research & Development efforts made by the company.

★ Industrial and labour relations.

★ New projects anvil, if any and plans for future growth and expansion.

★ Modernisation and technology upgradation.

★ The pattern of share holding. If majority of the shares of a company are held by the owners of the company, then few shares would be available in the market and causes for rise in the price of the share when a company performs well.

★ Take over threats against the company, if any

B. FACTORS Vis-a-Vis Industry

★ The strengths and weakness of the industry to which the company belongs.

★ The opportunities for and threats against the industry to which the company belongs.

★ The total licensed and installed capacities of the industry.

★ The total present and the expected future demand for the products of the industry.

★ The policies of the Government regarding the industry.

★ Price controls if any, for the products of the industry.

C. Determinants of the market sentiments

The following factors will determine the market sentiments:

★ The Political environment.

★ The Economic climate.

★ The Fiscal Policy of the Govt.

★ The Global environment.

★ The Technological environment.

★ Industrial support.

★ War and Natural Calamities.

★ The Effect of other Stock Exchanges.

Guidelines for Better Investment

Guidlines to investors;

The following guidelines are helpful for maximising expected return and minimising risk of investment by the investors;

1. Increase in investment can be made only in the case of profit making companies.
2. Always define the limits of loss and target profit.

3. One has to admit his past mistakes and make revisions in the portfolio after a careful review.

4. Every investor should expect the reasonable appreciation in the price of a scrip that he expects.

5. Buy shares of reputed companies backed by *Top Class Management.*

6. Every investor should pursue a policy of *dversification* and consolidation of his portfolio with reference to the relevant data.

7. In the stock market an investor with patience, usually makes handsome *profits.*

8. An investor should normally *sell* the shares of a particular company, if its market price does not *react* to good news

9. Every investor should exercise a policy of phased accumulation and disinvestment when the share price of a company is about to decline.

10. An investor expects appreciation in value of the investment based on the fundamental analysis, and he should purchase shares in small lots and reduce nis average purchase price when the prices are falling. If his prediction proves accurate, the price of the share would soon start raising this would result in a good returns.

11. If the share price *moves up* and croses the level estimated by the investor, he should sell a part of his holdings and book profits or reduce the average purchase price.

12. *Do a careful risk* - reward analysis. Buy shares when you estimate a substantial rise in prices, with a relatively low risk of fall in prices due to *unforeseen developments.*

13. Always invest in shares of a company whose share prices rise in a falling market, such shares demonstrate a high inherent strength.

14. Share prices should be carefuly judged by estimating their *potential value.*

15. If an investor receives a *tip* for a particular industry he should invest in a company which got good prospects in that sector.

16. Do not invest in ''*inactive*'' shares, generally it is difficult to encash them.

17. Do not increase investment of funds in the loss making companies and need to revise such investment by adopting the diversification of porfolio.

18. Do not keep more than 12 *companies* shares in a portfolio.

19. Do not keep *odd lots.*
20. Do not wait for the *peak/bottom* prices in the share market for sell or buy decision.
21. Do not make a decision solely on the tips of information.
22. Do not go against the *trend* in respect of growth shares.
23. Do not buy shares at high prices when the market is *bullish.*
24. Do not invest in shares of companies bringing in *unknown* products or technology.
25. Do not invest in shares of companies with *chronic labour problems.*
26. Do not invest in *unlisted shares* or shares of closely held companies.

Selecting the Growth oriented industries:

An investor can identify the growth potential of an industry by analysing the following factors.

1. Statistical analysis of past performance.
2. Assesement of the intrinsic value of the company and an industry.
   a) Demand/supply position of the industry.
   b) Profitability.
   c) Development of new products.
   d) Nature of industry.
   e) Evaluation of management expertise.

REVIEW PROBLEMS

Illustration No.1: A company's dividend is to grow at 0.28 for the first two years and 0.18 for the following 3 years and to level off at 0.09 there after. The required rate of return is 0.12. The company currently pay, a dividend of Rs.1.50 per share. Determine the fundamental value of the share of the company.

Solution:

Fundametal Value of a Share

Year	Previous dividend	Growth rate	projected dividend •	Present value Factor 12%	Present value
(1)	(2)	(3)		(5)	4×5=(6)
1	1.50	0.28	1.92	0.893	1.714
2	1.92	0.28	2.45	0.797	1.952
3	2.45	0.18	2.89	0.712	2.057
4	2.89	0.18	3.41	0.636	2.168
5	3.41	0.18	4.02	0.567	2.279
Price based on projected years dividend (134)•					10.170 Value of Stock

$$\text{Present Value of Equity} = \frac{\text{projected dividend for year 5}}{(\text{Required rate of return - level of risk})}$$

** Dividend for year 5 + growth rate of dividend @18%

= 3.41+0.61= 4.02

* Projected dividend = Dividend for year 1 + growth rate of dividend

$= 1.50 + 1.50 \times 0.28 = 1.50 + 0.42 = 1.92$

Current year projected dividend = 4.02

Required rate of return = 0.12

Level off risk = 0.09

$$PV_e = \frac{4.02}{(0.12 - 0.09)}$$

$$= \frac{4.02}{0.03} = 134^{\bullet}$$

Illustration No.2: The following data is related to the projections of a company with regard to dividends. The company expects that the dividends to grow at a 0.25 rate for the next two years and 0.16 for the following three years and to level off at 0.08 there after. Required rate of return is 0.14. The company currently pays a dividend of Rs.2.00 per share. What is the fundamental value of the share?

Solution:

Fundamental Value of a Share;

Year	Previous dividend	Growth rate	Projected dividend	Present value Factor @14%	Present value
(1)	(2)	(3)		(5)	4×5=(6)
1.	2.00	0.25	2.50	0.877	2.1925
2.	2.50	0.25	3.13	0.769	2.4069
3.	3.13	0.16	3.62	0.675	2.4435
4.	3.62	0.16	4.19	0.592	2.4804
5.	4.19	0.16	4.86	0.519	2.525
Present value of stock					12.04564

Price based on projected current year dividend.

$$\text{Present Value of Equity} = \frac{\text{Currentyear projected dividend}}{\text{(Required rate of return - level of risk)}}$$

Current year projected dividend = 4.86
Required rate of return = 0.14
Level off risk = 0.08

$$PV_e = \frac{4.86}{(0.14-0.08)}$$

$$= \frac{4.86}{0.06} = \boxed{\text{Rs.81.0}^\bullet}$$

Illustration No.3: Mr. Agarwal bought 100 shares of VXL ltd. at Rs.125 per share. He held the shares for 3 years and sold at Rs.180 per share. The company paid Rs.1.50 dividend per share in each of the 3 years. What is the total return earned from this investment?

Solution:

Applying the approximation method

$$\text{Rate of Return} = \frac{\text{Average Annual Income}}{\text{Average investments}}$$

$\therefore$ Average Annual Income = $\dfrac{\text{Capital gains + Annual dividend for 3 years}}{2}$

Capital gains = Sale price - Purchase price

= 180 - 125 = Rs.55

Dividend per share = Rs.1.50 for 3 years Rs.4.50

$\therefore$ AAI = $\dfrac{\text{Rs.55} + \text{Rs.4.50}}{2} = \dfrac{59.5}{2}$ = Rs.19.83

Average investment = $\dfrac{125+180}{2}$ =Rs.152.50

AAI = Rs. 19.83 = $\boxed{\text{Rs.19.83}}$ = 0.13 or Say 13%

AI = Rs.152.50

Rate of Return = $\dfrac{\text{AAI}}{\text{AI}} = \dfrac{19.83}{152.50}$

Illustration No.4: Mr. suresh bought 100 shares of ABC Ltd., at Rs.140 per share. He holds the shares for 3 years and sold at Rs.220 per share. The company paid Rs.3.00 dividend per share in each of the 3 years. What total return did Suresh earn from his investment?

Solution:

Applying the approximate method

Average Investment = $\left(\dfrac{140+220}{2}\right)$

= $\dfrac{360}{2}$ =Rs.180

Rate of Return = $\dfrac{\text{Average Annual Income}}{\text{Average Investments}}$

Average Annual Income = $\dfrac{80}{3}$ +3 = Rs.29.66

Average investment = 180.

$\therefore$ Rate of Return = $\dfrac{29.66}{180}$ =0.1647 or 16.4%

Total Return to Suresh is 16.4%

Illustration No.5: Given below are the basic data relating to seven scrips listed in the stock Exchange. You are required to construct a portfolio with four scrips for a total invesmtent of Rs.1.00 lakh explain the reasons for your selection.

SCRIPS PARTICULARS

Particulars	M	N	O	P	Q	R	S
1.Back ground	60 year good track record	100 year good track record	60% good track record	20% good track record	30% good track record	55% good track record	80% good track record
2.Industry	Power	Textile	Personal care	Fertilisers	Food products	Chemicals	diversi fied
face value	Rs. 10	Rs. 10	Rs. 10	Rs. 10	Rs. 10	Rs. 10	Rs. 10
current market Price	192	125	229	15	235	203	256
EPs for 99-2000	13	27	5	5	6	12	8
EPs for 2000-01	12.75	30	5.60	75	9	2	3
EPs for 99-2000	2.70	5.60	7.70	2	5.60	7	6
EPs for 2000-01	2.80	5.60	5	2	7	7	3
High value in 52 weeks	230	380	320	30	440	310	340
PE ratio	16	4	52	2	46	12	28
Sensitive to Government	High	High	Medium	High	Medium	High	Medium
Market Lot (No.of shares)	100	100	100	100	100	100	100

Solution:

From the above data we have to select a portfolio of four scrips out of the seven. The total funds available for investment are Rs.1 lack. The selection of four scrips based on the following.

a) Current trends in the industry.

b) Earnings yields.

c) Dividend yields.

d) Potential for capital appreciation.

The reason for using earning yields as a decision criteria, instead of EPs is that, EPs does not recognise the effect of increase in equity capital as a result of retention of earnings.

Company	Industry	EPs Rank	DPS Rank	PE Ratio	D/P Ratio	Rank
P	Fertilisers	5	6	1	28.57	5
Q	Food products	4	1	6	77.77	3
R	Chemical	2	1	3	31.81	4
S	Diversified	7	4	5	100	1
M	Power	3	5	4	21.96	6
N	Textiles	1	2	2	18.66	7
O	Personal care	6	3	7	89.28	2

Illustration No.6: Given below are the financial data relating to two scrips in the steel industry with a paid - up value of Rs.10 per share. Based on the data presented, indentify the scrip you would select by giving reasons.

Year	1997 Company		1998 Company		1999 Company		2000 Company		2001 Company	
Particulars	M	N	M	N	M	N	M	N	M	N
	Rs.		Rs.		Rs.		Rs.		Rs.	
Face value	10	10	10	10	10	10	10	10	10	10
Book value	15.20	26.35	17.70	29	19.99	36.80	23.30	41.10	25.10	47.25
EPs	2.85	2.30	5.52	2.98	5.90	8.98	8.12	6.96	6.34	9.20
Dividend per share	2.50	1.00	3.00	2.00	4.00	3.00	3.50	2.00	4.00	3.50

Solution: Paid up value of both scrips is Rs.10 per share. it is assumed that investors are rational and risk averse. They prefer the security that provides the highest return for a given level of risk and they want risk premium for given additional risk. In the question, we are given with the data related to return to the equity holders which is reflected by earning per share (EPs). Therefore for the given level of return what is the scrip that would be preferred or risk. Let us first calculate the risk of two securities based on EPs.

Let x be the stream of earnings per share **(EPs)** generated by company M. Let y be the stream of earnings per share (EPs) generated by company N. Calculation of Risk (σ).

Year	x	y	x	x^2	y	y^2
1997	2.85	2.30	-2.896	8.352	-3.784	14.318
1998	5.52	2.98	-0.226	0.051	-3.104	9.634
1999	5.90	8.98	0.154	0.023	2.896	8.384
2000	8.12	6.96	2.374	5.635	0.876	0.767
2001	6.34	9.20	0.594	0.3528	3.116	9.709
	28.73	30.42	0	14.4138	0.000	42.814

Mean value of EPS for Scrip $(\overline{x}) = \dfrac{\sum x}{N}$

$\sum x$ = Rs. 28.73

N = 5

$$\overline{x} = \frac{28.73}{5}$$

= Rs.5.746

Mean value of EPs for scrip N $= \dfrac{\sum y}{N}$

$\sum y$ = Rs. 30.42

N = 5

$$\overline{x} = \frac{30.42}{5}$$

= Rs.0.084

The risk of a security with regards to its earnings can be quantified and measured. It can be symbolically presented by "σ" (Sigma).

Standard deviation of scrip M:

$$\sigma_x = \sqrt{\frac{\sum x^2}{N}}$$

$\sum x^2$ = 14.41

N = 5

$$\sigma_x = \sqrt{\frac{14.41}{5}}$$

$$\sigma_x = \sqrt{2.88}$$

$$\sigma_x = 1.70$$

Standard deviation of Scrip N:

$$\sigma_y = \sqrt{\frac{\sum x^2}{N}}$$

$$\sum y^2 = 42.81$$

$$N = 5$$

$$\sigma_y = \sqrt{\frac{42.81}{5}}$$

$$\sigma_y = \sqrt{8.562}$$

$$\sigma_y = 2.93$$

Interms of risk, security of company M is better as it is having a lower standard deviation of 1.70 as compared to stand deviation of 2.93 of company N. The lower is the value, the lower will be the risk of the security for expected return. Calculation of Co-efficient of variation

$$cv_M = \frac{\sigma x}{\bar{x}} \times 100 \qquad \sigma x = 1.70 \qquad \bar{x} = 5.74$$

$$= \frac{1.70}{5.74} \times 100 = 29.58\%$$

$$cv_N = \frac{\sigma y}{\bar{y}} \times 100 \qquad \sigma y = 2.93 \qquad \bar{y} = 6.084$$

$$= \frac{2.93}{6.084} \times 100 = 48.15\%$$

On the basis of comparison of co-efficient of variation of two companies, it can be concluded that the scrip "M" earnings are less variable (more consistent and stable) as compard to scrip "N" because the Co-efficient of variation of scrip "M" is less than the scrip "N". From the data of the book value and EPs it seems that "N" is more leveraged company as compared with "M" hence, those who do not want to face higher risk, are adviced to go for scrip "M".

The average dividend per share is more for company "M" based on the above analysis, we would select the scrip of company "M" for investment as it is less risky and it pays more average and consistent returns. Further, it is noted that the dividend per share paid by the company "M" is showing an increasing trend. For some investors, who prefer capital appreciation in view of low tax rate on long term capital gains for such investors the decision for selection of a scrip is based on book values of a company. The book value of the scrip "N" is increasing rapidly and it is much higher than that of the scrip "M" there fore, those who are looking for capital gains should go for the scrip "N".

Illustration No.7: As a holder of **RIL** company equity share, your are given a right to subscribe the new issue of equity to raise capital to expand plant fecilities. The announcement of the rights issue was made on August 1, for owners with a record date of August 31. The subscription price for the new stock was set at Rs.60 per share. Each equity share holder is allowed to buy one new equity share at the subscription price for every 8 shares of equity. The market price of the share on August 7 was Rs.69.

A) What was the theoretical value of rights on August 7.

B) If the price is not changed what should be the value of right on September 1.

C) What value would the rights have on September 16.

D) Would you expect that the market price and theoretical price are to be same in the future? why? or why not?

Solution:

A) The theorilical value of the right issue on August 1 was Rupee 1 from the following calculations.

$$\text{Valuation of Right} = \frac{\left(\begin{array}{c}\text{Market price}\\ \text{as on desired date}\end{array}\right) - \left(\begin{array}{c}\text{Subscripti on price}\\ \text{of the new stock}\end{array}\right)}{\text{Allotment ratio} + 1}$$

Market price as August 7 = Rs.69.

Subscription price of the New stock Rs.60.

Allotment Ratio = 8 shares for every one share.

$$\frac{69-60}{8+1} = \frac{9}{9} = \text{Rs.}1$$

B) On September 1 the rights would be expected to have a value of Rupee 1.

C) The rights would have no values on September 16, since the rights will expire as the previous day only. After the last date of subscription, the unsubscribed right do not have any value.

D) Generally we would not expect that the market price and theoritical are to be identical, due to demand conditions for the particular share.

Illustration No. 8: A company has the following Capital Structure

a) 10,000 equity shares of Rs.10 each Rs.1,00,000

b) 2,000, 10% preference shares of Rs.100 each Rs.2,00,000

c) 2,000, 10% debentures of Rs.100 each Rs.2,00,000

Calculate the earning per share for each of the following levels of "EBIT"

a) Rs.1,00,000

b) Rs.60,000

c) Rs.1,40,000

The company is in 50% tax bracket. Calculate also the financial leverage taking EBIT levels.

Solution:

Calculation of earning per share (EPs)

Particulars	Situation-A	Situation-B	Situation-C
EBIT	1,00,000	60,000	1,40,000
(-) Interest on debentures at 10%	20,000	20,000	20,000
PBT (Profit before tax)	80,000	40,000	1,20,000
(-) Income tax at 50%	40,000	20,000	60,000
Profit after tax	40,000	20,000	60,000
(-) Preference divident at 10%	20,000	20,000	20,000
Earnings available to equity shareholders	20,000	0	40,000

$$\text{EPS} = \frac{\text{Profits After Taxes}}{\text{No. of equity shares}}$$

Situation-A;

$$= \frac{20,000}{10,000} = \text{Rs.}2$$

Situation-B;

$$= \frac{0}{10,000} = \text{Rs.}0$$

Situation-C;

$$= \frac{40,000}{10,000} = \text{Rs.}4$$

Calculation of Financial Leverage at different situations:

$$\text{Financial Leverage} = \frac{\text{Operating profit}}{\text{Profit before tax}}$$

FL at Situation-A;

$$= \frac{1,00,000}{80,000} = 1.25$$

FL at Situation-B;

$$= \frac{60,000}{40,000} = 1.50$$

FL at Situation-C;

$$= \frac{1,20,000}{60,000} = 2$$

Illustration No.9: A company has the following capital structure:

20,000 equity shares of Rs.10 each Rs.2,00,000

4,000 10% preference shares of Rs.100 each Rs.4,00,000

4,000 10% Debenture of Rs.100 each Rs.4,00,000

Calculate EPs for each of the following levels of EBIT:

a) Rs.2,00,000

b) Rs.1,20,000 and

c) Rs.2,80,000

The company is in 50% tax bracket. Calculate the financial leverage taking EBIT levels under all the situations.

Solution: Table showing computation of earning per share;

Particulars	Situation-A Rs.	Situation-B Rs.	Situation-C Rs.
EBIT	2,00,000	1,20,000	2,80,000
Less interest (-) on debentures @ 10%	40,000	40,000	40,000
PBT	1,60,000	80,000	2,40,000
(-) Income tax @ 50%	80,000	40,000	1,20,000
PAT	80,000	40,000	1,20,000
(-) Preference dividend @ 10%	40,000	40,000	40,000
Earnings available to equity shareholders	40,000	0	80,000

$$\text{Earnings per Share} = \frac{\text{Earnings available to equities share holders}}{\text{No. of equity shares}}$$

Situation-A;

$$= \frac{40,000}{20,000} = \text{Rs.}2$$

Situation-B;

$$= \frac{0}{20,000} = \text{Rs.}0$$

Situation-C;

$$= \frac{80,000}{20,000} = \text{Rs.}4$$

Calculation of Financial Leverage at different situations:

$$\text{Financial Leverage} = \frac{\text{Operating profit}}{\text{Profit before tax}}$$

FL at Situation-A;

$$= \frac{2,00,000}{1,60,000} = 1.25$$

FL at Situation-B;

$$= \frac{OP}{PBT} = \frac{1,20,000}{80,000} = 1.5$$

FL at Situation-C;

$$= \frac{OP}{PBT} = \frac{2,80,00}{2,40,00} = 1.16$$

Illustration No. 10: The capital structure of a company consists of ordinary share capital of Rs.10 lack (shares of Rupees 100 par value) and Rs.10 lack of 10% debentures, sales increased by 20% from 1 lack units to 1,20,000 units. The selling price is Rs.10 per unit, variable cost, amount is Rs.6 per unit and fixed expenses are Rs.2 lack. The income-tax is assumed to be 50% you are required to calculate the following;

A) The EPs at the level of 1 lack units and 1,20,000 units.

B) The Degree of operating liverage at 1 lack units and 1,20,000 units.

C) The Degree of financial liverage at 1 lack units and 1,20,000 units.

Solution:

Calculation of EPs for 1,00,000 and 1,20,000 units;

Particulars	1,00,000 units Rs.	1,20,000 units Rs.
Sales (@ Rs.10 per unit)	10,00,000	12,00,000
(-) Variable cost (@ Rs.6 per unit)	6,00,000	7,20,000
Contribution	4,00,000	4,80,000
(-) Fixed Cost	2,00,000	2,00,000
operating profit	2,00,000	2,80,000
(-) Interest (@ 10%)	1,00,000	1,00,000
PBT	1,00,000	1,80,000
(-) Income Tax (@ 50%)	50,000	90,000
PAT (Earnings available to Equity shareholders)	50,000	90,000

$$\text{EPs at sales of 1,00,000 units} = \frac{50,000}{10,000} = \boxed{\text{Rs.5}}$$

$$\text{EPs at sales of 1,20,000 units} = \frac{90,000}{10,000} = \boxed{\text{Rs.9}}$$

Operating Leverage at 1,00,000 units;

$$\text{Operating Leverage} = \frac{\text{Contribution}}{\text{OperatingProfit}}$$

$$= \frac{4,00,000}{2,00,000} = 2$$

Operating Leverage at 1,20,000 units;

$$= \frac{4,80,000}{2,80,000} = 1.714$$

Financial Leverage at 1,00,000 units;

$$\text{Financial Leverage} = \frac{\text{Operating profit}}{\text{Profit before tax}}$$

$$= \frac{2,00,000}{1,00,000} = 2$$

Financial Leverage at 1,20,000 units;

$$\text{Operating Leverage} = \frac{\text{Operating profit}}{\text{Profit before tax}}$$

$$= \frac{2,80,000}{1,80,000} = 1.55$$

Illustration No.11: Suppose a firm has a capital structure comprising of ordinary shares amounting to Rs.10,00,000. The firm now wishes to raise additional Rs.10,00,000 for expansion. The firm has four alternative financial plans.

A) It can be raised the entire amount in the form of equity capital.

B) It can raise 50% as equity capital and 50% as 5% debentures.

C) It can raise amount of Rs. as 6% debentures.

D) It can raise 50% equity capital and 50% preference capital.

Further, assume that the existing **EBIT** is Rs.1,20,000 the tax rate is 50%, outstanding ordinary shares are 10,000 and the market price per share is Rs.100 under all the four alternatives which financial plan should the firm select?

Solution:

Calculation of EPs under various financial plans

(Rs.)

PARTICULARS	A (Equity)	B (Equity+Deb-)	C (Deb)	D (Equity+Dref)
EBIT	1,20,000	1,20,000	1,20,000	1,20,000
(-) Interest @ 5%	---	25,000	60,000	---
PBT	1,20,000	95,000	60,000	1,20,000
(-) Income tax(50%)	60,000	47,500	30,000	60,000
PAT	60,000	47,500	30,000	60,000
Less: Preference dividend	---	---	---	25,000
Earning available to equity share holders	60,000	47,500	30,000	45,000

$$\text{EPs} = \frac{\text{Earning available to Equityshareholders}}{\text{No. of Equity Shares}}$$

Alternation-A;

$$= \frac{60,000}{20,000} = 3\%$$

Alternation-C;

$$= \frac{30,000}{10,000} = 3\%$$

Alternation-B;

$$= \frac{47,500}{15,000} = 3.17\%$$

Alternation-D;

$$= \frac{30,000}{15,000} = 2.33\%$$

SUMMARY

Security analysis (Fundamental analysis)

Investment claimate in an economy can be analysed from the Gross National Product and its components. Economists, Stock analysts, Financial analysts and investors deal in tems of GNP, as a measure of economic ativity. Investment success is more likely to be found in grouping and strongly competititive industries. The growth of industry depends upon three stages. **The pioneering stage, expasion stage and stagnation stage.** The specific market and economic environment may enchance the performance of a company for a period of time. The elements of the company analysis includes **Analysis of Marketing Activities, Accounting Policies, Dividend Policies, Capital Structure, Financial Analysis, Operating Efficiency, Quality of Management.** We also covered the Guidelines for better investment to investors, which is more useful to the general readers. These market tips will helpful to the common man before going to make an investment decision. The following guide lines are helpful for maximising expected return and minimising risk of investment by the investors.

a) Increase in investment can be made only in the case of profits making companies.

b) Always define the limit of loss and target profit.

c) Buy shares of reputed companies backed by top class management

d) In the stock market an investor with patience usually makes handsome profits.

e) Investors must be careful in analysis Risk & Return.

f) Share prices should be carefully judged by estimating the potential value.

g) Investors are advised not to invest in inactive shares.

h) The investors should maintain a portfolio with not more than 12 companies.

i) It is better not to invest in odd lots.

j) The investor should not invest in unlisted shares or shares of closely held companies.

QUESTIONS

1. What is fundamental analysis?
2. As an investment consultant which scrip would you recommend to buy by your client.
3. Explain the industry analysis and nature of industry.
4. Write an essay on analysis of company for selecting a good company scrip.
5. Give an example of an industry you feel has positive competitive conditions for your selections as an industry to make investment. Why have you selected this industry?
6. What are the short comings of the Traditional Approache of Investment analysis?
7. What are the utilities of cash flow analysis?
8. What do you mean by external analysis and internal analysis?

9. What are the differences between vertical analysis and horizontal analysis.

10. Explain the factors which affect market price of a share?

11. Can we say "stock market activities are temparament of psychology"?

12. What do you mean by the Ratio analysis? How the ratios are helpful in picking of a better scrip from the market?

13. Expain the following terms.

    a) E.P.S.

    b) PE Ratio

    c) Payout policy

    d) Company analysis

    e) Economic Indicatiors

EXCERCISE

Question No.1: The capital structure of ABC Ltd.consists of an ordinary share capital of Rs.20,000,000 (shares of Rs.100 par value) and Rs.5,00,000 of 10% debentures,sales increased by 20% from 2,00,000 units to 2,40,000 units. The selling price is 20% per unit, variable cost 12% per unit and fixed expenses amount to Rs.4,00,000. The income tax rate is assumed to be 50% you are required to calculate the following.

1) The EPs of the levels 2,00,000 & 2,40,000 units:

(Ans: Rs.28.75; Rs.36.75)

Question No.2: Determine the earnings per share (EPs) of a textiles company which has operating profit (EBIT) of Rs.1,60,000.

Its capital structure consists of the following securities;

10% debentures	Rs.5,00,000
12% debentures	Rs.1,00,000
equity shares (of Rs.10 each)	Rs.4,00,000

The company is in the 55% tax bracket.

1. Determine the firms EPs.
2. Determine the per centage change in EPs associated with 30% increase and 30% decrease in EBIt.

(Ans: Rs.9.38; 30% increase Rs.14.78; 30% decrease Rs.3.97)

Question No.3: The following data relate to two companies A Ltd. & B Ltd.

Capital employed	A Ltd	B Ltd
Equity share capital (Rs.10 shares)	5,00,000	2,50,000
9% debentures	---	2,50,000
Earnings before interest and tax	1,00,000	1,00,000
Return on capital employed	20%	20%

Both the companies the return on the total capital employed is same but their earnings per share in A Ltd. is much less than as comparied to "B" Ltd.,

You are required to state for the satisfaction of the share holders of A Ltd., the reasons for such lower earnings per share on their capital, assume the tax at 50%.

(Ans: A Rs.1; B Rs.1.55)

TECHNICAL ANALYSIS

Technical analysis is the study of *Market Action* for the purpose of forecasting future price trends. The term market action includes the *three* principal sources of information available to the *technician - price, volume and interest.* Technical Analysis can be frequently used to supplement the fundamental analysis. It discards the fundamental approach to intrinsic value. Changes in price movements represent shifts in supply and demand position. Technical Analysis is useful in timing a buy or sell order. The technician must *(a) identify the trend and (b) recognise the trend.* The technical analysis does not claim **100%** of success in predictions. It helps to improve the knowledge of the probabilities of price behaviour and provides for investment. Its reward can be realised more quickly, but in long run, it may be more disappointing. It requires attention and discipline, with quality stocks held for the long-term. Technical analysis especially **charts,** provide the best and most convenience method of comparison.

In stock market all fundamental factors are discounted by the market and reflected in prices. In stock market, present trends are influenced by the past trends. Analysis of historical trends and "Random Walk Theory" has been found to be *not applicable* by the technical analysts. The trends in stock market share prices are divided into 3 kinds viz., *Primary, Secondary and Minor.* The Primary trend is a long term trend for *one year.* The Secondary trend for *few weeks/months* and the minor trend for *daily basis.*

The stock market is different from other markets, as there is a continuous buying and selling bid and offer rates. The entry and exit in the market will there fore, make all the difference to the spread between buying and selling prices and the profit or losses timing of investment is therefore of vital importance for trading in the stock market.

The technical approach is based on the following three premises:

1. Market action discounts every thing.
2. Prices move in trends.
3. History repeats itself.

1. Market action discounts everything

This statement is the cornerstone of technical analysis. According to Newton's frist law of motion that "Everything will continue in its state of rest or motion unless it is acted upon by another external force". The technical analysis is simulator to the Newton's first principle. If we understand this principle, it will be easy to understand the technical analysis also. The technical analyst believes that anything that can possibly affect the market price of a security such as fundamentals, political, psycological or otherwise is actually reflected in the price of that security. There fore, it is also called as market discounts everything. The price of a security on any day is the result of various factors, which have influenced such price on that day.

2. Prices move in trends

Price trend is the basic concept in technical analysis. The whole purpose of charting the price action of a future market is to identify trends in the early stages of their development for the purpose of trading in the direction of those trends. In fact, the techniques used here to identify and follow existing trends. There is a coroliary to the premise that prices move in trends - a trend in motion is more likely to continue than reverse.

3. History repeats itself

Predictions for the future are all based on history. Charts are made on the assumption that past figures and data help in extrapolation for the future. Another way of saying this is that projections for the future can be done only after a complete understanding of the past or that the future is just a repetition of the past.

Technical Analysis is a tool which should be used with fundamental analysis and most important with commonsense. In technical analysis a significant factor is volume. The technical approach uses a variety of methods to take investment decisions. These methods can broadly be categorised as follows:

1. Dow Jones Theory
2. Random Walk Theory
3. Formula Plans.
4. Variable Ratio Formula Plans
5. Matrix Approach

1. Dow Jones Theory

The Dow Jones Theory is the oldest and considered to be the most popular of all technical market studies. It was first published as a stock market average by Charles Dow on July 3, 1884. Although it has its fair share of critics, it is known to nearly every one who has had any association with the stock market and is respected by most. It is absolutely technical in approach and is built upon and concerned with nothing but the stock market action itself. Including nothing from business statistics on which the fundametalists depend, Charles Dow the original promulgator of this theory, had not intended that this theory is to be a device for forecasting the stock market or as a guide for investor but rather to serve as a barometer of business trends. The Dow theory is that its signals are given 'too late.' In spite of all this, the Dow theory remains one of the foundations of modern technical market study.

The Dow theory is based on industrial averages. It is a well-known fact that securities of established companies tend to go up or down together. Charles Dow is belived to have the first to recognize this concept of industrial averages and to make an effort to express the general trend of the securities market in terms of the average prices of a few selected representative stocks.

The basic tenets of the theory are as follows:

1. The averages discount everything.
2. The three market trends.
3. Major trends have three phases.
4. The averages must confirm to each other.
5. Volume must confirm the trend.
6. A trend is assumed to be in effect until it gives definite signals that it has reversed.

1. The Averages Discount Everything

The theory states that every possible factor affecting supply and demand and thus, the market prices, must be reflected in the averages.

Even natural calamities are considered though, these can neither be anticipated nor their exact affect is estimated. Thus, when they occur, they are quickly discounted and assimilated into the price action.

2. The Three Market Trends

The trends in stock prices are depending upon business conditions, demand & supply, performance of corporate sector, working results of individual organisations etc., The trends in the stock market can be found as **"down trend"** and **"up trend"**. According to Dow, up trend means, the market may have a pattern of rising peaks and troughs a down trend would just be the reverse with the peaks and troughs. Trends are categorically divided into three heads the primary, secondary and minor. Among them the most significant trend is the primary or major trend which usually last for more than a year and possibly for several years. Dow believed that primary trends reflect the basic mood of the market. The secondary or intermediate trends represent corrections in the primary trend and usually last for three weeks to three months. These corrections usually retrace one-third to two-third of the previous trend. The minor trend lasts for less than three weeks and represents short-term fluctuations.

3. Three Phases of Major Trends

Dow categorized major trends into three distinct phases. For the bullish market, the first phase is called the accumulation phase and takes place, when astute investors begin buying securities as the seeming adverse economic news has finally been discounted by the market. Then the second phase begins, when keen followers of trends notice the bullish trend and begin to participate in the buying. Prices advance rapidly and business news improve. The third and final phase is characterized by active public participation when the news of increased market activity gets around. During the last phase, the astute investors who had initiated the first phase begin to 'disload' as the market in a boom.

4. The averages must conform to each other

At the time of formulation of the theory, Dow had been concerned only with the Industrial and Rail Road averages. He felt that no important bull or bear market signal could take place unless both the averages gave the same signal. The signals did not have to occur simultaneously, but the closer they got the better. When contradictory trend signals were given, the previous trend was assumed to be still in effect.

5. Volume must confirm the trend

In other words, volume should expand in the direction of the major trend. For the up trend; volume should expand or increase as the prices move higher and diminish as prices dip. It would be the other way for the down trend, where volume would increase, when prices drop and decrease when they rise.

6. A trend is assumed to be in effect until it gives definite signals that it has reversed

This particular Dow tenet has evoked a lot of criticism but when correctly understood, all it does is warn against changing market position too soon or 'jumping the gun'. It does not imply that one should delay action by even a single unnecessary minute once a signal of change of trend has appeared, but it only asks the investor to be sure before he attempts to alter his market position. As a matter of fact, the market is never stationary, it is always in a state of flux.

The application of the Dow theory or, for that matter, of any trend theory in practice for determining the point of 'buy' and 'sell' is an easy task. The crux is to be able to distinguish between a normal secondary correction in an existing trend and the first leg of a new trend in the opposite direction. Technicians differ in their opinion of the exact points of 'buy' or 'sell'. The following figures illustrate the determination of these points. The reversal pattern is referred to as failure swing.

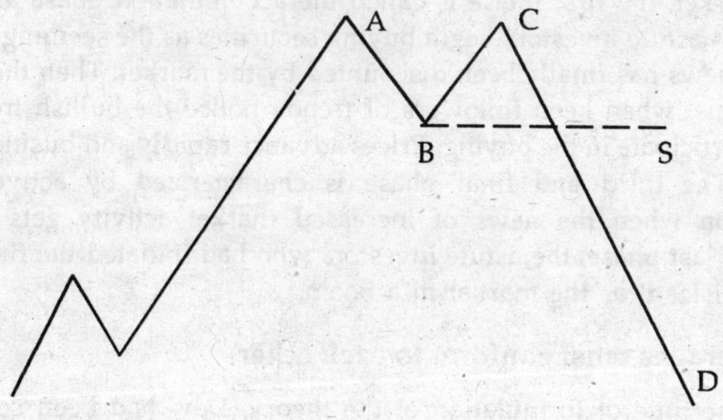

Fig.1.A Failure Swing

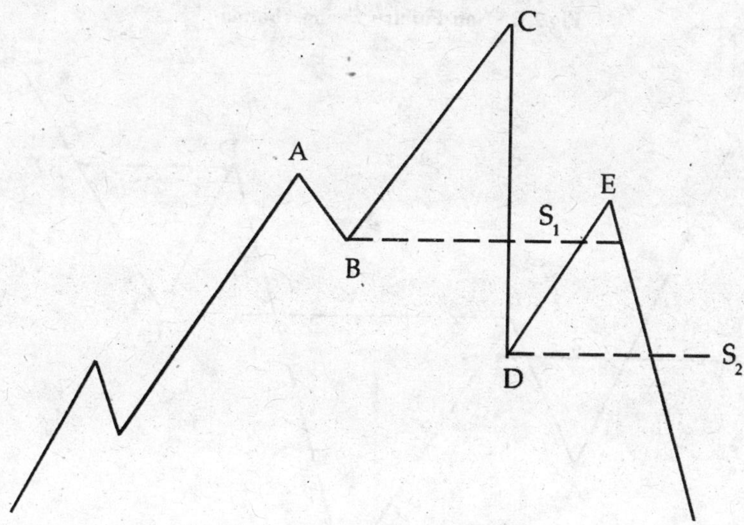

Fig.1.B. Non-failure Swing

Figure 1.A and Figure 1.B refer to bull market conditions changing over to bearish conditions and hence the question of 'when to sell' arises. In Fig 1A, peak C fails to overcome the previous peak A and the trough D also falls below B. So the signal to sell is constituted at S. In Fig 1B peak E exceeds A before falling below B. Technicians differ in their opionion as to whether the signal to sell is constituted at S1 or S2.

Figure 2.A and Figure 2.B refer to bear market conditions changing to bullish and hence the question is 'when to buy?''

In Figure 2.A the trough at C fails to fall below A and peak at D is also higher than B. So the 'buy' signal is constituted at B1.

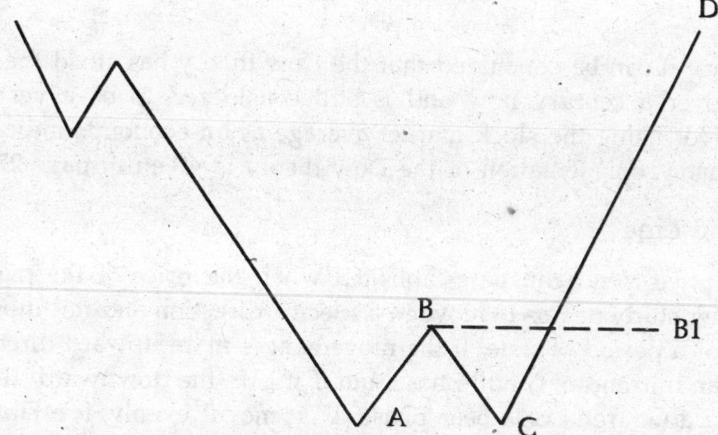

Fig.2A: Failure swing (bottom)

Fig.2.B. Non-Failure Swing (bottom)

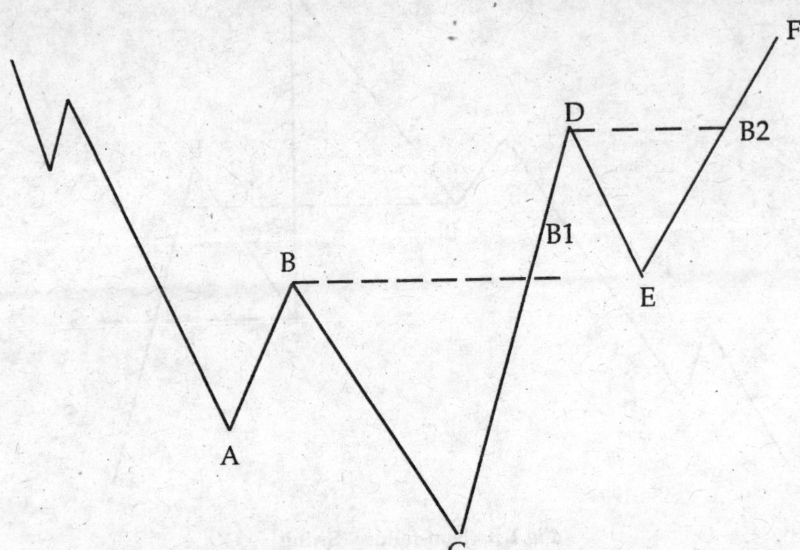

In Figure 2.B, peak D is higher than the previous peak F and B and the successive troughs E is higher than C, indicating a reversal in the bearish trend. 'Buy' signals are constituted at B1 and B2.

Though the Dow theory has worked well in identifying major bull and bear markets, it has not completely escaped criticism. As mentioned, its signals are 'too late.' Generally, a Dow reversal signal is given in the second phase of an uptrend as a previous intermediate peak is penetrated; hence, about 25 per cent of the initial reversal move is missed by the late signal. To answer this, one can only say that at the time of formulation of the theory, it was not intended that the Dow chart would indicate 'buy' 'and 'sell' points. It was intended to anticipate and indicate bull and bear markets only.

Hence it can be concluded that the Dow theory has stood the test of time for over a century now and is still considered to be a very good technique for using the stock market average as an economic indicator. A diagrammatic representation of the Dow theory is given in page 273.

The Trend Line

A price trend can be established when the price of the particular share under study begins to move in a specific direction and this movement persists for a period of time. If the movement is in an upward direction, it is called an uptrend or a bull phase, but if it is in the downward direction, it marks a downtrend or a bear phase. If it moves evenly, it establishes a horizontal trend. These trends may be illustrated.

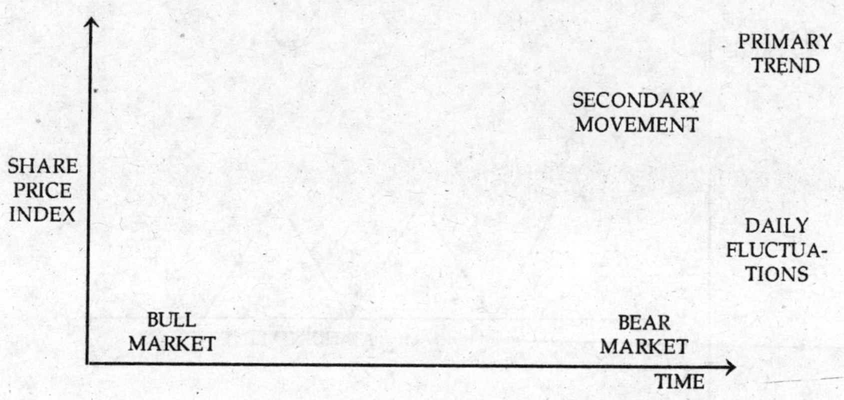
SHARE
PRICE
INDEX
PRIMARY
TREND
SECONDARY
MOVEMENT
DAILY
FLUCTUA-
TIONS
BULL
MARKET
BEAR
MARKET
TIME

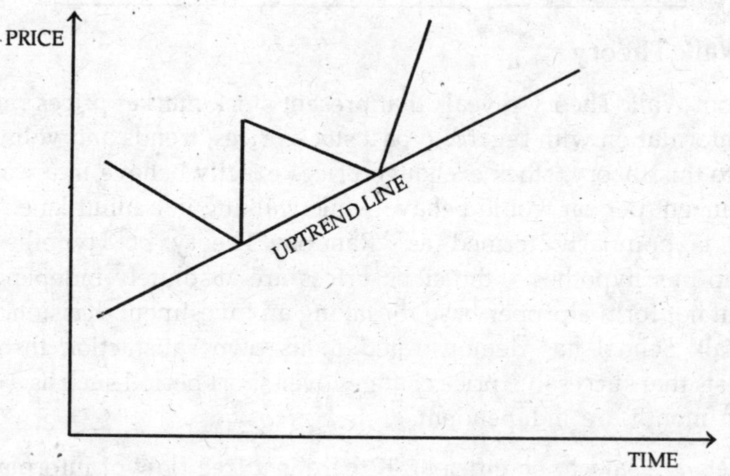
PRICE
UPTREND LINE
TIME

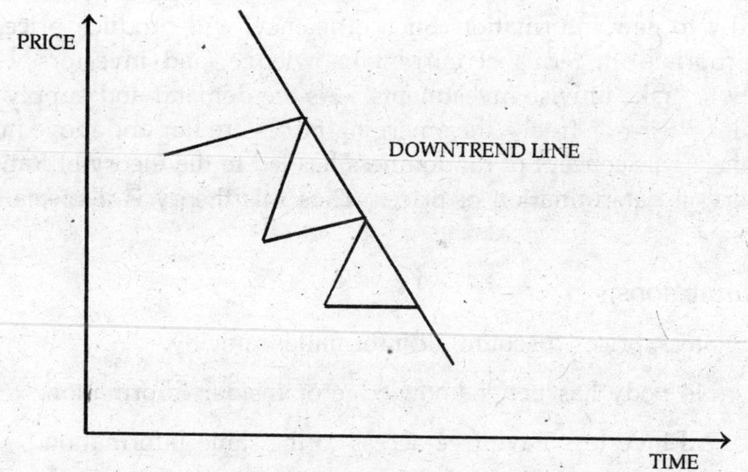
PRICE
DOWNTREND LINE
TIME

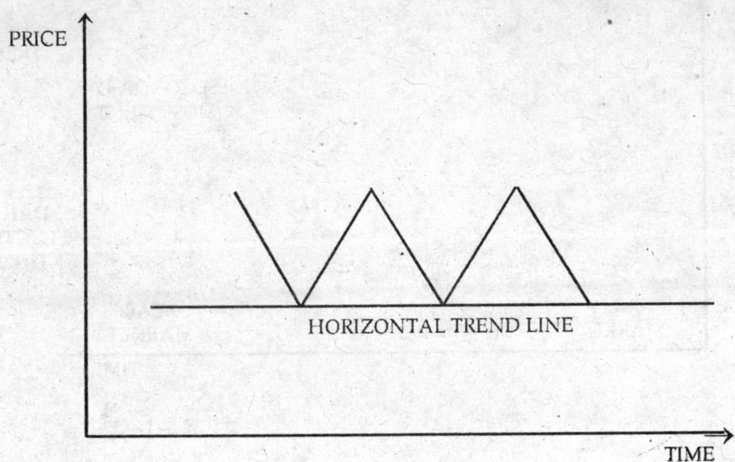

Random Walk Theory

Random Walk Theory reveals that present stock market prices reflect all known information with regard to past stock prices, trends and volumes. According to this theory, stock exchange prices exactly behave in a way in which a drunken person would behave while walking in a blind lane. This view point is popularly termed as "Random Theory or Hypothesis". According to this hypothesis, the stock prices are absolutely independent and they can not form a proper base for taking an investment decision. The Random Walk School has demonstrated to its own satisfaction through empirical tests that successive price changes over short period such as a day, a week or a month are independent.

Markets are said to be efficient, if there is a free flow of information and markets absorb this information fully and quickly. "Efficiency means the ability of the capital market to function, so that price of securities react rapidly to new information. Such efficiency, will produce prices that are, 'Appropriate' in terms of current knowledge, and investors will be less likely to make unwise investments". As the demand and supply forces are playing their role freely, the emerging prices are fair and move in a random manner. This concept of randomness has led to the theory of Random Walk Theory in determination of prices. Thus this theory is a specially devised theory.

Assumptions;

1. Stock prices discount all information quickly.
2. No body has better knowledge or insider information.
3. All investors have free access to the same information.
4. Market can not be influenced by institutional investors.

5. The flow of information is free and unbiased.
6. No one can influence the market.
7. Market quickly adjusts itself based on demand and supply factors.
8. Investors behave in rational manner.
9. Share prices move in an independent manner.

In an efficient market, all the relevant information is reflected in the current stock price. Information can not be used to obtain excess return: such information has already been taken into account and absorbed in the prices. All prices are correctly stated and there are no "bargains" in the stock market.

Forms of Random Walk Hypothesis

Tests of the market efficiency are essentially tests of whether the three general types of information - past prices, other public information, and inside information - can be used to make above average returns on investments. This theory can be divided into the following three forms viz.,

A) Weak form,

B) Semistrong form, and

C) Strong, form

A) Weak Form

This is the first form of the Random Walk Hypothesis. As the past prices are already absorbed by the market, the present prices move independent of the past, which is the analysis of the Random Walk Hypothesis. Prices have no memory, and prices of yesterday have nothing to do with tomorrow. It is an important property of a market that one might do as well flipping a coin as spending time by analysing past price movements.

If the Random Walk Hypothesis is empirically confirmed, we may assert that the stock market is weak-form of efficient. In this case any predictions done by chartists based on past price patterns is worthless.

Random Walk Theorists usually take as their starting point, the model of a perfect securities market in which a relatively large number of investors, traders, and speculators compete in an attempt to predict the course of future prices.

Reflecting the historical development, the weak form implies that the knowledge of the past patterns of stock prices does not aid investors to attain improved performance. Random Walk theorists view stock prices are mcving randomly about a trend line which is based on anticipated earning power.

The statistical information to provide support for the weak form of the efficient market hypothesis are discussed here under:

i) Filter Rules

ii) Serial Correlation

iii) Run Test

i) Filter Rules: The use of chartsis essentially a technique for filtering out the important information from the unimportant price and volume of data are supposed to tell the entire story we need to know to identify the important "action" in stock prices. "If a stock moves up with per cent, buy it and hold it long; if it then reverses itself by the same per centage, sell it and take a short position in it. When the stock reversed itself again by per cent cover the short position and buy the stock long". The size of the filter varied from 0.5 to 50 per cent.

ii) Serial Correlation: Security price changes do not appear to have any momentum or inertia which causes changes of a given sign to be followed by changes of that same sign, the filter rules should have, detected this pattern if it existed. However, security prices may follow some sort of a reversal pattern in which price changes of one sign tend to be followed by changes of the opposite sign. Filter rules might not detect a pattern of reversals. Serial correlation (or auto correlation) measures the correlation co-efficient between a series of numbers with lagging in the same time series. Trends or reversal tendencies in security price changes can be detected with serial correlation. We can measure the correlation between security price changes in period "t" (denoted P) and price changes in the same security which occur "k" periods later and are denoted pt +k; k is the number of periods of lag. They are long-term upward trend in security prices, so if one period covers a number of years a possitive serial correlation should be observed. The existence of patterns in short terms (Daily, weekly, monthly) price changes which can be used to earn a larger trading profit.

iii) Run Test: Filter rules and serial correlation may not pickup the sensitive price changes that technicians use for making decisions. That is, price changes may be random most of the time but occassionally become serially correlated for varying period of time. To examine this possibility, run tests may be used to determine, if there are "runs" in the price changes.

A run is a set of consecutive prices of the same sign. A time series, such as prices of stocks can be tested to see whether there are dependencies among the data merely by looking at the number of runs in the series.

If a price increase of any size is designated by "+" and decrease in price by "-" any pattern might be observed over time.

Hypothetical shares	Number of Runs
A	+ + + + + + ...2
B	+- + - + - + - + - 10
C	- - + - + + + - - - + ...6

The pattern for share A reflects continuing trend. If the price of the share has been increasing (decreasing) it will probably continue to move up (or down). Share B shows the opposite behaviour, a tendency of price reversal from the preceding period. Share A has very few runs but share B has many. Share C represents an unpredictable sequence, evidenced by a number of runs to the number expected by chance in a totally random series. Since each observation is counted equally regardless of size, run analysis removes potential problems of non-normality in identifying independence.

Yesterday's prices do not tell us much about tomorrow's or at least not enough to consistently make unusual returns based merely on price data.

B) Semistrong Form

The semistrong form of the efficient market hypothesis says that current prices of stocks not only reflect all informational content of historical prices but also reflect all publicly available knowledge about the corporations being studied. The semistrong form says that efforts by analysts and investors to acquire and analyze public information will not yield consistenty superior returns to the analyst.

C) Strong Form

The strong form of the efficient market hypothesis maintains that not only publicly available information is useless to the investor or analyst, but all information is useless specifically, no information that is available be it public or "inside", can be used to earn consistently superior investment returns. Many of the tests of the strong form of the efficient market hypothesis deal with tests of mutual fund per formance.

Empirical Tests of the Semistrong Form

The semistrong form says that current stock prices will instantaneously reflect all publicly available information. These tests attempt to analyze, if an analyst using such data when they become available to him can successfully use this information to obtain superior investment results.

Fama, Fisher, Jensen and Roll[1] made a major contribution with their study of the semistrong form hypothesis. They tested the speed of the market's reaction to a firm's announcement of a stock split and the accompanying information with respect to a changed in dividend policy.

Ball and Brown[2] conducted another test in this area by analyzing the stock market's ability to absorb the informational content of reported annual earnings per share information. In their study the authors examined stock price movement of companies that experienced "good" earnings reports as opposed to the stock price movements of companies that experienced "bad" earnings. A "good" earnings report was reflected in earnings per share figure that was higher than the previously forecast earnings per share and conversely a "bad" earnings report was indicated earnings per share figure that was lower than had been forecost previously. They found that those companies with "good" earnings reports experienced price increases in their stock and those with "bad" earnings reports experienced stock price declines. The intersting result was that about 85 per cent of the informational content of the annual earnings announcement was reflected in stock price movements prior to the release of the actual annual earnings figure.

The random walk model says nothing about relative price movements that is, about selecting securities that may or may not perform better than other securities. It says nothing about decomposing price movements into such factors as market, industry, or firm factors. Certainly, it is entirely possible to detect trends in stock prices after one has removed the general market influences or other influences; however, this in no way would reflect the random walk model. We will in fact be dealing with relative prices and not with absolute prices, which lie at the heart of the Random Walk hypothesis. Further, more these "trends" provide no basis for forecasting the future.

There seems to be a misunderstanding by many to the effect that believing in random walk means that one must also believe by analyzing stocks, and consequently stock prices, is a useless exercise, for if indeed stock prices are random, there is no reason for them. This is very wrong. The random walk hypothesis is entirely consistent with an upward or downward movement in price.

---

1. *Eugene F. Fama etc.* "The adjustment of stock prices to New Information," International Economic Review 10, no.1 (February 1969) pp.1-21)
2. *Ray Ball and Phillip Brown,* "An Empirical Evaluation of Accounting Income Number," Journal of Accounting Research 6 (Autumn 1968); pp.159-78)

3. Formulae plans

The formulae plans provide an automatic timing device for the investor. These plans are therefore suitable for all types of investors big or small.

The following are some basic types of formulae plans;

a) Rupee cost averaging plan.

b) Modified rupee avaraging plan.

c) Ratio Formula plan.

d) Constant Ratio Formula plan.

a) Rupee Cost Averaging Plan

This is also termed as rupee averaging or strict rupee averaging plan It is the simplist type of formula plan. This plan consists of investing a regular intervals, a fixed rupee amount in selected securities or group c securities at equal time intervals regard less of the market conditioı investor buys more securities at low prices than at high prices. Compariso of an average price per share, under "Rupee" averaging and averagir market price are presented in the table given below:

Market price per share Rs.	Quarterly investment Rs.	No.of shares pruchased	Cumulative average cost per share (Rs)	Cumulative average market pric per share (R
200	2000	10.0	200.00	200.00
180	2000	11.1	189.87	196.00
160	2000	12.5	178.56	180.00
140	2000	14.3	167.00	170.00
120	2000	16.7	154.80	160.00
100	2000	20.0	141.84	150.00
120	2000	16.7	138.20	145.72
140	2000	14.3	138.40	145.00
160	2000	12.5	140.52	146.66
180	2000	11.1	143.68	150.00
200	2000	10.0	147.46	154.54

Advantages

This plan has the following advantages;

i) According to this plan an investor can acquire securities at a lo average price.

ii) Implementation of this plan is very simple and mechanical. There is no need to think every time "*what to buy and when to buy*".

Limitations

This plan will prove reasonably in terms of subsequent market levels. The posibility of the things rests on certain limitations.

i) The plan takes a long period of stock price cycle.

ii) This plan will not take into consideration of certain elements psycology/economic position in a bear market.

2. Modified Rupee Averaging Plan

Under this plan, the investor is required to put an equal amount of money in various fixed list of securities in a paticular period of time. However, earlier several modifications were made to this plan to have the existing rupee averaging plan. The following are the some of such modifications:

i) An investor may invest a fixed amount every time, but may continuously vary the number of securities purchased. For example, if the investor has fixed sum of Rs.50,000 to be invested bi-annually, the securities purchased in the second halfyear may be different from those purchased in the first half year or he may even sell some of the over-priced stocks and replace them by reinvesting in the more shares of the companies.

ii) The investor may buy the same securities each time but may vary the timing of his investment during the year. For example an investor may have decided to invest *Rs.50,000* every year. However, within the year, he may make the investment on different dates which suits more conveniently without affecting the total level of investment in a portfolio.

3. Ratio Formula Plans

Under the Ratio Formula plan, the sale of securities is made gradually in bullish market and purchases are made in bearish market. This plan makes the investor an alteration of investment between different securities, to counter the market psycology. If an investor follows this plan he may switch over from shares to debentures or debentures to shares. This plan specifies in advance about the timing amount of transactions to be deployed in the market.

4. Variable Ratio Formula Plan

Under this plan investor has to sell the shares in raising market and buy the bonds in their place. He may reduce the praportion of his portfolio according to the price flactuations. As per this plan the one should make a

forecast about the normal price line and he should expect actual prices. The investor should frame the norms to buy, sell, and holding period.

For example the investor may like to keep 50% investment in shares at normal price. He may fix up 1, 2 and 3 zones above this normal line with percentage of investment in shares at 40, 30 and 20. Similarly, he may keep 1, 2 &3 zones below the normal line, with percentage of investment in shares at 60, 70 and 80 respectively. These price zones will determine the behaviour of the finance manager as regards purchasing and selling of the shares constituting his investment portfolio.

For example, if the prices of the shares move up ward from the normal or trend line to zone 1, then he will reduce his percentage of investment in shares from 50 to 40 per cent. Similarly, if the prices of the shares move down ward from the trend line to zone 1, he will increase his investment in shares to 60% by disposing part of his investment in fixed yield bearing securities.

5. Matrix Approach

The Matrix Approach is useful to an organisation, who can spare funds for a long period. This approach is used in making investment decisions. For example a large amount of cash flows are not immediately reinvested in long term projects. The funds are kept for some time and later on together with funds raised through long-term loans are invested in suitable projects. Therefore, the time gap will be utilised in a suitable channel to take advantage of opportunitic return. In this approach the investor may give high priority to safety, liquidity, yield, image etc., These elements are alloted maximum 100 marks. The various channels are awarded marks on the basis of their characterstics. A channel which scores highest marks will be selected.

Investment Matrix

Investment channel	Investment Criteria				Total Marks (400)
	Liquidity 100 marks	Safety 100 marks	Yield 100 marks	Image 100 marks	
Fixed deposit with a Bank	100	100	50	50	300
Fixed deposit with a Company	80	80	90	40	290
Shares in XY Ltd.	90	80	90	80	340
Loan to a film distributor.	30	20	100	30	180

The above table revels that the shares in XY Ltd, attracts 340 marks out of 400. Therefore, it is better to invest in the form of shares in XY Ltd.

SUMMARY

In this chapter, we have learnt a general aspects with regard to key factors for buying of a particular scrip. A number of tests have been available to obtain the intrinsic value of a share. Technical analysis is one of the tools in arriving intrinsic value of a particular scip. It is the study of market action. It is useful for forecasting the future trend. The technical analysis discards the fundamental analysis while assessing the intrissic value of a scrip. But the technical analysis does not give 100% guarantee in selection of a better scrip. It is not useful for long term purpose of investment. Technical analysis provides charts which are useful in comparsion of two scrips. Technical analysis approach is based on three premises i.e., market discounts every thing, prices move in trends, history may always repeat it self. The technical analysis approach consisting of Dow Jones Theory, Random Walk Theory, Formula plans, Variable Ratio Formula Plans and Matrix Approach. Dow Jones theory explains about the price movements of the stocks in securities market. This theory is the basic foundations of modern technical analysis. Dow Jone theory is a device for better forecasting stock market prices and services as a guide to the investors. It is not a barometre. Random walk theory reveals that the present stock market digests the all explored news information. This theory also indicates that the stock prices are independent and do not have proper base for taking an investment decision. Formula plans indicate the timing of investment in the stock market. It clearly reveals that when one can enter and exit from stock market. The Variable Ratio Formula Plan discusses about the switch over to equity and debentures according to the market prices. It is a tool for alteration of portfolio Matrix approach suggests that a company can earn better return from their ideal fund. It informs about the utilisation of funds until the project commencement.

QUESTIONS

1. What is Technical Analysis? How does it deffer from Fundamental Analysis?
2. Would you advice an investor according to Technical Analysis for an investment decisions?
3. What is the trend analysis? How it is useful for selection of a share?

4. Define the Random Walk Theory. Discuss how far it is useful to the investors in taking of an investment decision?

5. Discuss the important factors which generally have a bearing on investment decision.

6. Explain the Dow Jones Theory, How far it is useful in Portfolio Management?

7. Explain how the formula plan is useful to the Finance Manager at the time of purchasing the scrips.

8. Write short notes on the following;

   a) Investment matrix approach

   b) Run Test

   c) Filter Rules

   d) Rupee Cost Averaging Plan

   e) Ratio Formula Plan

   f) Constant Ratio Formula Plan

1. *Portfolio Management*

1

PORTFOLIO MANAGEMENT

INTRODUCTION

The various concepts of portfolio management such as, portfolio, portfolio management, portfolio strategy, portfolio rebalancing, portfolio theory, Markowiz, Randomwak, CAPM, Efficient market theory, intrinsic value, unsystematic risk, thin market, systematic risk, security market line, risk aversion, hedging, growth stocks, financial risk, financial engineering, efficient portfolio, efficient market hypothesis, efficient market, earnings multiplier model, diversification, alpha, current yield, characteristic line capital market line, broad market, Beta (β) etc., are presented below:

Portfolio

A set or combination of securities held by an investor. A portfolio comprising of different types of securities and assets.

Portfolio Management

It is a process of encompassing many activities of investment in assets and securities. The portfolio management includes the planning, supervision, timing, rationalism and conservatism in the selection of securities to meet an investors objectives. It is the process of selecting a list of securities that will provide the investor with a maximum yield constant with the risk he wishes to assume.

Portfolio Strategy

It is a process to construct the portfolio with a strategy taking into consideration of investing in a right security selecting a right sector, grabbing a growth scrip at right time.

Portfolio Rebalancing

It is a method to incorporate the latest changes arise in the market with reference to portfolio components.

Portfolio Theory

It is a body of knowledge, which has been quantifying the expected return and risk of the portfolio.

Markowitz Theory of Portfolio Management

This theory is associated with the expected return and level of risk exposure with the portfolio.

Random Walk Theory

It is a theory based on the behaviour of stock exchange prices.

Captial Asset Pricing Model (CAPM)

This theory reveals the return on each security is related to the total risk.

Efficient Market Hypothesis

This hypothesis reflects the intrinsic value of a security. This theory is also known as Random Walk Theory.

Earnings Multiplier Model

The model states that the price of a stock is equal to the product of its earnings and a multiplier.

Diversification

Investment in more than one risky asset with the primary objective of risk reduction and maximising the return.

Alpha

It is the difference between actual earned return and expected return at a level of systematic risk.

Current Yield

The yield on a security resulting from dividing the interest payment or dividend on it by its current market price.

Characteristic Line

A regression line representing the relationship between the return on an individual security and the return on the market portfolio.

Capital market line

The relationship between expected rate of return and risk of an efficient portfolio.

Broad market

The market which attracts funds in greater volume and from many investors.

Beta (β)

It is a measure of volatility faced by an asset or a portfolio or a project return.

Variance

It is a measure of total risk. It is represend by squaring the standard deviation (σ^2)

Stock Index Futures

Futures contracts on stock indices.

Stock Index Options

Option contracts on stock market indices.

Arbitrage

A simultaneous purchase and sale of a security in different markets to derive benefit from price differential.

Efficient Market Theory

A market in which asset prices reflect all available information quickly and accurately. In such a market the new information is absorbed by market participants and incorporated into market prices quickly.

Intrinsic Value

It is the present value of the stream of benefits expected from the asset. It also referred as the fair value or reasonable value.

Unsystematic Risk

This is also called as diversifiable risk. It is the risk attributable to factors unique to the security and the company to which the security belongs.

Thin Market

The market in which there are only few buyers and sellers for a security.

Systematic Risk

The risk that cannot be diversified. It is also called as market risk.

Security Market Line

The line representing the relationship between risk and return for individual and an efficient portfolio.

Risk aversion

It is the attitude of the investor, who prefers less risk than more risk.

Hedging

Processes of buying and selling of securities in different markets simultaneously to gain out of the price differences

Growth stocks

The shares on which return has been increasing and is expected to increase in future.

Financial risk

The risk which arises from the use of debt capital in the capital structure of a company.

Financial engineering

Developing new financial products by innovation.

Efficient portfolio

A portfolio which generates more expected return at an accepted low level of risk.

Liquidity

The extent to which an asset may quickly be converted into cash with least administrative and other costs.

Long position

A position in which the investor is entitled to receive an asset in future. It is the position of a buyer of the securities.

Margin

It is the part of a transaction's value that customer must pay to initiate transaction.

Market Maker

A business concern that acting as principal, buys and sells securities.

Net Present Value

It is the present value of benefits minus present value of costs of the investment.

Opportunity cost

The rate of return that can be earned on the best alternative investment it is the next best use of resources.

Option contract

An agreement that confers the right to buy or sell an asset at a set price at some future date. The right is exercisable at the discretion of the option buyer.

Put option

An option that gains its holder the right to sell an asset at a fixed price during a certain period.

Repo (Repurchase agreement)

An agreement between buyer and seller for the sale of securities to reverse the transaction in the future at a specified date and price.

Risk

It refers to variability of return. It is measured by standard deviation or beta co-efficient.

Risk Premium

The difference between the expected rate of market returns and the risk free rate of return.

Annuity

A fixed amount of cash to be received in every year for a given period of time.

Ask Price

The price at which the specialist or dealer offers to sell shares.

Badla (Contango)

It is a percentage of interest paid by the buyer of shares for the postponement of the transfer of those shares from one settlement day to the next settlement day.

Bear Market

A market dominated by operators who have a pessimistic view of the future, period of time during which indicators of the stock market decline.

Bid

A predetermined quantity of securities that is offered for sale and sold or tendered to the highest bidder.

Blue Chip Stock

Stocks or shares of the highest quality, with long record of earnings and dividends, shares of well known, stable, mature companies.

Bonds

Contractual liabilities that obligate the issuer to pay a specified amount at a given date in the future, generally with periodic interest payments in the interim at a fixed rate.

Book Value

The cost price of an asset less accumulated depreciation.

Bull Market

The market in which prices are going up and the market sentiment is highly optimistic.

Call Option

An option that gives its holder the right to buy an asset at a fixed price during a certain period.

Deep Market

The market in which there are always sufficient orders for buying and selling at both below and above the market price.

Forward Contract

An agreement between two parties to exchange an asset for cash at a predetermined future date for a price that is specified today.

Yield

The rate of discount which makes the present value of the stream of future returns plus the terminal value of the asset equal to the current market price of the asset.

Traditional Theory of Portfolio Management

It deals with the evaluation of return and risk conditions in each security.

Modern Portfolio Theory

It deals with the maximisation of returns through a combination of different securities.

Dominance

The combination of equity with riskless financial assets to enhance the value of a portfolio.

Standard Deviation

It is the measure of the variability of a distribution around its mean it is square root of variance.

Expected Return

The weighted average of possible returns with weights being the probabilities of occurrence.

Probability Distribution

It is a set of possible values that a random variance can assume and their associated probabilities of occurrence.

Co-efficient of Variation

It is a measure of risk. It is the variability of two or more financial assets which will be compared for taking a decision. It is the ratio of the standard deviation of a distribution to the mean of that distribution.

Co-variance

A statistical measure indicates the degree to which two variables move together.

Correlation Co-efficient

A standardised statistical measure of the linear relationship between two variables.

Price/Earnings ratio

The market price per share of a firm's common stock divided by the most recent 12 months of earning per share

Tax shield

A tax deductible expense.

Indifference curve

A line representing all combinations of expected return and risk that provides an investor with an equal amount of satisfaction.

Sunk costs

Unrecoverable past outlays that cannot be recovered and should not affect present actions or future decisions.

Interest Rate Risk

The variation in the market price of a security caused by changes in interest rates.

Perpetuity

An ordinary annuity whose payments or receipts continue forever.

Discount Rate

Interest rate used to convert future values to present values

Present Value

The current value of a future amount of money evaluated at a given interest rate.

Future Value

The value at some future time of money, or a series of payments, evaluated at a given interest rate.

Compound Value

Interest paid on any previous interest earned, as well as on the principal borrowed.

Maturity

The life of a security, the amount of time before the principal amount of a security becomes due.

Yield Curve

A graph of the relationship between yields and term to maturity for particular securities.

Sharpes Portfolio Theory

This theory deals with the reduction of the market risk and maximise the returns for a given level of risk. It takes into consideration the total risk of portfolio.

PORTFOLIO MANAGEMENT

Portfolio is a collection of different securities and assets. Portfolio is a basket of investments held by an individual investor, Foreign Institutional Investor /or a corporate body. Portfolio management involves a proper investment decision with regard to what to buy and sell. It involves proper money management. Portfolio management reduces risk and increases return. Portfolio management renders the services to satisfy the asset preference of investors.

Professional portfolio manager is a highly talented, skilled research staff member. After the success of mutual funds in portfolio management, a number of brokers and investment consultants who are professionally qualified have become portfolio managers. Portfolio manager is an important person, who holds the financial future dreams of millions of investors. Crores of rupees and the dreams of millions of investors are at the disposal of portfolio managers.

Objectives of Portfolio Management/Investment

The objective of portfolio management is to maximise the return and minimise the risk. These objectives are categorised into;

1. Basic objectives
2. Subsidiary objectives.

1. Basic Objectives

The basic objectives of the portfolio management further divided into two kinds viz., (a) maximise yield, (b) minimise risk. The aim of the portfolio management is to enhance the return for the level of risk to the portfolio owner. A desired return for a given risk level is being stated. The level of risk of a portfolio depends upon many factors. The investor who invests the savings in the financial asset, requires a regular return and capital appreciation.

2. Subsidiary Objectives

The subsidiary objectives of investment is expecting a reasonable income, appreciation of capital at the time of disposal, safety of the investment and liquidity etc., The objective of investor is to get a reasonable return on his investment without any risk. Regularity of income at a consistent rate is desired by any investor. However, it may not always be possible to get such income. Every investor has to dispose his holding after a stipulated period of time for a capital appreciation. Capital appreciation of a financial asset is highly influenced by a strong brand image, market leadership, guaranteed sales, financial strength, large pool of reserves, retained earnings and accumulated profits of the company. The idea of growth stocks is the right issue in the right industry, bought at the right time. *The safety of the investment* is desired by a portfolio management. The portfolio objective is to take the precautionary measures about the safety of the principal even by diversification process. The safety of the investment calls for careful review of economic and industry trends. *Liquidity* of the investment is most important, which may not be neglected by any investor/portfolio manager. An investment is to be liquid, it must have *''termination and marketable''* facility at any time.

Scope of Portfolio Management

Portfolio management is a continues process. It is a dynamic activity. The following are the basic operations of a portfolio management;

a) Monitoring the performance of portfolio by incorporating the latest market conditions.

b) Identification of the investor's objective, constraints and preferences.

c) Making an evaluation of portfolio income (comparison with targets and achievements).

d) Making revision in the portfolio.

e) Implementation of the strategies in tune with investment objectives.

Nature of Portfolio Management

Portfolio Management is a dynamic concept. A portfolio is not merely a collection of unrelated assets. Portfolio management involves a regular, scientific analysis, right jüdgement and timely action. The main objective of portfolio management is to help the investors with the better professional services as given below:

1. Portfolio should be constructed according to the investors objectives.
2. Constructed portfolio shall be reviewed from time to time in view of latest market developments.
3. The portfolio evaluation should be done according to risk and return.

SEBI Guidelines to Portfolio Management

SEBI has issued detailed guidelines for portfolio management services. The guidelines have been made to protect the interest of investors. The salient features of these guidelines are given here under;

1. The nature of portfolio management service shall be investment consultant.
2. The portfolio manager shall not guarantee any *return* to his clients.

3. Client's funds will be kept in separate bank account.
4. The portfolio manager shall act as trustee of client's funds.
5. The portfolio manager can invest in money or capital market.
6. Purchase and sale of securities will be at prevailing market price.

Powers of SEBI

The Securities and Exchange Board of India has the following powers to control and manage the portfolio managers:

1. The portfolio manager shall submit to *SEBI* such reports, returns and documents as may be prescribed.
2. *SEBI* may investigate the affairs of a portfolio manager such as *inspection of books of accounts, records etc.,*
3. *SEBI* has full authority in the event of violation of any provision to *suspend or cancel* the license.
4. No exemptions will be given under any circumstances to portfolio manager.

General responsibilities of a portfolio Manager

Following are the some of the responsibilities of a portfolio manager;

1. The portfolio manager shall act in a judiciary capacity with regard to the client's funds.
2. The portfolio manager shall transact the securities within the limitations placed by *the client*.
3. The portfolio manager shall not derive any direct or indirect benefit out of the clients funds.
4. The portfolio manager shall not pledge or give a loan of securities held on behalf of clients.
5. The portfolio manager shall ensure proper and timely handling of complaints from his clients.

Cancellation of Registration of a Portfolio Managers

The registration of a portfolio manager may be cancelled if;

1. The portfolio manager involves in manipulation, or price rigging or cornering
2. The financial position is un sound.

3. The portfolio manager is *involved guilty in fraud.*

4. The portfolio manager is guilty of repeated defaults.

Code of conduct of portfolio Managers

The following code of conduct shall be followed by every portfolio manager in India as per the Regulation *13 of SEBI.*

1. A portfolio manager shall maintain a high standards of integrity and fairness.

2. The client's funds should be deployed as soon as he receives.

3. A portfolio manager shall render all times *high standards,* and unbiased service.

4. A portfolio manager shall not make any statement which is likely to be harmful to the interest of other portfolio managers.

5. A portfolio manager shall not make any *exaggerated* statement.

6. A portfolio manager shall not disclose to any client or press any confidential information about his client, which has come to his knowledge.

7. A portfolio manager shall always provide true and adequate information.

8. A portfolio manager should render the best possible advice to the client.

Objectives of Investors

The following are the objectives of investors;

1. Safety of their investment.
2. Maximum regular return
3. Liquidity
4. Minimisation of risk.

An investor may decide on the basis of a detailed study of *Market information* that the shares he has sold earlier are worth buying again. The current prices may be higher than the price at which he has relinquished them. It is better to buy shares at *higher prices* in a rising market than to hold on to shares in a *falling market*. The *growth potential* of a company may improve due to a rising trend in *sales or profits, modernisation and expansion, changes in Government policies* and other such factors.

Portfolio Investment Process

The ultimate aim of the portfolio manager is to reduce the risk and increase the return to the investor in order to reach the investment objectives of an investor. The manager must be aware of the investment process. The process of portfolio management involves many logical steps like portfolio planning, portfolio implementation and monitoring. The portfolio investment process applies to different situations. Portfolios are owned by different individuals and organisations with different requirements. Investors should buy when prices are very low and sell when prices rise to levels higher than their normal fluctuations.

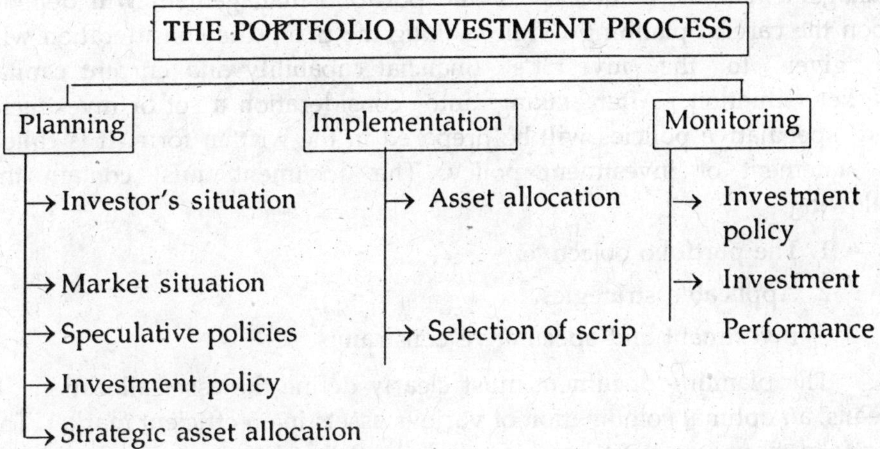

Applying the different steps for portfolio investment process can be complex and opinions are divided for maximisation of wealth to the investors. Many differences exist between present investment theory and empirical results and which have often contradictory results the following some basic principles should be applied to all portfolio decisions.

1. The quantum of risk to be acceptable.
2. The profits will vary along with variability of risk.
3. Individual securities affect the aggregate portfolio.
4. Portfolio should provide a sound liquidity position.
5. Diversification of a portfolio may decrease the risk level.
6. Portfolio should be tailored to the needs of investors.
7. Follow the passive investment startategy/or an active speculative strategy.

Portfolio investment process is an important step to meet the needs and convenience of investors. The portfolio investment process involves the following steps;

1. Planning of portfolio.
2. Implementation of portfolio plan.
3. Monitoring the performance of portfolio.

1. Portfolio Planning & Implementation

Planning is the most important element in a proper portfolio management. The success of the portfolio management will depend upon the careful planning. While making the plan, due consideration will be given to the investor's financial capability and current capital market situation. After taking into consideration a set of investment and speculative policies will be prepared in the written form. It is called as statement of investment policy. The document must contain the following;

1. The portfolio objective.
2. Applicable strategies.
3. Investment and speculative constraints.

The planning document must clearly define the asset allocation. It means, an optimal combination of various assets in an efficient market. The portfolio manager must keep in mind about the difference between basic pure investment portfolio and actual portfolio returns. The statement of investment policy may contain these elements. The portfolio planning comprises the following situations for its better performance.

a) Investor conditions

b) Market situation

c) Investment/strategic speculative policies.

d) Investment policy.

e) Asset Allocation.

A) Investor conditions

The portfolio shall be planned according to needs and convenience of portfolio owners. The needs of the owners are different, where it is depended upon their age, accepted level of risk, portfolio liquidation, their future requirements etc., *For ex: a 60 year old man with small amount of saving money* has a short term horizon, ability to accept little investment level of risk, needs protection against *short-term inflation. In contrast a young man investing for his retirement at 25 years have a long-term investment horizon, ability to accept a higher level of risk, and a need for long-term inflation*. Therefore, knowing the purpose of the portfolio investment makes it possible to begin sketching out appropriate investment/speculative policies. While preparing the investment planning the total economic position of the investor should be thoroughly observed. *The investor's knowledge* of various instruments also has as important impact on portfolio. The investor also must understand about the equity returns, short term bond returns, deviation of bond international investment environment, exchange rate risk etc., If the investor is unable to understand the nature and extent of a scrips *short and long-term risk* the scrip should not be held. The portfolio management's success, finally lies with the *tolerance* which the portfolio owner has of investment risk. It is clearly a typical aspect of developing a proper investment strategy. Investment theories are largely based on future at which the portfolio will be liquidated. The theoretical approach always reveals the *Standard Deviation* of the security portfolio's value at a particular date. But it depends upon important practical investment considerations. Therefore, the investor shall have understanding capabilities about *investment horizon, his reactions to portfolio results, and the nature and extent of security risk.*

B) Market Situations

The portfolio owner must known the latest developments in the market. He may be in a position to assess the potential of future returns on various capital market instruments. The investors expectation may be two types, *long-term expectations and short-term expectations*. The most important investment decision in portfolio construction is asset allocation. *Asset allocation* means the investment in different financial instruments at a percentage in portfolio. Generally the portfolio managers will allocate the funds among *1) Equity Shares, 2) Fixed Income Securities, 3) Money Market Investment, 4) Real Estate Investment, 5) Global Depository Receipts*. Some investment strategies are static. The portfolio requires changes according to investor's needs and knowledge. A continuous changes in portfolio leads to *higher* operating cost. *For ex:* The Mutual Funds, FIIs, spend large sums of money as brokerage charges. Thus, the portfolio owner should define the time period for rebalancing investment strategy. But this strategic rebalancing period is clearly difficult to make. Generally the potential *volatility* of equity and debt market is *2 to 3 years*. The another type of rebalancing strategy focusses *on the level of prices of a given financial asset.*

C) Speculative Policies

The portfolio owner may accept the speculative strategies in order to reach his goals of earning to maximum extant. If no *speculative* strategies are used the management of the portfolio is relatively easy. Speculative strategies may be categorised as *asset allocation timing decision or security selection decision.* Small investors can do by purchasing mutual funds which are indexed to a stock. Organisation with large capital can employ investment management firms to make their speculative trading decisions. If any portfolio owner wishes to involve in speculative strategies through *timing and security* selection, outside professional managers are more likely to provide better performance oriented services. Individual investors with small amount of capital cannot avail the speculative strategies.

D) Investment Policy

The investment policy of a portfolio is called as "*Statement of Investment policy.*" The statement of investment policy plays a vital role in the better portfolio management. The policy should be in the written form. The statements of investment policy can be amended regularly according to the needs of the investor. The statement of investment policy is the constitution of a portfolio. The document is more important and it may be frequently reviewed. The statement of investment policy should be prepared after the investor has fully investigated all major aspects of a portfolio. The investment policy statement has the following benefits;

1. Written document clearly defines all the affairs of selecting a better portfolio.
2. The evaluation of performance of the portfolio.
3. The *document* indicates the discipline and stability of a portfolio in long run.
4. It is a guiding force, and suggests the portfolio manager "*what to do, when to do, how to do.*"

The portfolio objective is the important element for a better investment planning. A clearly defined objective gives a direction towards achieving the targeted performance. Theoretically, the objective is to *minimise risk and maximise return* of the portfolio for a specified period.

The portfolio objectives usually are related to achieving the greatest return for a given risk level. The constraints of the portfolio reduces the chances of achieving the targeted portfolio objective. Generally every portfolio faces the following *constraints;*

1. Return-Risk relationship.
2. Types of instruments.
3. Taxation
4. Diversification.
5. Asset allocation.

1. Return-Risk Relationship

If the portfolio objective states that a high level of return, the important constraint is to accept the high level of risk also. The risk level may be found as a *''portfolio beta''* or *''The standard deviation''* of portfolio returns. But in practice such measures are not commonly used at present.

2. Types of Instruments

The manager of portfolio should have a clear understanding of the various types of securities which are available in the market. *For ex:* if *60%* of assets are to be invested in debt instruments; the manager should thoroughly know about the various instruments which are available in market and understand the duration of time, tax features, default risk etc.,

3. Taxation

Generally, the investors who do not pay taxes may wish to exclude the purchase of securities. Investors with average marginal tax rates may wish to include the statement. The portfolio can be reviewed periodically during the course of a year in order to identify possible tax benefits. Liquidity needs vary considerably among investors.

4. Diversification

The investment policy statement should be prepared in such a way that it must include the desired extent of diversification. The diversification can also include the following aspects:

1. The quantity of securities to beheld.
2. The maximum percentage of each security in the portfolio.
3. The variance of the portfolio returns.

5. Asset Allocation

The price levels of certain asset, industries or companies are temporarily be *too high or too low*. Portfolio holdings should depart from the asset mix called for asset allocation. The another type of active speculation involves the selection of securities within a given asset class. The allocation will call for broad diversification through an indexed holding.

Portfolio objectives and planning

The portfolio investment process involves the various situations, constraints and objectives. The portfolio owned by an organisation and an individual will differ. The portfolio objective is determined by the investment strategy, diversification and selection of investments. Before designing the portfolio, the manager should kept in mind about the basic facts of an investor. *i.e. the age, responsibilities, health, portfolio needs, his taxation status, accepted level of risk, the need for income, liquidity.* The investor's psychological attitude, personal and financial information may be helpful in designing of better portfolio.

Planning is the most important element in preparation of a better portfolio. Planning is a part of *risk-averse* process. Planning, a portfolio depends upon the accepted risk of an investor. The accepted risk may be influenced by the size of portfolio, return, time horizon, kinds of assets, tax factors, investor's financial capabilities etc., The *goal* may be growth or income oriented, the investors psychologically may be ready to earn *high current income, and high capital appreciation* or both even go together. The investor may choose any one of the factors. The investment strategy will depend upon portfolio objectives. The portfolio objectives may be achieved by;

a) Maintenance of liquidity

b) Balancing between income tax and capital gains tax.

c) Maintaince of a balance between equity and debt instruments.

d) Adjustment between high dividend earning and growth companies.

The ultimate aim is to minimise risk and maximise return. Risk and return are correlated. Construction and diversification of a portfolio reflects quite opposite attitudes. The general investment policy is to *buy equity shares only.* Investor may decide to buy *growth shares* rather than *quality growth shares.* The investor may further concentrate on speculative shares rather than quality growth shares. Most of the investors may opt for diversification to reduce the *Volalility of returns.* After deviding the portfolio objective the portfolio may be constructed according to needs and tastes of investor. Security analysis will play an important role. The following factors should be kept in mind by the investors while analysing the securities;

1. Application of fundamental and technical analysis.
2. Analyse the financial statements and predict intrinsic value.
3. Locate high dividend and low levered companies.
4. Inside information from concerned companies.
5. Identify the financial muscle companies.
6. High priority to stock broker, merchant banker's advice.
7. Assessing the real value of a share.

Portfolio management requires a periodic supervision of buy and hold philosophy, market sentiments for getting of high returns. For investment success, the timing is most important, and it depends upon enter and exit from stock market. Investors must be quickly responsive to market changes. The investor should take advantage of *over price or under price situations.*

Elements of Portfolio Management

The following are the elements of portfolio Management;

1. The portfolio should reflect the investor's objectives, preferences, constraints, his tastes which helps the formulation of the investment policy.
2. According to the investment policy different strategies are to be developed and implemented for construction of a portfolio.
3. Continuous evaluation of a portfolio and monitoring the performance can increase the returns.

PORTFOLIO MANAGEMENT

Portfolio consists of a collection of financial assets such as equity shares, bonds, treasury bills, debentures. The collection of properties may also be treated as portfolio. It refers to the various assets of an investor which are to be considered as a unit. According to SEBI rules 1993, it may be defined as "The total holding of securities belonging to any person."[1] A portfolio is therefore, not merely a collection of unrelated assets but a carefully blended asset combination within a framework. It is not desirable to invest the entire funds in a single security. Hence, the investment shall spread to different prospecting sectors with a time horizon. It is preferred that every security be viewed in a portfolio context. The expected return of a portfolio will depend upon the individual's security returns which contains the portfolio.

Portfolio management is a process encompassing many activities of investment in assets and securities. Portfolio management is a dynamic and flexible concept. The individual securities have their own risk and return characteristics. Portfolio analysis "Considers the determination of future risk and return in holding various blends of individual securities."[2] The portfolio analysis begins where the security analysis ends. Security analysis is the part of portfolio management. Security analysis refers to how to select a best scrip, at what price, at what time etc., But portfolio management involves the level of risk and return associated with the portfolio. It develops many techniques to escape the risk and increase its returns by the process of portfolio rebalancing. Portfolio management involves a continuous monitoring, evaluation, and performance, technique as a weapon to meet the investment target.

Differences between security analysis and portfolio management

The following are the differences between security analysis and portfolio Management;

i) Security analysis includes the security valuation. But the portfolio management includes valuation of risk, and expected return.

ii) Security analysis will commence before the buying of a different securities, whereas portfolio management commences after construction of a portfolio.

iii) The objective of security analysis is to findout the "intrinsic" value of a security. The intrinsic value is the actual worth of a financial asset. The objective of portfolio management is to maximise the returns and minimise the risk to the investor.

iv) The security analysis will make a perfect planning about selection of the industry, company for investment. Portfolio planning is the selection of best securities to meet the personal needs and desires of the investors.

v) The security analysis only recommends the sector, company scrip, time, etc., but the portfolio management will make more perfect assurance to the investors regarding the capital appreciation and regular returns.

vi) Security analysis is based on three main schools of thought i,e. Fundamental Analysis, Technical Analysis, Efficient Market Theory. The fundamental analysis is a tool to identify over valued and under valued securities. The technical analysis centres around studying the price movement of the stock and drawing inferences from them and then predicting the market price. The efficient market theory is based on the efficiency of the capital markets. Hence, the security analysis is mainly concentrated about selection of different alternatives of financial assets to construct an efficient portfolio.

The construction of a best portfolio will depend upon a careful security analysis. The portfolio management always thinks about the returns and rewards of a different financial assets which are fully involved with systematic and unsystematic risk. The portfolio management is mainly concentrated on the stock behaviour in the market. Selection of a particular scrip or financial asset is the responsibility of a security analyst. But the portfolio manager's obligation is to show best returns to the portfolio owner with a combination of different kinds of financial assets. Portfolio analysis indicates the determination of future risk and return in holding a different set of individual securities. The portfolio analysis contains the important lements as presented below;

1. Return on portfolio
2. Risk of a portfolio.

1. Return on portfolio

The portfolio value is highly influenced by return of individual securities. Each security in a portfolio contributes return in the proportion of its investment in security. Thus, the portfolio value may increase and the targeted goals can be achieved. The return on portfolio is the weighted average of the expected returns, from each securities with a proportionate weights of the different securities in the total investment. The return on portfolio depends upon the selection of financial asset which was made according to the investor's perception. The efficiency of a portfolio is highly influenced by a number of factors, i.e. investor's objective, investor's risk presumption, safety of investment, capital appreciation, liquidity of financial asset, hedging, time horizon set out by investor, constraints regarding diversification by the investor etc.

The data of the following table reveals the calculation of 4 portfolio's return and risk.

Security	proportion of funds invested in each security (weights)	Expected return on each security	Contribution of each security to return
X	35%	13%	4.55
Y	30%	18%	5.40
Z	20%	23%	4.60
A	15%	15%	2.25
	100%		16.8%

The above portfolio yields 16.8% return on an average of 4 kinds of securities.

The portfolio risk can be calculated by using the measures such as standard deviation and variance. These can be calculated by applying the following formula;

$$\text{Standard deviation} = \sqrt{\sum(x-\overline{x})^2} = \sqrt{\sum x^2}$$

$$\text{variance} = \sum(x-\overline{x})^2 = \sum x^2$$

x = Is the expected return on security '*X*'

$\overline{x}$ = Is the mean or the weighted average return on the security 'X'

$\therefore$ The co efficient of variance = $\frac{\sigma}{\overline{x}} \times 100$

The following table will explain the calculation of standard deviation for a given portfolio.

Securities	Return	Probability
1	7%	0.30
2	11%	0.55
3	15%	0.15

Ans:

(1)	Return (2)	Probability (3)	Weighted return (2×3)	Return deviation from mean	weighted deviations squared
1	7%	0.30	0.021	-0.033	0.001
2	11%	0.55	0.060	0.007	0.001
3	15%	0.15	0.022	0.047	0.002
		1.00	0.103		0.004

Average expected return 0.103 or 10.3 (mean)

The return deviation can be obtained as follows.

For Security 1 = (0.07-0.103) = -0.033

For Security 2 = (0.11-103) = 0.007

For Security 3 = (0.15-0.103) = 0.047

$\sigma^2 = 0.004$

$\sigma = \sqrt{\sigma^2} = \sqrt{0.004}$

$\sigma = 0.063$ or 6.3%

$\therefore$ The Co-efficient of Variation = $\frac{\sigma}{\overline{x}} \times 100 = \frac{6.3}{10.3} = 61\%$

2. Risk on a Portfolio

Risk is the most important element in portfolio management. Risk is reflected in the variability of the returns from zero to infinity. The risk on a portfolio is different from the risk on individual securities. The expected return of a portfolio depends on the probability of the returns and their weighted contribution to the risk. This is the essence of risk. Risk means, the probability of various possible bad outcomes from a constructed portfolio. The measurement of risk in portfolio involves (a) finding of average absolute deviation(b) standard deviation. These elements can be explained with following illustrations:

The probabilities of each of the returns of a portfolio are given below. Calculate the absolute deviations for the given portfolio.

Event	Return	Probability
1	0.20	-10
2	0.25	22
3	0.30	27
4	0.25	12

Estimation of absolute deviation;

Event (1)	Return (2)	Proba-bility (3)	Absolute return (2×3) (4)	Probability deviation (5)	(x) absolute deviation (5×2) (6)
1	0.20	-10	-2.0	-24.6	4.92
2	0.25	22	+5.5	7.4	1.85
3	0.30	27	+8.1	12.4	3.72
4	4 0.25	12	+3.0	-2.6	0.65
			+14.6		11.14%

Probability deviation can be calculated as follows (column.5);

- 10 - 14.6 = - 24.6

22 - 14.6 = + 7.4

27 - 14.6 = + 12.4

12 - 14.6 = - 2.6

∴ The measure of absolute deviation is 11.14%

Traditional Theory of Portfolio Management

Traditional portfolio theory deals with the evaluation of return and risk conditions of each security. It reveals the subjective nature. The value of a particular scrip depends upon the quantum of amounts of dividends declared by the company, the price earnings ratio. The EPS the holding period etc., It recognises specific type of risk and non risk factors. It was based on the risk. The risk can be measured for each individual security by calculating the standard deviation. It is further, suggested that the lowest standard deviation value security should be choosen. The highest value of standard deviation reveals the involvement of high risk component of that security.

Traditionally, portfolio selection has been viewed as an art form, perhaps ever a craft. The selection of security must be preceded by attenation to financial planning. The financial planning requires a careful consideration about the needs and provisions of the investor. The investor before entering the market, will have to look after the basic living expenses, savings, insurance and shelter costs. Then the investment in securities may be proved as a purposeful activity. Financial discipline is the most important element to the investors who want to be successful in stock market. The traditional approach recognises several basic tenets[1] for building a best portfolio. First, the investor prefers large to smaller returns from securities. Second, the way to achieve this goal is to make more risk. Third, the ability to achieve higher return depends upon the investor's judgment of risk and his ability to assume specific risks.

The traditional theory also takes into consideration the factors like, *interest rate risk, purchasing power risk, financial risk, taxation, and market ability*. Generally, the investors are interested for higher returns from securities. Therefore, they will have to face high risk also,. The investor ability to achieve high returns will depend upon many factors among them, the quantum of risk level to be faced is an important one. Portfolios are presumably constructed by employing securities associated with varying degrees of risk and non - risk factors. Spreading money among many securities can reduce the risk.

Assumptions

The traditional theory is based on the following assumptions.

a) It assumes that the market is inefficient.

b) It also thinks that the fundamentalists can take advantage of market inefficiency situation.

---

1. *Harry Saurian,* Investment Management, Prentice Hall, 1973.

c) It felt that the fundamentalists can earn quick profits.

d) It considers that the fundamentalists will expect the potential growth of a particular company for predicting the future trend of the share prices.

The traditional theory suggests the following;

1. An investor should make sufficient provision of money after all adjustments of his family expenses.
2. The investor must strictly stick on to financial discipline.
3. The investor should take greater protection for inflation.
4. The success of the investment game will depend upon the investor's psychology rather than the stock market gimmicks.

Modern Portfolio Theory (MPT)

The modern portfolio theory indicates the maximisation of returns through a combination of different securities. This theory tells us that risk can be reduced by combining low risk securities with high risk. This theory depends upon the concept of diversification. It believes that risk can be reduced by diversification. Modern theory of portfolio was based on research work of *Hary Markowitz and William Sharpe.*

Assumptions

Modern portfolio theory is based on the following assumptions;

1. It is based on assumption of free and perfect flow of information.
2. It believes that markets are perfect and absorbs all information quickly.
3. The riskiness of a financial asset in portfolio is to be seen in the context of market related risk or portfolio risk, but not in isolation

It also indicates that the returns are the same whenever you enter the market. This theory uses of Beta for measuring the market risk. The basis of a modern portfolio theory depends upon the following factors;

A) Diversification

B) Concept of dominance

C) The role of Beta

A) Diversification

Diversification means, investment of funds in more than one risky asset with the basic objective of risk reduction. The lay man can make good returns on his investment by making use of technique of diversification. The modern portfolio theory generally assumes of the following three forms of diversification.

1. Simple diversification.
2. Over diversification.
3. Efficient diversification.

1. Simple diversification

It involves a random selection of portfolio construction. The common man could make better returns by making a random diversification of investments. It is the process of altering the mix ratio of different components of a portfolio. The simple diversification can reduce unsystematic risk. The research studies on portfolio found that *10 to 15* securities in a portfolio will bring sufficient amount of returns. Further, this concept reveals that the prediction should be based on a scientific method.

2. Over diversification

Investors have the freedom to choose many investment alternatives to achieve the desired profit on his portfolio. However, the investor shall have a great knowledge regarding a large number of financial assets spreading different sectors, industries, companies. The investors also more careful about the liquidity of each investment, return, tax liability, the performance of the company etc., Investors find problems to handle the large number of investments. It involves more transaction cost and more money will be spent in managing over diversification. If any investor involves in over diversification, there may be a chance either to get higher return or exposure to more risk. All the problems involved in this process may result in inadequate return on the portfolio.

3. Efficient diversification

Efficient diversification means a combination of low risk involved securities and high risk instruments. The combination will only be finalised after considering the expected return from an individual security and its inter relationship with other components in a portfolio. The securities shall have to be evaluated and thus diversification to be restricted to some extent. Efficient diversification assures the better return at an accepted level of risk.

The modern portfolio theory indicates that the risk can be reduced by a balanced diversification. But, diversification requires a high talent, knowledge of industries, companies, product lines, business environment, indepth analysis about market share, growth areas, potential profit companies, etc.. Therefore, the modern portfolio theory hopes in diversification to achieve the desired goals.

B) Concept of Dominance

The return of the portfolio depends upon the accepted level of risk. If the investor wants to increase the return he will have to accept a higher level of risk also. The portfolio managers have more freedom in building up of a better portfolio. He has the opportunity to add risk free financial assets in his portfolio. Generally, the risk free instruments are available freely in the market like a government bond or bank deposit. If he incorporates such risk free financial assets, he lowers the risk of the portfolio, but, also correspondingly lowering of expected return. The concept of dominance shows that the equities can be combined with bonds or other riskless financial assets to enhance the returns and minimise the risk.

C) The Role of Beta

Beta is a measure of volatility faced by an asset or a portfolio. It measures the systematic risk. It is also called as market risk. "The systematic risk can be reduced by beta. It measures sensitivity of the return of one asset to the market return. Any financial asset will have a total return consisting of two elements; 1. Risk free return 2. Risk premium. Risk free return means a return which faces little loss of liquidity for the period of investment. Risk premium is a return for risk taking and it varies from asset to asset.

Modern portfolio theory explains that, diversification reduces the total risk, subject to company's unsystematic risk. The Beta's importance lies for managing non-diversifiable part of risk. In the capital market, different financial assets are available like equity, debentures, public sector bonds and Government securities. Among these instruments equities are most risky, followed by debentures which is less risky and the PS bonds & Govt. Securities are least risky. Different financial assets will have different risk characteristics. Money market instruments like treasury bills, commercial bills, are less risky. The risk characteristics of various financial assets are different. Generally the following major asset classes are used for portfolios by mutual funds and professional fund managers;

a) Equity shares.

b) Bonds, debentures.

c) Money market instruments.

Usually, investors differentiate among four goals; current income, growth in *current income, capital appreciation, and preservation of capital.* No investor wants to lose money. But every one wants to get more returns from the market through an efficient portfolio. Therefore the search for capital gains inevitably involves risk of loss of capital, high income is frequently associated with high risk. The modern portfolio depends upon the factors like *investment strategy, risk management strategy, duration of the portfolio, target return, etc.*

The investment strategy will depend upon the investor's background. Investor's database is the main element for designing a better investment strategy. The investors, want a regular income or capital appreciation or a mixture of both income and appreciation. Asset allocation is the another important factor in investment strategy process. Risk management strategy indicates the risk elimination from the efficient portfolio. The duration concept can be explained by taking the life or maturity period of the asset. The ideal duration period of any portfolio is 5 years. The target return will be achieved by the portfolio through the accepted level of risk. The difference between traditional portfolio theory and modern portfolio theory are presented below.

Traditional Portfolio Theory	Modern portfolio Theory
1. It deals with the evaluation of return and risk conditions in each security.	1. It deals with the maximisation of returns through a combination of different types of financial assets.
2. It is based on measurement of standard deviation of a particular scrip.	2. It is based on mainly diversification process.
3. It assumes that market is inefficient.	3. It assumes that market is perfect and all information is known to public.
4. It gives more importance to standard deviation.	4. It gives more importance to beta.

The following are some of the important Modern Portfolio theories:

1. Markowitz Theory of Portfolio Management.
2. Sharpe's Theory of Portfolio Management
3. Capital Asset Pricing Model (CAPM).

MARKOWITZ THEORY OF PORTFOLIO MANAGEMENT

The modern portfolio theory was developed by *Dr. Hary M. Markowitz* in 1952. He generated a number of portfolios within a given amount of investible funds. He started with the idea of risk aversion of average investors. It is a model based on a theoretical frame work for analysis of risk and return. He used the standard deviation for measurement of risk. He also utilised the relationship between securities for selection of better asset mix in a portfolio. His entire work led to the concept of efficient portfolio. An efficient portfolio is expected to yield the highest return for low level of risk. According to Markowitz "*A portfolio is said to be efficient, if it is expected to yield the highest possible return for the lowest risk or a given level of risk.*"[1] A portfolio is not efficient if there is another portfolio with high return and low risk. An investor can reduce the risk by diversification of his investment portfolio. Markowitz model is a theoretical frame work for the analysis of risk return choice. If an investor wants to build an efficient portfolio, first he has to chose an expected return level with a minimum risk level.

The portfolio selection is not a simple choice of any one security or securities, but a right combination of securities. He emphasised that quality of a portfolio will depend upon the quality of individual assets in a portfolio. Therefore, the combined risk of two different financial assets is not the same like the separate risk of two assets. Risk and reward are two important elements considered by a general investors. The return may vary depending on , circumstances. Risk is measured by the variance of the distribution which are called as variance and co-variance. As per the modern port folio theory the expected return, the variance of these returns and co-variance of the returns of the securities within the portfolio are to be considered for the choice of a portfolio. A set of efficient portfolio earns by the process of combining various securities, whose combined risk is lowest for an accepted level of return.

Assumptions

The Assumptions: *Markowitz* theory is based on the following assumptions:

1. Investors behave rationally
2. Investors know all the information about the market situation.
3. Investors choose higher returns to lower level of risk.
4. The markets are efficient and they absorb information quickly and perfectly.

1. Investment Management, *V.A. Avadhani*, P.No. 582, 1999. Himalaya Publishing House.

5. Investors are risk averse.
6. Investors can reduce their risk by adding new investments in the portfolio.
7. Investors will get a higher rate of return if they adopt the efficient portfolio model.
8. By combining all the financial assets, the return on various securities as to be correlated to each other.
9. Investors decisions are based on expected return and their variance.

The Modern portfolio theory indicates that the risk can be reduced by diversification. It believes in perspective of combination of securities under constraints of risk and return. Modern portfolio theory is the combination of securities to get the most efficient portfolio. The efficiency of a portfolio is based on the quality of analysis and predictions of the market. *Return is always chased by Risk."*

A combination of securities may help to spread risk over manay securities. The inter relationship between securities may be specified only broadly. Ex: The relation between auto stocks and tyre stocks, utility stocks and steel, cement stocks etc.

A portfolio consisting of two stocks is probably less risky than one holding either stock alone. But the combination of two securities are more important in portfolio construction. Markowitz's approach to build up with good portfolio possibilities has its roots in risk return relationships. The investor's attitude towards portfolios depends exclusively upon;

a) Expected return and risk.

b) Quantification of risk.

Risk is the statistical notation of variance, or standard deviation of return. These simple assumptions are strong and disrupted by many traditional theorists.

Impact of combining two securities

Holding two securities is probably less risky than holding either security alone. It is possible to reduce the risk of a portfolio by incorporating into it a security whose risk is greater than that of any of the investments held initially. But it will depend upon the quantum of ratio of two securities. Therefore, the measurement of expected return on portfolio can be calculated through the following formula.

I. Measurement of expected return on portfolio

$$R_p = \sum_{i=1}^{N} X_i R_i$$

where;

R_p = expected return to portfolio

X_i = Proportion of total portfolio invested in security " i "

R_i = Expected return to security " i ".

n = Total number of securities in portfolio.

II. Co-variance of two securities

The interactive risk of two securities is called as "co-variance." If the rates of return of two securities move together, then their interactive risk is called as co-variance is positive. If the rates of returns are independent co-variance is zero. Inverse movements results in negative co-variance. The co-variance of two securities is presented in the following formula;

$$\text{Co - variance} = \text{COVxy} = \frac{1}{N}\sum^{N}(Rx - \overline{R}x)(Ry - \overline{R}y)$$

COV_{xy} = Co-variance between x and y securities.

R_x = Return on security x.

R_y = Return on security y.

$\overline{R}x$ = Expected return on security x

$\overline{R}y$ = Expected return on security y

No = Number of portfolios.

III. Co-efficient of correlation between two securities

It is a measure to indicate the similarity or dissimilarity in the behaviour of two securities return.

$$r_{xy} = \frac{\text{co - variance of x and y}}{\sigma_x \sigma_y}$$

r_{xy} = Coefficient of correlation between x and y securities.

Cov_{xy} = Co-variance between x and y securities.

$$Cov_{xy} = \frac{1}{N}\sum^{N}(R_x - \overline{R}_x)(R_y - \overline{R}_y)$$

$\sigma x \sigma y$ = The standard deviations of x and y securities.

R_x = Return on security x

R_y = Return on security y

$\overline{R}_x$ = Expected return on security x

$\overline{R}_y$ = Expected return on security y.

Full Co-variance model

Markowtiz model is called as full co-variance model. According to this approach the portfolio return will depend upon the different types of security purchase. The effect of one security purchase over the effect of the other security is taken into consideration and then the results are measured by three important variables *i.e.*''*Return, standard deviation and coefficient of correlation.*" Co-variance of the securities will help in finding out the interactive risk between securities. The return on securities increases or decreases, when the co-variance is positive. If rate of return on securities is independent, there is no relation between two securities return, then the *co-variance is zero.* If the returns on different securities are inversely related to each other, the co-variance will become *negative.* Therefore, the co-variance will depend upon the rate of return on securities.

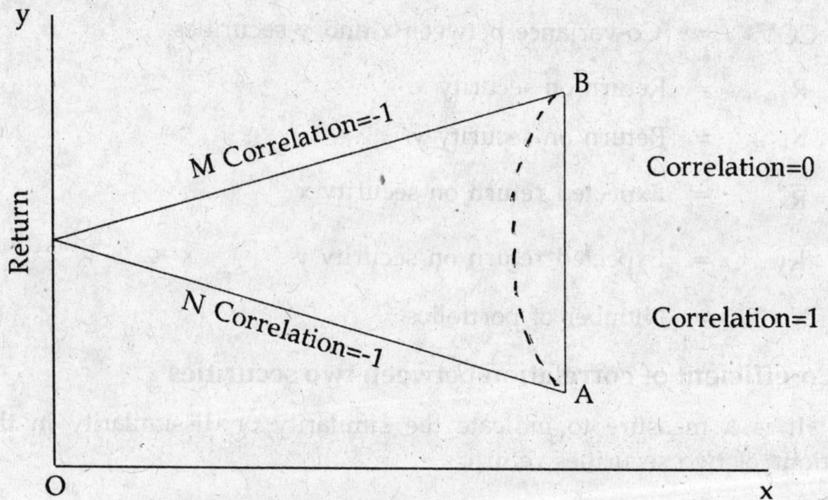

The above diagram shows inverse relationship between M and N.

a) M has higher return than N with equal risk when the risk is reduced to zero.

b) Securities at BDE provide better return than ACE when correlation is '*O*'

c) A and B are positively Correlated.

Markowitz model concludes that efficient frontier portfolio is to be considered by the investors. The model also reveals the least portfolio risk at a particular level of return and his analysis is depicted in the form of diagram of securities as presented below.

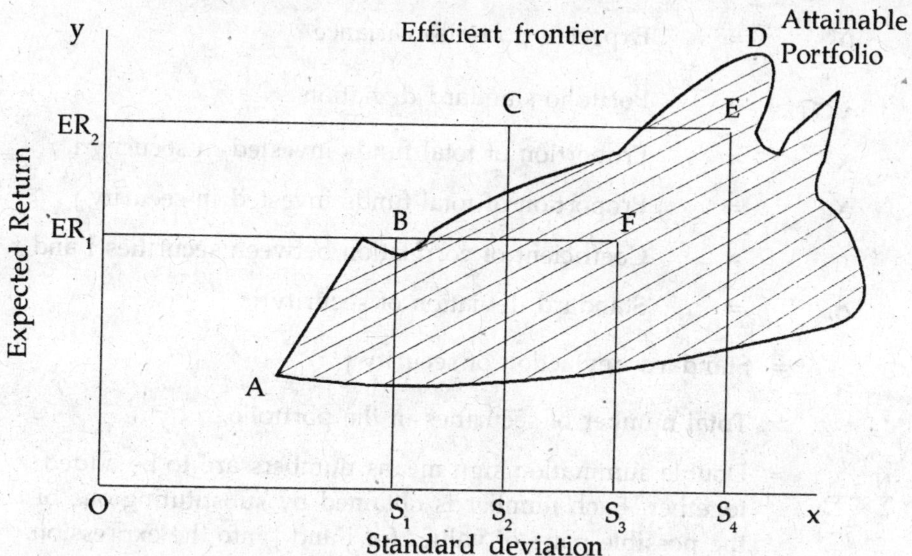

The shaded portion of area indicates attainable set of portfolio combination it can be constructed from a given number of securities. According to the diagram the securities BCD stands on the efficient line AD are treated as the portfolios on the efficient frontier ABCD is a boundary of the attainable set. The efficient frontier appears as a budge or Arc. Only those assets which perfectly positively correlated will generate an efficient frontier. The diagram further reveals that the portfolio B dominates portfolio F and C dominates E because the return is the same but the risk greater at F and E.

Impact of 3 securities on portfolio

Portfolio composed of some proportions of three securities namely A, B and C. AD represents all portfolios composed of AB, AC represents of all portfolios composed of B and C and soon. All these security pairs may have correlation coefficients less than +1.0. The risk return in a three security case uses the same formula for expected portfolio return indicated earlier.

$$RP = \sum_{i=1}^{N} XiRi$$

The portfolio standard deviation depends upon the standard deviations of return for its components, their correlation co-efficients and the proportions invested. It can be calculated through the following formula;

$$\sigma_p^2 = \sum_{i=1}^{N} \sum^{N} x_i x_j x_{ij} \sigma_i \sigma_j$$

σ_P^2	=	Expected portfolio variance
$\sqrt{\sigma_P^2}$	=	Portfolio standard deviation
X_i	=	Proportion of total funds invested in security i
X_j	=	Proportion of total funds invested in security j
r_{ij}	=	Coefficient of correlation between securities i and j
σ_i	=	Standard deviation of security i
σ_j	=	Standard deviaction of security j
N	=	Total number of securities in the portfolio.
$\sum_{i=1}^{N} \sum_{j=1}^{N}$	=	Double summation sign means numbers are to be added together. Each number is obtained by substituting one of the possible pairs of values for i and j into the expression.

for N = 2

$$\sigma_p^2 = x_i x_j\ r_{1.1}\sigma_1\sigma_1 + x_1 x_2 r_1 r_{1.2}\sigma_1\sigma_2 + x_2 x_1 r_{2.1}\sigma_2\sigma_1 + x_2 x_2 r_{2.2}\sigma_2\sigma_2$$

Thus $r_{1.2} = 1 \quad r_{1.3} = 1 \quad r._{2.3} = 1$

$$\sigma_p^2 = x_1^2\sigma_1^2 + x_2^2\sigma_2^2 + 2x_1x_2r_{1.2}\sigma_1\sigma_2$$

because $r_{ij}\ \sigma_i\sigma_j = Cov_{ij}$

We can simplify, further to $\sigma_p^2 = \sum_{i=1}^{N} \sum_{j=1}^{N} x_i x_j Cov_{ij}$

For building up the efficient set of portfolio as laid down by Markowitz, the investor need to look into these important parameters.

a) Expected return

b) Variance of returns

c) Covariance (variance of one asset return to other asset returns)

REVIEW PROBLEMS

Illustration No. 1: Monex owns a portfolio of two securities with the following expected returns, standard deviations and weights.

Security	*Expected return*	*Standard deviation*	*Weight*
X	11%	14%	.30
Y	14%	19%	.70

What are the maximum and minimum portfolio standard deviations for varying levels of correlation between two securities?

Solution:

$$\sigma_p = \left[x_A^2\sigma_A^2 + x_B^2\sigma_B^2 + 2x_A x_B r_{AB}\sigma_A\sigma_B\right]^{1/2}$$

σ_p = Standard deviation of a portfolio

x_A^2 = Proportion of weight of security x

σ_A^2 = Standard deviation square of a security x

x_B^2 = Proportion of weight of a security y

σ_A^2 = Standard deviation square of security x.

σ_B^2 = Standard deviation square of a security y

σ_A = Standard deviation of x security

σ_B = Standard deviation of y security

r_{AB} = Correlation of two securities x and y

x_A^2 0.30 $x_B^2 = 0.70$ $r_{AB} = +1$ Correlation between x and y securities. (Maximum level)

$\sigma_A^2 = 14^2$ $\sigma_B^2 = 19^2$

$\sigma_A = \sqrt{14}$ $\sigma_B = \sqrt{19}$ $r_{AB} = -1$ Correlation between x and y securities (Minimum level)

by substituting the values in the formula, we can get

$$\sigma_P = \left[(0.3)^2(14)^2 + (0.7)^2(19)^2 + 2(0.3)(0.7)(14)(19)r_{AB}\right]^{1/2}$$

by simplifying the values

$$= [(0.09)(196) + (0.49)(361) + 2 \times 55.86\ r_{AB}]^{1/2}$$

$$= [17.64 + 176.89 + 111.72\, r_{AB}]^{1/2}$$

$$= [17.64 + 176.89 + 111.72\, r_{AB}]^{1/2}$$

The portfolio standard deviation will be at maximum when the correlation between x and y is +1.0. Therefore;

$$= \left[17.64 + 176.89 + (111.72 \times 1)\right]^{1/2}$$

$$= \left[17.64 + 176.89 + 111.72\, r_{AB}\right]^{1/2}$$

$$= [306.25]^{1/2}$$

$\sqrt{306.25} = 17.5\%$. The portfolio standard deviation will be at maximum level.

The correlation between securities x and y is +1.0. Then the minimum level of standard deviation as follows by substituting the values we can get

$$\sigma_p = \left[17.64 + 176.89 + 111.72 \times -1\right]^{1/2}$$

$$= \left[17.64 + 176.89 - 111.72\right]^{1/2}$$

$$= \left[17.64 + 65.17\right]^{1/2}$$

$$= \sqrt{82.81} = 9.1$$

Illustration No.2: A portfolio consisting of 5 securities is listed below. Calculate each stock's expected return. By using the individual security's expected return, compute the portfolio's expected return.

Stock	Intial investment	Expected end of period investment value	Proportion of portfolio's intial market value
M	Rs.10,000	Rs.14,000	18%
N	Rs. 5,000	Rs. 8,000	8%
O	Rs. 8,000	Rs.10,000	14%
P	Rs.20,000	Rs.24,000	38%
Q	Rs. 7,000	Rs.10,000	10%

Solution:

The portfolio's expected return will be calculated by the following formula;

$$\overline{R}_p = \sum_{i=1}^{n} (x_i R_i)$$

$\overline{R}_p$ = Expected return on portfolio

n = Number of securities in portfolio

x_i = Proportion of portfolio's intial market value

R_i = Expected rate of return on individual securities

The expected return and the proportion of portfolio's intial market value can be found in the following table;

Stock	*Return* (E – I)[1]	*Percentage (Return) (Ri)*
M	Rs.14,000-10,000 = Rs.4,000	$4{,}000 \times 100 \div 10{,}000 = 40\%$
N	Rs.8,000-5,000 = Rs.3,000	$3{,}000 \times 100 \div 5{,}000 = 60\%$
O	Rs.10,000-8,000 = Rs.2,000	$2{,}000 \times 100 \div 8{,}000 = 25\%$
P	Rs.24,000-20,000 = Rs.4,000	$4{,}000 \times 100 \div 20{,}000 = 20\%$
Q	Rs.10,000-7,000 = Rs.3,000	$3{,}000 \times 100 \div 7{,}000 = 42.86\%$

$\therefore$ Ri = 40% Ri = 60% Ri = 25% Ri = 20% Ri = 42.86%

Xi = 18% Xi = 8% Xi = 14% Xi = 38% Xi = 10%

1. E = Expected end of period investment value
2. I = initial investment

10,000 - 4,000 profit

100 - ?

$$\frac{100 \times 4{,}000}{10{,}000} = 40\%$$

$\therefore \overline{R}_p = \sum_{i=1}^{5} (X_i R_i)$ by substituting the values in the formula we can get

$$\overline{R}_p = (0.18 \times 40\%) + (0.08 \times 60\%) \mid (6.14 \times 25\%) \mid (0.38 \times 20\%) \mid (.10 \times 42.86\%)$$

$$\overline{R}_p = (7.2) + (4.8) + (3.5) + (7.6) + (4.3)$$

by simplifying the values $\overline{R}_p = 27.4\%$

Illustration No.3: Mr. Anand owns three securities and has estimated return in following joint probability distribution;

Out come	Security x	Security y	Security z	Probability
1	13	-14	0	0.12
2	10	-4	8	0.17
3	3	0	10	0.27
4	-1	2	14	0.26
5	6	8	9	0.18

Calculate the portfolio's expected return if, Anand invests 30% in security x, 30% in security y and 40% in security z. Assume that each security return is completely uncorrelated with the returns of the other securities.

Solution:

The expected returns of the securities in the portfolio are as follows;

$\overline{R}_x = (\text{Px return})$ P = Probability

$\overline{R}x = (0.12 \times 13) + (0.17 \times 10) + (0.27 \times 3) + (0.26 \times -1) + (0.18 \times -6)$

$= 1.56 + 1.70 + 0.81 - 0.26 + -1.08$

$= 4.07 - 0.26 + 01.08 = 2.73$

$\overline{R}x = 2.73$

$\overline{R}y = (0.12 \times -14) + (0.17 \times -4) + (0.27 \times 0) + (2.6 \times 2) + (0.18 \times 8)$

$\overline{R}y = -1.68 - 0.68 + 0 + 0.52 + 1.44$

$\overline{R}y = -2.36 + 1.96$

$\overline{R}_y = -0.4$

$\overline{R}z = (0.12 \times 0) + (0.17 \times 8) + (0.27 \times 10) + (0.26 \times 14) + (0.18 \times 9)$

$\overline{R}z = 0 + 1.36 + 2.7 + 3.64 + 1.62$

$\overline{R}z = 9.32$

$\therefore Rx = 2.73 \; Ry = -0.4 \quad R_z = 9.32$

$\therefore$ expected return on the portfolio of securities

$$\therefore \overline{R}_p = \sum_{i=1}^{n} (x_iR_i)$$

$\overline{R}_p$ = Expected return on portfolio

x_i = Proportion of portfolio's investment

R_i = Expected rate of return on individual security

$x_i = 30\%,\ x_i = 30\%, x_i = 40\%, R_i = 2.73, R_i = -0.4, R_i = 9.32$

$\overline{R}p = (0.3 \times 2.73) + (0.30 \times -0.4) + (0.4 \times 9.32)$

$\therefore$ expected return on total portfolio is 4.427

Illustration No. 4: Given the following information about two securities calculate the covariance between two securities and correlation between them.

Particulars	*Stock x*	*Stock y*
1. Return (%)	7 or 11	13 or 5
2. Probability	0.5 each return	0.5 each return
3. Variance (%)	4	16
4. Standard deviation (%)	2	4

Solution:

At the first instance, calculate expected return on each security.

$\therefore$ Expected return on $x = (P \times R)$

P = Probability R = Return on security

Calculation of correlation between two securities.

$$r_{xy} = \frac{Cov.xy}{\sigma_x \sigma_y}$$

r_{xy} = Co-efficient of correlation of x and y.

Cov_{xy} = Covariance between x and y.

σ_x = standard deviation of x

σ_y = standard deviation of y

The values are as follows;

Cov.xy= -8.

$\sigma_x = 2.$

$\sigma_y = 4$

$$\therefore r_{xy} = \frac{-8}{(2)(4)} = \frac{-8}{8} = -1$$

If the Coefficient of Correlation between two securities is -1.0, then a perfect negative correlation exists.

Illustration No.5: Consider the following three securities and the relevant data on each.

Particulars	Stock1	Stock2	Stock3
1. Expected return	12	14	10
2. Standard deviation	12	17	7

3. Correlation Co-efficients

Stocks 1,2 = 0.4

Stocks 2,3 = 0.5

Stocks 1,3 = 0.6

What are portfolio risk and return if the following proportions are assigned to each stock? stock 1 = 0.3 stock 2 = 0.3 stock 3= 0.4 .

Solution:

The portfolio return can be calculated through the formula.

$$R_p = \sum_{i=1}^{N} x_i R_i$$

R_p = Return on portfolio.

x_i = Proportion of portfolio investment

R_i = Expected rate of return on security.

x_i = 0.3 x_i = 0.3 x_i = 0.4 R_i = 12 R_i = 14 R_i = 10.

R_p = (0.3)(12)+(0.3)(14)+(0.4)(10)

R_p = 3.6+4.2+4.0= 11.8.

The following formula will help for calculation of portfolio risk;

$$\sigma_p^2 = x_1^2\sigma_1^2 + x_2^2\sigma_2^2 + x_3^2\sigma_3^2 + 2x_1x_2r_{1.2}\sigma_1\sigma_2 + 2x_2x_3r_{2.3}\sigma_2\sigma_3 + 2x_1x_3r_{1.3}\sigma_1\sigma_3$$

The values are as follows:

x_1 = 0.3 σ_1 = 12 r_1 = 0.4

x_2 = 0.3 σ_2 = 17 r_2 = 0.5

x_3 = 0.4 σ_3 = 7 r_3 = 0.6

$$\sigma_p^2 = (0.3)^2(12)^2 + (0.3)^2(17)^2 + (0.4)^2(7)^2 + 2(0.3)(0.3)(0.4)(12)(17) + 2(0.3)(0.4)(0.5)(17)(7) + 2(0.3)(0.4)(0.6)(12)(7)$$

(0.09)(144)+(0.09)(289)+(0.16)(49)+2(0.09)(81.6)+2(0.06)119+2(0.072)(84)

= 12.96+26.01+7.84+14.69+14.28+12.09

= 87.87

σ_p = $\sqrt{87.87}$ = 9.37

ER = (0.5x(7)+(0.5x(11)

ER_x = 3.5+5.5=9

ER_y = (0.5)(13)+(0.5)(5)

= 6.5+2.5 = 9

∴ Expected return on stock x is 9

executed return on stock y is 9

Calculation of covariance between two securities is as follows;

$$\mathrm{Cov}_{xy} = \frac{1}{N}\sum^{N} \left[R_x - \overline{R}_x\right]\left[R_y - \overline{R}_y\right]$$

Cov_{xy} = Covariance between x and y.

R_x = Return on security x

R_y = Return on security y

$\overline{R}_x$ = Expected return on security x

$\overline{R}_y$ = Expected return on security y.

N = number of observations.

Particulars	*Return*	*Expected return*	*Difference*	*Product*
Stock x	7	9	-2	
Stock y	13	9	+4	(-2x+4)=(-8)
Stock x	11	9	+2	
Stock y	5	9	-4	(+2 x -4 = -8)

by substituting the values in the formula:

$R_x = 7 \quad \overline{R}_x = 9 \quad R_y = 13 \quad \overline{R}_y = 9$

$$\mathrm{Cov} = \frac{1}{2}\left[(7-9)(13-9)+(11-9)(5-9)\right]$$

$$\mathrm{Cov} = \frac{1}{2}\left[(1-2)(4)+(2)(-4)\right]$$

simplifying the values $= \frac{1}{2}(-8)+(-8)$

$= \frac{1}{2}(-16) = -8$

Covariance between two securities is -8

Illustration No.6: Calculate the covariance and coefficient of correlation from the following data. Stocks are x and y and their returns and expected returns are given below.

Particulars	*expected return*	*return*
stock x	16	20
stock y	28	20
stock x	24	20
stock y	12	20

Solution:

For calculation of covariance and coefficient of correlation, at first, arithmetic mean should be calculated and then standard deviation.

stock x	stock y	dx	dy	dx^2	dy^2
16	28	-4	+8	16	64
24	12	+4	-8	16	64
40	40			32	128

Calculation of arithmetic mean;

$$\bar{x} = \frac{\Sigma x}{n} \qquad \bar{y} = \frac{\Sigma y}{n}$$

$$\bar{x} = \frac{40}{2} = 20 \qquad \bar{y} = \frac{40}{2} = 20$$

Calculation of standard deviation;

$$\sigma_x = \sqrt{\frac{dx^2}{n}} \qquad \sigma_y = \sqrt{\frac{dy^2}{n}}$$

$$\sum dx^2 = 32 \qquad \sum dy^2 = 128$$

$$n = 2 \qquad n = 2$$

$$\sigma_x = \sqrt{\frac{32}{2}} \qquad \sigma_y = \sqrt{\frac{128}{2}}$$

$$= \sqrt{16} = 4 \qquad = \sqrt{64} = 8$$

$$\sigma_x = 4 \qquad \sigma_y = 8$$

Calculation of Co-variance;

$$Cov_{xy} = \frac{1}{N}\sum_{t=1}^{N}(r_{xi} - \bar{r}_x)(r_{yi} - \bar{r}_y)$$

r_{xi} = Return on x security

$\bar{r}_x$ = Arithmetic mean of x security

r_{yi} = Return on y security

$\bar{r}_y$ = Arithmetic mean of y security.

	Return	*Expected return*	*Difference*	*Product of difference*
stock x	16	20	-4	$\rightarrow -4 \times +8 = -32$
stock y	28	20	+8	
stock x	24	20	+4	$\rightarrow +4 \times -8 = -32.$
stock y	12	20	-8	

$r_{xi} = 16, \quad r_{xi} = 24$

$\bar{r}_x = 20m \quad \bar{r}_x = 20$

$r_{yi} = 28, \quad r_{yi} = 12$

by substituting the values in the formula;

$$CV = \frac{1}{2}(16-20)(28-20) + \frac{1}{2}(24-20)(12-20)$$

$$CV = \frac{1}{2}(-4)(+8) + \frac{1}{2}(4)(-8)$$

$$CV = \frac{1}{2}(-32) + \frac{1}{2}(-32)$$

$$CV = -16 \pm 16 = -32$$

Calculation of correlation; $r_{xy} = \frac{cov.xy}{\sigma_x \sigma_y}$

r_{xy} = Coefficient of correlation.

$Cov.xy = -32 \qquad \sigma_x = 4 \sigma_y = 8$

$$r_{xy} = \frac{-32}{4 \times 8} = \frac{-32}{32} = -1$$

Correlation coefficient is negative and they are perfectly negatively correlated with a value of 1.

Illustration No.7: Given the following data, calculate the covariance of returns for assets x and y.

State of the market	*Probability*	*Annual returns* x	y
1	0.30	7%	8%
2	0.20	12%	-2%
3	0.10	-6%	10%
4	0.40	9%	-7%

Solution

a) The first step is calculation of expected return of portfolio.

b) The second step, calculation of co-variance between two securities.

c) Final step requires calculation of coefficient of correlation.

a) The expected return of the portfolio can be calculated through the following formula;

$$R_p = \sum_{i=1}^{n} (x_i R_i)$$

R_p = Expected return on portfolio.

X_i = Proportion of portfolio's investment.

R_i = Expected return on individual security.

X_i = 0.30 X_i = 0.20 X_i = 0.10 X_i = 0.40.

Ri_x = (7) Ri_x = 12 Ri_x = -6 Ri_x = -7

by substituting the values in the formula, we can get expected return;

$$E_{rx} = (0.30) \times 7 + (0.20)(12) + (0.10)(-6) + (0.40)(-7)(2.1) + (2.4) + (-0.6) + (-2.8)$$

on simplification 4.5+-3.4 = 1.1%

E_{ry} = (0.30)(8)+(0.20)(-2)+(0.10)(10)+(0.40)(-7)

= (2.4)+(-0.4)+(1)+(-2.8)

= 2.4+ -0.4+1 $\pm$ 2.8

= 3.4 $\pm$ 3.12

= 0.28 or 2.8%

The co-variance can be calculated;

Probability	rx	ry	(rx-er)	(ry-er)	products.
(1)	(2)	(3)	(4)	(5)	(4 × 5=6)
0.30	7	8	(7-1.1)=5.9	(8-2.8)=5.2	0.30 × 5.9 × 5.2=9.20
0.20	12	-2	(12-1.1)=10.9	(-2-2.8)=-4.8	0.20 × 10.9 × -4.8=-10.46
0.10	-6	10	(-6-1.1)=-7.1	(10-2.8)=7.2	0.10 × -7.1 × 7.2=-5.11
0.40	9	-7	(9-7)=-16	(-7-2.8)-9.8	0.40 × -16 × -9.8=62.72
					+71.7
					- 15.57
				Cov.xy	56.13

Correlation Coefficient = $r_{xy} = \dfrac{Cov.xy}{\sigma_x \sigma_y}$

$$\sigma_x = \sqrt{\sum(x-\bar{x})^2}$$

$$^2_x = 0.3(7-1.1)^2 + 0.20(12-1.1)^2 + 0.10(-7.1-1.1)^2 + 0.4(9-7)^2$$

$$^2_x = 0.3(5.9)^2 + 0.20(10.9)^2 + 0.10(-7.1)^2 + 0.40(9-16)^2$$

$$^2_x = 0.3(34.81) + (0.20)(118.81) + 0.10(50.41) + 0.40(256)$$

$$\sigma^2_x = 10.44 + 23.76 + 5.041 + 102.4 = 141.64$$

$$\sigma^2_x = 141.64$$

$$\sigma^2_x = \sqrt{141.64} = 11.90$$

by substituting the above table values, σ_y can be found as (column. No.5);

$$\sigma^2_y = 0.30(5.2)^2 + 0.20(-4.8)^2 + 0.10(7.2)^2 + 0.40(-9.8)^2$$

$$\sigma^2_y = 0.30(27.04) + 0.20(23.04) + 0.10(51.84) + 0.40(96.04)$$

$$= 8.112 + 4.608 + 5.184 + 38.41 = 56.32$$

$$\sigma^2_y = \sqrt{56.32} = 7.50$$

Cov.xy = −69.09 $\sigma_x = 11.90$

$\sigma_y = 11.90$

$$\therefore \text{ Correlation} = r_{xy} = \frac{\text{Cov.xy}}{\sigma_x \sigma_y} = \frac{56.13}{11.9 \times 7.5} = \frac{56.13}{89.25}$$

$$= r_{xy} = +0.63$$

SHARPE'S PORTFOLIO THEORY

The another modern portfolio theory is Sharpe's model. This model was developed by William Sharpe. He simplified the method of diversification of portfolios. Sharpe published a model simplifying the mathematical calculations done by the Markotwiz model. According to Sharpe's model,[1] the theory estimates, the expected return and variance of indices which may be one or more and are related to economic activity. This theory has come to be known as Market Model.

Assumptions

Sharpe's portfolio theory is based on the following assumptions:

1. The securities returns are related to each other.
2. The expected return and variances of indices are the same.
3. The return on individual securities is determined by unpredictable factors.

Sharpe's single index model will reduce the market related risk and maximise the returns for a given level of risk. Sharpe's model will take into consideration the total risk of portfolio. The total risk consists of both systematic and unsystematic risk. The risk may be eliminated by diversification. If the diversification is perfect and unsystematic risk is negligible, then it is very easy to overcome the systematic risk.

The return on security's increase or decrease is depending upon a great extent in the market index. The movement of security return shows the correlation with the market index. The individual security's return is determined by the following equation;

$$R_i = \alpha_i + \beta_i + e_i$$

1. *Fisher* and *Jordan*, security analysis and portfolio management, P.No.575, Prentice Hall of India, 1996

R_i = Expected return on security

α_i = Alpha Coefficient

β_i = Beta Coefficient

I = The level of market return index

e_i = Error(residual risk of a company)

Beta is a measure of volatility faced by a financial asset or a portfolio or a project return.

Alpha (α) is the measurement of difference between actual earned return and expected return at a level of systematic risk.

Sharpe's index model takes into consideration the regression equation through beta coefficient (β) and alpha(α). Alpha and beta will remain constant and calculation of expected return on the portfolio can be calculated as follows;

$$E_p = \sum_{i=1}^{n} w_i(\alpha_{pi} + \beta_{iI}) = E_p = \sum_{i=1}^{n} w_i(\alpha_i + \beta_{iI})$$

E_p = expected return on portfolio

w_i = proportion of security i in the portfolio.

α_i = alpha of security i

β_i = Beta of security i

I_i = market index estimate

Alpha and beta are the tools to find the total risk in a portfolio. The regression coefficient comprises the value of alpha through the following equation;

$$y = a + bx$$

y = regression coefficient.

a = alpha

b = beta.

Sharpe's index gives more importance for regression analysis through beta and alpha analysis. The following table reveals the meaning of various elements involved in a portfolio;

Variable	*Relationship to Market*	*Concept*
Alpha	positive	stock performance is better than market.
Alpha	zero	stock performance is on par with market.
Alpha	negative	stock performance is worse than market.
Beta	higher than 1	stock performance is worse than market. (very risky)
Beta	zero	stock performance is on par with market.
Beta	lower than 1	stock performance is better than market.
e-epsilon	higher than 1	stock performance is worse than market.
e-epsilon	zero	stock performance is equal to market position.
e-epsilon	less than 1	stock performance is better than market.

Beta is measured by market movements. A well diversified portfolio is influenced by the market movement. The market can be considered by the following fundamental factors which enhances the price of a particular scrip;

1. Goodwill of the enterprise.
2. Financial planning of the company.
3. Profitability of the enterprise.
4. Market situation.
5. Liquidity of the stock in market.
6. Survey of stock. (past trend, history of the company).

Optimal Portfolio

According to sharpe, the beta ratio is the most important in a portfolio. Beta is a measure for determining risk and return for stocks and portfolios. Therefore, the optimal portfolio is directly relate to the beta. It is excess return to beta ratio. The security's excess return over beta ratio can be calculated from the following formula:

$$ER = \frac{R_i - R_f}{\beta_i}$$

R_i = Expected return on stock i

R_f = Risk free rate of return.

β_i = Rate of return expected to change on stock i with 1% change in market return.

Sharpe's model with specific risk which comprises of systematic and unsystematic risk. It also includes extra market co-variance. The extra market co-variance is an independent and it shows attendently of the stock to move together. The co-variance lies in between the systematic and specific risk. The optimal portfolio may be selected by finding out the cut off rate for each security. The securities which have rank higher than the cut off rate will be selected. The calculation of cut off rate involves the following process;

a) Analyse different risk return ratios of stocks considered for selection.

b) Ranking all the securities according to higher excess return to beta and less return to beta.

The desirability of any security is directly related to its excess return to beta ratio.

c) Find out the cut off rate for each security.

The cut off rate is more important in selection of optimal portfolio. The cut off rate C_i for security i can be calculated by the following formula;

$$C_i = \frac{V_m \sum_{i=1}^{1} \frac{(R_i - R_b)\beta_i}{E_i}}{1 + V_m \sum_{i=1}^{1} \frac{\beta i^2}{E_i}}$$

C_i = Cut off rate

R_i = Expected return on stock.

R_b = Return received from riskless

β_i = Systematic risk

E_i = Specific risk (unsystematic risk)

V_m = Extra market variance

Selection of securities with high rank above the cut off rate is common for all securities. The stock with excess return is to be a ratio greater than cut-off rate should be selected for inclusion in optimal portfolio.

REVIEW PROBLEMS

Illustration No.1: From the following information, calculate the cut off rate according to sharpe's model. The risk free rate of return is 6%. The extra market variance is 10%.

Security	Expected return	Beta	Unsystematic risk(ei)
A	26	2.0	27
B	18	1.5	22
C	30	1.8	24
D	20	3.0	35
E	22	2.5	40
F	24	2.8	45
G	28	2.3	25

Solution:

The calculation of expected return and then ranking of securities is shown below:

- The calculation of expected return:

$R_f = 6\%$

Security (1)	R_i (2)	B_i (3)	e_i (4)	$R_i - R_b$ (5)	Expected return $5 \div 3$ (6)
A	26	2.0	27	26-6=20	10
B	18	1.5	22	18-6=12	8
C	30	1.8	24	30-6=24	13.33
D	20	3.0	35	20-6=14	4.66
E	22	2.5	40	22-6=16	6.40
F	24	2.8	45	24-6=18	6.42
G	28	2.3	25	28-6=22	9.56

The expected return is then ranked to findout the cut off rate for each security(e_i) for which the following table is prepared;

Ranking of Securities

Ranked securities	Expended return	$\frac{(R_i - Rb)}{ei}$	$\sum_{i=1}^{1} \frac{(R_i - R_b)B}{ei}$	$\frac{B^2}{ei}$	$\sum_{i=1}^{1} \frac{B^2}{ei}$ (Cumulative data)
(1)	(2)	(3)	(4)	(5)	(6)
1-C	13.33	(30-6/24)1.8=1.8	1.80	0.16	0.16
2-A	10.00	(26-6/27)2.0=1.48	3.28	0.15	0.31
3-G	9.56	(28-6/25)2.3=2.04	5.32	0.21	0.52
4-B	8.00	(18-6/22)1.5=0.81	6.13	0.10	0.62
5-f	6.42	(24-6/15)2.8=1.12	7.25	0.17	0.79
6-e	6.40	(22-6/40)2.5=1.00	8.25	0.15	0.94
7-d	4.66	(20-6/35)3=1.20	9.45	0.25	1.19

Explanation to Column No.4 (Cumulative data available in column No.3)

1.80+1.48 = 3.28

3.28+2.04 = 5.32

5.32+0.81 = 6.13

6.13+1.12 = 7.25

7.25+1.00 = 8.25

8.25+1.20 = 9.45.

Explanation to Column No.5

1st rank security (C) $B^2 = \frac{1.8^2}{24} = 3.24 \div 24 = 0.16$

2nd rank security (A) $B^2 = \frac{2.0^2}{27} = 0.15$

3rd rank G = $2.3^2 \div 25 = 0.21$

4th rank B = $1.5^2 \div 22 = 0.10$

5th rank F = $2.8^2 \div 45 = 0.17$

6th rank E = $2.5^2 \div 40 = 0.15$

7th rank D = $3^2 \div 35 = 0.25$

Calculation of "C" value for **1st rank security (C);**

$$C_i = V_m \sum_{i=1}^{1} \frac{\frac{(R_i - R_b)B}{e_i}}{1 + V_m \sum_{i=1}^{1} \frac{B^2}{ei}}$$

$$V_m = 10\% \frac{(R_i - R_b)B}{ei} = 1.8 \qquad \frac{B^2}{ei} = 0.16$$

1st rank substituting the values in the formula as follows;

$$C_i = \frac{10(1.8)}{1 + 10(0.16)}$$

$$Ci = \frac{18}{1 + 1.6}$$

$$Ci = \frac{18}{2.6} = 6.92$$

2nd rank calculation of "C" value for 2nd rank security - A;

$$V_m = 10 \frac{(R_i - R_b)B}{ei} = 3.28 = \frac{B^2}{ei} = 0.15$$

$$= \frac{10(3.28)}{1 + 10(0.15)} = \frac{32.8}{2.5} = 13.12$$

3rd rank security G $= \frac{10(5.32)}{1 + 10(0.21)} = 53.2 \div 3.1 = 17.16$

4th rank **security B** $= \frac{10(6.13)}{1 + 10(0.10)} = 61.3 \div 2 = 30.65$

5th rank **F** $= \frac{10(7.25)}{1 + 10(0.17)} = 26.85$

$$6\text{th rank E} = \frac{10(8.25)}{1+10(0.15)} = 82.5 \div 2.5 = 33$$

$$6\text{th rank D} = \frac{10+(9.45)}{1+10(0.25)} = 94.5 \div 3.5 = 27$$

The securities "C" for which the expected return is greater than their cut off rate C_i is to be selected for an optimal portfolio and the ratio in percentage (P_i) can be arrived by using the cut off rate of lower ranked security selected as the common cut off rate all selected securities.

Ranked securities	Expected return	c_i	Securities selected	z_i B-ei
1 C	13.33	6.92	1-C	1.8-24(13.33-10)0.24
2 A	10.00	13.12	-	-
3 G	9.56	17.16	-	-
4 B	8.00	30.65	-	-
5 F	6.42	26.85	-	-
6 E	6.40	33.00	-	-
7 D	4.66	27.00	-	-

Illustration No. 2: Kotak Mahindra Finance recently used reports from various security analysts to develop inputs for the single index model. Out put derived from the single index model consisting of the following efficient portfolios;

Portfolio	expected return(ER)	standard deviation
1	10%	4%
2	12%	7%
3	15%	9%
4	19%	14%
5	22%	19%

a) If the risk free rate of return is 7% which portfolio is the best?

b) If the company assumes that the investments would like to earn an expected 12% with a standard deviation of 5%, is this possible ?

c) If the company accepts 10% standard deviation, what would be the expected portfolio return and how the company can achieve it?

Solution:

a) The best portfolio can be found when we compare its returns with the risk free rate of return a it 7% :

$ER_1 = 10$ $ER_2 = 12$ $ER_3 = 15$ $ER_4 = 19$ $ER_5 = 22$ Rb = 7

$\sigma_1 = 4$ $\sigma_2 = 7$ $\sigma_3 = 9$ $\sigma_4 = 14$ $\sigma_5 = 19$

Portfolio	(ER-Rf)/ σ
1	(10-7)/4 = 0.75
2	(12-7)/7 = 0.71
3	(15-7)/9 = 0.88
4	(19-7)/14 = 0.85
5	(22-7) 19 = 0.78

Portfolio 3 is the optimal portfolio because its expected return is higher

b) A standard deviation of 5% results in an expected return of only. 11.4%.

ER = Rf + 6(OPR)

ER = expected return

Rf = Risk free rate of return Rf = 7%

σ = standard deviation σ = 5%

OPR = Optimal Portfolio return OPR = 0.88.

ER = 7% + 5% (0.88)

ER = 7 + 4.4 = 11.4%

c) ER = Rf + σ (OPR); substituting the values in the formula;

Rf = 7% σ = 12%, OPR = .88

ER = 7% + 10% (0.88)

= 7% + 8.8 = 15.8%

The optimal portfolio standard deviation is 9

Therefore, the desired standard deviation is 10

$$\therefore \sigma p = \frac{\text{desired}\sigma}{\text{optimal portfolio}\sigma}$$

$$= \frac{10}{9} = 1.11$$

The debt equity mix ratio may be in 1.11%

Illustration No.3: How many inputs are needed for a portfolio involving 85 securities if the co-variance is computed through Sharpe's method.

Solution:

The number of inputs are needed as follows:

Sharpe's = $(N \times 3) + 2$

N = Number of securities = 85

Sharpes model = $(85 \times 3) + 2$

= 255 + 2 = 277

Illustration No. 4: From the following data using the five years of monthly returns the regression statistics were generated using the market model and a broad equity index.

Security	α	σ	ROI
ABC	-0.31	15%	0.52
DEF	0.25	6%	0.30
GHI	0.03	13%	0.48
JKL	0.30	6%	0.90
INDEX	0.00	5%	1.00

a) Calculate an estimate of β (Beta) for each security.

b) What is the market model beta's during next five year period?

c) Assuming that the return on market portfolio is 8% and the risk free rate is 10% calculate the equilibrium expected return on each security.

d) Assume that each security is the only holding of the portfolio calculate required expected returns.

e) Calculate the beta of a portfolio consisting of an equal investment in each security.

Solution: a) Calculation of β for each of the following securities;

∴ β = Beta

σ = Standard deviation of a security

I = Index standard deviation

ROI = return on investment.

Calculation of Beta for security ABC;

σ = 15% Iσ = 5%   ROI = 0.5

B = (15 ÷ 5) (0.52) = 1.56

Calculation of Beta for security DEF;

B = (6 ÷ 5) (0.30) = 0.36

Beta for GHI security:

σ = 13%   Iσ = 5%   ROI = 0.48

B = (13 ÷ 5) (0.48) = 1.248.

Beta for JKL security:

σ = 6%   Iσ = 5%   ROI = 0.90

B = (6 ÷ 5) (0.90) = 0.90

Beta for Market Index:

σ = 5%   Iσ = 5%   ROI = 1.00.

B = (5 ÷ 5) (1.00) = 1.00

b) Beta estimates less than 1.0 will probably increase towards 1.0 Beta estimates larger than 1.0 will probably decrease towards 1.0

c) Calculation of the equilibrium expected return on securities;

Security	*ER*
ABC	Rf + B(Rm) Rf = 10% B = 1.56 Rm = 8% 10 + 1.56(8) = 22.48
DEF	Rf = 10% B = 0.36 Rm = 8% ER = 10 + 0.36(8) = 12.88
GHI	Rf = 10% B = 1.248 RM = 8% ER = 10 + 1.248(8) = 19.98
JKL	Rf = 10% B = 0.90 Rm = 8% ER = 10 + 0.90(8) = 17.2
INDEX	Rf = 10% B = 1.00 Rm = 8 ER = 10 + 1.00(8) = 18.

ER=Rf + B (Rm)   Rf = risk free rate of return B = Beta

Rm = return on market portfolio.

d) Calculation of required expected return on securities;

Required expected return = Rf + (σ) (Rm)/Market σ

∴ r.e.r. for ABC security = Rf=10% σ =15% Market= σ 5% Rm=8%

= 10 + 15 (8)/5 = 10 +15 (1.6)

= 10 +24 = 34.

Calculation of required rate of return on DEF security;

Rf = 10 Rm = 8% market σ = 15% σ = 6%

= 10 + 6 (8)/15

= 10 + 6 (0.53)

= 10 + 3.18 = 13.18%

Calculation of required rate of return on GHI security;

Rf=10 Rm=8 market σ =15% σ =13%

= 10 + 13 (8)/15

= 10 + 13 (0.53)

= 10 + 6.89 = 16.89%

Calculation of required rate of return on JKL security;

Rf=10 Rm=8 market σ =15 σ =6%

= 10 + (6) (8)/6

= 10 + 6 (1.33)

= 10 + 7.99 = 17.99% or 18%

e) Calculation of beta of a portfolio consisting of an equal investment in each security;

$\beta mp = w_1(B_1) + w_2(B_2) + w_3(B_3) + w_4(B_4)$

βmp=Beta of a market portfolio

w_1 = Proportion of the investment in each security

w_1 = 0.25, w_2 =0.25, w_3 =0.25, w_4 = 0.25

B_1 = 1.56 B_2 =0.36 B_3 =1.248, B_4 = 0.90

βmp = 0.25(1.56) + 0.25 (0.36) + 0.25 (1.248) + 0.25 (0.90)

= 0.39 + 0.09 + 0.31 + 0.22 = 1.01

Illustration No. 5: From the following information calculate the residual variance of each of the following stocks on the assumption of the risk index model.

Stock	Beta	Portfolio weight	Expected return	Total variance
A	0.60	0.30	0.50	0.09
B	0.75	0.35	0.30	0.07
C	0.95	0.35	0.25	0.05

Market variance = 0.07

a) What is the beta factor of the three stocks portfolio?

b) Compute the variance of the given portfolio.

c) What is the expected return on the portfolio?

Solution:

The residual variance can be found by applying the following formula;

$\sigma_i^2 = \beta^2 + \sigma_m^2 + \sigma^2 ei$ or

$\sigma_{ei}^2 = \sigma_i^2 - \beta^2 \sigma_m^2$

σ^2 = variance β^2 = betasquare $\sigma^2 m$ = marketvariance

$\sigma^2 ei_a$ = residualvariance of stock a

$\sigma^2 i_a$ = variance of the stock a

$\beta^2 = (0.60)^2$ $\sigma_i^2 = 0.09$ $\sigma^2 m = 0.07$

$\sigma^2 ei_a = 0.09 - (0.60)^2 (0.07) = 0.90 - 0.025 = 0.875$

$\sigma^2 ei_b = 0.07 - (0.75)^2 (0.07) = 0.75 - 0.039 = 0.711$

$\sigma^2 ei_c = 0.05 - (0.95)^2 (0.07) = 0.05 - 0.063 = -0.013$

a) The beta factor for the portfolio or the weighted average beta of the 3 stocks can be calculated as follows;

$$\beta_p = x_a \beta_a + x_b \beta_b + x_c \beta_c$$

β_p = Beta of the portfolio.

x_a = weight of portfolio of the 'A' stock

β_a = Beta of the 'A' security

x_b = Weight of the portfolio of 'B' stock

β_b = Beta of the 'B' security

x_c = Weight of the portfolio of 'C' stock

β_c = beta of the 'C' security.

$x_a = 0.30$ $x_b = 0.35$ $x_c = 0.35$

$\beta_a = 0.60$ $\beta_b = 0.75$ $\beta_c = 0.95$

Substituting the value in the formula we can get;

$\beta_p = (0.30)(0.60) + (0.35)(0.75) + (0.35)(0.95)$

$\beta_p = 0.18 + 0.26 + 0.33 = 0.77$

b) The variance of the portfolio can be computed by the following formula;

$$\sigma_p^2 = \beta_p^2\sigma_m^2 + \sigma^2 ep$$

$$\beta^2 p\sigma^2 m + \sigma^2 ep$$

$\sigma^2 p$ = variance of the portfolio

$\beta^2 p$ = Beta square of the portfolio

$\sigma^2 m$ = market variance

$\sigma^2 ep$ = residual variance

$\sigma^2 = \beta^2 p\sigma^2 m + \sigma^2 ep$

$\therefore \beta^2 p = 0.77^2 \sigma^2 m = 0.07$

$\therefore \beta^2 p\sigma^2 m = 0.772 + 0.07$

$= 0.5929 + 0.07 = 0.663$

$\sigma^2 ep = (w_1)^2(\sigma^2 ea) + (w_2)^2(\sigma^2 eb) + (w_3)^2(\sigma^2 ec)$

$w_1^2 = 0.302 w_2^2 = 0.352 w_3^2 = 0.35$

$\sigma^2 ei_a = 0.875 \sigma^2 ei_b = 0.711 \sigma^2 ei_c = -0.013$

$= (0.30)^2(0.875) + (0.35)^2(0.711) + (0.35)^2(-0.013)$

$= 0.09(0.875) + 0.123 \times 0.711 + 0.123 \times (-0.013)$

$= 0.079 + 0.87 + -0.001$

$= 0.166 + -0.001 = 0.165$

$\sigma^2 p = 0.663 + 0.165 = 0.83$

c) The expected return on the portfolio can be calculated by the following formula;

$$Erp = X_a E(R_a) + X_b E(R_b) + X_c E(R_c)$$

$X_a = 0.30$ $X_b = 0.35$ $X_c = 0.35$

Er_a = expected return on security 'A' = 0.50

Er_b = expected return on security 'B' = 0.30

Er_c = expected return on security 'C' = 0.25.

Substituting the values in the formula we can find expected return on portfolio;

Er_p = 0.30 (0.50) + 0.35 (0.30) + 0.35 (0.25)

= 0.15 + 0.10 + 0.088 = 0.338 or 33.8%

Illustration No.6: From the following information which is based on assumption of the single index model calculate the beta factor of stock 1.

$\beta_2 = 1.50$ $\sigma^2 m = 0.42$ $Cov R_1 R_2 = 0.07$

Solution:

Based on the assumption of the single index model, we can calculate the co-variance between two stocks as follows;

$$Cov(R_1 R_2) = \beta_1 \beta_2 \sigma^2 m$$

$$\therefore \beta_1 = \frac{Cov.(R_1 R_2)}{\beta_2 \sigma^2 m}$$

Co-variance $R_1 R_2 = 0.07$ $B_2 = 1.50$ $\sigma^2 m = 0.42$

$$\beta_1 = \frac{0.07}{1.50 \times 0.42}$$

$$\beta_1 = \frac{0.07}{0.63} = 0.11$$

Illustration No.7: The standard deviation of return is 6% on equity shares of A Ltd 5% for X Ltd. and 4% for the market portfolio. A company's correlation coefficient for the market is +0.09 and X Ltd to the market is 0.7 what is the beta coefficient for A Ltd and X Ltd..?

Solution:

Beta can be calculated by applying the following formula;

$$\text{Beta} = \frac{(r)(\sigma)}{\sigma_m}$$

r = Coefficient of correlation of the stock.

σ = Standard deviation of the stock.

σ_m = Standard deviation of the market portfolio.

$$\beta_a = \frac{(r_a)(\sigma_a)}{\sigma_m}$$

$r_a = 0.09$ $\sigma_a = 6\%$ $\sigma_m = 4\%$

$$\text{Beta}_a = \frac{(0.09)(0.06)}{0.04} = \frac{0.0054}{0.04} = 0.135$$

$$\text{Beta}_x = \frac{(r_x)(\sigma_x)}{\sigma_m}$$

$r_x = 0.7$ $\sigma_x = 5\%$ $\sigma_m = 4\%$

$$\text{Beta}_x = \frac{(0.7)(0.05)}{0.04}$$

$$= \frac{0.035}{0.04} = 0.875$$

Illustration No.8: From the information given below, calculate the beta of the two securities, A and B, assume that these securities constitute the market portfolio. Their weights and variances are 0.65, 170 and 0.35, 310 respectively. The co-variances of two securities is 190.

Solution:

Calculation of variance of the given portfolio is presented below;

$$\sigma^2 m = x_a^2 \sigma_a^2 + x_b^2 \sigma_b^2 2x_a x_b C_{ab}$$

$\sigma^2 m$ = Market variance

x_a^2 = Proportion of security a in the portfolio

σ_a^2 = Standard deviation of the security 'a'

$x_{b.}^2$ = Proportion of the security "b" in the portfolio.

σ_b^2 = Standard deviation of the security 'b'.

C_{ab} = Co-variance of the two securities.

Substituting the values in the formula we can get market variance then, we will have to calculate the co-variances of securities and betas.

$\sigma^2 m = x_a^2 = (0.65)^2 \quad x_b^2 = (0.35)^2 \quad \sigma_a^2 = 170 \quad \sigma_b^2 = 310$

$\sigma_m^2 = (0.65)^2(170) + (0.35)^2(310) + 2(0.65)(0.68)190$

$= 0.423 \times 170 + 0.122 \times 310 + 167.96$

$= 71.91 + 37.97 + 167.96$

$= 277.84.$

In the two security market model case, the calculation of σ_{am} is presented below:

$$\sigma_{am} = w_1 \times \sigma_1^2 + w_2 \sigma_2^2$$

$w_1 = 0.65 \quad \sigma_2^1 = 170 \quad w_2 = 0.35 \quad \sigma_2^2 = 310$

$\sigma = 310 = 0.65 \times 170 + 0.35 \times 310$

$\sigma = 110.50 + 108.5$

$\sigma = 219$

CAPITAL ASSET PRICING MODEL (CAPM)

This portfolio theory is concerned with the analysis of risk and return and the process by which an efficient portfolio can be achieved. Normally, the investors will have to include more securities in order to reduce the risk. The principles of portfolio management discuss the relationship between capital market theory and capital asset pricing model. Capital market theory is concerned with the pricing of assets in the market. It is a major extension of the portfolio theory of Markowitz.[1] Portfolio theory is a description of the rational investors behaviour in building an efficient portfolio. The capital asset pricing model was developed by Sharpe and Lintener in 1960. It is based on economic model. It aims the investor at maximising the utility of wealth. "The capital asset procing model is a reletionship explaining how assets should be priced in the capital markets."[2] It reveals the relationship between the expected return, unavoidable risk and the valuation of securities. The unavoidable risk means, the risk which cannot be avoided by diversification. If a security does not provide adequate return, then the security will not favour the investor. Therefore, its market value will fall. It indicates the following important assets:

a) The desired rate of return on all financial assets depends upon the component of riskless rate of return.

b) The investors are generally risk averse.

c) Investors are concerned with unavoidable risk.

In this model the company's risk is eliminated and only the market risk remains. The market should be a free, with a large number of players who are influenced fairly and accurately by the demand and supply forces generated by free flow of correct and perfect information. This information is digested by the market immediately and prices are fair and competitive. Therefore, the price of a share is determined as in action system and the market is the best performer and no individual can out perform the market.

This model reveals that the company risk and the market risk are related by a variable called ''*Beta*." The following equation of security. valuation presents the concept of "Beta".

$$(R_i - R_b) = \beta_i(R_m - R_b)$$

R_i = Required rate of return.

R_b = Risk free rate of return

RM = Market risk

1. **William sharpe,** "Capital Asset Prices; A theory of Market Equilibrium Under Conditions of Risk" Journal of finance (sept.19 64) pp 425-42.
2. **Fisher & Jordan,** Security Analysis & Portfolio Management, P.No.636. Prentice Hall 1999.

β_i = Constant.

$R_i - R_b$ = Risk premium of the scrip.

The CAPM attempts to measure the risk of a security in the portfolio. The CAPM can be used to examine the risk and return of any type of financial assets. The model further, explains that the total risk of a portfolio can be bifurcated into systematic and unsystematic risk. Systematic risk can be eliminated through diversification, unsystematic risk cannot be eliminated and is correlated with that of the market portfolio. A portfolio may be efficient if there is no unsystematic risk.

Assumptions

The CAPM model is based on the following assumptions;

1. Investors are known all the market information and fluctuations.
2. The information available in the market will be digested by capital markets.
3. Investors are risk averse
4. There are no transaction costs and there no restictions on investments.
5. Investors have homogeneous expectations regarding risk and return on securities.
6. Risk is the variance of expected portfolio returns.
7. Investors have identical time horizon.
8. Ignorance of liquidity and new issues of securities.

For valuation of a securities, the firms usually apply the capital asset pricing model (CAPM), because no other method provides this type of evaluation. The CAPM is of special interest to managers whose firms are closely held, pay no dividends. Managers are often use the corporate cost of capital as the required rate of return for new capital investment.

Generally, the investors are concerned with non-diversifiable risk, where the companies have used the CAPM in the following three related ways;

a) To determine hurdle rate for investments.
b) To assess the required return for each division of the business unit.
c) To valuate the performance of the divisions of units.

The CAPM has been used to select securities to construct portfolios and evaluate portfolio or equity share performance. Securities which show super returns are considered as under valued. These securities are attracted by investors. Under valued securities may be some times called as "Positive Alphas". The securities which were over valued are considered as "Negative Alpha" selecting securities beta has been used to control risk level of a portfolio. The relationship between the expected return of a security and its contribution depends upon the attitudes of the investors.

The model reveals that the market is in equilibrium position and the expected rate of return for a given level of risk is equal to the required rate of return.

Security Market Lines (SML)

Security Market Line reveals the relationship between the required rate of return (R_i) and Non-diversified risk. The CAPM identifies a security return with risk free rate as a proportional to the expected net market return.

All securities in equilibrium plot along a straight line called the security market line. The unsystematic risk may be diversified by the construction of an efficient portfolio. The following diagram presents a SML which has beta in the portfolio.

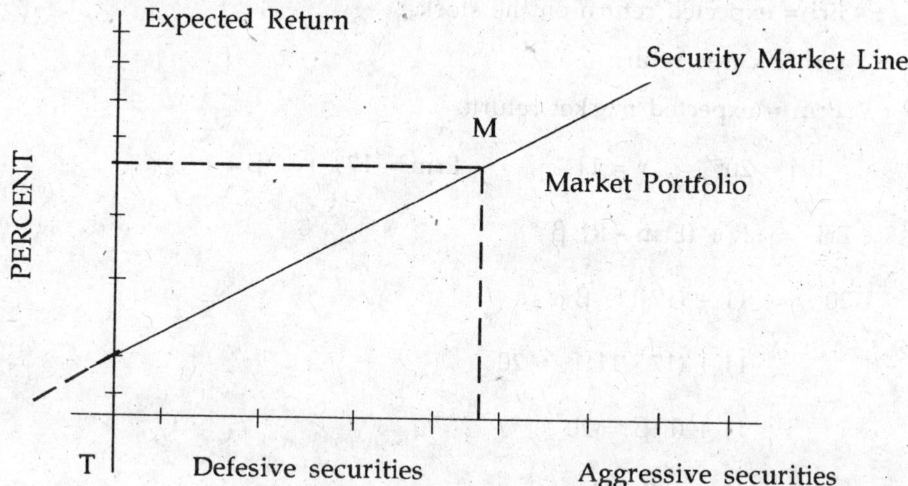

The above diagram presents a SML, it has beta as the independent variable and the expected return of portfolios and individual securities as the dependent variable. The SML has a positive slope indicating the expected return which increases with risk. The risk of a riskless asset T, is zero, therefore T is the point at which the SML crosses the vertical axis, y intercept point. The risk of the portfolio relates to market is 1. therefore, the point beta equals 1, is associated with the expected market return.

REVIEW PROBLEMS

Illustrations No.1: Rajesh auto has a beta of 0.90. If the expected market return is 18% and the risk free rate of return is 9%. What is the appropriate required rate of return?

Solution:

The required rate of return can be calculated by the following formula:

=Risk free rate of return+(market return-Risk free rate of return)×Beta.

Market return=18%; Risk free rate of return = 9% Beta = 0.9

Substituting the values in the formula;

$= 9\%+(18\%-9\%)\times 0.9$

$=9\%+(9\%)\times 0.9=9\%+8.1$

$= 17.1\%$

Illustration No. 2: If r = 11% E(rm) = 17% (market return) and return on the stock is 20% what is implicit Beta (β) of this stock?

Solution:

$$Eri = R+(Erm-R)\beta$$

Eri = expected return on the stock..

r = risk free return

Erm = expected market return.

$\therefore$ Eri = 20% r = 11% Erm = 17% β = ?

$$\begin{aligned} Eri &= R + (Erm - R)\ \beta \\ 20 &= 11 + (17\text{-}11)\ \beta \\ &= 11 + (17 - 11)\beta = 20 \\ &= 11 + (6)\beta = 20 \\ &= 11 + 6\ \beta = 20 \\ &= 6\ \beta = 20 - 11 \end{aligned}$$

$$\beta = \frac{9}{6} = 1.5$$

Illustration No.3: The risk free return on a portfolio is 8%. The expected return on BSE index is 16% (and risk measured by standard deviation is 3%). How would you construct an efficient portfolio to produce a 14% expected return and what would be its risk?

Solution:

An efficient portfolio consists of investing in the market portfolio and risk free securities, by applying the following formula;

$$R_p = w(R_m) + (1-w)T$$

R_p = Expected return on portfolio.

W = Proportion of investment

R_m = Market return

T = Risk free return.

$R_p = 14\%$ $R_m = 16\%$ $T = 8\%$

Substituting the values in the formula;

$$14\% = W(16\%) + (1 - W)\,8\%$$

$$14 = 16W + 8 - 8W$$

$$14 - 8 = 16W - 8W$$

$$6 = 8W$$

$$w = \frac{6}{8}$$

$$\therefore \boxed{W = 75\%}$$

Therefore, 75% of the funds should be placed in market portfolio and the balance of 25% should be invested in risk free securities. The resulting portfolio risk can be calculated from the following formula;

$$R_p = T + \frac{(R_m - T)}{\sigma_m \sigma_p}$$

R_p = Expected return on portfolio

T = Risk free return

σ_m = Market risk

σ_p = Portfolio risk.

$R_p = 14\%$ $T = 8\%$ $R_m = 16\%$

substituting the values;

$$14\% = 8\% + \frac{16\% - 8\%}{3\%\sigma_p}$$

$$14\% = 8\% + \frac{8\%}{3\sigma_p}$$

$$6\% = \frac{8}{3\sigma_p} = \frac{6 \times 3}{8} = \sigma_p$$

$$\sigma_p = \frac{18}{8} = \boxed{2.25}$$

Illustration No.4: Venkat has Rs. 2,00,000 to invest. He is a fairly conservative person, so he sets a target β for his portfolio at 0.6. He then proceeds to analyse stocks and selects them based on his analysis. After careful analysis, he arrives at a group of 15 stocks with mean β of 1.8. Determine how he can weight his portfolio to reach his risk target.

$$w_p = \frac{\text{target beta}}{\text{average beta}}$$

$w_p = ?$ $\quad$ target = 06 $\quad$ averagebeta = 1.8

$$w_i = \frac{0.6}{1.8} = 0.33$$

Venkat should invest 1/3 rd of his money in the portfolio stocks. He should invest the remaining in treasury bills or some appropriately low risk security such as a money market fund.

Illustration No.5: From the following information find out which securities are over valued and under valued

R = 10% $\quad$ Erm = 16%

Stock	Eri	β
A	14%	1.2
B	16%	0.8
C	19%	1.3

Solution:

Over value and under value of a stock can be found by the following formula;

$$Er_A = R + (Erm - R) B$$

Er_A = Expected return on stock A

R = Risk free return

Erm = Market return

Eri = Return on investment.

∴ R=10% Erm=16% β=1.2

Er_A = 10 + (16 - 10) 1.2

= 10 + 6 × 1.2

= 10 + 7.2 = 17.2%

Er_b = 10 + (16 - 10) 0.8

= 10 + 6 x 0.8

= 10 + 4.8 = 14 .8%

Er_c = 10 + (16 - 10) 1.3

= 10 + 6 (1.3)

= 10 + 7.8

= 17.8%

Thus stock A, and C are over valued and stock B is under valued.

Illustration No. 6: From the following information calculate the return on securities and compare with the expected return by using security market line formula.

Security	*Expected return*	*Beta*
A	13%	1.25
B	14%	0.80
C	19%	1.55

The risk free return is 10% and market return is 16% (Rm)

Solution:

The return as securities can be found by applying the following formula;

$$R_A = Rf + \beta(R_m - R_i)$$

R_A = Return on security A

Rf = Risk free return

β = Beta of the stock

R_A = ? Rf = 10% β = 1.25 R_m = 16%

R_A = 10% + 1.25 (16 -10)

R_A = 10% + 1.25 (6)

R_A = 10 + 7.50 = 17.5%

$R_B = Rf + \beta(Rm - Ri)$

$= 10 + 0.80\ (16 - 10)$

$= 10 + 0.80\ (6)$

$= 10 + 4.8 = 14.8\%$

$R_c = 10 + 1.55\ (16 - 10)$

$= 10 + 1.55\ (6)$

$= 10 + 9.3 = 19.3\%$

$\therefore$ Security C only could get 19.3% which is higher than the expected return at 19%.

Illustration No.7: From the following data calculate the variance of two portfolios. The risk free rate is 9% market risk premium is 7% (standard deviation) standard deviation of market risk is 11%

a) Risk free investment 40% and risky fund 60%

b) Diversified portfolio with Beta of 1.7.

Solution:

The calculation of variance of a portfolio can be found by the following formula;

$$\sigma^2 = w(\text{market } \sigma) + Rf(0)$$

w=Proportion of risky fund in a portfolio.

Rf=Risk free rate W = 0.6 Rf = 0.4 $m^{\sigma} = 11\%$

$\sigma_1^2 = 0.6(11) + 0.4(0)$

$\sigma_1^2 = 6.6 + 0 = 6.6\%$

Portfolio (2)

$$\sigma_2^2 = \beta_2^2 \sigma m^2 + 0$$

$\beta_2^2 = 1.7^2 \qquad \sigma^2 = 11^2$

by substituting the value in the formula;

$= 1.7^2 \times (11)^2 + 0$

$= 2.89(121) + 0$

$\sigma_2^2 = 349.69$

$\sigma = \sqrt{349.69} = 18.7\%$

Illustration No. 8: From the following information calculate the stock equilibrium price.

The short-term government securities yield is 8 percent and the expected market return is 13%. Stock X's beta is 0.9 its growth rate is 5% and its last dividend was Rs.3.

Solution:

The equilibrium price of a security can be calculated by applying the following formula;

$R_x = R_f + B_x\ (R_m - R_f)$ and $P_o = D_o(1+g)/(R_x - g)$

R_x = Rate of return required on stock x

R_f = Risk free rate of return.

R_m = Return on market portfolio

B_x = Beta coefficient of stock x

g = Growth rate of dividend

Do = Last dividend per share.

R_f = 8% B_x =0.9 R_m = 13%

R_x = 8 + 0.9 (13 - 8)

R_x = 8 + 0.9 (5)

R_x = 8 + 4.5 = 12.50

Equilibrium price can be worked out as follows;

$$R_x = \frac{D_o(1+g)}{P_o} + g$$

$R_x = 12.5\%$ $$12.5\% = \frac{3(1+0.05)}{P_o} + 5\%$$

$D_o = 14.3$ $$12.5\% = \frac{3.15}{P_o} + 5\%$$

$g = 5\%$ $$12.5\% = 5\% = \frac{3.15}{P_o}$$

$P_o = ?$ $$7.5\% = \frac{3.15}{P_o}$$

$$Po = \frac{3.15}{0.075} = \text{Rs.}42.00$$

Illustration No.9: The beta coefficient of standard company is 1.4. The company is maintaining a 6% rate of growth in its earnings or dividends. The last dividend paid was Rs.3.00 per share. The risk free rate of return is 11% and the return on market portfolio is 16%. The current market price per share of the company is Rs. 18. What will be the equilibrium price per share of company?

Solution:

The expected rate of return is equal to $R_f + \beta(R_m - R_f)$

$R_f = 11\%$ $\beta = 1.4$ $R_m = 16\%$

$E(R) = R_f + \beta\,(R_m - R_f)$

$E(R) = 11+1.4(16-11)$

$= 11+1.4(5)$

$= 11+7=18\%$

Market price per share calculation:

$$E(R) = \frac{D_1(1+g)}{P_o} + g$$

ER=18% $g = 6\%$

D_1=Rs.3.00. $P_o = ?$

$$0.18 = \frac{3(1+0.06)}{P_o} + 0.06$$

$$0.18 = \frac{3+(1.06)}{P_o} + 0.06$$

$$\frac{3(1.06)}{P_o} = 0.18 - 0.06$$

$$\frac{3.18}{P_o} = 0.12$$

$$\therefore P_o = \frac{3.18}{0.12} = \text{Rs.}26.5$$

Illustration No.10: ABC Ltd., has a beta 1.65, the risk free rate of return is 12% and expected return on market portfolio is 18% the company pays a dividend of Rs. 2.50 per share and expected growth in dividends is 12% per annum.

a) What is the stock's required rate of return according to CAPM?

b) What is the stock's market price assuming the required return?

Solution:

a) The required rate of return can be calculated by the following formula;

$$R_p = R_f + \beta(R_m - R_f)$$

R_p = Required rate of return on portfolio

R_f = Risk free rate of return

β = Beta

R_m = Expected return on market portfolio.

R_f = 12% $\beta = 1.65$ $R_m = 18\%$.

by substituting the values in the formula we can get the required rate of return on portfolio;

$R_p = 12 + 1.65\ (18 - 12)$

$R_p = 12 + 1.65\ (6)$

$R_p = 12 + 9.9$

$R_p = 21.9\%$

b) The stock's perpetual dividend can be calculated through dividend growth model by the following formula;

$$P_o = \frac{D_1}{R_p - g}$$

D_1 = Dividend for current year.

R_p = Rate of return on portfolio.

g = Growth rate.

D = Rs.2.50; $R_p = 0.219$; g = 12%

$$P_o = \frac{2.50(12)}{(0.219 - 0.12)}$$

$$= \frac{2.80}{0.099} = \text{Rs.}28.28$$

Illustration No.11: Calculate $\beta 1$ and $\beta 2$ from the data given below.

year	Rs.	R_B	R_m	Rf (treasury bill rate)
1993	16	11	12	7
1994	-5	-1	-4	6
1995	18	14	13	8
1996	19	10	12	7
1997	23	12	14	8

Solution:

The systematic risk Beta can be calculated with the following formula;

$$\beta_1 = \frac{N \times \Sigma xy - \Sigma x \times \Sigma y}{N \times \Sigma x^2 - (\Sigma x)^2}$$

β_1 = Beta

N = No.of variables.

year	Rs.	R_B	R_m	Rf	y_1	y_1^2	y_2	y_2^2	x	x^2	xy_1	xy_2
(1)	(2)	(3)	(4)	(5)	(6)	(7)	(3-5)=8	(9)	(4-5)=10	11	12	13
1993	16	11	12	7	9	81	4	16	5	25	45	20
1994	-5	-1	-4	6	-11	121	-7	49	-10	100	110	70
1995	18	14	13	8	10	100	6	36	5	25	50	30
1996	19	10	12	7	12	144	3	9	5	25	60	15
1997	23	12	14	8	15	225	4	16	6	36	90	24
					Σy =35	Σy_1^2 =671	Σy_2 =10	Σy_2^2 =126	Σx =211	Σx^2 =211	Σxy =355	Σxy_2 =159

$\bar{y}_1 = \frac{35}{5} = 7 \quad \bar{y}_2 = \frac{10}{5} = 2 \quad \bar{x} = \frac{11}{5} = 2.2$

$\bar{y}_1 = Rs - Rb$

$\frac{1}{2} = Rb - Rf$

$x = R_m - Rf$

∴ All the above values are presented below;

$\overline{x} = 2.2$ 10th column.

$\Sigma x = 11,\ \Sigma x^2 = 211$ $\Sigma xy_1 = 355$ $\Sigma xy_2 = 159$ $\Sigma x_2 =$

$\overline{y}_1 = 7$ $\overline{y}_2 = 2$ $\Sigma y_2^2 = 126$ $\Sigma y_2 = 10$ $\Sigma y = 35$

For calculation β_1 the values can be substituted in the formula;

$$\beta_1 = \frac{5 \times 355 - 11 \times 35}{5 \times 211 - (11)^2}$$ by simplifying the equation;

$$= \frac{1755 - 385}{934} = 1.48$$

$$\beta_2 = \frac{N \times \Sigma xy_2 - (\Sigma x_2) \times (\Sigma y_2)}{N \times \Sigma x^2 - (\Sigma x)^2}$$

$$\beta_2 = \frac{5 \times 159 - 11 \times 10}{5 \times 211 - (11)^2}$$

$$\beta_2 = \frac{795 - 110}{1055 - 121} = \frac{685}{934} = 0.73$$

Illustration No.12: Electron's stock is expected to sell at Rs.80 a year hence it pays a dividend of Rs. 5 per share. If the stock's correlation is -0.4. $\sigma_x =$ 40% $\sigma_y =$ 20% Rf = 5%. Find out the beta value, expected return and present selling price of the stock.

Solution: Calculation of the beta value of the stock:

Beta value can be calculated by using the following formula;

$$\beta_x = \frac{\sigma x}{\sigma y} \times r$$

$\sigma_x = 40\%$ $\sigma_y = 20\%$ $r = -0.4$

$$\therefore \beta_x = \frac{40\%}{20\%} \times -0.4 = -0.8$$

Calculation of expected return:

$Er_p = Rf + \beta_x \times Rf$ $\quad Rf = 5\%$ $\quad \beta_x = -0.8$

$Er_p = 5\% + (-0.8 \times 5\%)$

$= 5\% \pm 4 = 1\%$

Calculation of present selling price of the stock $P_o = \dfrac{ESP + DPS}{1 + Er_p}$

P_o = Present selling price

ESP = Expected selling price   ESP=Rs.80

DPS = Dividend per share   DPS=Rs.5

Er_p = Expected return. Er_p =0.01

$= \dfrac{80+5}{1+0.01} = \dfrac{85}{1.01} = \text{Rs.}84.15$

Illustration No.13: From the following data calculate security market line.

Particulars	Expected return	Beta	Standard deviation
BSE index (market)	0.13	1.15	19
Risk less treasury bill	0.09	0.00	0
Scrip A	0.33	1.75	48
Scrip B	0.31	1.45	34
Scrip C	0.27	1.20	39

Solution: The equation of security market line is given below:

$$R_i = Rf + \beta(R_m - R_f)$$

Ri = return on investment

Rf = risk free rate of return

B = Beta of the investment

R_m = market return.

for scrip A: Rf = 0.09 β = 1.75 $R_m = 0.13$

$\therefore$ Ri = 0.09 + 1.75 (0.13 - 0.09)

= 0.09 + 1.75 (0.04)

= 0.09 + 0.07

= 0.16 or 16%

for scrip B: Rf = 0.09 β = 1.45 R_m = 0.13

Substituting the values in the formula;

= 0.09 + 1.45 (0.13-0.09)

= 0.09 + 1.45 (0.04)

= 0.09 + 0.058

= 0.148 or 14.8%

for scrip C: Rf 0.09 β = 1.20 R_m = 0.13

= 0.09 + 1.20(0.13 - 0.09)

= 0.09 +1.20 (0.04)

= 0.09 + 0.048

= 0.138 or 13.8%

Illustration No.14: from the following data calculate the expected return on a portfolio.

Security	*Expected return*	*% of fund invested*
1. Voltas	11%	30%
2. H L L	16%	30%
3. R I L	21%	40%

Solution: The formula for calculation of expected return on a portfolio is given below;

$$R_p = W_1R_1 + W_2R_2 + W_3R_3$$

R_p = expected return on portfolio

W = Weights

R = return on investment.

W_1 = 30% R_1 =11%

W_2 = 30% R_2 = 16%

W_3 = 40% R_3 = 21%

Substituting the above values in the formula;

$R_p = 0.3 \times 11 + 0.3 \times 16 + 0.4 \times 21$

3.3 + 4.8 + 8.4 =16.5%

Illustration No.15: from the following information calculate the implicit Beta of the stock.

$r = 11\%$ $Er_m = 17\%$ (market return)

Expected return on the stock = 20%

Solution: The implicit cost of Beta can be calculated through the following formula;

$Eri = R + (erm - R)\ \beta$

Eri = Expected return on investment

$R = 11\%$ $erm = 17\%$ $\beta = ?$ $Eri = 20\%$

$20 = 11 + (17 - 11)\ \beta$

$20 = 11 + (6)\ \beta$

$20 = 11 + 6\beta$

$6\beta = 20 - 11 = 9$

$$\beta = \frac{9}{6} = 1.5$$

PORTFOLIO CONSTRUCTION AND MANAGEMENT

Portfolio Construction

The holding of different securities and financial assets is called as ''*portfolio*''. The retention of different financial instruments depends upon their ''*Risk and Return*'' characteristics. Investment decision will depend upon factors such as preference of the investors, their needs objectives, financial capability, the psychological factor, age, profession, level of accepted risk, their abilities to understand the stock market. Knowledge of the nations economy, potential savings, taxation, time horizon, investment habits, etc., Port folio theory concerns with the allocation of different types of assets. *Portfolio construction* refers to allocation of total investible funds among a wide variety of financial instruments or assets. The objective of portfolio theory is *to minimise risk or maximise return*, subject to a number of *constraints*. The investors would like to have the priorities like *capital appreciation, regular income, marketability, safety, and security*. These characteristics vary between different instruments and assets. The investor's motive for savings are varied depending on the individuals profile. *Ex: Contribution to provident fund, pension funds, provision for insurance, contingencies etc.,*

After designing the portfolio strategy, the construction and allocation of funds will lead to the building up of the portfolio. There after the portfolio requires a constant review and revision with a view to know the result of the portfolio on a continuous basis. This is called as monitoring of portfolio. Finally once in a quarter or half year, the portfolio performance is evaluated for its success by comparing the actual achievements with the targets fixed. Therefore, the evaluation of portfolio's efficiency is a continuous process and the evaluation helps for revision of a portfolio. The following factors are important while constructing a portfolio;

a) Risk

b) Enter & Exit from stock market

c) Diversification.

d) Risk return analysis.

1. Risk

Risk is an estimation of the degree of happening of the loss. It is usually done by assigning probabilities on the basis of past data. The risk can be defined as "The chance of future loss that can be foreseen."[1]

All investments have risks. The risk arises due to number of elements. The risk can be measured by the degree of standard deviation of returns. The risk involved in time horizon called ''*Liquidity premium.*'' The retention of security is subject to the repayment of principal amount called ''*default premium.*'' The risk arises due to variability in interest rates, business default, financial collapse, purchasing power changes. All the above risks are part of ''*systematic risks*'' which lead to a risk premium. All these risks are market related risk. There is another type of risk, relating to a group of industries or firms called group related risk. The risk which related to a particular company called ''*Specific risk*''. The risks are to be rewarded by a higher return in the market that can be secured on risk free assets.

According to the Markowitz[2] Model, usually the investors are risk averse. The portfolio should be designed as to maximise return for a given level of risk. The level of risk-return in a portfolio consisting a satisfactory level called ''*efficient portfolio.*'' It is possible through a detailed analysis of information on each security in terms of expected return and expected risk. Efficient portfolio is a well diversified combination of many securities with a low degree of risk. In efficient portfolio, a wide varieties of industries, different companies with various characteristics are to be chosen.

---

1. Hampton John. ''*FDM*'' P.22
2. **H.M.Markowtiz,** Portfolio Selection,(Johan wiley 1950)

2. Enter & Exit from stock Market

Time is the most important factor in making of investment in the market. Enter at *under price* situation and exit from market in *over price* position of a particular scrip. Generally every portfolio will have time horizon for a short-period or long-term-basis. Capital gains is considered long term if equity investment is for atleast *one year* and other types of investments for at least *three years*. It is more useful to prepare an investment strategy for a medium time period of *3 to 5 years*. The portfolio is to be carefully assessed for every regular period of time, the past experience shows the rise and fall of prices which is in reflection of '' *sensex*'' above the normal inflation rate of 10% per annum.

Portfolio Management comprises *three* major categories of activities. *Asset allocation, Asset Revisions, Selection of Asset (blue chip)*. It is more beneficial to the investors who enter the market when it is *declining share prices* and exit from the market where the share prices are *over heated*. Buying of a right scrip, at a right time, at right price, correct assessment of a scrip for its intrnsic value may be helpful in getting success in stock market. It may be advisable that enter the stock market at ''*bears phase*'' and exit from the market at ''*bullish phase*''. The time to buy cyclical stocks during depreassion period and selling them in prosperity situation is also advisable. There are no stocks that can be safely put away without periodic evaluation. A continuous evaluation of portfolio makes more confidence to the investor to come out with success from stock market. The future is unpredictable the best way to invest is to hedge and control risk if possible. It is better to ''*buy on the rumour time, sell on the news time*''. It would be a good time for long term investors to buy the stock at depressed prices.

c) Diversification

Generally, the success of a portfolio depends upon the accepted level of risk, the higher the risk, higher is the return, Risk in portfolio can be eliminated to some extent by a proper diversification into a number of scrips. If portfolio has been constructed with wide number of scrips to different industries, then the portfolio is involved in high risk horizon. Therefore, the portfolio manager should not be chosen a wide areas of industries, he may concentrate on limited industries. The diversification secures the results when the number of scrips chosen should be limited to *12-15*. Diversification only can secure reduction of risk and maximisation of returns with a divergent qualities in terms of *performance, product lines, management, marketing etc.*,

d) Risk-Return Relationship:

In the management of a portfolio, risk management is most important element. The portfolio should be constructed to minimise the risk and maximise the return. The company's related risk can be eliminated but market risk cannot be reduced. All the risk-return is subject to variation and the objective of the portfolio manager is to reduce the variability. Usually, the higher the risk that the investor takes, the higher is the return.

Efficient Portfolio

Markowitz's model is a theoretical frame work for the analysis of risk-return choices. Decisions are based on the concept of efficient portfolios. Efficient portfolio means, a portfolio which has the largest expected return for a given level of risk or the smallest risk for a given level of expected return. An investor's final choice out of the efficient set depends on his tastes. An investor might select an optimal portfolio from available resources. A number of portfolios on the efficient frontier are called as *''Carner portfolios.''* A corner portfolio can be defined as one in which either can adding a new security or dripping a financial asset from the existing efficient portfolio. This process is continued until each corner portfolio becomes efficient portfolio.

For construction of an efficient portfolio the portfolio manager has to conceptualise various combinations of investments in his basket of investment. The risk on the portfolio is to be estimated by measuring the standard deviation of different portfolio returns. The standard deviation around the expected return can be worked out as below.

Return (in Percent)	Porbability of getting the Return	Expected Return (in percent)	Standard deviation of expected return (in percent)
6	0.05	$6 \times 0.05 = (0.30)$	$(6\text{-}9.4)^2 \times .05 = 0.578$
8	0.35	$8 \times 0.35 = (2.80)$	$(8 - 9.4)^2 \times 0.35 = 0.686$
10	0.45	$10 \times 0.45 = (4.50)$	$(10 - 9.4)^2 \times 0.45 = 0.162$
12	0.15	$12 \times 0.15 = (1.80)$	$(12 - 9.4)^2 \times 0.15 = 1.014$
	1.00	Weighted average (9.4)	$\sigma = 1.562$ Variance 2.44

The *standard deviation on an average* for each possible return is 1.56% from the expected return of *9.4%*. The deviation of *1.562* could be either side of the expected return.

Monitoring and Evaluation of Performance of a Portfolio

Portfolio monitoring is a continuous and on going assessment of present portfolio and the portfolio manager shall incorporate the latest developments which occurred in capital market. The portfolio manager should take into consideration of *investor's preferences, capital market conditions and expectations.* Monitoring the portfolio is up-grading activity in asset composition to take the advantages of *economic, industry and market conditions.* The market conditions are depending upon the Government policy. Any change in Government policy would reflect the stock market, which in turn effects the portfolio. The continuous revision of a portfolio depends upon the following factors;

1. Change in Government policy.
2. Shifting from one industry to other
3. Shifting from one company scrip to another company scrip.
4. Shifting from one financial instrument to another (Equity to Debt) or (Debt to equity).
5. The half yearly/yearly results of the corporate sector.

Risk reduction is an important factor in portfolio. It will be achieved by a diversification of the portfolio, changes in market prices may have necessiated in asset composition. The composition has to be changed to maximise the returns to reach the goals of investor.

1. Asset composition (Equity preference Debentures, PSU Bonds, Govt. securities)
2. Industry groups (Information technology, Auto mobiles, Plastic, Petrochemicals)
3. Blue chip Companies.

Portfolio Revision

Once the portfolio is constructed, it undergoes changes due to changes in market prices and reassessment of companies. Portfolio revision means alteration of the composition of debt/equity instruments, shifting from one industry to another industry, changing from one company to another company. Constant market changes necessitate readjustment of portfolio. Any portfolio requires monitoring and revision. Portfolio activities will depend on daily basis keeping in view the market opportunities. Portfolio revision uses some theoretical tools like *security analysis, Markowitz model, Risk-Return evaluation etc.,*

EVALUATION OF PERFORMANCE OF THE PORTFOLIO

The ability of a portfolio manager depends upon the absorption of latest developments which occurred in the market. The ability of expectations if any. We must able to cope up with the wind immediately. Investment analysts continuously monitor and evaluate the results of the portfolio performance. The expert portfolio manager shall show superior performance over the market and other factors. The performance also depends upon the timing of investments and superior investment analysts capabilities for selection. The evolution of a portfolio always followed by revision and reconstruction. The managers will have to assess the extent to which the objectives are achieved. For evaluation of portfolio, the manager shall keep in mind the secured average returns, average or below average as compared to the market situation. Selection of proper securities is the first requirement. Diversification of a portfolio is the second requirement. Markowitz model or Sharpe's single index model will reduce the market risk and maximise the returns for a given level of risk. The evaluation of a portfolio performance can be made based on the following methods;

a) Sharpe's Measure

b) Treynor's Measure

c) Jensen's Measure

a) Sharpe's Measure

The objective of modern portfolio theory is maximisation of return or minimisation of risk. In this context the research studies have tried to evolve a composite index to measure risk based returns. The credit for evaluating the systematic, unsystematic and residual risk goes to *Sharpe, Treynor and Jensen.* Sharpe measures total risk by calculating standard deviation. The method adopted by Sharpe is to rank all portfolios on the basis of evaluation measure. Reward is in the numerator as risk premium. Total risk is in the denominator as standard deviation of its return. We will get a measure of portfolio's total risk and variability of returns in relation to the risk premium. The measure of a portfolio can be done by the following formula;

$$SI = \frac{Rt - Rf}{\sigma f}$$

SI = Sharpe's Index

Rt = Average return on portfolio

Rf = Risk free return

σ f = Standard deviation of the portfolio return.

Illustration: Find out the portfolio performance by using Sharpe's model from the following data.

Portfolio	Average return	Standard deviation	Risk free rate
A	25%	5%	12%
B	30%	9%	12%

The portfolio performance can be find out by the following formula;

For portfolio - A; $SI = \frac{Rt - Rf}{\sigma f}$

SI = Sharpe's Index Rt = 25

Rt = average return on portfolio Rf = 12

Rf = Risk free return $\sigma f = 0.05$

σf = standard deviation

$$\therefore SI = \frac{.25 - .12}{0.05}$$

$$= \frac{.13}{0.05} = 2.6$$

The Sharpe's index for portfolio A = 2.6

For B portfolio;

Rf = 0.12 6 $\sigma = 0.09$ Rt = 0.30

$$SI_B = \frac{0.30 - 0.12}{0.09}$$

$$SI_B = \frac{0.18}{0.09} = 2$$

according to the calculated ''*portfolio* A'' has a better performance.

b) Treynor's Measure

The Treynor's measure relates a portfolio's excess return to non-diversifiable or systematic risk. The Treynor's measure employs beta. The Treynor based his formula on the concept of characteristic line. It is the risk measure of standard deviation, namely the total risk of the portfolio is replaced by beta. The equation can be presented as follows;

$$T_n = \frac{R_n - Rf}{\beta_m}$$

T_n = Treynor's measure of performance

R_n = Return on the portfolio

Rf = risk free rate of return

β_m = Beta of the portfolio (A measure of systematic risk)

Illustration: Calculate portfolio performance of the following X and Y securities by using Treynor's method.

Portfolio	Return	B_n	rf
X	22	0.6	11
Y	26	1.2	11

Solution: Treynor's measure of performance can be computed as follows;

For Portfolio X: $T_n = \frac{R_n - Rf}{\beta_m}$

R_n =0.22 rf=0.11 β_m =0.6

$$T_{nx} = \frac{0.22 - 0.11}{1.2} = \frac{0.11}{0.6} = 0.183$$

$$\text{For Portfolio Y} = \frac{0.26 - 0.11}{1.2} = \frac{0.15}{1.2} = 0.125$$

Portfolio X is better than Y because $T_nx > T_ny$

Jensen's Measure:

Jensen attempts to construct a measure of absolute performance on a risk adjusted basis. This measure is based on CAPM model. It measures the portfolio manager's predictive ability to achieve higher return than expected for the accepted riskiness. The ability to earn returns through successful prediction of security prices on a standard measurement. The Jensen measure of the performance of portfolio can be calculated by applying the following formula;

$$(R_p = Rf + (R_{MI} - Rf) \times \beta)$$

R_P = Return on portfolio

R_{MI} = Return on market index

Rf = Risk free rate of return.

Illustration: From the following data, calculate the portfolio performance measure according to Jensens model.

Portfolio	Return on portfolio	Portfolio Beta
1	20%	1.5
2	17%	1.1
3	23%	1.8
Market Index	18%	1.03

Market Beta : 1.00

Risk free rate of return : 10%

Solution: The return of 3 portfolios on the basis of CAPM are as follows;

$$Rp = Rf + (R_{mi} - Rf)\beta$$

For portfolio-I

R_{MI}=20%Rf=10% B=1.5

by substituting the values in the formula;

R_P = 10+(20 -10) × 1.5

R_P = 10+(10) × 1.5

R_P = 10+15 = 25%

For portfolio-II

= Rf=10% R_{MI}=17% B=1.1

Rp = 10+(17-10) × 1.1=17.7%

For portfolio-III

=10+(23-10) × 1.8=33.4%

The measure of performance = Actual vs estimated:

I = 20% - 25% = 5%

II = 17% - 17.7 = 0.7%

III = 23 -33.4 = 10.4%

Here, the portfolio III performance is outstanding.

PROBLEMS

Illustration No.1: The portfolio return and risk for three growth oriented firms for the specified period are listed below.

Growth firm	Return	Risk
X	17%	18%
Y	15%	20%
Z	14%	13%

Rank each firm by Sharpe's index of portfolio performance if risk free rate of return is 9%.

Solution: Sharpe's index of portfolio performance can be calculated by the following formula;

$$SP = \frac{\overline{R}_p - Rf}{\sigma_p}$$

SP = Sharpe's measurement of performance

$\overline{R}_p$ = Return on portfolio

Rf = Risk free rate of return.

σ_p = Risk

Calculation of Sharpe's index performance for x growth firm;

$\overline{R}_p$ =17% R=9% σ_p =18%

$$SP_x = \frac{17-9}{18} = \frac{8}{18} = 0.44$$ Ist rank

$$SP_z = \frac{14-9}{13} = \frac{5}{13} = 0.38$$ IIrd rank

$$SP_y = \frac{15-9}{20} = \frac{6}{20} = 0.33$$ IIInd rank.

Illustration No.2: From the following data, calculate the risk adjusted performance of each of the investment funds using the Sharpe's measure? Assume that the Government Treasury Bills yield a constant rate of return at 8%.

Year	*X (return)*	*Y (return)*	*Z (return)*
1997	6	6	4
1998	0	3	-7
1999	-3	-2	-10
2000	10	12	16
2001	7	7	5

Solution: With the given data, first, we must calculate the averages for all the security returns.

Calculation of arthmetic mean for the given data;

Year	x	$\bar{x} = 4$ dx	dx^2	y	dy	dy^2	z	dz	dz^2
1997	6	+2	4	6	0.8	0.64	8	2.8	7.84
1998	0	-4	16	3	-2.2	+4.84	-3	-8.2	67.24
1999	-3	-7	49	-2	-7.2	+51.84	-8	-13.2	174.24
2000	10	6	36	12	6.8	46.24	20	14.8	219.04
2001	7	3	09	7	1.8	3.24	9	3.8	14.44
	+23		114	+28		106.80	+37		482.80
	-03			-02			-11		
	Σx = +20			+26			+26		

$$\bar{R}_x = \frac{\Sigma x}{n} = \frac{20}{5} = 4 \qquad \bar{R}_y = \frac{26}{5} = 5.2 \qquad \bar{R}_z = \frac{26}{5} = 5.2$$

$$\therefore \bar{R}_x = 4 \qquad \sigma^2_x = 114 \qquad \therefore \sigma x = \sqrt{114} = 10.67$$

$$\bar{R}_y = 5.2 \qquad \sigma^2_y = 106.80 \qquad \sigma y = \sqrt{106.80} = 10.33$$

$$\bar{R}_z = 5.2 \qquad \sigma^2_z = 482.80 \qquad \sigma z = \sqrt{482.80} = 21.97$$

$$SP_x = \frac{\bar{R}P_x - R}{\sigma p} = \bar{R}P_x = 4 \qquad R = 7 \qquad \sigma p_x = 10.67$$

$$\therefore \frac{4-7}{10.67} = \frac{-13}{10.67} = -0.28 \qquad \text{IIIrd rank}$$

$N = 5 \quad \Sigma xy = 243 \quad \Sigma x^2 = 203$

$\alpha = y - \beta x$

$$\beta = \frac{N\Sigma xy - \Sigma x.\Sigma y}{N\Sigma x^2 - (\Sigma x)^2}$$

$$= \frac{5 \times 243 - (-3)(6)}{5 \times 203 - (-3)2} = 1.226$$

$\alpha = y - \beta x$

$\alpha = 1.26 - 1.226(-0.6) = \boxed{1.93}$

Year	r_i	r_m	R_f	$x = (r_m - r_f)$	$y(r_i - r_f)$	xy	x^2
1	17	14	10	4	7	28	16
2	13	11	8	3	5	15	9
3	15	12	9	3	6	18	9
4	-3	-2	11	-13	-14	182	169
5	9	7	7	0	2	0	0
				-13	+20		$\Sigma x^2 = 203$
				+ 10	− 14		
				-3	+6		

$$\therefore \bar{x} = \frac{\Sigma x}{n} = \frac{-3}{5} = -0.6$$

$$\bar{y} = \frac{\Sigma y}{n} = \frac{6}{5} = 1.2$$

PORTFOLIO ANALYSIS

The main aim of portfolio analysis is to give a cautious direction to the risk and return of an investor on a portfolio. Individual securities have risk return characteristics of their own. Therefore, portfolio analysis indicates the future risk and return in holding of different individual instruments. The portfolio analysis has been highly succesful in tracing the efficient portfolio. Portfolio analysis considers the determination of future risk and return in holding various blends of individual securities. An investor can sometimes reduce portfolio risk by adding another security with greater individual risk than any other security in the portfolio. Portfolio analysis is mainly depends on *Risk and Return of the portfolio.* The expected return of a portfolio should depend on the expected return of each of the security contained in the portfolio. The amount invested in each security is most important. The portfolio's expected holding period value relative is simply a weighted average of the expected value relative of its component securities. Using current market values as weights, the expected return of a portfolio is simply a weighted average of the expected returns of the securities comprising that portfolio. The weights are equal to the proportion of total funds invested in each security. The formula for expected return of a portfolio is as follows;

$$\overline{R}p = \sum_{i=1}^{n} wi\overline{R}i$$

$\overline{R}p$ = The expected return on portfolio

n = The total number of securities in the portfolio

w = The proportion or weight of total funds invested in security 'j'

$\overline{R}_i$ = expected return for security 'j'

Portfolio risk is concerned with the probability of actual yield being less than o, that is the probability of loss. A useful measure of risk should take into account both the probability of various possible bad out comes. Two measures are used for claculation of risk i.e., the average absolute deviation and the standard deviation. The average deviation can be calculated with the help of expected return. Then, each possible outcome is analysed to determine the amount by which the value deviates from the expected return. Portfolio risk can be reduced by diversification. The standard deviation for a portfolio will depend on the variance and co-variance of the individual and two securities respectively. If, the number of securities in a portfolio increases, the covariance term becomes more important relative to the variance terms. Covariance[1] is a statistical measure of the degree to which two variables move together. A positive value means that on average, they move in the same direction, correlation is a standardised statistical measure of the linear relationship between two variables. Its range is from -1.0 (perfect negative correlation), through 0 (no correlation) to +1.0 (perfect positive correlation). The correlation positive indicates that the returns from two securities generally move on the same direction. The negative correlation implies that the securities move in

1. Financial Management, Vanhorne, P.No.97, Prentice Hall, 1997.

opposite directions. A "o" correlation implies that the returns from two securities are uncorrelated. They show no tendency to vary together in either in positive or negative linear fashion. Therefore, the correlation between two stocks is generally positive, lessthan 1.0. Assuming that investor puts his funds in few securities, the holding period return of the portfolio is shown as follows;

Security	Percentage of funds invested in each security	Expected return for holding period	Return on each security
A	20	13%	2.60
B	30	18%	5.40
C	25	23%	5.75
D	25	8%	2.00
	100	Weighted return	15.75%

Beta(β)

Beta describes the relationship between the stocks return and the market index return. This can be positive or negative. It indicates about the percentage chage in the price of the stock regressed (correlated) to the percentage changes in the market index. Beta can be defined[1] "An index of systematic risk. It measures the sensitivity of a stock's returns to changes in returns on the market portfolio. The beta of a portfolio is simply a weighted average of the individual stock beta as in the portfolio". If beta has changed 1% then market index will lead to one percentage change in price of a stock, if beta is zero, stock price is unrelated to the market index. If the beta is minus one, it indicates a negative relationship with the market index. If the market goes up by 1 percent, the stock price will fall by 1%. It measures the systematic market related risk, which can not be eliminated by diversification. If the portfolio is efficient, beta measures the systematic risk effectively. On the other hand, alpha and epsilon measure the unsystematic risk, which can be reduced by efficient diversification.

Rho

Rho may be called as covariance or correlation coefficient. Rho measures the relationship between two stocks. If there is no relation between two securities, the coefficient of correlation can be zero. If the coefficient is +1, it indicates that both the securities are in upward movement. On the other Rho is -1 the direction of the movement will be opposite as between stock price and the market index.

---

1. Financial Management, Vanhorne, P.No.102, Prentice Hall, 1997.

The equation of Rho is presented below:

$$P = \frac{Cov.(xy)}{\sigma x \sigma y} = \sum_{x=1}^{n} \frac{R \times i - \overline{R}_i}{\sigma i} \times \frac{R \times j - \overline{R}_j}{\sigma r} \; p \times ij$$

$\overline{R}_i$ = Expected return on 'i' security

$\overline{R}_j$ = Expected return on 'j' security

n = Total number of joint observations

p_{ij} = Joint probability of 'i' and 'j' securities

Coefficient of Correlation can be calcualted by the following formula;

$$r_{xy} = \frac{C_{xy}}{S_x S_y}$$

r_{xy} = Coefficient of Correlation

C_{xy} = Covariance between x and y

S_x = Standard deviation of x returns

S_y = Standard deviation of y returns

or

$$r_{xy} = \frac{\text{Covariance}}{\sigma_x \sigma_y}$$

Regression equation

The basic equation for calculating risk can be formulated in the form of a regression equation given below.

$$y = a + b \times .e^{i}$$

Y = Return on the security in a given period.

a = The intercept where the regression line crosses the y axis.

b = Is the slope of the regression line.

e = error term containing all residuals.

The following graph will illustrate the regression equation:

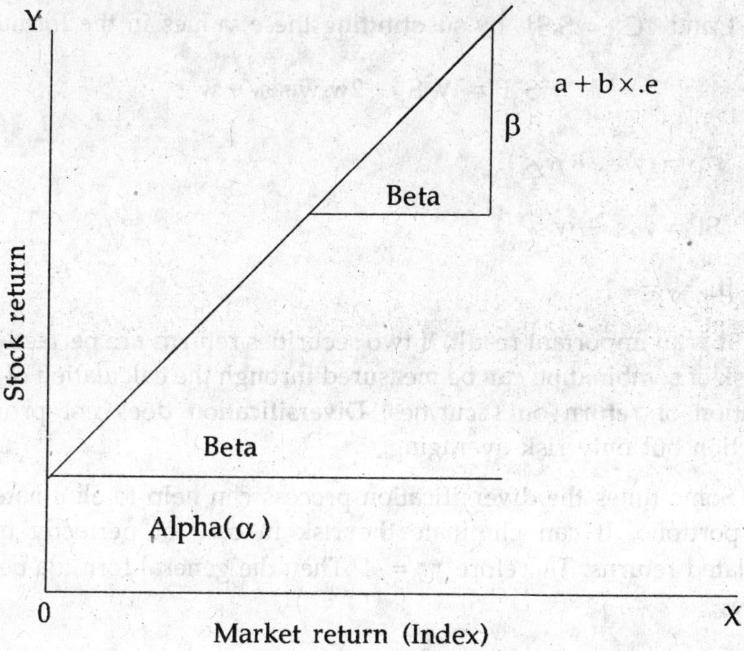

Alpha

Alpha measures the unsystematic risk of the company. It is the difference between actual earned return and expected return at a level of systematic risk. If Alpha is a positive return, then that scrip will show higher returns. If the Alpha is zero then there is no difference between expected and actual return of a security.

Diversification

The risk can be eliminated by a proper diversification. But diversification may not be useful in all situations. Sometimes, the diversification may help to eliminate the risk or may not be. The following formula may help, when the correlation of returns is positive. It is the effect on risk when the two securities are combined. The general formula is;

$$V_p = w_x^2 v_x + 2 w_x w_y c_{xy} + w_y^2 v_y$$

V_p = The variance of return for the portfolio

w_x = The proportion of the the funds invested in security x.

w_y = The proportion of the funds invested in security y

c_{xy} = The covariance between the return on security x and the return on y security

N = The number of securities in the portfolio

If there is a perfect positive correlation between two securities so $r_{xy} = +1$ and $C_{xy} = S_xS_y$, by substituting these values in the formula;

$$S^2P = W_x^2S_x^2 + 2w_xw_yS_xS_y + w_y^2s_y^2$$

$$S^2p = (w_xS_x + w_yS_y)$$

$$SP = w_xS_x + w_yS_y$$

If $r_{xy} = +1$

It is an important result. If two securities returns are perfectly positive the risk of combination can be measured through the calculation of standard deviation of return on securities. Diversification does not provide risk reduction but only risk averaging.

Some times the diversification process can help to eliminate the risk of a portfolio. It can eliminate the risk in case of perfectly negatively correlated returns. Therefore $r_{xy} = -1$. Then the general formula becomes as follows;

$$S^2P = W_x^2S_x^2 - 2w_xw_yS_xS_y + w_y^2s_y^2$$

it can be factored to obtain.

$$S^2P = (w_xS_x - w_yS_y)^2 \quad \text{If } r_{xy} = -1$$

This can be represented as below;

$$w_x = \frac{S_yW_y}{S_x}$$

If the two securities returns are perfectly negatively correlated, it is possible to combine them in a manner that will eliminate all risks. Some risks can be reduced by pooling of all securities. It has the important task of investment manager for selecting a better securities.

Un correlated returns

Some times the risk can be reduced by pooling of all the securities. Combining of different securities needs a high talented skill by a portfolio manager. The different types of securities offers wide variety of returns and risk to the portfolio. If the returns are uncorrelated between two securities the general formula becomes as follows;

$$S^2P = w_x^2s_x^2 + w_y^2s_y^2 \quad \text{If } r_{xy} = 0$$

If the diversification process helps the portfolio to reduce the risk either of a single security or components of securities. It will remain the same irrespective of the number of securities in the portfolio. If all returns are uncorrelated the general formula becomes;

$$S^2P = w_1^2 s_1^2 + w_n^2 s_n^2$$

Sp = Standard deviation of the return on portfolio

w_1 = The proportion of invested in securities of a portfolio funds

w_2 = The proportion of funds invested in security of a portfolio.

s_1 = Standard deviation of the return for security 1

s_2 = Standard deviation of the return for security 2.

N = The number of securities included in portfolio.

Diversification provides substantial risk reduction, when the components of a portfolio are uncorrelated. If the investor wants to reduce the overall risk of the portfolio, enough securities are to be included. This process may be called as portfolio insurance. The portfolio construction is a highly skilled task before a fund manager. Some situations require a combination of risky and riskless securities. Ex: If security A return is certain, and the B security return is uncertain. Therefore $s_A = 0$ and the combination becomes as follows;

$$SP = W^2 A_o + 2w_A w_B o + w^2 B s^2 B$$

Therefore;

$SP = w_B s_B$ If $s_A = 0$

If a risky security is combined with a risk less one, the risk of the combination is proportional to the amount invested in the risky component. Investing in a risk less security is on par with lending of money. Usually the borrowed fund is a costly investment and it enhances the leverage. If the borrowed capital is invested in a risk alternative, then the leverage increases the expected return on investment. Some times the expected return may decline with unfavorable out come. Borrowing increases risk and expenses. Leverage increases risk and return. The individual investors can borrow from a number of sources. The borrower has to meet the cost of fund. The interest rate will depend upon number of factors *i.e.,* The length of time involved, the amount of money borrowed the purpose of loan, the lender, the collateral etc. There is a chance that the loan amount will not be repaid in full and on time, the rate charged of course be higher and the loan will be risk less.

Choosing The Best Portfolio

There are various possible portfolios available on the efficient frontier. The investor has to choose and build a portfolio. In order to select best portfolio. The risk return preferences of the investors are to be analysed. The diagram shows the risk-return trade off or the risk-return indifference curve for investor.

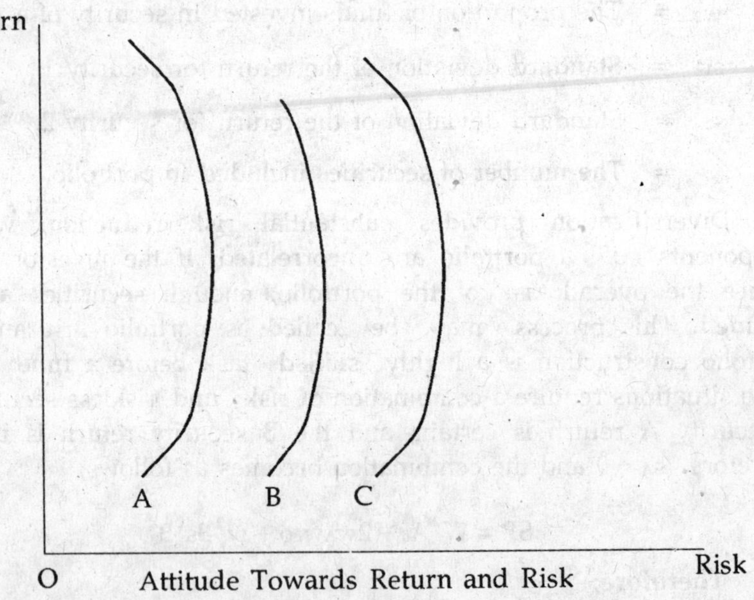

In the above diagram, the indifference curves C_1, C_2, C_3 are shown. All the points lying on a particular indifference curve represent different combinations of risk and return which provide same level of utility or satisfaction to the investors. An investor may have a present satisfaction level represented by the indifference curve C_1 but if the satisfaction level increases, then the investor will move to indifference curve C_2 or C_3. Thus, an investor at any particular point of time will be indifferent between combinations of S_1 and S_2 or between combinations of S_3 and S_4 or between the combinations of S_5 and S_6. The efficient frontier can now be combined with the indifferent curves to determine the investor's optimum portfolio. Given the efficient frontier risk return indifference curve and the tangency point of efficient frontier with the indifferent curve. This tangency point mark the highest level of satisfaction that the investor can attain. This has been presented in the following graph.

Graph showing the efficient portfolio;

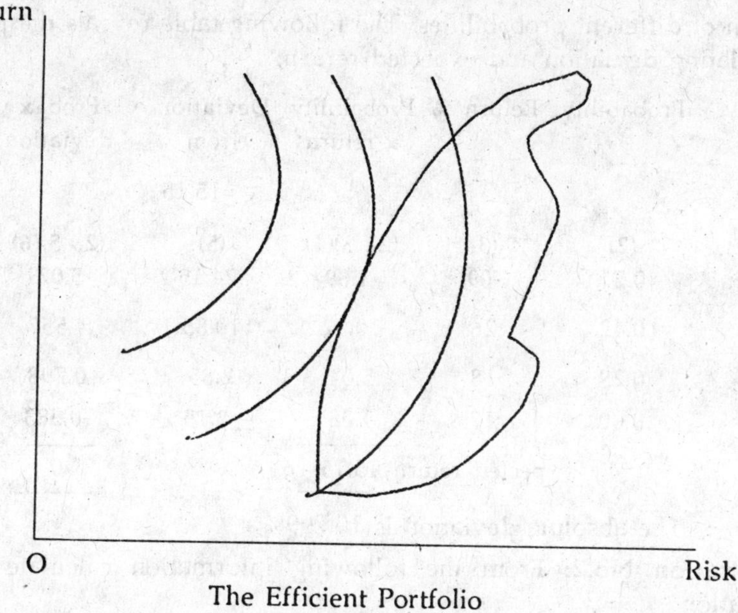

The Efficient Portfolio

In the graph R is the tangency point and is also the efficient portfolio. At this portfolio, the investor will be able to get the best possible level of satisfaction and the best combination of risk and return. Another combination say x, though, lies on the same indifference curve C_2, cannot be attained as it is outside the portfolio region. Further, combination "X" is also not optimal because it is not giving the required level of satisfaction to the investor though it is within the portfolio region. An investor having other sets of indifference curve will possibly have some other portfolio as his efficient portfolio.

REVIEW PROBLEMS

Illustration No.1: From the following data calculate mean and absolute deviation

Event	Probability	Return
a	0.21	-9
b	0.42	26
c	0.28	18
d	0.9	12

Solution:

The average absolute deviation can be calculated through expected return of different probabilities. The following table reveals the process of calculating deviation and expected return;

Event	Probability	Return %	Probability x return	Deviation from $\overline{x}$=15.15	Prob. x deviation	Prob. y absolute deviation
(1)	(2)	(3)	(2 x 3)(4)	(5)	(2 x 5)(6)	(7)
a	0.21	-09	-1.89	-24.15	-5.071	5.071
b	0.42	26	10.92	10.85	4.557	4.557
c	0.28	18	5.04	2.85	0.798	0.798
d	0.09	12	1.08	-3.15	-0.283	0.283
		expected return	15.15		0	10.709

∴ The absolute deviation is 10.709%

Illustration No.2: From the following information calculate standard deviation

Event	Probability	Return %
a	0.21	-09
b	0.42	26
c	0.28	18
d	0.09	12

Solution:

The standard deviation can be calculated through the following table;

First, we must calculate the average and measure. The deviations from the mean.

Event	Probability	Return %	Probability x return	Deviation from $\overline{x}$=15.15	Deviation squared	Prob. x deviation square
(1)	(2)	(3)	(2 x 3)(4)	(5)	(2 x 5)(6)	(2 x 6)(7)
a	0.21	-09	-1.89	-24.15	583.22	122.47
b	0.42	26	10.92	10.85	117.72	49.44
c	0.28	18	5.04	2.85	8.12	2.27
d	0.09	12	1.08	-3.15	9.92	0.89
		expected return ($\overline{x}$)	15.15			175.07

$\therefore$ Standard deviation $= \sqrt{175.07}$

$= 13.23$

The deviations from $\overline{x}$ were arrived as follows (explanation to column No.5);

-09 - 15.15 = -24.15

26 - 15.15 = 10.85

18 - 15.15 = 2.85

12 - 15.15 = -03.15

Illustration No.3: Calculate the covariance and coefficient of correlation from the following data. Stocks are x and y and their returns and expected returns are given below:

Particulars	Return	Expected return
stock x	16	20
stock y	28	20
stock x	24	20
stock y	12	20

Solution:

First calculate standard deviation, then covariance is to be calculated.

Calculation of standard deviation;

X	Y	dx	dy	dx^2	dy^2
16	28	(16-20=-4)	(28-20=(+8))	16	64
24	12	(24-20=+4)	(12-20=(-8))	16	64
Σx 40	Σy 40			32	128

$\overline{x} = \frac{\Sigma x}{n}$ $\quad \overline{y} = \frac{\Sigma y}{n}$

$= \frac{40}{2} = 20$ $\quad = \frac{40}{2} = 20$

$\overline{x} = 20$ $\quad \overline{y} = 20$

The following formula can be applied for calculation of standard deviation;

$$\sigma_x = \sqrt{\frac{\Sigma dx^2}{N}}$$

$$\sigma_y = \sqrt{\frac{\Sigma dy^2}{N}}$$

σ_x = Standard deviation of x stock

dx^2 = Squared deviations from arithmetic mean of x stock

n = No.of securities

σ_y = Standard deviation of y stock

dy^2 = Squared deviations from arithmetic mean of y stock.

Therefore, the values may be substituted in the formula.

$\Sigma dx^2 = 3$ $\Sigma dy^2 = 12$

$\sigma_x = \sqrt{\frac{32}{2}}$ $\sigma_y = \sqrt{\frac{128}{2}}$

$\sigma_x = \sqrt{16}$ $\sigma_y = \sqrt{64}$

$\sigma_x = 4$ $\sigma_y = 8$

The next step is calculation of Covariance;

Stock	Return	Expected return	Difference	Product of differences
(1)	(2)	(3)	2-3=(4)	
x	16	20	-4	
y	28	20	+8	$-4 \times 8 = 32$
x	24	20	+4	
y	12	20	-8	$4 \times -8 = -32$

$$\text{Covariance} = \frac{1}{2}(R_x - ER_x)(R_y - ER_y) + \frac{1}{2}(R_x - ER_x)(R_y - ER_y)$$

R_x = Return on x stock

ER_x = Expected return on X stock

R_y = Return on y stock

ER_y = Expected return on stocky.

Covariance $= \frac{1}{2}(16 - 20)(28 - 20) + \frac{1}{2}(24 - 20)(12 - 20)$

$= \frac{1}{2}(-4)(+8) + \frac{1}{2}(4)(-8)$

$= \frac{1}{2}(-32) + \frac{1}{2}(-32)$

$= -32$

Calculation of Correlation: $r_{xy} = \frac{Cov.xy}{\sigma_x \sigma_y}$

r_{xy} = Coefficient of correlation

σ_x = Standard deviation of stock x

σ_y = Standard deviation of stock y

Cov.xy= -32

$\sigma_x = 4$

$\sigma_y = 8$

Substituting the values in the formula;

$$\therefore r_{xy} = \frac{-32}{4 \times 8} = \frac{-32}{32} = -1$$

Correlation coefficient is negative and they are perfectly negatively correlated with a value of 1.

Illustration No.4: From the following information calculate the expected return and standard deviation for two companies.

	Company-A		Company-B	
	Expected return	Probability	Expected return	probability
1	8	0.3	10	0.2
2	12	0.5	16	0.5
3	14	0.2	20	0.3

Solution:

Calculation of expexted return for Company-A presented below;

Company - A

Return	Probability	Weighted probability return
(1)	(2)	1 x 2 (3)
8	0.3	2.4
12	0.5	6.0
14	0.2	2.8
		11.2

∴ The expected return for company A is 11.2%

The calculation fo standard deviation of **Company-A** is given below:

Outcome	Weighted probability return	Deviations from expected return (11.2-er)	Squared deviation	Products of Weighted probabilities and squared deviations
(1)	(2)	(3)	(4)	(5)
1	2.4	11.2-8=3.2	$3.2^2 = 10.24$	$10.24 \times 0.3 = 3.072$
2	6.0	11.2-12=-0.8	$-0.8^2 = 0.64$	$0.64 \times 0.5 = 0.320$
3	2.8	11.2-14=-2.8	$-2.8^2 = 7.84$	$7.84 \times 0.2 = 1.568$
				4.960

∴ Standard deviation for company A = $\sqrt{4.960}$

$\therefore \sigma_A = 2.23\%$

Calculation of expected return for Company -B;

Return	Probability	Weighted probability return
(1)	(2)	$1 \times 2 = (3)$
10	0.20	2.00
16	0.50	8.00
20	0.30	6.00
	expected return	16.00

Calculation of standard deviation for Company B;

Outcome	Weighted probability return	Deviations from expected return	Squared deviations	Products of Weighted probabilites and deviations squared
(1)	(2)	(3)	(4)	(5)
1	2	16-10=6	$(6)^2=36$	$36 \times 0.2 = 7.2$
2	8	16-16=0	$(0)^2=0$	$00 \times 0.5 = 0$
3	6	16-20=-4	$(-4)^2=16$	$16 \times 0.3 = 4.8$
				12.0

$\therefore$ Standard deviation = $\sqrt{12}$

= 3.46

The risk and return of company B is higher.

Illustration No. 5: Given below are the returns of Voltas and BSE sensex for 5 year period. Calculate Beta, Alpha, residual variance and correlation.

Year	Return on Voltas (y)	Return on BSE sensex (x)
1	0.3	0.1
2	0.4	0.2
3	0.5	0.3
4	0.6	0.4
5	0.7	0.5

Solution:

Calculation of beta $(\beta) = \dfrac{n\Sigma xy - (\Sigma x)(\Sigma y)}{n\Sigma x^2 - \Sigma(x)^2}$

The values can be calculated as follows:

Year	x	y	xy	x^2	y^2
1	0.10	0.30	0.03	0.01	0.09
2	0.20	0.40	0.08	0.04	0.16
3	0.30	0.50	0.15	0.09	0.25
4	0.40	0.60	0.24	0.16	0.36
5	0.50	0.70	0.35	0.25	0.49
	$\Sigma x=1.50$	$\Sigma y=2.5$	$\Sigma xy=0.85$	$\Sigma x^2=0.55$	$\Sigma y^2=1.35$

$$\bar{x} = \frac{\Sigma x}{n} = \frac{1.5}{5} = 0.3 \qquad \bar{y} = \frac{\Sigma y}{n} = \frac{2.5}{5} = 0.5$$

$\therefore$ $n = 5$ $\quad \Sigma xy = 0.85$ $\quad \Sigma x = 1.50$ $\quad \Sigma x^2 = 0.55$

$\Sigma y = 2.5$ $\quad \Sigma y^2 = 1.35$

$$\beta = \frac{(5 \times 0.85) - (1.5 \times 2.5)}{5 \times 0.55 - (1.50)^2}$$

$$= \frac{4.25 - 3.75}{2.75 - 2.25} = \frac{0.5}{0.5} = 1$$

$$\therefore \quad \beta = 1$$

Calculation of α***;***

$$\alpha = y - \beta x$$

α = Alpha $\qquad \beta = 1$

$y = \bar{y} = 0.5$ $\qquad x = \bar{x} = 0.3$

Substituting the values in the formula;

$\alpha = 0.5 - 1\ (0.3)$

$= 0.5 - 0.3 = 0.2$

Calculation of residual variance;

It can be calculated by the following formula;

$$e^2 = \frac{\Sigma y^2 - \alpha \Sigma y - \beta \Sigma xy}{n}$$

$\Sigma y^2 = 1.35$ $\quad \alpha = 0.2$ $\quad \beta = 1$ $\quad n = 5$ $\quad \Sigma xy = 0.85$ $\quad \Sigma y = 2.5$

Substituting the values in the formula;

$$e^2 = \frac{1.35 - 0.2 \times 2.5 - 1 \times 0.85}{5}$$

$$e^2 = \frac{1.35 - 0.50 - 0.85}{5}$$

$$e^2 = \frac{1.35 - 1.35}{5}$$

$$e^2 = \frac{0}{5} = 0$$

Calculation of correlation:

$$r = \frac{\Sigma xy}{\sqrt{\Sigma x^2 . \Sigma y^2}}$$

r = coefficient of correlation.

$\Sigma xy = 0.85$ $\Sigma x^2 = 0.55$ $\Sigma y^2 = 1.35$ $r = \frac{0.85}{\sqrt{0.55 \times 1.35}}$

$$= \frac{0.85}{\sqrt{0.743}} = \frac{0.85}{0.86} = 0.98$$

Calculation of variance of Voltas:

$\overline{y} = \frac{\Sigma y}{n}$ $\Sigma y = 2.5$ $n = 5$

$$= \frac{2.5}{5} = 0.5$$

Return	Deviation from 0.5(y)	Deviations squared y^2
0.3	-0.2	0.04
0.4	-0.1	0.01
0.5	0	0
0.6	0.1	0.01
0.7	0.2	0.04
		$\Sigma y^2 = 0.10$

$$\text{Variance} = \sigma^2 = \frac{\Sigma y2}{n}$$

$$\therefore \sigma^2 = \frac{0.10}{5} = 0.2$$

$$\sigma = \sqrt{0.02} = 0.144$$

systematic variance = variance x r

variance = 0.02 r = 0.98

Systematic variance = 0.02×0.98 = 0.0196

Unsystematic variance/Unexplained residual = variance - systematic variance

= 0.02 - 0.0196 = 0.0004

$\therefore$ Total variance = Systematic variance + Unsystematic variance

0.0196 + 0.0004 = 0.02

Variance of BSE index:

Return	$\overline{x}$ =0.3 x	x^2
0.1	0.20	0.04
0.2	0.10	0.01
0.3	0	0
0.4	0.10	0.01
0.5	0.20	0.04
n=1.5		Σx^2 =0.10

$$\overline{x} = \frac{\Sigma x}{n} = \frac{1.5}{5} = 0.30$$

variance $\sigma^2 = \frac{\Sigma x^2}{n}$ $\Sigma x^2 = 0.10$ n=5

$$\sigma^2 = \frac{0.10}{5} = 0.02$$

$$\sigma^2 = 0.02$$

$$\sigma = \sqrt{0.02} = 0.144$$

Illustration No.6: From the following data, calculate the co-variance of returns for securities x and y.

State of the market	Probability of occurrence	Annual returns	
		x	y
1	0.3	7%	8%
2	0.2	12%	-2%
3	0.1	-6%	10%
4	0.4	9%	-7%

Solution:

Before the calculation of covariance of returns, the expected return on stock should be calculated by the following formula;

$$Er_x = \sum_{x=1}^{N} px^{rx}$$

Expeçet return for x security;

$Er_x = (0.3)\ (7) + (0.2)\ (12) + (0.1)\ (-6) + (0.4)\ (9)$

$\therefore\ er_x = 2.1+2.4 \pm .6 + 3.6$

$er_x = 8.1 - 0.6$

$er_x = 7.5\%$

Expected return for y security;

$\Sigma ry = (0.3)\ (8)+(0.2)\ (-2)+(0.1) \times 10+0.4 \times -7$

$\Sigma ry = 2.4 - 0.4 + 1.0 - 2.8$

$= 3.4 - 3.2 = 0.2$ or 2%

Co-variance can be worked out by the following formula.

$$Cov.xy = (\sum_{1}^{N} r_{xt} - \bar{r}x)(r_{yt} - \bar{r}y)$$

The required values are to be obtained from the following table;

Calculation of covariance;

Prob.	r_x	r_y	$r_x - Er$	$r_y - Er$	$1 \times 4 \times 5 = (6)$
(1)	(2)	(3)	(4)	(dx^2)	(5) (dy^2)
					$(prob \times rx - Er \times ry - er)$
0.3	-7	8	(7-7.5)=-0.5	(8-0.2)=7.8	-1.17
0.2	12	-2	(12-7.5)=+4.5	(-2-0.2)=-2.2	-1.98
0.1	-6	10	(-6 -7.5)=-13.5	(10-0.2)=9.8	-13.23
0.4	9	-7	(9-7.5)=+1.5	(-7-0.2)=-7.2	-4.32

$Covariance = probability \times rx - Er \times ry - er$

$\therefore$ Covariance= -20.27

Co-efficient of correlation can be calculated by applying the following formula;

$$r_{xy} = \frac{Cov.xy}{\sigma_x \sigma_y}$$

$\therefore$ Cov.xy=-20.27 σ_x=? σ_y=?

Now, we have to calculate σ_x and σ_y with the above values;

σ_x^2 = prob × (dx^2) +prob. (dx^2) +prob. $(dx^2)^n$

= $0.3 \times (-0.5)^2 + 0.2 (4.5)^2 + 0.1 (-13.5)^2 + 0.4 (1.5)^2$

= $0.3 \times 0.25 + 0.2 \times 20.25 + 0.1 \times 182.25 + 0.4 \times 2.25$

= 0.075 + 4.05 + 18.22 + 0.9 = 23.24

$\sigma_x = \sqrt{23.24}$ =4.8%

σ_y^2 = $0.3 (7.8)^2 +\text{-}0.2 (-2.2)^2 + 0.1 (9.8)^2 + 0.4 (-7.2)^2$

σ_y^2 = 18.25+0.97+9.60+20.73=49.55

σ_y^2 = 49.55

$\sigma_y = \sqrt{49.55}$ =7.01

σ_x =4.8 σ_y =7.01

$$r_{xy} = \frac{-20.7}{4.8 \times 7.01} = \frac{-20.7}{33.68} = -0.61$$

Illustration No.7: From the following information calculate coefficient of correlation and covariance of returns.

Year	Return (x)	Return (y)
1	10	12
2	-7	-10
3	16	20
4	18	22
5	22	16

Solution:

For calculation of coefficient of correlation, the following formula is applied.

$$r_{xy} = \frac{N\Sigma xy - \Sigma x.\Sigma y}{\left[(N.\Sigma x^2) - (\Sigma x)^2\right]\left[(N.B\Sigma y^2) - (\Sigma y)^2\right]^{\frac{1}{2}}} N$$

The values of the above formula can be drawn from the table;

Return x	Return y	x^2	y^2	xy
10	12	100	144	120
-7	-10	49	100	70
16	20	256	400	320
18	22	324	484	396
22	16	484	256	352
Σx =59	Σy =60	Σx^2 =1213	Σy^2 =1258	Σxy =1258

N = 5, Ex = + 59, Ey = +60

x^2 =1213, y^2 =1384, Σxy =1258

$$r_{xy} = \frac{51258 - 5960}{\left[(5 \times 1213) - (59)^2\right]\left[(5 \times 1384) - (60)^2\right]^{\frac{1}{2}}}$$

$$= \frac{6290 - 3540}{\left[(6065) - (3481)(6920) - (3600)\right]^{\frac{1}{2}}}$$

$$= \frac{2750}{(2584)(3320)^2}$$

$$= \frac{2750}{(8578800)}$$

$$= \frac{2750}{2928.97}$$

r = 0.938

Calculation of covariance of returns:

$$Covxy = \frac{1}{N}\sum_{t=1}^{N} (r_{xi} - \bar{r}_x)(r_{yi} - \bar{r}_y)$$

year	return x	return y
1	10	12
2	-7	-10
3	16	20
4	18	22
5	22	16
	$\Sigma x = 59$	$\Sigma y = 60$

$\bar{x} = \frac{\Sigma x}{n} = \frac{59}{5} = 11.8$ $\quad\quad$ $\bar{y} = \frac{\Sigma y}{n} = \frac{60}{5} = 12$

Substituting the values in the formula;

$$= \frac{1}{5}\left[(10-11.8)(12-12) + (-7011.8)(-10-12) + (16-11.8)(20-12) + (18-11.8)(22-12) + (22-11.8)(16-12)\right.$$

$$= \frac{1}{5}\left[(0) + (-18.8)(-22) + (4.2)(8) + (6.2)(10) + (10.2)(4)\right]$$

$$= \frac{1}{5}(0 + 413.6 + 33.6 + 62 + 40.8)$$

$$= \frac{1}{5}\ (550) = 110$$

Illustration No.8: Mr. Dinesh has a portfolio of five securities. The expected rate of return and amount of investment in each security is as follows:

Security;	M	N	O	P	Q
Expected return;	0.12	0.10	0.13	0.11	0.11
Amount invested;	40,000	20,000	60,000	50,000	30,000

Compute the expected return on Dinesh's portfolio.

Solution:

The expected return on Dinesh portfolio can be calculated as follows;

$$erp = \left(\frac{\text{Amount invested}}{\text{Total portfolio}} \times \text{expected return}\right)$$

$= (40{,}000/2{,}00{,}000)\ 0.12 + (20{,}000/2{,}00{,}000)\ 0.10 + (60{,}000/2{,}00{,}000)$

$+ (50{,}000/2{,}00{,}000)\ 0.11 + (30{,}000/2{,}00{,}000)\ 0.11$

$= \frac{1}{5}\ (0.12) + \frac{1}{10}\ (0.10) + 0.3 \times 0.13 + \frac{1}{4}\ (0.11) + 0.15 \times 0.11$

$= 0.2 \times 0.12 + 0.10\ (0.10) + 0.3 \times 0.13 + 0.25 \times 0.11 + 0.15 \times 0.11$

$= 0.024 + 0.01 + 0.039 + 0.0275 + 0.0165$

$= 0.024 + 0.01 + 0.039 + 028 + 0.016$

$= 0.118$ or 11.8%

Illustration No.9: Calculate the Portfolio return from the following proportions of each stock, stock 1 = 0.3 stock 2 = 0.3 and stock 3 = 0.4 and the returns of them are 12, 14, and 10 respectively.

Solution:

The return on the portfolio can be calculated by the following formula;

$$R_p = \sum_{i=1}^{N} x_i R_i$$

n = Total number of securities in portfolio.

R_p = Return on the portfolio

x_i = Weight of the security in portfolio

R_i = Return on the security.

R_p = (0.3) (12) + (0.3) (14) + (0.4) (10)

R_p = 3.6 + 4.2 + 4.0 = 11.8%

Illustration No.10: The following information provide two companies returns for the past ten years.

Company	% return during year									
	1	2	3	4	5	6	7	8	9	10
A Ltd.,	39	26	-8	4	16	30	-9	27	19	6
B Ltd.,	30	27	-14	3	12	28	0	17	29	8

a) Calculate the standard deviation of each companies returns.

b) Calculate the correlation coefficient of the companies returns.

c) If you had placed 50% of your money in each company, then what would be the standard deviation of your portfolio and the average yearly return?

d) What percentage of investment in each would result in the lowest risk?

e) Assume a risk free return of 6% you would like to and that only one of the two companies. Which would be the better to invest?

Solution:

a) Calculation of Mean and standard deviation of two companies:

$$\bar{x}_A = \frac{\Sigma x}{n} \qquad \bar{y}_B = \frac{\Sigma y}{n} \qquad \sigma = \sqrt{\frac{\Sigma x^2}{n}}$$

Company A				Company B				
Year	Return (X)	$(\bar{x}=15)$ (x)	x^2	Year	Return (Y)	$(\bar{y}=14)$ y	y^2	xy
1	39	24	196	1	30	16	256	224
2	26	11	121	2	27	13	169	143
3	-08	-23	529	3	-14	-28	784	664
4	04	-11	121	4	03	-11	121	121
5	16	1	01	5	12	-02	04	-02
6	30	15	225	6	28	14	196	210
7	-09	-24	576	7	0	0	0	0
8	27	12	144	8	17	03	09	36
9	19	04	169	09	19	15	5	60
10	06	-09	81	10	08	-06	36	54
n =10	Σx =150		2010		Σy =140		1800	Σxy =490

$$\bar{x} = \frac{150}{10} = 15 \qquad \bar{y} = \frac{\Sigma y}{n} = \frac{140}{4} = 4$$

$$\sigma_x = \sqrt{\frac{\Sigma x^2}{n}} \qquad \sigma_y = \sqrt{\frac{\Sigma y^2}{n}}$$

$$\sigma_x^{\,2} = 2010 \qquad \Sigma y^2 = 1800$$

$$n=10 \qquad n=10$$

$$\sigma_x = \sqrt{\frac{2010}{10}} = \sqrt{201} = 14.17\% \qquad \sigma_Y = \sqrt{\frac{1800}{10}}$$

$$\sigma_Y = \sqrt{180}$$

$$\sigma_y = 13.41\%$$

$$\therefore \quad \bar{x}_A = 15 \qquad \bar{y}_B = 14$$

$$\sigma_A = 14.17 \qquad \sigma_B = 13.14\%$$

b) Calculation of coefficient of correlation of the companies returns

The coefficient of correlation can be calculated by the following formula;

$$r = \frac{\Sigma xy}{N\sqrt{A}.\sqrt{B}}$$

$$\Sigma xy = 490; \qquad \sigma_A = 14.17; \qquad \sigma_B = 13.14 \qquad N=10$$

$$r = \frac{\Sigma xy}{\sigma A \sigma B} = \frac{490}{10 \times 14.17 \times 13.14} = \frac{490}{10 \times 186.19} = \frac{490}{1861.9} = 0.26$$

$$= \frac{\sqrt{1572}}{3.16}$$

$$= \frac{\sqrt{1572}}{3.16} = \sqrt{497.46} = 22.30$$

$$r = \frac{Cov.xy}{\sigma x \sigma y} \qquad Cov.xy = 22.30 \quad \sigma x = 14.17 \qquad \sigma y = 13.41$$

$$r = \frac{22.30}{14.17 \times 13.41}$$

$$= \frac{22.30}{190.01} = 0.11.$$

c) Calculation of standard deviation when 50% of funds invested:

$$\sigma_P = w_1^2 \times \sigma_1^2 + w_2^2\sigma_2^2 + 2w_1w_2\sigma_1\sigma_2 r$$

$w_1 = 0.5$ $\sigma_1 = 14.17$ $w_2 = 0.5$ $\sigma_2 = 13.41$ $r = 0.11$

Substituting the values in the formula;

$$\sigma_P = 0.5^2 \times 14.17^2 + 0.5^2 \times 13.41^2 + (2 \times 0.5 \times 0.5 \times 14.17 \times 13.41 \times 0.11)$$

$$\sigma_P = 0.25 \times 200.78 + 0.25 \times 179.82 + 10.45$$

$= 50.19+44.95+10.45$

$= 105.59$ **or** 1.05%

The expected return on portfolio can be calculated through the following formula;

$Er_P = w(\overline{R}_x) + w(\overline{R}_y)$ $w=0.5$ $\overline{R}_x = 15$ $\overline{R}_y = 14$

$Er_P = 0.5(15)+0.5(14)$

$=7.5+7.0=14.5\%$

d) Using the minimum variance equation and let w stand for company A;

$$W_A = \frac{\sigma_2^2 - \sigma_1\sigma_2 r_{1.2}}{\sigma_1^2 + \sigma_2^2 - \sigma_1\sigma_2 r_{1.2}} \quad \sigma_1 = 14.17 \quad \sigma_2 = 13.41 \quad r_{1.2} = 0.11$$

$$W_A = \frac{13.41^2 - 14.17 \times 13.41 \times 0.11}{14.17^2 + 13.41^2 - 14.17 \times 13.41 \times 0.11}$$

$$= \frac{179.82 - 20.92}{20.78 + 179.82 - 20.92}$$

$$= \frac{158}{359.68} = 0.44$$ **or** 44%

W_B = 56% (100-44)

e) For holding of a better return scrip, first we must calculate risk-slope of the two companies and then comparison of two companies should be made.

For Company A = $\frac{\overline{x} - Rf}{\sigma}$ $\overline{x}$ =15 Rf=6 σ =14.17

$$= \frac{15-6}{14.17} = \frac{9}{14.17} = 0.63 \text{ per Unit of } \sigma$$

for Company B = $\frac{14-6}{13.41}$

$$= \frac{8}{13.41} = 0.59\% \text{ per Unit of } \sigma$$

The values of both the companies are same, but A company is bettor for investment.

Illustration No.11: Samsung Corporation is planning to invest in a security that has several possible rates of return. Given the following probability distribution returns, whatis the expected rate of return? Compute standard deviation.

Probability (p)	Return (R)
0.10	-12%
0.20	07%
0.30	12%
0.40	27%

Solution:

The expected rate of return can be calculated by the following formula;

$$Er = R \times p$$

Probability (P)	Return (R)	Expected return (ER)	weighted return $(ER-R)^2 \times P$
(1)	(2)	$1 \times 2 = (3)$	$(3-2)^2 \times 1 = (4)$
0.10	-12%	-1.2%	$(15.8-12)^2 \times 0.10$=77.28
0.20	07%	1.4%	$(15.8-07)^2 \times 0.20$=15.48
0.30	12%	3.6%	$(15.8-12)^2 \times 0.30$= 4.33
0.40	27%	10.8%	$(15.8-27)^2 \times 0.40$=50.17
		(ER) 15.8%	σ^2 =147.26
			σ =12.13

Illustration No.12: Smt. Vani is considering an investment in one of the two securities. The following information is given , as a financial adviser which investment is better, based on risk and return? give your suggestion which security do you recommend?

Security A		Security X	
probability	Return	Prob	return
0.30	21%	0.20	24%
0.40	17%	0.30	8%
0.30	13%	0.30	16%
		0.20	-7%

Solution:

Calculation of risk and return for two scrips is presented below:

Investment in security A				Investment in security B.			
Prob.	Return	Expected return	Weighted deviation $(ER-R)^2$	Prob.	Return	Expected return	Weighted deviation $(ER-R)^2$
(1)	(2)	$1\times 2=3$	4	5	6	$5\times 6=7$	8
0.30	21	6.3	$(17-21)^2.3=4.8$	0.20	24	4.8	$(10.6-24)^2.2=35.9$
0.40	17	6.8	$(17-17)^2.4=0$	0.30	8	2.4	$(10.6-8)^2.3=2.02$
0.30	13	3.9	$(17-13)^2.3=4.8$	0.30	16	4.8	$(10.6-16)^2.3=8.74$
		(ER)=17	$\sigma^2=9.6$	0.20	-7	-1.4	$(10.6-7)^2.2=61.95$
						+12	$\sigma^2=108.61$
						-1.4	
						10.6	

$\sigma^2 = 9.6$ $\qquad \sigma = \sqrt{108.61}$

$\therefore \sigma_A = \sqrt{9.6} = 3.09$

Therefore, the investment of security A provides the highest reward for the lowest risk.

Illustration No.13: Mr. Harish is evaluating a security. 1 year treasury bills currently paying 10%. from the following information calculate the expected return and its standard deviation. Can he invest in this security?

Probability :	0.15	.30	.40	.15
Return :	13%	5%	8%	3%

Solution:

Probability(p)	*Return(R)*	*Expected return*	*Weighted deviation*
(1)	(2)	$1 \times 2 = (3)$	$(ER-R)^2$ P
0.15	13	1.95	$(7.1\%-13)^2$ .15=5.22
0.30	5	1.50	$(7.1\%-5)^2$ .30=1.32
0.40	8	3.20	$(7.1\%-8)^2$ .40=0.32
0.15	3	0.45	$(7.1\%-3)^2$ .15=2.52
		7.1%	σ^2 =9.38

$\therefore \quad \sigma = \sqrt{9.38} = 3.06$

Mr. Harish should not invest in this security. The level of risk is higher for a return which is equal to the rate offered on treasury bills.

Illustration No.14: From the following information findout the security and portfolio value relatives. The amount of investment is Rs.22,350.

Security	No. of shares	Current price per share	Expected end of periodshare value
A	100	18	21
B	150	23	25
C	200	43	47
D	250	28	34
E	100	15	20

Solution:

Calculation of security and portfolio value relatives;

Security	Current value	Proportion of current value holding (2 ÷ 22350)	Current price	Expected end of period value per share	Expected holding period value	Contribution to portfolio expected holding period value
(1)	(2)	(3)	(4)	(5)	5 ÷ 4 = (6)	3 × 6 = (7)
A	1800	0.08	18	21	1.1666	0.094494
B	3450	0.155	23	25	1.0869	0.168469
C	8600	0.384	43	47	1.0930	0.419712
D	7000	0.313	28	34	1.2142	0.380044
E	1500	0.067	15	20	1.3333	0.089331
	22350	1.000				1.15205

Calculation of security and portfolio holding period returns;

Security	Proportion of current value of portfolio	Expected holding period return (%) (3) from the above column (6)	Contribution to portfolio expected holding period return
(1)	(2)		2 × 3 = (4)
A	0.081	16.66	1.349
B	0.155	8.69	1.346
C	0.384	9.30	3.571
D	0.313	21.42	6.704
E	0.067	33.33	2.233
	1.0000		15.203%

TIME VALUE OF MONEY

Money has a time value. The basic objective of the finance manager of a company is to maximise shareholder's wealth in an appropriate period of time. The finance manager will have to take a right decision for investment. The investors form their opinion about the firm on the basis of information available to them. While taking the decision the finance manager must keep time factor in mind. The finance manager shall know the various valuation concepts such as. "Compound value concept, Annuity concept, present value concept." All the concepts are based on the money value. A rupee today is much more valuable than a rupee tomorrow. The time value of money is one of the central ideas in finance. Time value of money becomes important and some times vital consideration in decision making. Valuation concept may be categorised into the following two types;

1. Compound value concept.
2. Present value concept.

1. Compound value Concept

In this concept, the interest earned on the principal amount becomes a part of principal at the end of the compounding period. Compound value can be defined as "The process of determining the terminal value of an amount when compound interest rate applies. It can be on a continuous basis or at a fixed time intervals."[1]

"The process of finding the future value of a payment or series of payments when applying the concept of compound interest."[2]

For ex: If Rs.1,000is invested at 15% compound interest for 2 years. The return for the 1st year will be Rs. 150/- and for the second year interest will be on Rs.1,150/- (1,000+150).The total amount of interest due at the end of 2nd year will be Rs. 173 approximately. The general equation used to calculate the compound value of time after "N" *years* is given below;

$$A = P(1+i)^n$$

i = interest rate

P = Principal amount at the beginning of the period.

A = Amount at the end of period "n"

n = number of years.

In multiple compounding periods the compound value can be calculated with the help of the following formula;

$$A = P(1 + i/m)^{mn}$$

A = Amount after at the end of period 'n'

m = No. of times per year compounding is made

P = Principal amount at the beginning of the period

i = Interest rate

n = number of years for which compounding is to be done.

---

1. *L.M. Bhole,* Financial Markets and Institutions " P.No.32, 1999. Tata Mc Graw.
2. *I.M.Panday.* Financial Management, P.No.269, 1999, Vikas Publishing House Pvt. Ltd.

Illustration: Calculate the compound value when Rs.10,000 is invested for 3 years and the interest on it is compound at 15% p.a. semi annually.

Solution:

$$A = P(1 + i/m)^{mn}$$

$$A = Rs.10,000(1 + 0.15/2)^{2\times3}$$

$$A = Rs.10,000(1 + 0.075)^{6}$$

$$= 10,000(1.075)^{6}$$

$$= 10,000 \times 1.543$$

$$= \boxed{Rs.\ 15,433}$$

2. Present value Concept

The present value concept helps to estimate the present worth of a future payment adjusted for the time value of money. The present value concept is quite opposite to the compounding value concept. The interest can be earned on the idle money. This return is called as discounting rate. A positive rate of interest, the present value of future rupee will always be lower.

The present value can be defined as "Any asset or security derives its value from cash flows it is expected to generate in future. The present value of the future or delayed pay off can be found by multiplying the pay off by the discount factor which is less than one."[1] It may be expressed as follows;

$$\text{Discount factor} = \frac{1}{1 + \text{discount rate}}$$

The present value of money can be found in the following kinds;

a) PV after "N" years

b) PV of a series of cashflows

c) PV of an annuity.

d) PV of perpectual annuity.

a) PV after "N" years

From the discussions regarding rupee worth, the value of Rs.1 received after a time period, is less than that its present worth. Hence an

1. *L.M. Bhole,* Financial Institutions & Markets, P.No. 33, 1999 Tata Mac-Graw.

investor will like to part away with a sum that is less than Re.1 to get Re.1. after a time period. To find the amount that he is willing to part away with that amount. The following formula can be used to get the value;

$$Pv = \frac{A}{(1+i)^n}$$

Pv = The present value of cash flows.

i = interest rate

A = Amount at the end of the period.

n = number of year.

For ex: if a depositor expects to get Rs.1000 after one year at the rate of 10%, the amount he will have to forego at present can be calculated as follows;

$$Pv = \frac{A}{(1+i)^n}$$

A = Rs.1,000 $Pv = \frac{1,000}{(110)} = \text{Rs.}909.09$

i = 10%

b) PV of a Series of Cashflows

In this method, to estimate the present value of future series of returns, the present value of expected inflows will calculated. The present value of series of cash flows can be represented by the following formula;

$$P = \frac{A_1}{(1+i)^1} + \frac{A_2}{(1+i)^2} + \frac{A_3}{(1+i)^3} + ... + \frac{A_n}{(1+i)^n}$$

OR

$$P = \sum_{t=1}^{n} \frac{At}{(1+i)}$$

PV = Sum of individual present values of cash flows.

A_1, A_2, A_3 & An = Clash flows at the end of different time periods

i = Discounting rate

Illustration: You are required to find out the PV of future cash inflows that will be received over next four years assuming the discount rate is at 10%.

Year ;	1	2	3	4
Cashflows (Rs.);	10,000	20,000	30,000	40,000

Solution:

In order to compute the present value of four years cashflows we can find the PV of each cashflows.

Present Value of Cashflows

Year	Cashflows (Rs)	PV. factor at (10%)	Present value
1	10,000	0.909	9090
2	20,000	0.826	16,520
3	30,000	0.751	22,530
4	40,000	0.683	27,320
Present Value of series of Cashflows			75,460

c) PV of annuity

The present value of an annuity can be calculated by multiplying the annual annuity amount by the sum of the present value factors for each year of the annuity, for which the present value annuity table is used.

Illustration: Calculate the present value of Annuity of Rs.5000 received annually for 4 years, if the discounting rate is 10%.

Solution:

Year (1)	Cashflows (2)	PV. factor (3)	Present value (2×3)
1	5000	0.909	4545
2	5000	0.827	4135
3	5000	0.751	3755
4	5000	0.683	3415
		3.170	15,850

$\therefore$ The PV = $3.170 \times 5{,}000 = 15{,}850$.

d) Present value of a perpetual Annuity

An investor is interested to findout the present value of his investment, when he is going to get a constant returns year after year. An annuity of this kind is available forever is called perpetuity. For ex: if a donor invests a certain sum of money at which a constant interest is received an year after year. This return amount will be given as award to the merit students. This type of annuity continuous forever. The PV of perpetuity can be computed with the following formula;

Present value of perpetuity = A/i

A = Amount of return; i = Discount rate

Illustration: Mr. Raj intends to have a return of Rs.10,000/- per annum for perpetuity. The discount rate is 20%, calculate the present value of this perpetuity.

Present value of perpetuity = A/i

A = 10,000/- $P = \frac{10,000}{20\%}$ = Rs.50,000

i = 20%

The data reveals that Mr. Raj should invest Rs.50,000 at 20% to get annual return of Rs. 10,000 forever.

SUMMARY

Portfolio is a collection of different securities. It is a basket of investment held by an individual investor/FII/or a corporate body. It involves a proper investment decision making. It reduces risk and increase returns. Portfolio management is becoming now as a profession. Portfolio managers are required to get license from SEBI. The portfolio managers services are available in two kinds (a) Discretionary nature and (b) Non-discretionary nature. Discretionary nature of service renders under a contract agreement with client. Non-discretionary nature means the manager should work according to the directions of his client. There are two objectives regarding portfolio management *viz.,* (a) Basic objectives (b) subsidiary objectives. The portfolio investment process involves 3 steps. planning, implementation, and monitoring. Money has a time valve. The win of the finance manager is to maximise the share holders wealth in appropriate period of time. Time value of money becomes important and some times vital consideration in decision making process. Valuation concept may be divided into two kinds *i.e. Compound Value Concept and Present Value Concept.* The two concepts help to find out the returns for a particular period to take a right decision at right time.

Portfolio management has not been developed upto 1950. It has been developed as a systematic body of knowledge. Portfolio enhances the expected return and reduces risk. The theory of portfolio reveals investment process to deploy the funds in market. The portfolio theory developed by Markowtiz, studies the risk and return involved in a portfolio and their inter-relationship. Markotwiz theory was further developed by william Sharpe. The Sharpe theory reveals that the portfolio return will depend of upon the degree of beta of the portfolio. Therefore, Sharpe's model deals with performance and quality of a portfolio. The another theory of portfolio is called as Capital Asset Pricing Model (CAPM). This model reveals that how assets should be priced in the capital markets. The CAPM is based on economic model. It aims at enchancing the wealth of investor. The CAPM further analyses the relationship between expected return of a portfolio and beta.

Portfolio construction refers to allocation of total investment amount among a wide range of financial assets. The objective of portfolio theory is to minimise risk or maximise return subject to a number of constraints. Risk, enter & exit from a stock market, diversification, risk-return analysis are the important factors while constructing a portfolio. Portfolio monitoring is a continuous and ongoing assessment of present portfolio and the portfolio manager should in corporate all the latest developments occurred in capital market. The main aim of portfolio analysis is to give a cautious direction about the risk and return to the investor on a portfolio.

QUESTIONS

Short Question:

I) What is a portfolio?

II) What is portfolio management?

III) What is portfolio diversification?

IV) Define Portfolio Risk?

V) What is efficient frontier?

VI) What is capital market line?

VII) What difference do you find between securities analysis and portfolio management?

VIII) What β is CAPM?

IX) How do you measure the Portfolio risk?

X) What is B? How it will be measured?

XI) How optimum portfolio is selected?

XII) What are the assumptions of Markowitiz Model?

XIII) What is the market risk?

XIV) What is Alpha? Distinguish between negative & positive Alpha?

XV) What are the differences between systematic and unsystematic risk.

Essay Questions:

1. Explain the evolution of portfolio management services in India.
2. Define portfolio management and explain risk-return relationship found in a portfolio.
3. Write the various steps involved in investment process of a portfolio.
4. What do you mean by portfolio theory? Explain theMarkowtiz Model?
7. What is the Capital Asset Pricing Model approach ? Explain critically the CAPM.
8. Discuss the concepts of portfolio construction and what are the steps involved in construction of a better portfolio.

EXERCISES

CAPM;

Problem No.1: If you invest Rs.10,000/- in Sarabia Pharmaceuticals (β =1.5) and Rs.20,000/- in the Arvinda Textiles (β =1.2), the risk free rate of return is 10% and the expected market return is 16%;

a) What are the β and the expected rate of return of your portfolio?

b) If you want to reduce the Beta of your portfolio to 1.0. What is the investment that you have to make in Transport corporation of India (β 0.8) to achieve this objective?

c) If you decide to invest in risk free securities to reduce the Beta of your portfolio to 1.0 what investment would you make in risk free securities?

Ans.: a) β_P =1.3 Er_P =0.178 b) Rs.45,000

c) Rs.9000 d) Rs.6000.

Problem No.2: Security XYZ has a beta of 1, the risk free rate of return is 10% and the market premium is 8%. What is the required rate of return on security xyz according to the security market line equation?

Ans: 0.18

Problem No.3: Uma group of Industries has a beta of 1.25 and pays no dividends. The risk free rate is 10%, the expected market return is 20%. The investor expects that the share is to be worth Rs.50 in one year. Using the CAPM, find the value of the share today.

Ans: Rs.40.82

Problem No.4: A Ltd. Security has a β of 0.7 and security X Ltd., has a beta of 1.3. Find the risk free rate of return, If the expected rates of return are 10% and 14% respectively.

Ans: 5.33%

Problem No.5: The rate of return on Government securities is 7% and the expected market return is 12%. Stock A's beta is 0.8 its growth rate is 4% and its last dividend per share was Rs.2.00 What would be the stock's equilibrium price?

Ans: Po= 29.71

Problem No.6: From the following information, calculate $Beta_1$ and $Beta_2$ of the stocks.

year	Rs	R_B	R_M	Rf
1999	15	10	11	6
2000	-06	-2	-5	5
2001	18	9	11	6
2002	22	11	13	7

Ans: β_1 =1.48 β_2 =0.73

Problem No.7: The following information belonging to 3 securities, calculate the return on securities.

Security	ER	β
A	14%	1.20
B	15%	0.75
C	20%	1.50

The risk free rate of return is 9% and market return is 15%.

Ans. : RA = 16.2%

RB = 13.5%

RC = 18%

Problem No.8: The following information is given to you, analyse the same as a financial analyst and find out whether the stocks were placed undervalued or over valued?

Stock	Expected return	Beta
A	13	1.10
B	15	0.75
C	18	1.25

Ans: Er_A=15.6% Er_B=13.55 Er_C=16.5%

A & B are undervalued and C is overvalued.

Markowitz Model:

Problem No.9: From the following information calculate the portfolio variance.

Instruments	Proportion	σ	r
Equity	25%	0.1689	0.45
Bonds	50%	0.0716	0.35
Real Estate	2.5%	0.0345	0.20

Ans: $\sigma^2 p$ = 0.00488

σ = 0.0698 or 6.98%.

Problem No.10: The following information is related to two companies stocks, Calculate the covariance and correlation between two investments.

Stock A Ltd.,	Stock X Ltd.,	Probability
12	-12	0.10
15	-7	0.15
20	5	0.20
10	10	0.25
05	12	0.30.

Ans: Covariance = - 22.68

Correlation = - 0.49

Problem No.11: Smt. Vani owned 5 securities at the beginning of the year. The following information is available, What is the expected return on the investment portfolio for the year?

Security	Current price	Share amount	Expected price at the end of the year
X	Rs.50	100	Rs.65
W	Rs.30	150	40
Y	Rs.20	75	25
Z	Rs.25	100	32
A	Rs.40	125	47

Ans: The initial value of the portfolio is Rs.18,500 Expected return on portfolio 19.47%

Portfolio Analysis;

Problem No.12: From the following information, determine the average returns for stock A Ltd. and the BSE over a given period and also calculate standard deviations of returns for both stock A and BSE.

Year	BSE	Stock A Ltd.,
1	-26.5%	-14.0%
2	37.2%	23%
3	23.8%	17.5%
4	-7.2%	2%
5	6.6%	8.1%
6	20.5%	19.4%
7	30.6%	18.2%

Assuming that;

a) The situations 1 to 7 years is expected to be holding period.

b) What is the risk free rate of return of the stock at equilibrium situation.

Ans: The arithmetic average rate of return of stock A Ltd. 10.6%

The Arthematic mean of BSE=12.1%; σ_A=13.1%; σ BSE=22.6%

b) 8.6%

Problem No.13: XYZ portfolio had a following rate of return 15%, 23%, 11%, -3% and 37% over the last five year period. What were the arithmetic mean rate of return and the variance of the returns?

Ans: Variance = 338.24

Problem No.14: From the available information Smt. Vani is considering an investment in one of the two securities. As an investment analyst which investment is better, based on risk and return? Advice the client.

Security	*MNO*	*Security*	*PQR*
prob.	return	prob.	return
0.30	19%	0.20	22%
0.40	15%	0.30	6%
0.30	11%	0.30	14%
		0.20	-5%

Ans: $\sigma_{MNO}=3.09$ $\sigma_{PQR}=9.11$

Problem No.15: The following information is provided and the client approached you for advice in selecting a portfolio of assets based on the following data.

Year	stock x	y	Return from z
1998	0.14	0.18	0.14
1999	0.16	0.16	0.16
2000	0.18	0.14	0.18

The creation of portfolio is by investing equal proportions of 50% in each of two different securities. As a financial analyst you are required to find the following measurements;

a) What is the expected return on each portfolio.

b) What is the expected return on each of security's for the given period.

c) What is the standard deviation of each security's return?

d) How would you characterise the correlation between the returns on its two assets.

Ans: a) ER_x, ER_y, $ER_y=0.16$

b) ER_x, ER_y, $ER_y=0.16$

c) $\sigma_{xy}=0$ $\sigma_{xz}=0.0164$ $\sigma^2_{yz}=0$

d) x and y negative correlation, x and z are positive, y and z are negative correlation.

Problem No.16: Miss. Gowthami holds a two stock portfolios. Stock PQR has a standard deviation of returns of 0.6 and stock MNO has a standard deviation of 0.4. The correlation is 0.25. She holds equal amounts of each stock. Compute the portfolio standard deviation for two stock portfolio.

Ans: $\sigma p = 0.4$.

Problem No.17: Mr. Harish earns returns of 8%, 11% and 15% over the last 3 years. What is the arithmetic mean for these annual returns?

Ans: 11.33%.

Problem No.18: Mr. Dinesh under takes a series one year investment starting with Rs. 70,000. The investment become a worth of:

a) after completion of 1 year Rs.78,400

b) after completion of two years Rs.87,810

c) after completion three year Rs.11,015

Calculate the annual arithmetic rate of return.

Ans: 12%.

Problem No.19: Mr. Netheesh holds the stocks x and y. The returns and expected returns of the scrips are given below. Calculate the covariance and Co-efficient of Correlation.

Stock	Return	ER
x	14	18
y	26	18
x	22	18
y	10	18

Ans: $\overline{x}=18$ $\overline{y}=18$

Cv=-32 $r_{xy}=-1$

Problem No.20: Suresh has invested in a stock of Hindusthan lever Ltd. The following information is provided to you to calculate correlation, Residual variance, Alph and Beta.

Year	Return on HLL stock	Return on NIFTY
1997	0.2	0.1
1998	0.3	0.2
1999	0.5	0.3
2000	0.4	0.4
2001	0.6	0.5

Ans: Correlation 0.966 Variance of HLL = 0.02

e^2 =0.04 Variance of NIFTY=0.144

α =0.04 β =0.9

Problem No.21: Mr. Anand holds two scrips in his portfolio. The returns on two scrips are presented below. Calculate the co efficient of co-relation and co variance of returns.

return on scrip (Blue star)	return on scrip (Lyods)
8	10
-9	-12
14	18
16	20
20	24

Ans: Correlation 0.94

Covariance of returns:110.

Problem No.22: Vasu holds two securities of reputed companies. From the available information, as a financial analyst how would you advice about his movements in a highly volatile stock market? Calculate the expected returns and standard deviation as a measure of risk of the two scrips. Which is to be better for return and risk estimates.

Out Come	Nestle Ltd., (ER)	Prob.	Ponds India Ltd. (ER)	prob.
1	6	0.3	8	0.2
2	10	0.5	14	0.5
3	12	0.2	18	0.3

Ans: Expected return of Nestle Ltd., 9.2% Ponds India Ltd.14.0%. Risk and return of Ponds India Ltd. is higher.

Misce:

Problem No.23: The following information is available in respect of the return from security x under different economic conditions.

Economic Conditions	Return	Probability
Good	22	0.1
Average	18	0.4
Bad	12	0.3
Poor	5	0.2

Find out the expected return of the security and the risk associated with that.

Ans: Average expected return 14%

Standard deviation 2.74%.

Case study - An analysis of IBP Ltd[1]

Generating funds through disinvestment of stakes in public sector units is among the top priorities of the Central Government during the current financial year. And IBP is high on the list of those PSUs in which strategic partners would soon be introduced through divestment. This petroleum sector, PSU, which has interests in refining and marketing of petroleum products, has already received encouraging response from potential candidates interested in picking up the 33.58% stake that would soon be up for divestment. Infact, of the 13 parties now left in the race, there are a couple of Fortune 500 companies too, besides some domestic PSUs and private groups such as Reliance,etc.

IBP has a large retail marketing network with over 1200 petrol pumps spread across the country. Its long term borrowings stood at just about Rs. 375 crore. This amount can comfortably be repaid once IBP receives its due amount of Rs. 350 crore from the oil co-ordination committee. There after, the PSU would be debt free. Also, the company has been able to bring down its workforce by almost 500 people, following successful completion of a couple of voluntary retirement schemes.

On the other side, the date of deregulation of the petroleum sector is also nearing. The administered price mechanism would be dismantled from April 2002. Therefore, considering the retail marketing network of

1. *The Economic Times*, "Changing rules to prop up value", Dt: 15/10/2001

IBP and steady oil prices of $ 21-22 abarrel ruling currently. In the light of these two future major challenges for IBP, we check out on how well it is positioned to respond to the unfolding developments.

Shareholding pattern

Currently, IBP has an equity capital of Rs.22.15 crore of this, the government plans to offer 33.58% equity stake for divestment later this year. Infact, if the IBP chairman's statement is to be believed, the entire process would be completed latest by the end of this calendar year. According to the company's current shareholding pattern 59.6% of its equity is held by the government. Another 21.6% rests with financial institutions. About 0.4% of the equity is with the employes of the company while the remaining 18.15% equity rests in the hands of the public.

Thus, following the divestment, governments stake in IBP would be diluted to 26% and effectively a change in management control would take place in the company. Infact, with the SEBI regulations of 20% open offer for minority share holders, the winner to the bid for IBP's stake could effectively end up with a total stake of upto 53% of the PSU's equity.

Disinvestment factor

The parties looking for the **33.58%** stake in IBP have always found the company is an excellent platform in the petroleum sector, especially due to its wide retail marketing network. Yet, several tricky issues pertaining to the PSU have depend the interest of parties keen on acquiring government's stake in IBP. One such issue is the **61%** equity held by IBP in Balmer Laurie, lubricants, speciality chemicals, freight containers etc. Balmer Lawrie is not currently doing too well. For the last quarter ended june, 2001, its net profit had dropped to Rs. 0.27 crore. As a result, potential parties interested in buying out the Government stake in IBP had insisted on hiving off IBP's stake in Balmer Lawrie predinvestment. This has been now sorted out, by deciding to hive off the 61% stake that IBP holds in Balmer Lawrie infavour of a newly in corporated company, which would be divested later. This step may now see IBP drawing more favourable response from potential bidders.

Another major issue relates to bank guarantees. Earlier the final bid winner was to furnish bank guarantees to the tune of Rs.2000 crore towards prospective investments in refineries, terminals and other petroleum related infrastructure over the 10 years post-divestment. But this move was resisted not only by the prospective bidders but also by some ministries, which suggested that the amount should be lowered to Rs.500 crore. Bidders view this astant amounting to a contingent liability that would be reflected in their balance sheets. Besides, there is uncertainty regarding the areas of future growth too. However, this issue too has now been set to rest by the ministries concerned. Once this is thorough, most roadblocks in the divestment of IBP would have been just cleared.

FINANCIAL DATA

(Rs.in crores)

	June 2001 (3 months)	June 2000	12 months March 2001
1. Sales	2231.09	2042.63	8388.41
2. Operating exp.	2201.72	2011.34	8263.17
3. Operating profit	35.70	37.57	176.97
4. Interest	13.25	18.79	82.56
5. Gross profit	22.45	18.78	94.41
6. Depreciation	8.78	10.46	33.19
7. PBT	13.67	8.32	61.22
8. Tax	2.03	0.83	7.00
9. Net profit	11.64	7.49	54.22
10. Equity capital	22.15	22.15	22.15

While these are some issues which have delayed the divestment process to some extent, IBP's strengths in retail marketing and its low debt equity ratio of 1.2:1 and manageable work force (it has been reduced by 20% over the past two years) have helped to draw encouraging response from potential bidders like Caltax, Shell, Total Fina, Reliance Petroleum and BHP, among others some PSUs too continue in the race for the 33.58% of stake in IBP.

Financial Performance

IBP has been able to register steady growth over the recent years in its financial performance in terms of turnover as well as bottom line. During the financial year upto March 2001, the Company's sales turnover breached the **Rs.8000** crores mark. Turnover stood at **Rs.8388** crores up 23% compared to the preceding *financial year.*

Beside, IBP was able to record a significant break through during the financial year, with its debt equity ratio falling considerably to 1.2 : 1 level down from **1.7 times** in the preceding financial year. This resulted in substantial savings in interest costs.

At the net profit level, the company improved its net profit by almost **30%** to **Rs.54.22** crores. However in line with the industry trends, operating margins continued to remain low at 1-2 percent of net sales. It may be highlighted that, recognising the strength of its vast retail network, the PSU turned aggressive by keeping the growth of the lubricants segment at well above industry average for three successive years. In the last financial year too, when there was a negative growth in the lubricants segment, IBP recorded negative growth of 8-9 percent better than average industry growth of 12 - 13%.

IBP's growth in top line slipped during the April-June 2001 quarter. By mopping up sales of **Rs.2231.09 crore** in this quarter, the PSU registered an improvement of 9% over the previous year corresponding quarter.

However, even though operating profits slipped marginally during this period, gross profit shot up nearly **19.5%** encouraged by lower interest costs of **Rs.13.25 crore** against Rs.18.79 crore in April June - 2001. At the net profit level, IBP registered a rise of almost **55%** compared to the first quarter of previous financial year.

Out look

IBP is now on the verge of effecting some major changes in the running of the company. One of these is the change in management control as a result of the divestment process. The stock quotes at around **Rs.300.** The company has a little over 1/3 rd of its capital to offer for divestment. With many overseas gaints in the race for the cake and roadblocks slowly getting cleared, the disinvestment could fetch any thing between **Rs.300 crore** to **Rs.400 crore** to the government,if the final winner in the disinvestments process offers between **Rs. 400 per share** to **Rs. 500 per share.**

With the change in management control, the strategic partners may well take a fresh look at the company's future priorities. Also, the date for the deregulation of the petroleum sector(April 2002) draws closer. The demand - supply position of petro products too will play a crucial part in the performance of the company and its scrip.

However, at the current price, the stock has a good chance to appreciate over the coming six months.

Divestment to decide IBP

Long-term trend	:	Market performer
Medium-term trend	:	Out performer
Short-term trend	:	Out performer

Price movements

IBP was among the first lot of PSUs, stocks which started trading on the bourse and has been an out performing stock during the last 18 months of the bear phase. Listed in 1990 at a level of **Rs.67,** the scrip saw a very sharp up ward movement in the 1992 bull run touching all time high of **Rs.530.** However, as the volumes data for that period is not available, the real strength of this upward movement cannot be gauged. In the subsequent bearish phase, the scrip retraced **90%** of its upward movement. It again caught the attention of the market in the 1994 bull run and moved upwards very sharply touching **Rs.474.** It corrected 27% of its upward before witnessing a pull back forming a lower top in sept. 1994. Soon after, the scrip came under the grip of bears and remained an under performer till mid 2000. The current interest in the scrip stems from its expected disinvestment by the government. It moved up from **Rs.85** and after touching a high of **Rs.390,** the scrip is currently placed at **Rs.312.** The scrip continues to be in the total control of bulls as it can be seen from the fact that even after the sept.11 attacks it has strongly out performed the market. The weekly charts and daily charts regarding the movement of share price presented below.

Weekly charts

The average and the trigger line on the weekly moving average convergence divergence **(MACD)** charts are converging as it gets ready to give a buy signal once again. The 12 week rate of change **(ROC)** is currently placed just below the equilibrium territory. Its upward movement into positive territory will give a bullish signal. The 5 week ROC has already given a buy signal as it inches into positive territory. The **14 week** relative strength index **(RSI)** is in the equilibrium territory and is moving in tandem with the scrip. The **5 week** RSI has also moved up sharply from the over sold territory and is placed in the equilibrium territory.

The weekly stochastic is also in buy mode and is currently in the equilibrium territory. The week **William R** is showing a similar trend and is in the equilibrium territory.

Daily charts

The **MACD** on the daily charts has given a buy signal as it moves into positive territory. The **12 day ROC** has turned south though still placed in the positive territory. The **14 day** RSI is also moving in tandem with the scrip and is currently placed in the equilibrium territory. The extreme short term oscillators of the scrip are in the over bought territory.

The 1st day William % R has once again turned down from just below the over bought territory indicating negative divergence.

Inference

The scrip is likely to out perform the market over the medium term while the long term trend is going to dependent on what is the final out come of its disinvestment.

Question

Based on the information, the reader is required to assess the potentiality of the scrip in future *i.e., prepare weekly charts, daily charts and expect the market price for a particular data.*

THE TALE OF TWO TECHS[1]

(A case analysis of WIPRO & HUGHES SOFTWARE)

WIPRO

The portfolio analysis consisting of three fundamental factors.

A) Financials

B) Operations

C) Out look.

A) Financial

Global IT services revenues for the second quarter grew 35% on a year and 9% on a sequential basis. But this would be misnomer, as there was a significant revenue contribution from bought out components. Of the $30 million that is expected to be booked in the current fiscal year, just $12 million would account for software services. The balance would be accounted for by hardware and software components, and subcontracted consulting services.

Without the **Lattice** contract, **WIPRO** revenues grew just 0.7% on a sequential basis. *Global iT* services contributed to 66% of the revenues in the quarter. Operating margins for global IT services saw a decline while that of domestic IT and consumer care businesses expanded in the quarter. This was essentially on account of bought out items. Excluding those, the operate margin would have been lower by 75 basis points on a sequential basis. The domestic IT business has seen a 218 basis points expansion on a sequential basis and 23 basis points expansion on a year on year basis.

1. "The tale of two techs" - Raji Goel, Investor guide, Dt: 22/10/2001. P.No.3 (suppl.)

Consumer business has recorded the highest jump in margins growing **225** basis points on a sequential basis and **579** basis points on a y-o-y basis.

On site rates rose by **4.6%** on a sequential basis while off share rates rose by **2.5%.** Realisations from new customers were **20%** higher than average realisations for the quarter due to a better mix of value added services. **WIPRO** added about **$ 34** million to its cash and cash equivalents during the second quarter, taking the total to **$ 134** million. It incurred capital expenditure of **$ 16** million in the last quarter. The receivables for IT services comedown to **58 days** of sales as compared **65 days** in the previous quarter. The financial data of the company presented below.

(Rs.in crore)

Cost Components	(1 st Quarter) 2000-2001	2001-02	(IInd quarter) 2001-2002 (F%)
1. Total Revenues	3081.4	755.2	847.9
2. Cost of revenues	1885	479.4	537.4
3. Other expenses	445	103	96.1
4. Amortisation of ESOPS	18.3	3.8	8.5
5. Operating profit	732.5	168.7	205.9
6. Other income	31.5	4.3	24.8
7. Tax	-	115	-
8. Net profit	649	173	210.9
9. Operating profit margin(%)	23.8	22.8	25.3
10. Net profit margin	23.9	22.9	27.2
Total revenues earned by the company as follows:			
a) Global IT services	-	415.7	560.1
b) Indian IT production&securities	-	232.4	172.3
c) Consumer care & lighting	-	78.8	74.3
d) Others	-	28.3	41.2
e) Total revenues	3081.4	755.2	847.9

B) Operations

WIPRO added **26** new clients in the quarter for its IT services business. Among the new units clients in cluded *Citibank, HSBC, Johnson Controls, Philip Morris, and Matsushita.* Wipro also started three new customer dedicated development centres. Besides, Wipro appears to have signed four new clients in october that include SCA packaging, visteon and a U.S. Life Insurance Company. Revenue from top 5 and top 10 clients increased to 30% and 44% respectively from 29 % and 112% respectively. In the previous quarter. Though the top client has changed from Nortel to Lattice, the share of the top client in total revenues remained at 8%.

The share of revenues from the US geography declined to 55% from 60% in the last quarter. The contribution of Europe moved up to 39% while the balance was contributed by Japan.

The contribution of R&D in global IT services remained the same at 52%. The telecom and ISP segment contributed 12% to the total revenues and moved up largely owing to the Lattice contract. The telecom and inter-networking segment catering to telecom companies and embedded systems and internet assess devices segment declined sequentially by 10% and 14% respectively, contributing 25% and 15% of the revenues. Package implementation was 6% of the revenue, having risen 63% on a sequential basis. This is a new growth area for WIPRO as it has set up an offshore centre for Mysap.com.

While there was a gross addition of 111 employees in the last quarter, there was a net decline of 384 professionals in the IT services division due to attrition and performance based separations. This has brought down the number of employees to 9411. This is a second quarter of consecutive decline in number of employees. The utilisation rates continued to be the same at 60%. The proportion of offshore work to the total declined to 48% from 50% in the last quarter. It is surprising that when the offshore model of Indian IT services companies is likely to result in higher revenues. WIPRO offshore revenues have actually declined.

C) Out look

While the management has a target of a 5% sequential growth in global IT services revenue for the December quarter, it would essentially be on account of the Lattice contract. There would be negligible sequential growth without the contract. Assuming a similar growth in the next quarter, Wipro would be able to report a 30% growth. This is significantly less than its previous guidance of a 40% growth. Wipro has indicated that it has factored in a further 10% decline from its telecom equipment customers. The company intends to invest up to $15 million in IT enabled services companies. It has decided to invest $10 million in Spectra Mind Services. Given the fact that 7 customers started billing after september 11 incidents, the out look for Indian IT services companies stands to be brighter. Wipro has followed a strategy that is exactly the reverse of Infosys. While the latter sacrificed pricing for volumes in the first quarter, Wipro did the reverse by weeding out low rate customers such as GE. At the same, Wipro's billing rates have been historically lower than that of Infosys and over half of its revenues come from R & D work. Wipro would be a beneficiary on account of its good offshore model and ability to win large contracts. R & D business is likely to remain constant and would not be susceptible to commoditisation, as skills are rarer in this segment.

For the current fiscal, wipro is estimated to post EPS of Rs.37, implying a 30% growth. Its stable business model, ability to get sequential rise in billing rates and win large orders are positives. Wipro still stands a risk of missing the renue targets. The scrips would be a buy only below Rs.1000 levels, when it would be quoting a PE of 27.

Hughes Software (Financials)

A huge 66% decline in bottom line on a sequential basis was the least one would expect from Hughes software. On the back of poor product revenues, its performance has been hit precisely at the point as a result of which it was deriving a higher PE multiple. The company declared revenues of Rs. 53.6 crore for the second quarter, a decline of 15% on a sequential basis but a 21% increase year on year basis. Net profit at Rs.6.3 crore posted a 66% decline on a sequential basis and a 5.2% decline on a year on year basis. Operating margins declined sharply on account of a fall in product revenues while expenses on products business continued to be high. Product revenues were Rs.7 crore in the second quarter against Rs.17.1 crore in the previous quarter. The decline was on account of lower number of product sales and lower average size of product deals. The average size of product deals declined to $ 66000 from $ 1,27,000 in the previous quarter.

The company also made a provision of Rs.1.8 crore on account of bad and doubtful debts. The accounts receivables worsened to 110 days during the second quarters as compared to 100 days in the last quarter. The receivables position for Non-Hangles Network Services (HNS) is close to five months of sales, a highly disturbing figure.

The cash position, however, stood at a comfortable Rs.69 crore at the end of last quarter.

Operations

Revenues from H N S continued to be strong with 8% sequential growth. HNS contributed 46% to the total revenues while Non-HNS and products contributed 41% and 13% respectively. Non-HNS and product revenues declined by 6% and 59% respectively, on a sequential basis. Hughes added three new customers in products and two new customers in services. Approximately 72% of the company's revenue came from Global 1000 clients. About 8 clients had revenue contribution of more than $1 million while 7 accounts had a revenue contribution between $ 0.5 million to $ 1 million.

The Company got a new contract from space way in a joint venture with H N S where it would be able to deploy 100 engineers. The number of employees increased to 1680 in the last quarter as compared to 1649 in the previous quarter, resulting in a net addition of 31 employees.

Out look

The company's second quarter results have demonstrated that its client base as well as business model have relatively lower revenue visibility, unpredictable product revenue streams and operating profit which is dependent on costs. With its heavy exposure to telecom vertical, there would be a lot of uncertainity associated with Hughes Software's revenues.

The company has given a guidance of 25% to 35% growth in revenues for financial year 2002 and net margins in the region of mid 20s. This would translate into flat net profits for the current fiscal. A sharp change in the guidance from a 60% growth to 25-35% growth within span of couple of months sinces lack of visibility and has been taken negatively by institutional investors.

Management has confirmed an order book of $ 4 million for products business, which would be executed over the second half of the current fiscal. The space way project would also result in a need for other business to grow up by 5% each for the next two quarters. Besides, if expenses are maintained at current levels, it would be able to achieve net margins of 25% implying a bottom line.

Question: Baoed on the above information you are asked to assess the protentabty of two company shares and suggest which company share is suitable for investment.

Security Analysis

SHOWING RESILIENCE[1]

A Case Analysis of Jaiprakash Industries Ltd.,

Jaiprakash Industries Ltd., has reported EPS growth of 143 percent during the financial year of 2001 and during FY 2002 the EPS is expected to grow by 126% JIL will under go a major change over FY 2002 onwards as it would be reporting numbers of the engineering division alone. Growth will be driven by the strong order book position of the engineering division. Valuation of JIL in different ways like the discounted cash flow, net asset value, replacement cost, etc., have the value of the enterprise at all over the current price of the stock.

1. A case study analysis of Jaiprakash Industries, the Economic Times, Dt: 22/10/2000.

The company is a Rs.2000 crores north India based conglomerate with interests in heavy civil engineering works, construction of dams sevarage, tunnels, underground power houses, manufacturing and marketing of cement, hospitality business and hydel power. The company has executed several big projects over the last 3 decades and has many more projects are to be executed over the next 5 to 6 years with a current order book position of over Rs.7000 crores. It has also executed several overseas projects in the past, particularly in Iraq and other Gulf Countries. It has a 2.5 million tonne Cement plant at Rewa, MP. Its wholly owned subsidiary Jaypee Rewa cement Ltd. has a 1.7 million ton cement plant located close to its own cement plant at Bela, MP. JIL's Bela cement plant operated at 97% capacity utilisation during FY 2001.

The Engineering division has been the cash cow for the company with successively rising sales and operating margins over 25% during the last 5 years. It is the cement division, which had played spoilsport with the company's financial performance due to marginal growth coupled with wafer thin operating margins.

The cement division had taken much of the sheen away from the engineering division clouding JIL's overall performance. But that is set to change as the management is intiating major restructuring to unlock value residing in the cement business. This should initiate a wealth creation process for JIL's stake holders. Also, the cement business is in for better days a head due to more remunerative cement prices and strong out performance in cement production growth in the Indian industry. In the first stage of the restructuring initiative, cleared by JIL board, the cement division is being merged with Jaypee Rewa Cement Ltd. effensive April 1,2001. The hive off will remove the burden of the cement division from the highly profitable engineering division operations, un locking hidden value of the engineering division's strong profitability, which gets corroborated by its financial results for FY 2001.

The hive off will create the largest cement capacity at a single location in the country. As a revamping initiative, the company may attract strategic investors for its cement business and sell off part of its stake. Cash inflows to the companu on account of the sale of stake in the revamped JRCL may be used by JIL to retire/repay debt, thereby further boosting the earnings stream due to substantial cut in interest costs. At present the scrip is under valued and can give good returns considering its future earnings growth potential driven by the restructuring initiatives and unlocking of value in the power business.

Current business profile: Engineering division

The JIL's engineering division specialises in hydro electric power projects, it has high technical competence. The company enjoys high margins due to manpower cost and high manpower loyalty, reflected in low employee turnover, lower overheads as compared to main competitors and expertise of executing complex projects located mostly in hilly terrain. The top management has huge accumulated experience of project execution. The company is now executing contracts worth about **Rs.7000 crore** on the order books of its engineering division. It has bagged the **Rs.4500 crore** Karcham wantagoo Project. The implementation agreement has been signed. The division is constructing 4 concrete dams, 1 rock fill dam and 6 power houses with aggregate capacity of **7320 mw** on behalf of state governments and PSUs.

Private Hydro power generation

JIL, through its subsidiaries Jaiprakash Hydro Power Ltd., and Jaiprakash Power Ventures Ltd. will be a major player in private Hydro power generation. It is involved in **1700 mw** environment friendly run of the river hydro power projects on the Build own operate **(Boo)** basis. Given the excellent returns in these projects, the subsidiaries will make wounderfull gains as the government assures a post tax return of **16%** on its equity **(pre tax return of 26%)**. I CICI has picked up a 28% equity stake in JHPL and has already invested **Rs.75 crore** out of the total commitment of Rs. 135 crore. JHPL is executing the **Rs.1620 crore** Bapsa Hydro Power Project.

Cement Division

Japyee group's cement plants have out performed the industry growth in a consistent manner over the last 2-3 years. During FY 2000 Japee group's cement production grew **23% vis-a-vis 15.1%** growth for the industry. During FY 2001 while all India cement production declined by **0.6%,** the decline in Jaypee group's cement production was limited to 0.3%. During the April - June 2001 quarter cement dispatches for Jaypee group were up by **8.47%** while all India cement dispatches were up by **2.33%** during the same period compared to the corresponding period last year. Given that in the past the cement division's performance had tended to drag JIL down the strong out performance will make a substantial difference to JIL's profitability. Also the improved utilisations will be extremely helpful in attracting strategic investors for the cement business. The strong growth in both cement sales and selling prices gives a strong upside to the Jaypee group future financial performance.

Outlook for the Engineering Division

JIL's engineering division contributed around **72%** of the company's turnover during FY 2001. The cement division constituted the rest. Once the cement business is hived off from April, 1 2001 the engineering division will comprise the entire turnover of JIL. The top line is projected to grow at **19%** in FY 2002. It would be driven by the strong order book position of the engineering division, with orders in hand of **Rs. 7000 crore** and impetus provided in budget **2001 to Tehri Hydel Power project** which is now slated to be completed a head of the earlier envisaged 2004.

Outlook for the Cement Division

JIL's cement division contributed around 28% of the company's turnover during FY 2001. A growth of 18% in cement sales during FY 2002 will give tremendous up side based on sharp improvement in cement prices. It may be noted that cement companies have already effected a price increase of **Rs.30** per bag since December 2000 and after the dip in cement prices during June 2001, cement manufacturers have again come together to under take production cuts and increase cement prices.

Key financials

JIL's sales have gone up **29%** during financial year 2001 while profit after tax is up **143%**. This was despite a change in accounting policy under which JIL will recognise retention money deducted by clients as revenue in the year in which it is released by the client after fulfilment of contractual obligation. The change in accounting policy reduced both income and profit by **Rs. 41.39 crore**. During the quarter ending June 2001, the company has commenced reporting financial for the engineering business alone. Consequent to the hive off of the cement division reported sales were down **15%** vis a vis the corresponding quarter last year. Net profit was up **85%** for the quarter ending June 2001 compared to the corresponding period last year.

Valuation

Employing the **DCF** model for JIL and its subsidiary JRCL yields a value substantially higher than the current market price. The D C F value is for stand alone JIL taking into account a conservative growth of average **12%** per annum over the next 10 years in the engineering business. Valuation on net asset value basis is over **Rs.100** per share and on replacement cost basis it would be substantially higher.

JIL has committed to invest **Rs.700 crore** in hydro power generation through its subsidiaries JHPL and JPVL. Equity investments in these projects have been valued by discounting the post-tax profit stream attributable to these equity investments. JHPL adds **Rs.50.30 crore** JIL and JPVI **Rs. 36.70 crore** to JIL's valuation on discounted basis. Combined, they add **Rs. 8700 crore** to JIL. In view of this the scrip looks under valued at current levels and may give good returns considering its expanding earnings stream and improvement in return on employed capital. Its engineering capabilities and strong order book position give it the necessary resilience in times of a gloomy economic out look.

Question: Based on the above facts analyse the company position and bringout the prospects for investment in the shares. Sub-stantiate your answer with appropriate information.

Unit-V

1. Management of Financial Derivatives

1

MANAGEMENT OF FINANCIAL DERIVATIVES

INTRODUCTION

The Indian economy has been experienceing a dynamic and new approach since 1991; steps were taken to correct various distortions and disorientations. The past four decades had proved that there could be both government failure and market failure. Realising this, the New Economic Policy aimed at correcting the imbalances and creating a more competitive environment to improve productivity and efficiency was announced. In the new economic environment a series of structural changes were under taken in financial sector to achieve the objectives. The financial sector reforms encompassed reform programmes in banking sector, capital market and removal of controls on issue of capital and issue pricing. The capital market reforms include the setting up of 'Securities and Exchange Board of India', Guidelines for mutual funds, permission to selected companies to raise capital from abroad with tax benefits, allowing foreign investors to invest in Indian capital market. The financial sector reforms are expected to give a boost to the economy by allocating funds for productive investment and capital formation. The operational investments in the financial system is expected to facilitate and expedite the process of market information.

The Indian stock market, inspite of being insulated from the international market is characterised by high price volatility. Speculations extends to non - specified shares also. Speculation dealings are supposed to be settled on a cash basis. In the case of new issues, before they are listed in the exchange, investors suffer due to the "grey market"[1]. However speculation is unavoidable as it is the driving force which builds up activity and ensures sustained interest of investors. The presence of speculator is useful for maintaining market continuity. The government seeks to control excessive speculation which leads haphazard price movements unrelated to fundamentals of securities.

1. *Grey* market means, an unofficial market out side the stock exchange.

Concept of Derivates

At present the Indian stock markets are not having any risk hedged instruments that would allow the investors to manage and minimise the risk. In industrialized countries apart from money market and capital market securities, a variety of other securities known as 'Derivatives' have now become available for investment and trading. "The derivatives originate in matheratics and refer to a variable which has been derived from another variable." "A derivative is a financial product which has been derived from another financial product or commodity." The derivatives do not have independent existence without underlaying product and market. "Derivatives are contracts which are written between two parties for a easily marketable assets." Derivatives are also known as deferred delivery or deferred payment instruments.

Definition of Derivatives

'A derivative is a financial product which has been derived from another financial product or commodity'.

D.G. Gardener defined the derivatives as 'A derivative is a financial product which has been derived from market for another product.' Derivatives are off balance sheet instruments, a fact that is said to obscure the leverage and financial might they give to the party. Derivatives are mostly secondary market instruments. Derivatives have little usefulness in mobilising fresh capital by the companies. The exchange traded derivatives are quite liquid and have low transactions cost. There is a lot of demand in India for derivatives trading. The values of derivatives and those of their underlying assets are almost non-existent in India. Steps have been taken by the authorities and NSE to introduce other derivatives. Derivatives would enhance further the speculative potential of the already highly speculative Indian stock market. The markets for derivatives are most likely to remain narrow and shallow. The derivatives market may function with a stability and honesty.

Growth of derivative markets

The derivative markets have been started in UK, USA and Europe in seventies. In 1988 Japan has started its topics options and in 1993 Hang Kang had its first options contract. The rapid growth of derivatives was due to need for hedging in trade, increased volatility in cash markets, improved technology and deregulation in the markets.

Functions of Derivatives

The primary purpose of the derivative instruments is not to borrow or lend funds but to transfer price lists associated with fluctuations, in asset's values. The derivatives provide 3 important economic functions.

1. Risk management
2. Price discovery.
3. Transactional efficiency.

Major Players of Derivatives

There are 3 major players in the derivatives trading.

a) Hedgers

b) Speculators

c) Arbitrageurs

a) Hedgers

The party which manage the risk is known as hedgers. Hedger seek to protect themselves against price changes in a commodity in which they have an interest.

b) Speculators

Speculators are the major players in the market, without whom the market probably would never exist.

c) Arbitrageurs

These are specialised in making purchases and sales in different markets at the same time and profits by the difference in prices between the two centres. Following of diagramme shows the plays of derivatives market.

The following diagram showing derivatives market players.

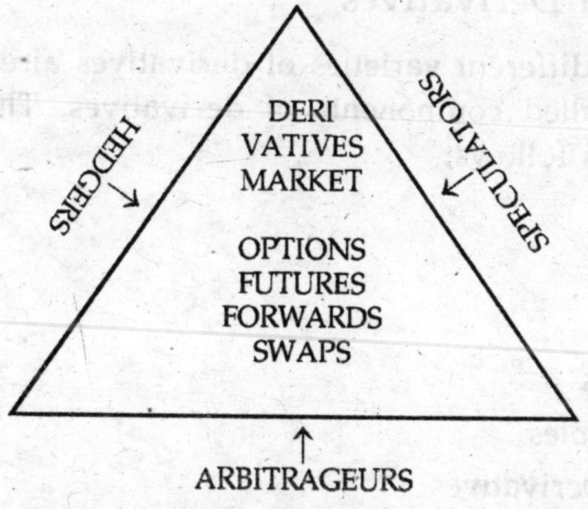

Derivatives Risks

Derivatives represent sophisticated instruments of finance that require education and comprehension. There are four inherent risks of derivatives.

a) Credit risk

b) Market risk

c) Legal risk

d) Operations risk

These risks should be clearly understood before establishing position in the derivatives markets. Derivatives are useful instruments that have essential numerous applications, but using them without an understanding of their nuances and behavior can lead for unanticipated risks.

Advantages of derivative markets

Following are the advantage of Derivates:

1. It increases the volume of transactions
2. Lower transaction cost in derivatives market
3. Increased hedge for investors in cash market.
4. Reduced risk of holding underlying assets
5. Increased liquidity for investors and growth of savings flowing into derivatives markets.
6. It leads to faster execution of transactions.
7. It enhances the price discovery process.

Components of Derivatives

There are different varieties of derivatives already inexistence and these are also called components of derivatives. The names of certain derivatives are as follows;

1. Futures
2. Options
3. Swaps
4. Warrants
5. Convertibles
6. Credit Derivatives
7. Swaptions.

Concept of Futures

Futures are agreements between two counter parties that fix the terms of an exchange. Futures are highly standardised contracts between the buyer and sellers or writers. Futures are not securities. Futures contracts provide for the delivery of contracted assets. Future markets are also called as **"paper market"** Futures are traded in auction markets organised by futures exchanges. They are transferable legal agreements and their terms are not changed during the life of the contract. They create obligation to make or take delivery at some future date. The trading is a similar to badla trading and it includes an interest component. The futures trading requires only margin deposit and not the full payment immediately.

Definition

A future concept is defined as a "Commitment to buy or sell at a specified future settlement date and a designated amount of a commodity or a financial asset. It is a legally binding contract by two parties to make or take delivery of commodity at a certain point of time in the future."

"A future contract is an agreement between a seller and buyer that calls for the seller to deliver to the buyer a specified quantity, grade of an identified commodity at a fixed time in the future and at a price agreed to when the contract is first entered into."

A future price in corporates the market belief about the likely course of assets undertaking price. Futures contracts are transferable specific delivery forward contract[1]. Futures contracts are on stock indices and not on individual stocks. Futures contracts increase the liquidity. The futures contract period of time may be in between 3 to 21 months abroad.

The salient features of futures market

Following are the features of futures market;

a) High-level counter re-trading

b) Small amount of physical exchange

c) Very high degree of leverage

d) Low level of default

Objectives of Future Contracts

Future contracts have the following objectives:

a) Hedging

b) Speculation

---

1. **Forward contract means an agreement between two parties to exchange an asset for cash at a predetermined future date for a price that specified today.)**

c) Price determination and discovery

d) Efficient allocation of resources

The salient features of Futures contract

The main features of futures contract are presented below:

1. Futures are traded only in organised exchanges.

2. Futures contracts required to have standard contract terms.

3. Futures exchanges have associated with clearing house.

4. Futures trading required margin payment and daily settlement.

5. Futures positions can be closed easily.

6. Futures markets are regulated by regulatory authorities like SEBI.

Various types of contracts in market for commodities and financial instruments. The different types of contracts are as follows;

A) Ready Delivery Contract

B) Forward Contract.

A) Ready Delivery Contract

It provides for delivery of goods/instruments and payment of a price, therefore either immediately or within 11 days after the time of contract. It leads to spot or cash transactions which take place at current prices of commodity.

B) Forward Contract

It is a contract for delivering the goods. These transactions are spot transactions. It is also know as "Specific delivery contract". They are deferred for execution to a future but fixed date.

Futures vs Forward

Futures and forward contracts are similar in many aspects. But there are many differences between these contracts. Futures contracts have several transactional advantages relative to spot and forward contracts. The following are the differeneces between Futures and Forward Contracts;

Futures Contract	Forward Contract
1. Trading is regulated	1. Trading is unregulated
2. Banks, corporations, individual investors, financial institutions, and speculators are active participants.	2. Participants are institutions.
3. Small amounts of money changes hands	3. No money changes hands until delivery of the contract
4. Trading is in competitive environment like "bids, offers, auctions".	4. Trading will be done by Telephone or Telex.
5. Settlements are made daily	5. Settlement will be made at a agreed fixed date
6. The delivery price is the spot price	6. The delivery price is the forward price
7. These contracts are standardised instruments.	7. These contracts are customised
8. This contracts are very small larger turnover.	8. These contracts are much in size.
9. These contracts are traded in recognised exchanges	9. These contracts can be traded on OTC and off the stock exchange
10. There are secondary market services.	10. There are no secondary markets.

Characteristics of futures

The quality of positive economic theory explains about its ability with precision clarity and simplicity. The main characteristics of futures explained by a good economic theory are as follows;

1. There is a limited number of actively traded products with futures contracts.
2. The trading unit is large and indivisible
3. It has no more than maturity of 3 months.
4. The success ratio of new contracts is about 25% in the world finan cial markets.
5. Futures are seldom used by farmers.

6. There are both commercial and non-commercial users of futures contract in interest rates and foreign exchange.
7. The main use of the futures by the commercial users is to hedge corresponding cash and forward positions.
8. The positions of the non-commercial users almost entirely speculative positions.
9. In foreign exchange futures, the positions of the commercials users are unbalanced.

Kinds of Futures

The following are the different kinds of futures;

A) Commodity Futures

B) Financial Futures

A) Commodity Futures

The commodity futures deal with trading in all domestic commodity future market. The value of commodity futures generally depends upon the price movements of market.

B) Financial Futures

Futures contracts based on a financial investment or a financial index are known as financial futures. Financial futures can be classified as;

1. Interest rate Futures.
2. Currency Futures.
3. Stock Index Futures.

1. Interest Rate Futures

These are written on the basis of interest rates or price indices of fixed interest securities. The characteristics of futures markets are presented below.

a) The trading unit is large and indivisible.

b) Futures are used by farmers (commodity future)

c) There are both commercial and non-commercial users (Foreign exchange)

d) Non-commercial users are entering into speculative position.

2. Currency Futures

This future is also called as "Foreign exchange future". They are traded on the basis of price of forex market. It deals with the price fluctuations of currency.

3. Stock Index Futures

Stock index futures contract, is a contract based on stock indices. Stock index future is a speculation tool. It is an inexpensive and highly liquid asset in the market. It is a tool for expression of an opinion about the general situation of the market. These contracts are more useful to portfolio managers to alter the **Risk-Return** distribution of their stock portfolios. The institutional investors can enter the market immediately, by purchasing stock index contracts. A stock index future's contract is an obligation to deliver on the settlement date an amount of cash. No physical delivery of stocks is made to buyers. In order to ensure that sufficient funds are available for settlement, both buyer and seller are required to put up a good faith, deposit or margin. The margin is not a down payment, and neither loan nor margin involves interest. The contract is marked to the market, daily and additional cash margin may be required depending upon the market movements. It is easy to see that the higher leverage afforded in the stock index, futures market is an essential attraction to both buyers and sellers. **Ex:** "Assume a contract is struck at 600 and the index moves up as high as 675 and down as low 560 prior to expiration. During this time, funds are being debited and credited each day from buyer to seller." In stock index futures contract, every day at the end of each trading session, each customer's position is marked to the latest settlement prices. Each customer's account is credited/debited according to price changes. If any variation is found, the customer has to adjust the cash. Sometimes the customers account shows any excess amount, that amount may be withdrawn by the customer. Ex: We are dealing with a "Sensex of 1800, contract. The original margin is Rs.20,000 and to maintain margin is Rs.10,000. Assure the contract is struck up with sensex at 1800. The next day the sensex moves upto 1810. The buyer receives Rs.18,000 from the seller's margin account **[(1810-1800) × 1800]** If during the contract the sensex moves from 1800 to 1780, the buyer owes the seller Rs.36,000. **[1800-1780] × 1800.**

Valuation of Stock Index Futures

The valuation of stock index futures is very simple and easy. It is explained with a simple scrip future. **Ex:** *an investor wants to hold the BSE sensex scrip for the next year. Then he will collect dividends, and his principal* *value will increase or decrease with the index.* At some price for the futures index, the investor can get exactly the same return by investing in treasury bills and make purchase a contract for future delivery of the index.

Return on index $= I_E - I_B + D$

I_E = Index price at expiration

I_B = Current index price

D = Dividends

Return on Futures $= F_E - F_B + R_F$

F_B = Future price at expiration

F_B = Current future price

R_F = Interest

Therefore, the following formula expresses the value of stock index future;

$$F_B = I_B + (R_F - D)$$

F_B = Current future price

I_B = Current index price

R_F = Interest

D = Dividend

The price of index should be equal to the price of futures at expiration.

Stock Index Arbitrage

Arbitrage means buying and selling of a commodity or asset in two different markets in order to get profit from price fluctuations from the two markets. Ex: *If the price of the gold in Mumbai is Rs.5,500 per 10 grams and the same in Chennai is Rs.5,600, therefore an opportunity exists to buy gold in Mumbai and sell in chennai to earn profit of Rs.100 per 10 grams.* Arbitrage makes market more efficient. Stock index arbitrage means buying a basket of stocks and selling futures when mispricing is occurred. It is not a risky. It requires large amount of capital in the futures contract. The most important part of the arbitrage comes in the pricing of these contracts. In the pricing of futures, the index dividend return and return on alternative investments should be kept in mind. Market sentiment also plays an important role in future pricing. However, every stock index arbitraguer has his own factors at that time like *the amount of capital available, transaction costs, the rate of return available from the arbitrage.*

The following are the different kinds of securities futures:

1. Futures on Fixed Income Securities.

2. Futures on Short-term Fixed Income Securities.

3. Futures on Long-term Securities.

1. Futures on Fixed Income Securities

Increasing rates of interest created new phenomenon in the capital market. Treasury bills, bonds, notes, other credit instruments bear a resemblance to the fluctuations. The prices are traditionally fluctuate inreaction to severe changes due to many factors. i.e., war, depression, weather, inflation etc., Fixed income futures have become an integral part of financing and investment and have transformed the whole process of interest rate risk management. The uses of fixed income futures for increasing and reducing exposures to the risk of changing interest rates.

2. Futures on Short-term Fixed Income Securities

Treasury bills, certificates of deposit and Euro-dollar futures are include in short-term fixed income futures. Treasury bill futures, CD's are not yet developed in India. The treasury bills are traded on a discount basis with the holder receiving the difference in the buying price and selling price or face value, as interest. The annual discount rate and yield as fixed income securities futures can be calculated as follows:

$$\text{The Formula for the Yield} = \frac{\text{(Face value - Price)}}{\text{Price}} \Big/ \frac{\text{No. of days to maturity}}{365}$$

Treasury bill futures trading is done in terms of prices and yield. The use of prices allows the futures to be put as the same price. Short term rates would be motivated to participate in treasury bills future market. The major users of the markets are banks, brokerage houses, and securities dealers. There are different types of treasury bills futures transactions show as arbitrage, speculation or hedging. Dealing in government securities involves constantly buying and selling of large amount of treasury bills. Dealers will analyse the treasury bills futures prices.

3. Futures on Long Term Securities

These futures contracts are very popular in America. But in India they are yet to be developed. Presently. these contracts call for delivery of security either issued or guaranteed by the Government. The following are the different types of securities under this category;

1. Treasury bonds
2. 10 years Treasury notes
3. 5 years Treasury notes
4. 91 days Treasury bills
5. Eurodollar time deposits

Recent Developments in Futures Trading

The bullish mood on bourses is continuing with the announcement of good second quarter[1] results by the corporates. The introduction of stock futures further boost sentiment and this was expected to prove the way for the return of retail investors who remained on the side lines.

The commencement of futures trading in **31** individual scrips heightened sentiment on stock markets. NSE and BSE commenced futures trading on individual shares from 9-11-2001. On NSE, the total number of futures contact on individual securities traded was 4503 with a value of Rs.89.15 crores. **L & T** was the most active contract with 1612 contracts being traded with a value of **Rs.33.33 crores. Satyam Computers** was the next most active futures contract with **593** contracts being traded with a value of **Rs.1069 crores.** However, among the 31 scrips in many cases, futures were traded at discount to the cash market, even with the bullish mood in market.

The introduction of then products will place India among the few countries that allow trading on single stock futures. It is expected that the introduction of leveraged products like single stock futures will inject the much needed liquidity into the Indian Capital Market as deferral products allow traders to carry forward their positions while taking a more long-term view of the market.

Moreover, stock futures will throw open up hedging and arbitrage opportunities to all market participants. Since, there are number of products based on the same underlying shares, there will be arbitrage opportunities between the underlying cash market, single stock futures and stock options.

2. Options

An option is a contract which involves the right to buy or sell securities at specified prices within a stated time. Option is a device for

1. "Scope for Retail investors" - *Ommen A ninan*, The Hindu, Dt:12/11/2001. P.No.18. Second quarter July - Sept.2001.

the gains from speculation. **"An option is a type of contract between two parties"**. Option is a derivative security used for the purpose of risk management in the investment market based on some securities. The largest option period is 9 months but it can be for a shorter period of 30 to 90 days. The contract unit can be of 100 shares or stocks. The minimum trading unit can be fixed at 100 contracts. The options are created and traded by the investors. The companies which issue assets underlying them have no responsibility in respect of their creation.

Characteristics of Options

The following are the main characteristics of options;

1. Options holders do not receive any dividend or interest.
2. Options yield only capital gains.
3. Options holder can enjoy a tax advantage.
4. Options are traded on O.T.C. and in all recognised stock exchanges.
5. Options holders can control their rights on the underlying asset.
6. Options create the possibility of gaining a windfall profit.
7. Options holder can enjoy a much wider risk - return combinations.
8. Options can reduce the total portfolio transaction costs.
9. Options enable with the investors to gain a better returns with a limited amount of investment.

In options trading, exercised date means, the date on which the buyer actually exercise the option. It is the price at which the option holder can buy or sell the underlying asset. Exercise price is also called as **"Striking Price"**. The options are mainly classified as:

a) Call option

b) Put option

A) Call Option

A call which is the right to buy shares under a negotiable contract and which do not carry any obligation. The buyers have the right to receive the delivery of assets are known as "call option".

B) Put Option

In this option the owner is the right to sell the underlying asset under a negotiable contract. Put Option holder has the right to receive the payment by surrendering the asset.

The writer of an option is a stock broker, member or a security dealer. The buyer of an option pays a price depending on the risk of underlying security and he as an investor or a dealer or trader.

Kinds of Options

There are a wide variety of options available in the market, they are;

a) Commodity Option

b) Currency Option

c) Stock Option

d) Stock Index Option

A. Commodity Option

Commodity option consumable enables the farmers to trade on general commodities market movements. They are traded based upon goods. The price movement of commodities will reflect the worth of Commodity Option.

B. Currency Option

The recent addition to options market has been the foreign currency exchange or currency options. It acts as a vehicle to protect against adverse exchange rate fluctuations. They are contracts that confers the right to buy or sell foreign currency at a specified price at some future date. The latest innovation in this contest is the futures options - a combination of future and options.

C. Stock Option

A complex variety options exists in the market - stock option is one of the options: Stock options may be on individual stocks or on various stock price indices. The stock option requires the actual delivery of stock upon exercise. The stock option is costly to some extent while comparing with stock index option. It involves most in stocks individual stock or group of an.

D. Stock Index Option

Stock index option enable investors to trade on general stock market movements. The stock prices movement will reflect in stock index option prices. In stock index option the transactions are settled by payment of cash. The amount of cash settlement is equal to the difference between the closing price of the index option price and the strike price of the option. The investment strategies with index options are similar to those for individual stock options.

Features of Options

The following are the features of Options;

1. The option is exercisable only by the owner namely the buyer of the option.
2. The owner has limited liability.
3. Owners of options have no voting rights and dividend right.
4. Options have high degree of risk to the option writers.
5. Options involving buying counter positions by the option sellers.
6. Flexibility in investors needs.
7. No certificates are issued by the company.
8. Options are popular because they allow the buyer profits from favourable movements in exchange rate.

A wide variety of options exists in the market, options are of the following types;

a) Call option.

b) Put option.

c) Writing option.

d) Spread option.

e) Gale options.

f) Double options.

A) Call option

A call which is the right to buy shares under a negotiable contract and which do not carry any obligation.

B) Put option

In the put option the owner is the right to sell the underlying asset under a negotiable contract.

C) Writing option

Writings options are two kinds.

1. Covered option.

2. Uncovered option.

Covered option is written against an owned stock position. Uncovered option may be written without owning the security.

D) Spread option

It is the process which involves the simultaneous purchase and sale of different options of the same security. Spread options may be two kinds.

a) Vertical spread.

b) Horizontal spread.

Vertical spread means purchase of two options with the same expiry date but different striking prices. Horizontal spread means, the striking price is the same but expiry dates are different.

Options may be purchased or sold by placing an order with a broker. An innovative development is eliminating a physical instrument. In options dealing no certificate is issued. This facilitates prompt settlements of transactions. In the absence of a certificate, each transaction and associated money activity must be handled as a book keeping entry.

Option prices are the result of the interaction of a number of different forces. There are six fundamental factors which influence the value of option.

a) Current Stock Price (s)

b) Striking Price (k)

c) Time to Expiration (t)

d) Stock Volatility (Stock prices fluctuation)

e) Rates of Interest

f) Cash Dividends

The striking price depends upon current stock price and the expiration date. The higher the stock price, the higher the call value. The stock volatility is an important determinant in value of an option. The higher volatility in stock market, then the stock will do either very well or very poorly, therefore, the higher volatility over the life time of a call, the higher its value relative to the stock. The another important determinant of a factor is "Interest Rates". The higher the interest rate, the lower the value of the striking price. A higher interest rate will have the same influence as a lower striking price. Higher interest rates tend to imply higher call prices. Cash dividends are also plays an important factor in valuation of an option. The higher the cash dividend prior to expiration, the higher the value of a put option.

Option strategies may be for hedging, speculation or spreading purpose. Hedging in option involves attempts to control risk. Speculation in options requires the purchase or the sale of an option without any position in the underlying stock. Spreading requires that the simultaneous purchase one option and the sale of another. The person doing the spreading is hedging. Spreading may be categorised as; ***(a)*** *bullish spread* ***(b)*** *bearish spread.* Bullish spread involves in buying the more expensive option and selling the cheaper option. The spread will show a profit if the prices rise. The same reverse direction is applied to bearish spread. In bearish spread, a profit anticipated if the stock price declines. In valuation of a option **"The Black-Scholes model"** is very important. Black and scholes have developed a device which assumes that the share returns are normally distributed. Let us, examine how the black-schole model is useful in valuation of an option.

Black-Scholes Model

Black and scholes developed a formula for determine the value of an option. The model is very popular in the market and it is useful to option holder to know the over priced or under priced of an asset. The model provides an excellent analysis in valuation of debt relation to equity. The equilibrium value of an option can be determined by the following assumptions;

1) There is no dividend payment on shares.
2) There is no interruption in market operations.
3) There are no transaction costs.
4) There are no taxes.
5) The share prices are not in volatile position.
6) The interest rates are constant.
7) The option is to be European type.

The Block-Scholes formula for estimating the fair value of a call option is as follows;

$$V_C = P_S[Nd_1] - \frac{P_x}{e^{(RF)(T)}}[Nd_2]$$

$$d_1 = \frac{I_n\left[\frac{P_S}{P_x}\right] + T\left[RF + \frac{\sigma^2}{2}\right]}{\sigma\sqrt{T}}$$

$$d_2 = \frac{I_n\left[\frac{P_S}{P_x}\right] + T\left[RF - \frac{\sigma^2}{2}\right]}{\sigma\sqrt{T}}$$

$$= d_1 - \sigma\sqrt{T}$$

P_S = The exercise price of the call.

e = 2.7183

R_F = Compounded annual risk free rate.

σ = The standard deviation of the continuously compounded annual rate of return on the share.

P_S = The current price of the share.

I_n = The natural log of the bracket number.

T = The time remaining to expiration on annual basis..

Nd_1, Nd_2 = The value of the cumulative normal distribution at d_1 and d_2.

After taking the dividends into consideration, the formula (Block Schole) should be as follows;

$$\dot{P}_S = P_S - \sum_{t=1}^{T} Dt/e^{RF \cdot t}$$

P_S = The current price of the share

$\dot{P}_S$ = Adjusted stock price

D_t = Declared/known cash dividend to be paid on day t from now

The Valuation of European Model

The valuation of an European model can be as follows by incorporating the Black Scholes call price.

$$= P_P = -P_S Nd_1 - \frac{P_X}{e^{RF} \times T} N - d_2$$

The following are the important factors in portfolio analysis in relation to the Black-Scholes call price.

1. Delta
2. Theta
3. Gamma
4. Vega
5. Rho

Deltas are an important by-products of the Black-Scholes Models. Deltas provide more useful information to the investors, who use options in portfolios. Delta means a change in option premium expected from a small change in the strike price.

Theta is used in options for the rate of change of the value of a portfolio as all the things remain constant theta is always negative for an option.

Gamma is useful in portfolio of an underlying assets. It is the rate of change of the portfolios delta with respect to the price of the underlying asset.

Vega is an option of portfolio, which is the rate of change of the value of the portfolios with respect to the volatility of the underlying asset.

The Rho is an option of portfolio which changes the value of a portfolio according to the interest rate. Rho measures the sensitivity of the value of a portfolio to interest rates.

The overall conclussions are that the Black-Scholes model provides excellent analysis to actual data and it serves as a useful valuation model.

Portfolio Insurance

Portfolio insurance is a device to protect the value of the basket of different assets. It was developed in mid 1980s as one of the most popular uses of options. If an investor holds a highly diversified portfolio, he needs some protection from the risk. Portfolio insurance is a strategy that provides to alter the amount of risk. The three important factors in portfolio insurance are; **(a)** loss is restricted to a prescribed extent, **(b)** the ratio of return on insured portfolio and uninsured portfolio, **(c)** the amount of investments of portfolios are restricted to market index. The portfolio insurance can be applied to two portfolios. The first portfolio may be assumed as the safe to the level of protection desired. This protection level is called as the floor and is the lowest value. The second portfolio having the difference between the total value of the portfolio and the floor is generally called as portfolio cushion. The assets of this portfolio consists of risky assets. The actual amount of investment between risky and risk free assets is determined by changing market fluctuations. A change in the market fluctuations offers the best opportunity to show the dynamic nature of portfolio insurance. We can expect that the rise and fall of the market takes over a time gap enough for the investors to rebalance the position.

3. Swaps

According to *A.K. Seth* "A swap is an agreement between two or more people or parties to exchange sets of cash flows over a period in future."

Swaps are agreements between two parties to exchange assets at predetermined intervals. Swaps are generally customerised transactions. The swaps are innovative financing which reduces borrowing costs, and to increase control over interest rate risk and forex exposure. The swap include both spot and forward transactions in a single agreement. Swaps are at the centre of the global financial revolution. Swaps are useful in avoiding the problem of unfavourable fluctuations in forex market. The corporates, commercial banks, institutional swaps, individual investors are now using the swaps more frequently. The following factors have influenced for the growth of swap market in India;

a) deregulation of financial policies.

b) growing global financial integration.

c) increasing volatility of interest and exchange rates.

The Swaps are associated with equity indices and physical commodities like oil and oil products. Swaps are concerned with exchange rates or interest rates. Swaps can penetrate savings in perfectly at free markets. Financial swaps are revolutionary especially for portfolio management. A swap is coupled with an existing asset or liability can radically modify effective risk and return. Swaps have had a major macro economic impact for giving the linkage between the Euro and domestic markets. The following are the various kinds of swaps available at present in the market;

1. Short Date Swaps
2. Syndicated Swaps
3. Hi-Tech Swaps
4. Draw Down Swaps
5. Puttable Swaps
6. Extendable Swaps
7. Collateralised Swaps
8. Cross Currency Interest Rate Swaps
9. Amortising Swaps

10. Options on Swaps
11. Variable Principle Swaps
12. Non-US bank Swaps
13. Dollar Swaps
14. Floating Rate Swaps

Short date swaps means where the floating and fixed rates are of less than two years. The corporate sector finds it attractive to do a swap out of one month. Syndicated swaps means arrangement of swaps in a large way at a competitive environment. Hi-tech swaps can give enormous value and flexibility in exposure, tax and earnings to management. Draw down swap is planned under a pre-committed floating rate financing system. The swap mainly depends upon a completion of a project. Puttable swap requires to sell a swap in 3 years. Extendable to 5 years. Collateralised swaps will depend upon the major credit risks in stock market. Cross currency interest rate swaps combine all aspects of both currency and interest rate swaps. Amortising swaps eliminates the potential exposure of foreign interest rates and currency rise. Options on swaps are traded in highly uncertain environment and in high volatile market. They are valuable and expensive. Variable principle swaps are tailored for the specific asset or liability of the counter party. non-US bank swaps deal with mainly of interest to Non-US banks in managing their dollar books. Dollar swaps are ranging from two years to 15 years.

4. Warrants

Warrant is a corporate created option to purchase a stated number of common shares at a specified price within a specified time. Warrants are attached to bonds/debentures and equity issues. Warrants generally have long term maturities. Warrants help companies in raising fresh capital. Warrants can be detached and traded separately. The maturity period of warrants is 3 to 10 years. Perpetual warrants are available in a broad. Warrants can be traded on the exchanges or over the counter. Warrants are similar to call options with some differences. Warrants are issued by companies and options are created by investors. Warrants are issued for long-term basis, but options expire to nine months. Options are standardised but warrants are not.

A warrant holder has no equity right in the firm. He does not receive dividends and does not have voting rights. Warrants are issued in the ratio determined by the company such as one warrant per one share. The difference between the actual price of a warrant and its minimum value is called as "premium". The warrant value depends upon the stock potential for rising the prices. A high dividend payout may also have an adverse effect on the price of a warrant. Many investors purchase the warrants for speculative purpose. Warrant market is a gambler's market. Warrants provide benefits both to the corporate sector and investors.

The following are the benefits to corporate sectors;

1. Warrants facilitate to raise funds to the corporate sector.
2. Their is no obligation to pay interest and repayment of principal.
3. Issue of warrants do not have flotation costs.

The following are the advantages to the investors;

a) Low investment.

b) Liquidity.

c) Capital gains opportunity.

The following formula can be used to value the warrant;

$$P_W = f(P_o, T_n, P_c, Di, F_c)$$

P_W = Market price of the warrant.

P_o = Option price of the equity price.

P_c = Current price of the equity share.

T_n = Duration of the issue.

Di = The ratio between shares outstanding and warrants.

F_c = The equity share price.

$$V = (P_c - P_o)N$$

V = The value of a warrant

P_c = Current price of the equity share

P_o = Option price of the equity share

N = No. of shares may be purchased with one warrant.

5. Convertible Debentures

Convertible debentures are more popular. Because, these are a hybrid securities. The debentures which may be converted into equity shares after a fixed date of time are called as convertible debentures. Until this period the convertible carries an interest rate as usual. The investments are more attractive as compared to fixed deposits. Convertible debenture combines high rate of return with the profitability of capital appreciation and the liquidity of shares.

Objectives of Convertible Debentures

Convertible debentures are the best devices to get utmost satisfaction of the share holders by the finance manager of the company. It should be issued by the companies when the actual pressure on funds requirement of the firm. The objectives of CDs are presented below:

1. A gradual dilution of EPS through CDs.
2. It is a tool of financing long term assets.
3. CDs are attractive during periods of dull market conditions.
4. CDs can attract a low underwriting commission
5. Banks may be willing to lend more money on CDs than equity shares.
6. The corporate sector can issue this instrument as a life boat/or like a parachute.
7. The companies can enjoy the advantages of debentures upto conversion time, afterwards they derive the advantages of equity share capital.

The main features of Convertible Debentures are presented below:

1. Conversion Price.
2. Conversion Ratio.
3. Quantum of Conversion.
4. Convertible Value.
5. Investment Value.
6. Timing of Conversion.
7. Premium.
8. Market Price.

1. Conversion Price

The debentures are converted into equity shares at the end of a specific period. The ratio at which the convertible debentures are exchanged for equity shares is known as conversion price. Conversion ratio is calculated by dividing the face value of a convertible debenture by its conversion price. Ex: *If the face value of a convertible debenture is Rs.100 and it is convertible into 2 equity shares of Rs.50 each, the conversion price is Rs.50 and the conversion ratio is 2 . The face value of equity is Rs.10 and the remaining Rs.40 is the premium.* The debentures may be fully converted or partly converted, it depends upon the terms of issue of debentures.

2. Conversion Ratio

The Conversion Ratio means the number of equity shares are issued for each convertible bond. Ex: if a company made a public issue of 15% convertible bonds of Rs.350 each for cash at par. Each bond face value is Rs.350 and had a conversion price of Rs.175 the conversion ratio is 2.

3. Quantum of Conversion

The Quantum amount of conversion will be based on some percentage of the face value of the debenture. The capital amount will be increased after the conversion amount transferred to capital account.

4. Convertible Value

The conversion value is based on the right to receive equity share. The convertible value of a debenture depends upon the conversion ratio and the market price of the share.

$$\text{Conversion Ratio} = \frac{\text{Issue price}}{\text{Conversion price}}$$

5. Investment Value of a Debenture

The value of a debenture is influenced by two factors, such as debenture value and the potential of the equity shares if converted. The debenture value depends upon two components, the investment value and the conversion value. The investment value is the market price based on yield to maturity. Investment value can be assessed with a fair accurate by a competent security analyst. The potential earnings of a company depends upon market environment.

6. Timing of Conversion

The period during which the conversion option is exercisable is called as "timing of conversion". This period may vary from one year to five years. It is better to the timing of larger conversion. The company can enjoy the benefits of "Pre-tax and earnings dilution" is possible when the larger period of timing of conversion.

7. Premium

If the market price of the convertible security is higher than its conversion value is called as **"premium"**. Some of the investors are risk averse. They can avoid risk by purchasing a convertible debenture/bond. Generally, a bond will sell at a premium over bond value. The amount of premium will depend upon the market value and conversion value. But the amount of premium can vary from issue to issue. The following factors may influence the premium;

a) Lower transaction costs on convertible bonds.

b) The amount of dividend.

c) The duration of the convertible bonds.

d) Option to buy equity shares directly.

8. Market Price

Market price of a convertible bond depends upon two components, conversion value and investment value. The convertible bond is the combination of bond and willing to buy a company's equity shares. In the stock market, if the value of share rises, then the value of convertible automatically fluctuates. Even the value of equity share fall the prices of the conversion will not fall.

Classification of Debentures

According to convertibility, debentures may be classified into three categories;

1. Fully convertible debentures (FCDs)
2. Partly convertible debentures (PCDs)
3. Non-convertible debentures (NCDs)

1. Fully Convertible Debentures (FCDs)

Fully convertible debentures are converted into equity shares of the company on the expiry of specific period. Convertible debentures may or may not carry any interest. According to SEBI guidelines the conversion is to be made at or after 18 months from the date of allotment but before **36 months.** The conversion is optional on the part of the debenture holders.

2. Partly Convertible Debentures (PCDs)

Partly convertible debentures' part face value will be converted into equity share and the remaining portion will be lying as a debt in the company. But the Debt portion will be redeemed at the expiry of certain period. The conversion should take place at or after **18 months.** The conversion is optional at the discretion of debenture holders.

3. Non-convertible Debentures (NCDs)

Non-convertible debentures do not confer any option on the holder to convert the debentures into equity share. NCDs are redeemed at the expiry of a specific period. The debentures which never convertible is called as NCD.

Advantages of CDs to the Corporate Sector

The following are the advantages to the corporate sector by issue of convertible debentures;

1. Tax benefits will be available to the company.
2. The companies are able to reduce its dependence on FIs and banks.
3. Funds are available at little cost.
4. Flexibility in maintenance of debt, equity ratio.
5. There may be steady increase in capital after each conversion.
6. FCDs/PCDs became more popular.
7. These instruments are having quick mobilisation power.

Advantages of CDs to the investors

The following are the advantages to the investors if they purchase the convertible debentures:

1. The investors will get a fixed return till conversion.
2. The debentures are listed in stock exchanges and enjoy a fair amount of liquidity.
3. The investors will get 100% security, because they are fully secured.
4. On conversion the investor can expect a handsome capital appreciation.

6. Credit Derivatives

Credit derivatives were developed in the U.S.A. It is a new financial instrument, which is developed for reducing credit risk. These derivatives are helpful to Commercial Banks, Finance Companies, to manage credit risk. Credit derivati[illegible] is an insurance against adverse changes in the quality of borrov[illegible] The credit derivatives are increasing exponentially. In the market, 3 t[illegible]es of credit derivatives are available. They are called as *Credit Swaps, Credit Options and Credit Linked notes.* **Credit swaps** are used by commercial banks. Banks can swap the payments from some of their loans for payments from a different institutions. It is also called as a loan portfolio swap. **Credit Option** means the investors can reduce the default risk by taking an insurance policy against their cr[illegible]dit amount. **A credit linked note** is another type of credit derivative. It is a combination of a regular bond and a credit option. This note assures to make regular interest payments. It also promises to pay a large amount when the bond matures. The credit derivative can reduce credit risk but also they expose the users of new financial risks. Credit derivatives are privately negotiated financial contracts. Credit derivatives are well developed after 1992.

The derivatives business has undergone significant structural changes over the years. The derivatives trading has increased phenomenally. Derivatives decrease risk not only for their issuers but also for the whole system.

7. Swaptions

The option on swaps known as swaptions. The swaption holders have a right to enter into swap contracts without obligation on or before the exercise date. In a put swaption, the holder is entitled to receive a fixed interest. In call swaption, the holder will have to pay a fixed interest. The premium shall be paid for obtaining swaption.

RBI Policy on Derivatives

The Reserve Bank of India has liberalised the policy on derivatives in Oct.1996. According to the guidelines issued by the RBI, the commercial banks can offer to hedge instruments to the corporates. They are presented below;

a) Authorised dealers in forex market can offer currency swaps, cross currency options and forward rate agreements.

b) The financial derivatives can be offered to book the overseas transactions.

c) Options will be allowed to sold to the customers by Authorised dealers only.

d) The authorised dealers are required to get the final approval by RBI.

e) Corporate bodies have to maintain and furnish reports to the RBI within a week.

SUMMARY

The new economic policy aimed at correcting the imbalances and creating more competitive environment to improve productivity and efficiency. In the new economic environment a series of structural changes were undertaken in financial sector to achieve the objective. The financial sector reforms encourage investors to invest in capital market. The reforms are expected to give a boost to the economy by allocating funds for productive purpose. The Indian stock market is characterised by high price volatile. Speculation is unavoidable and it is a driving force which builds up activity and assures sustained interest of investors. Derivatives have now become available for investment and trading. Derivatives are contracts. They are written between two parties. These are easily marketable assets. Derivatives are mostly secondary market instruments. They are quite liquid and have low transaction costs. The markets for derivatives are most likely to remain narrow and shallow. Different types of derivatives are available in the market namely; Futures, Options, Swaps, Warrants, convertible bond/debentures swaptions etc., Futures means an agreement to exchange a standard quantity of on a specified date in the future at a pre-determined price. Future contracts are transferable. They are traded in auction markets. There are many future contracts available. These are commodity futures, financial futures, stock index futures, interest rates futures and currency futures. Option is a contract which involves the right to buy or sell securities at specified prices within a stated time. Option is a device to get profits from speculation. Options can be divided into commodity option, currency option, stock option, stock index option, options on future etc., For valuation of option Black and Scholes have developed a formula. The formula provides an excellent analysis. Derivatives are important by products of Black and Scholes. Portfolio insurance is a device to protect the value of the basket of different assets. Swaps are agreements between two parties to exchange assets at predetermined intervals. Warrant is a corporate created option.

QUESTIONS

Short Questions

1. Explain the concept of Derivatives.
2. What are the advantages of derivative market?
3. What do you mean by Futures?
4. Explain the meaning of ready delivery contract.
5. What is forward contract?
6. Explain the concept of stock of index future?
7. What are the characteristics of futures on long-term securities?
8. Explain the concept of options?
9. Explain the difference between put option and call option?
10. What do you mean by portfolio insurance?

11. Explain the concept of swaps.
12. What is a Warrant?
13. What do you mean by credit derivatives?
14. What are the convertibles?
15. What is a convertion ratio?

Essay Questions

1. What do you mean by derivatives? How far is it useful to our capital market?
2. What do you mean by option? Explain different kinds of options?
3. What is Black and Schole model? How is it useful?
4. What are the differences between hedging and portfolio insurance?
5. Explain the importance of futures.
6. What are convertible debentures? Explain their various features
7. Explain the process of valuation of stock index futures?
8. What are the fundamental factors which influence the option price?
9. What do you mean by swaps? Explain the various kinds of swaps.
10. Explain the concept of a warrant? What are its advantages?
11. Explain the salient features of convertibles.

* * *